ベルセルク

BERSERK 18

BY
KENTARO MIURA
三浦建太郎

TRANSLATION
DUANE JOHNSON
LETTERING AND RETOUCH
REPLIBOOKS

DARK HORSE MANGA
DMP Digital Manga Publishing

PUBLISHERS
MIKE RICHARDSON, DARK HORSE MANGA
HIKARU SASAHARA, DIGITAL MANGA PUBLISHING

EDITORS
CHRIS WARNER, DARK HORSE MANGA
FRED LUI, DIGITAL MANGA PUBLISHING

COLLECTION DESIGNER
DAVID NESTELLE

ART DIRECTOR
LIA RIBACCHI

English-language version produced by
DARK HORSE MANGA and DIGITAL MANGA PUBLISHING.

BERSERK vol. 18 by KENTARO MIURA

© 1998 Kentaro Miura. All rights reserved. First published in Japan in 1999 by HAKUSENSHA, INC., Tokyo. English-language translation rights in the United States of America and Canada arranged with HAKUSENSHA INC., Tokyo through TOHAN CORPORATION, Tokyo. New text © 2007 by Dark Horse Comics, Inc. and Digital Manga, Inc. All other material © 2007 by Dark Horse Comics, Inc. Dark Horse Manga™ is a trademark of Dark Horse Comics, Inc. All rights reserved. No portion of this publication may be reproduced or transmitted, in any form or by any means, without the express written permission of the copyright holders. Names, characters, places, and incidents featured in this publication are either the product of the author's imagination or are used fictitiously. Any resemblance to actual persons (living or dead), events, institutions, or locales, without satiric intent, is coincidental.

Dark Horse Manga
A division of Dark Horse Comics, Inc.
10956 SE Main Street
Milwaukie OR 97222

darkhorse.com

Digital Manga Publishing
1487 West 178th Street, Suite 300
Gardena CA 90248

dmpbooks.com

To find a comics shop in your area, call the Comic
Shop Locator Service toll-free at 1-888-266-4226

First edition: July 2007

ISBN-10: 1-59307-743-2
ISBN-13: 978-1-59307-743-3

10 9 8 7 6 5 4 3 2 1
Printed in Canada

BERSERK

ベルセルク⑱

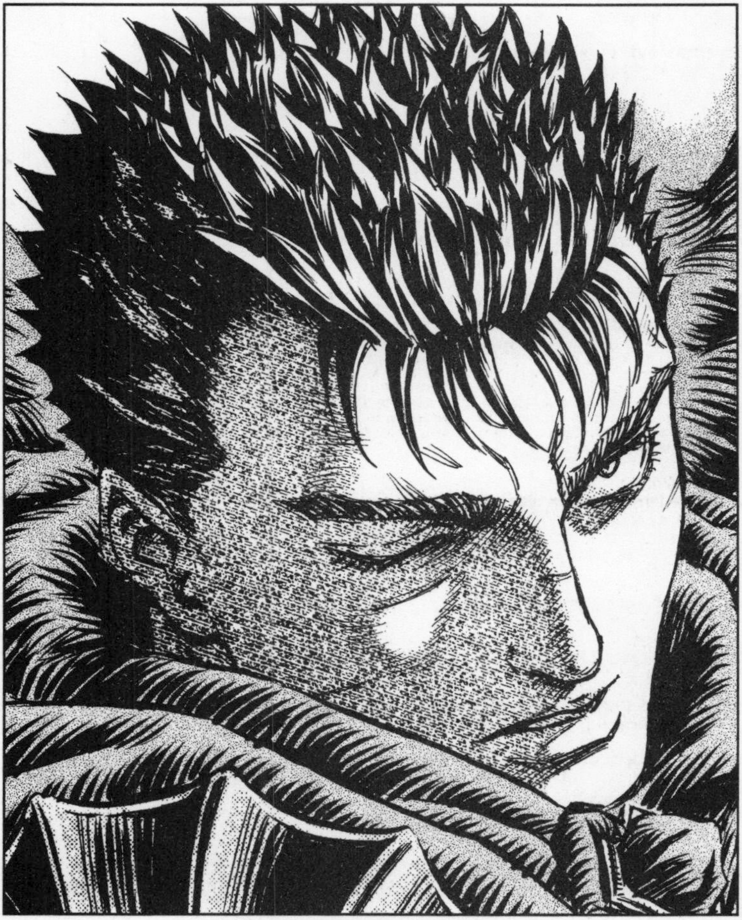

三浦建太郎

CONTENTS

CONVICTION ARC
BIRTH CEREMONY CHAPTER

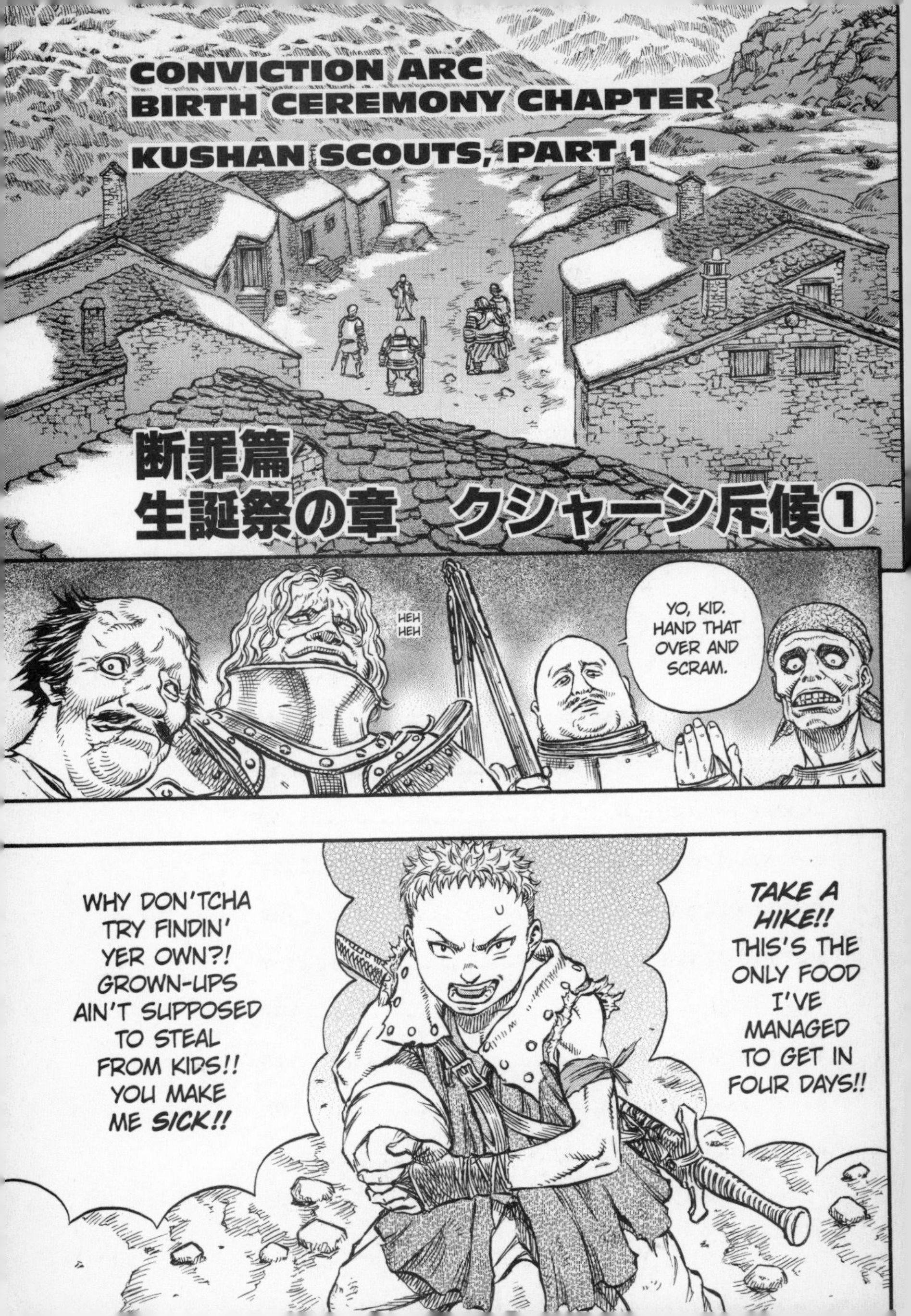
CONVICTION ARC
BIRTH CEREMONY CHAPTER
KUSHAN SCOUTS, PART 1
断罪篇
生誕祭の章　クシャーン斥候①
YO, KID. HAND THAT OVER AND SCRAM.
HEH HEH
TAKE A HIKE!! THIS'S THE ONLY FOOD I'VE MANAGED TO GET IN FOUR DAYS!!
WHY DON'TCHA TRY FINDIN' YER OWN?! GROWN-UPS AIN'T SUPPOSED TO STEAL FROM KIDS!! YOU MAKE ME SICK!!

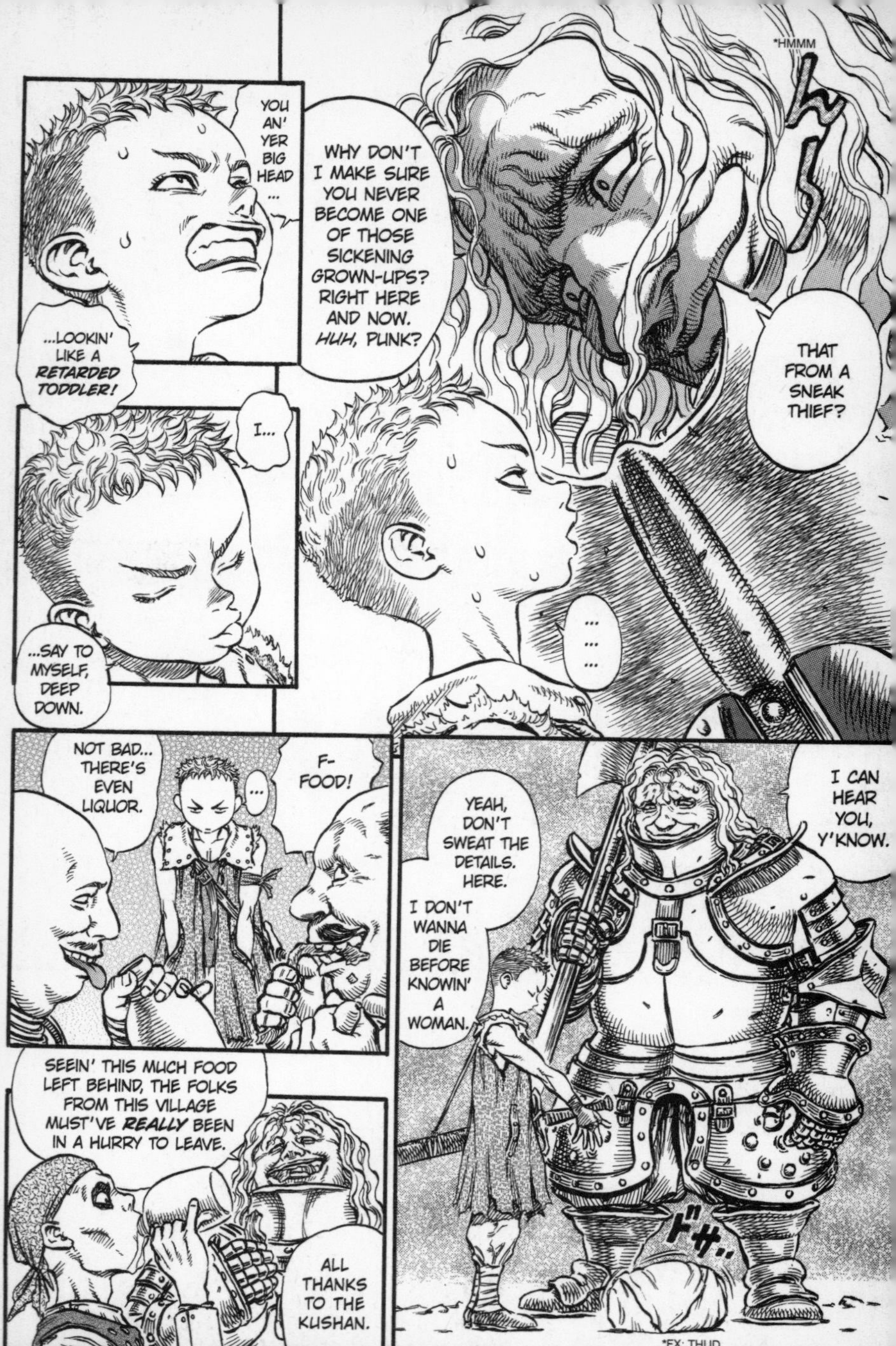
*HMMM
WHY DON'T I MAKE SURE YOU NEVER BECOME ONE OF THOSE SICKENING GROWN-UPS? RIGHT HERE AND NOW. *HUH*, PUNK?
THAT FROM A SNEAK THIEF?
... ...
YOU AN' YER BIG HEAD ...
...LOOKIN' LIKE A ***RETARDED TODDLER!***
I...
...SAY TO MYSELF, DEEP DOWN.
I CAN HEAR YOU, Y'KNOW.
YEAH, DON'T SWEAT THE DETAILS. HERE.
I DON'T WANNA DIE BEFORE KNOWIN' A WOMAN.
*FX: THUD
F- FOOD!
...
NOT BAD... THERE'S EVEN LIQUOR.
SEEIN' THIS MUCH FOOD LEFT BEHIND, THE FOLKS FROM THIS VILLAGE MUST'VE ***REALLY*** BEEN IN A HURRY TO LEAVE.
ALL THANKS TO THE KUSHAN.

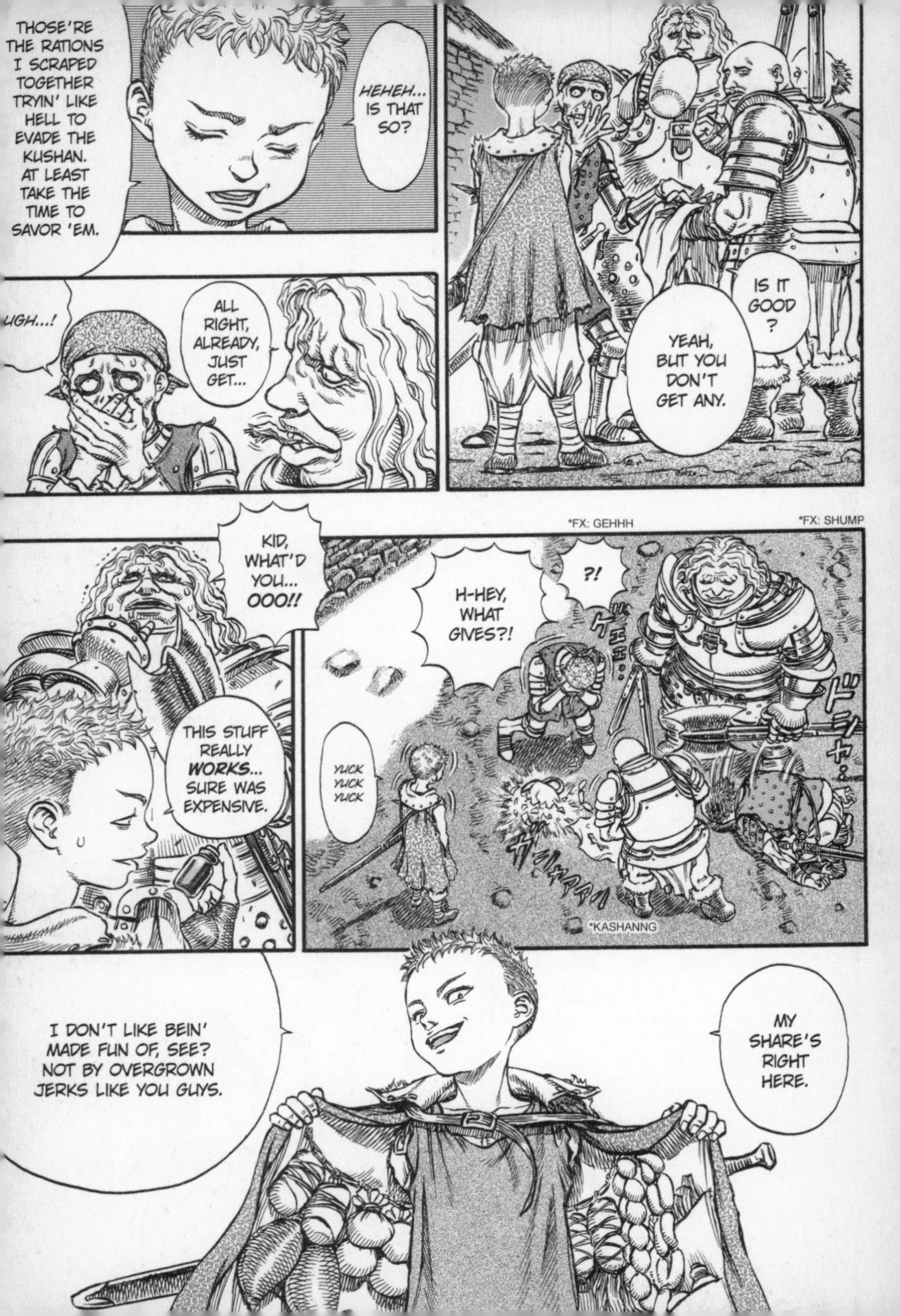
IS IT GOOD?
YEAH, BUT YOU DON'T GET ANY.
*FX: SHUMP
HEHEH... IS THAT SO?
THOSE'RE THE RATIONS I SCRAPED TOGETHER TRYIN' LIKE HELL TO EVADE THE KUSHAN. AT LEAST TAKE THE TIME TO SAVOR 'EM.
ALL RIGHT, ALREADY, JUST GET...
UGH...!
*FX: GEHHH
?!
H-HEY, WHAT GIVES?!
YUCK YUCK YUCK
*KASHANNG
KID, WHAT'D YOU... OOO!!
THIS STUFF REALLY WORKS... SURE WAS EXPENSIVE.
MY SHARE'S RIGHT HERE.
I DON'T LIKE BEIN' MADE FUN OF, SEE? NOT BY OVERGROWN JERKS LIKE YOU GUYS.

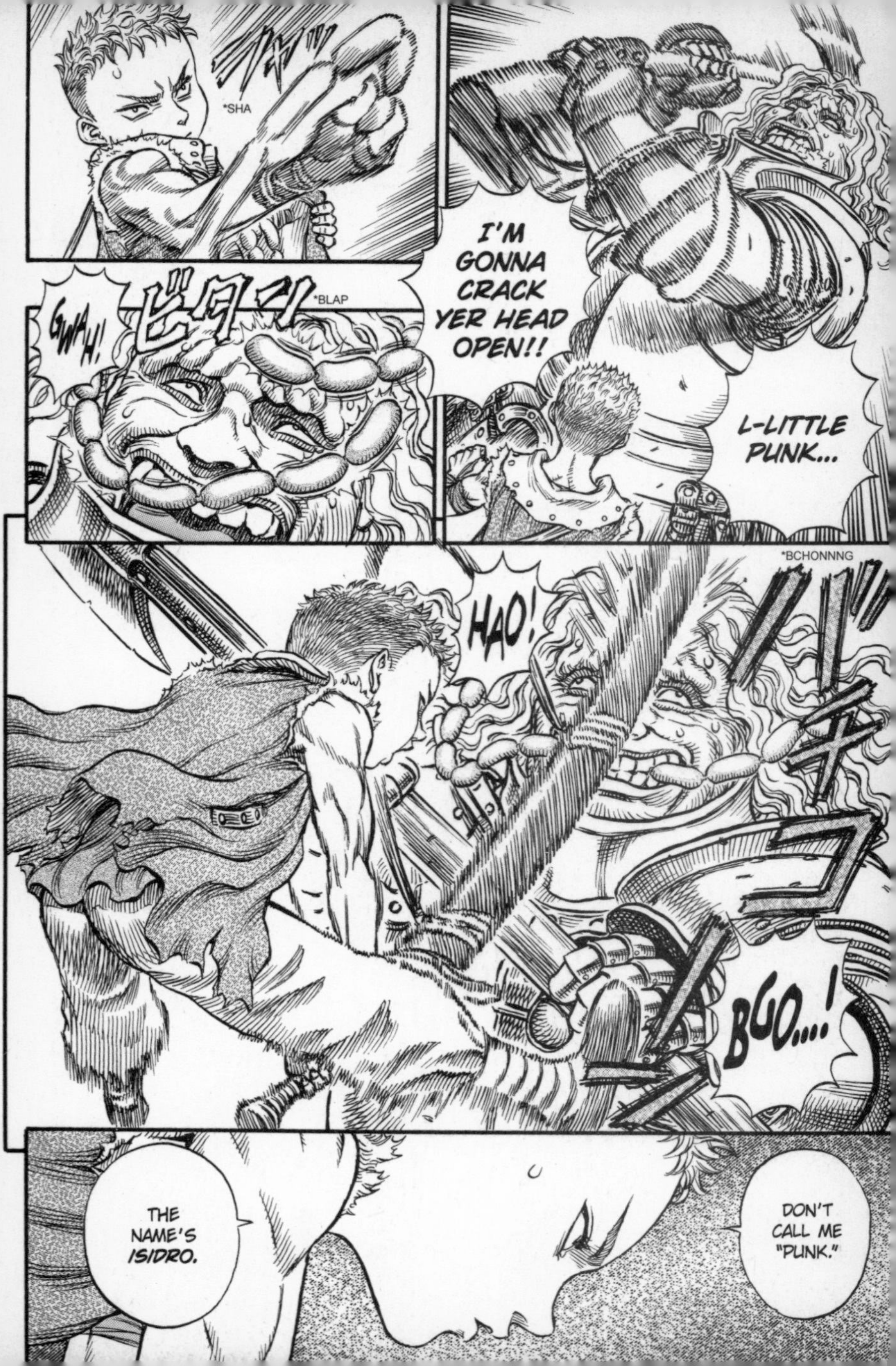
I'M GONNA CRACK YER HEAD OPEN!!
L-LITTLE PUNK...
*SHA
*BLAP
GWAH!
HAO!
*BCHONNNG
BGO....!
DON'T CALL ME "PUNK."
THE NAME'S ISIDRO.

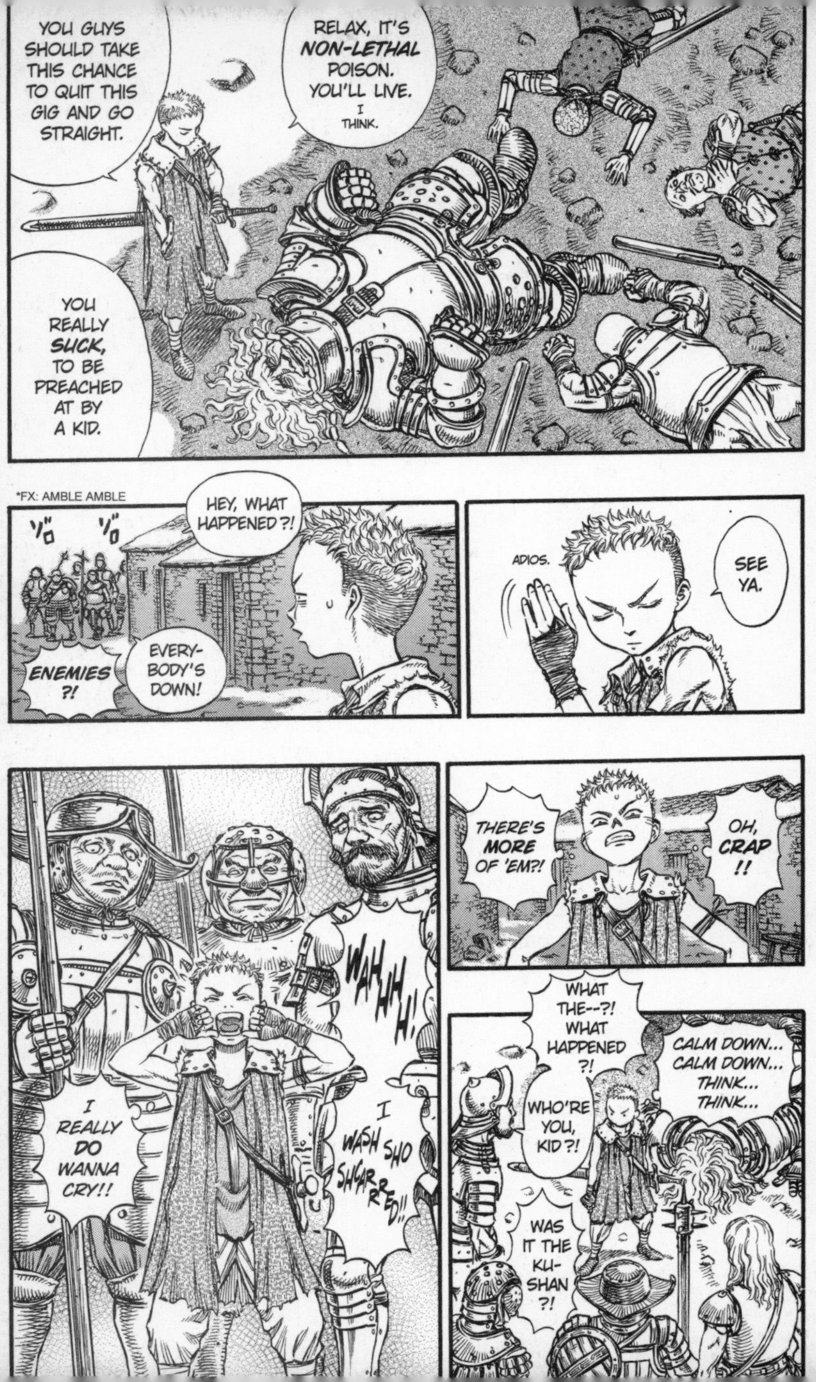
RELAX, IT'S NON-LETHAL POISON. YOU'LL LIVE.
I THINK.
YOU GUYS SHOULD TAKE THIS CHANCE TO QUIT THIS GIG AND GO STRAIGHT.
YOU REALLY SUCK, TO BE PREACHED AT BY A KID.
SEE YA.
ADIOS.
*FX: AMBLE AMBLE
ゾロ ゾロ
HEY, WHAT HAPPENED?!
EVERYBODY'S DOWN!
ENEMIES?!
OH, CRAP!!
THERE'S MORE OF 'EM?!
CALM DOWN... CALM DOWN... THINK... THINK...
WHAT THE--?! WHAT HAPPENED?!
WHO'RE YOU, KID?!
WAS IT THE KU-SHAN?!
WAHHHH!
I WASH SHO SHCARRRED!!
I REALLY DO WANNA CRY!!

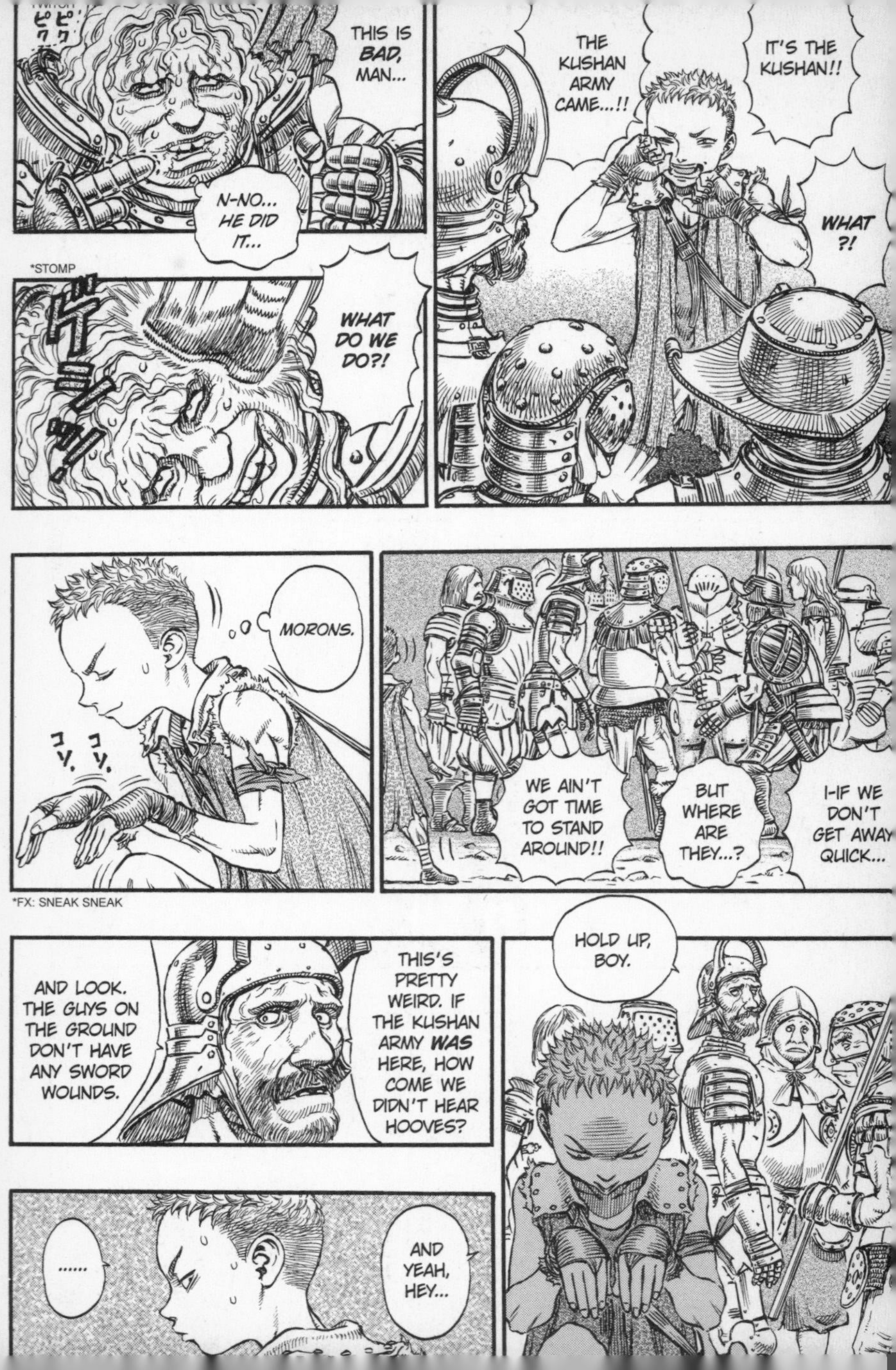
IT'S THE KUSHAN!!
THE KUSHAN ARMY CAME...!!
WHAT ?!
ピク ピク
THIS IS BAD, MAN...
N-NO... HE DID IT...
WHAT DO WE DO?!
ドシッ!!
*STOMP
I-IF WE DON'T GET AWAY QUICK...
BUT WHERE ARE THEY...?
WE AIN'T GOT TIME TO STAND AROUND!!
MORONS.
コソ コソ
*FX: SNEAK SNEAK
HOLD UP, BOY.
THIS'S PRETTY WEIRD. IF THE KUSHAN ARMY WAS HERE, HOW COME WE DIDN'T HEAR HOOVES?
AND LOOK. THE GUYS ON THE GROUND DON'T HAVE ANY SWORD WOUNDS.
AND YEAH, HEY...
......

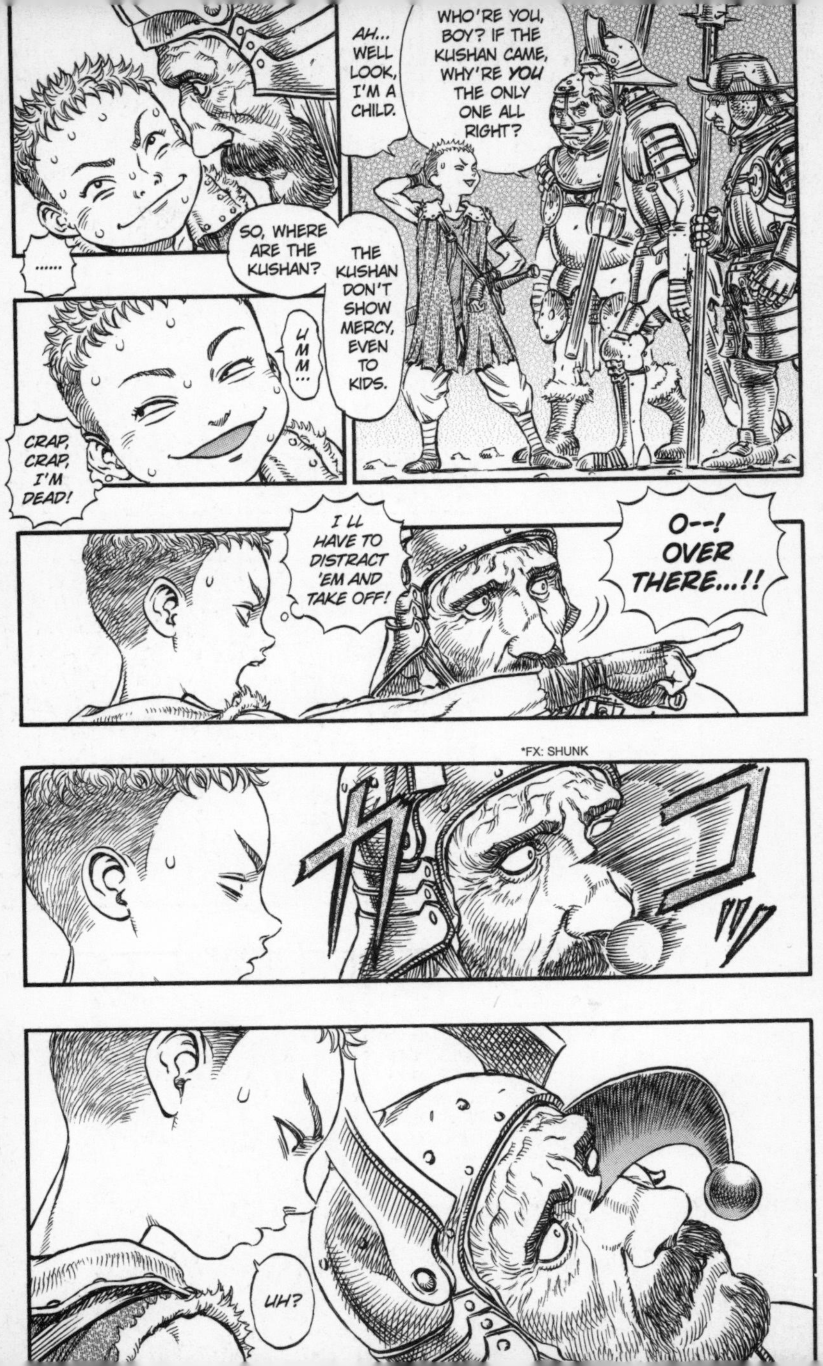
WHO'RE YOU, BOY? IF THE KUSHAN CAME, WHY'RE YOU THE ONLY ONE ALL RIGHT?
AH... WELL LOOK, I'M A CHILD.
THE KUSHAN DON'T SHOW MERCY, EVEN TO KIDS.
SO, WHERE ARE THE KUSHAN?
......
UMM...
CRAP, CRAP, I'M DEAD!
O--! OVER THERE...!!
I LL HAVE TO DISTRACT 'EM AND TAKE OFF!
*FX: SHUNK
UH?

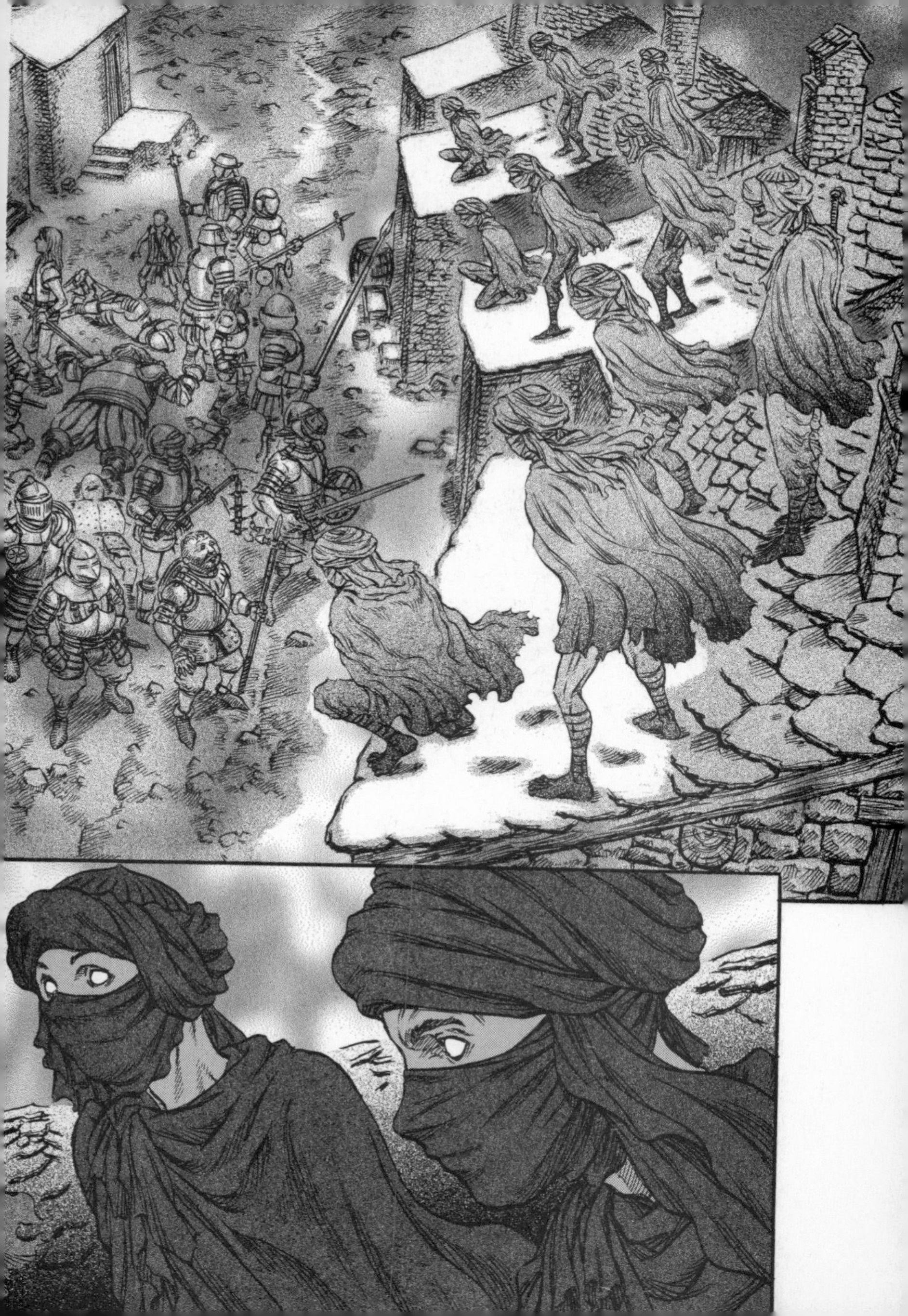

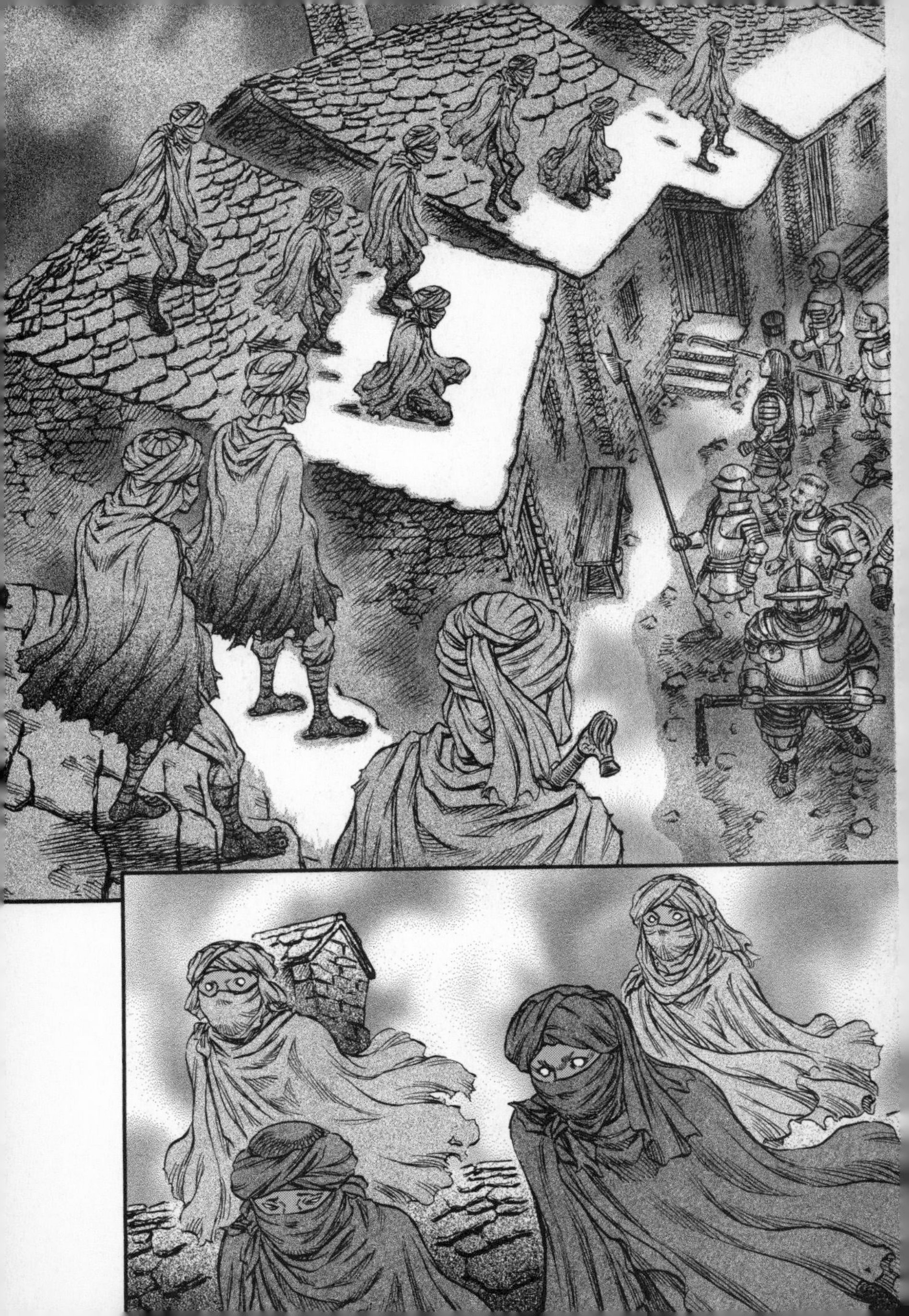

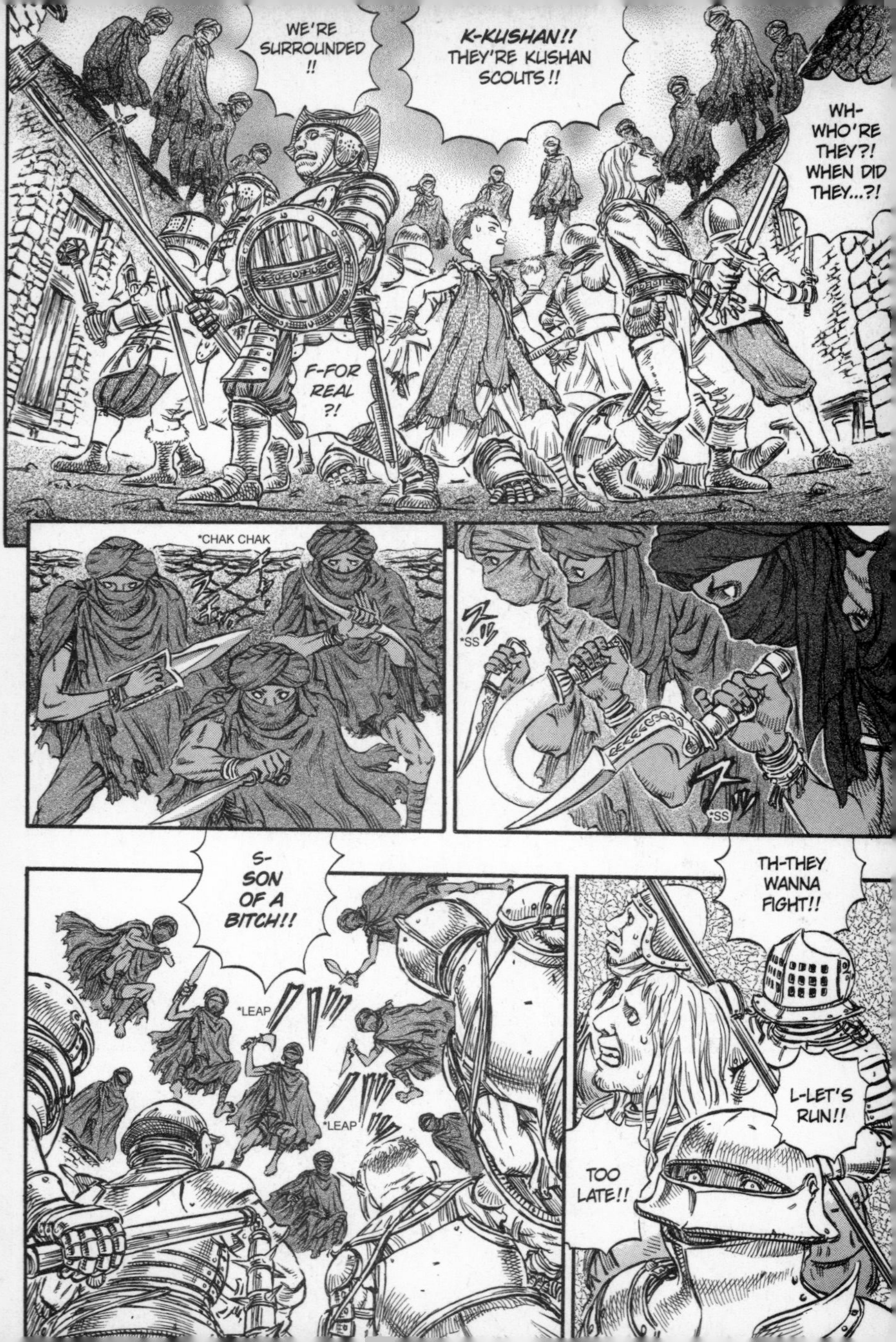
WH- WHO'RE THEY?! WHEN DID THEY...?!
K-KUSHAN!! THEY'RE KUSHAN SCOUTS!!
WE'RE SURROUNDED!!
F-FOR REAL?!
*SS
*SS
*CHAK CHAK
TH-THEY WANNA FIGHT!!
L-LET'S RUN!!
TOO LATE!!
S-SON OF A BITCH!!
*LEAP
*LEAP

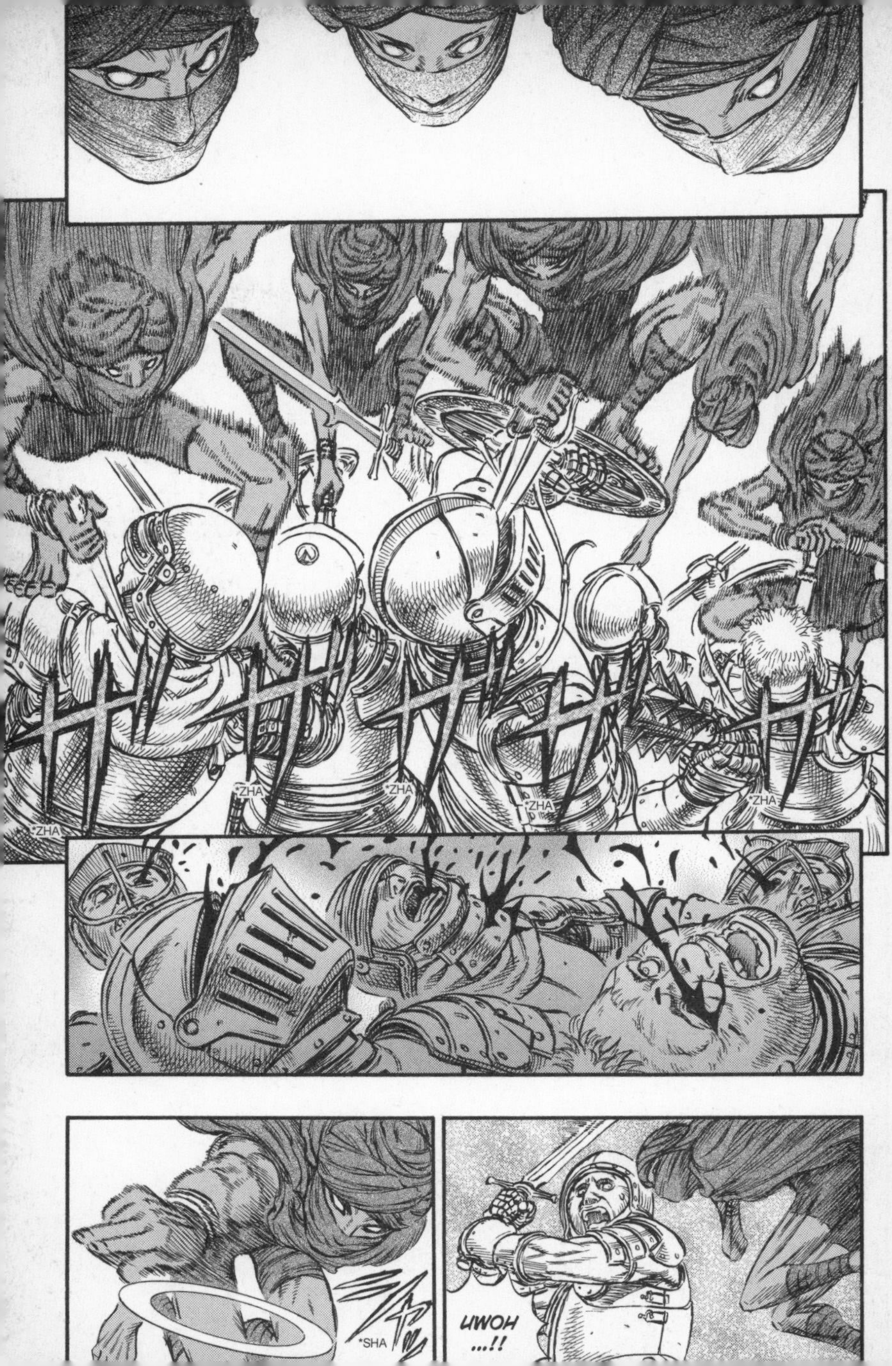
*ZHA
*ZHA
*ZHA
*ZHA
*ZHA
UWOH
...!!
*SHA

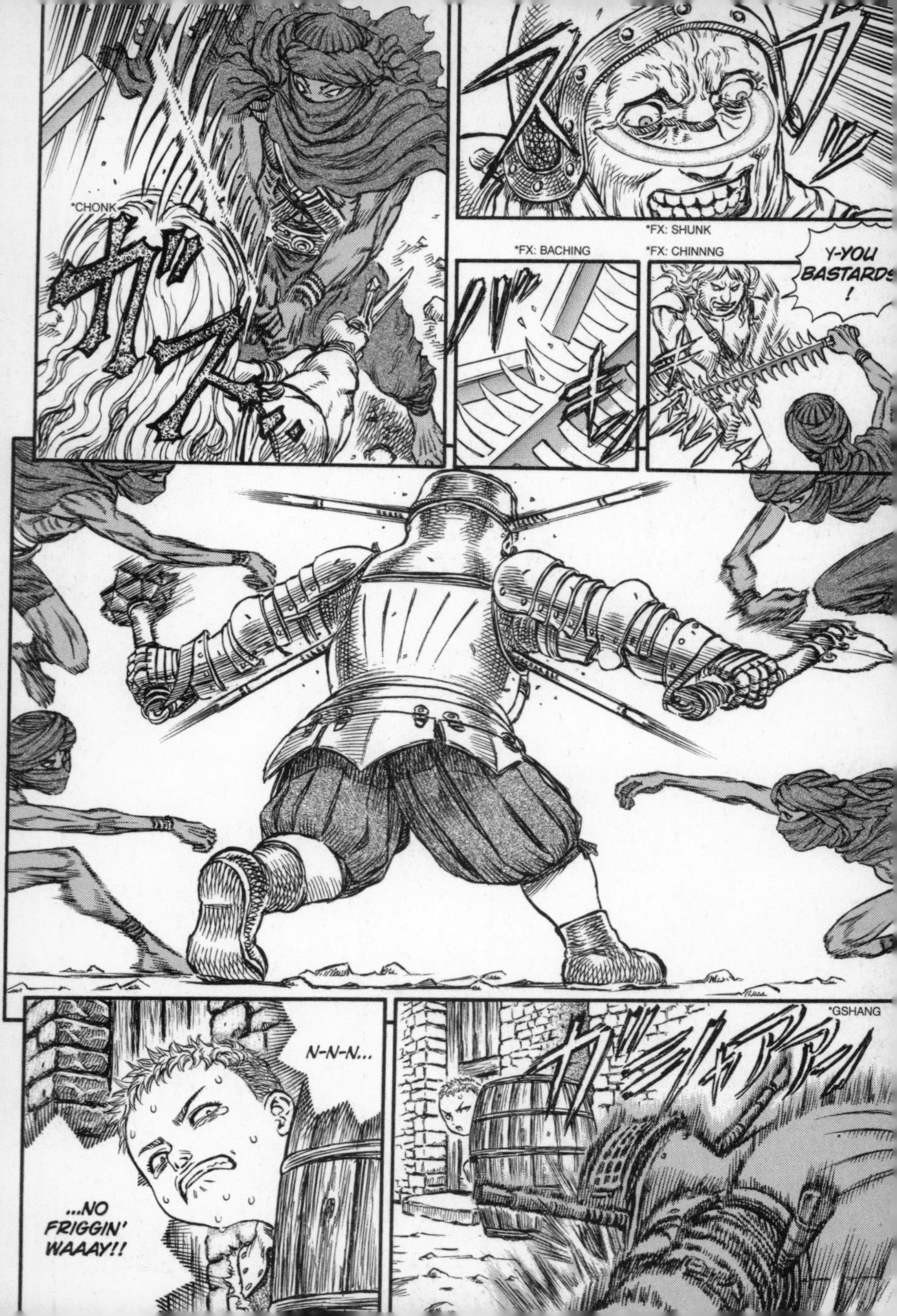
*FX: SHUNK
*FX: CHINNNG
Y-YOU BASTARDS!
*FX: BACHING
*CHONK
*GSHANG
N-N-N...
...NO FRIGGIN' WAAAY!!

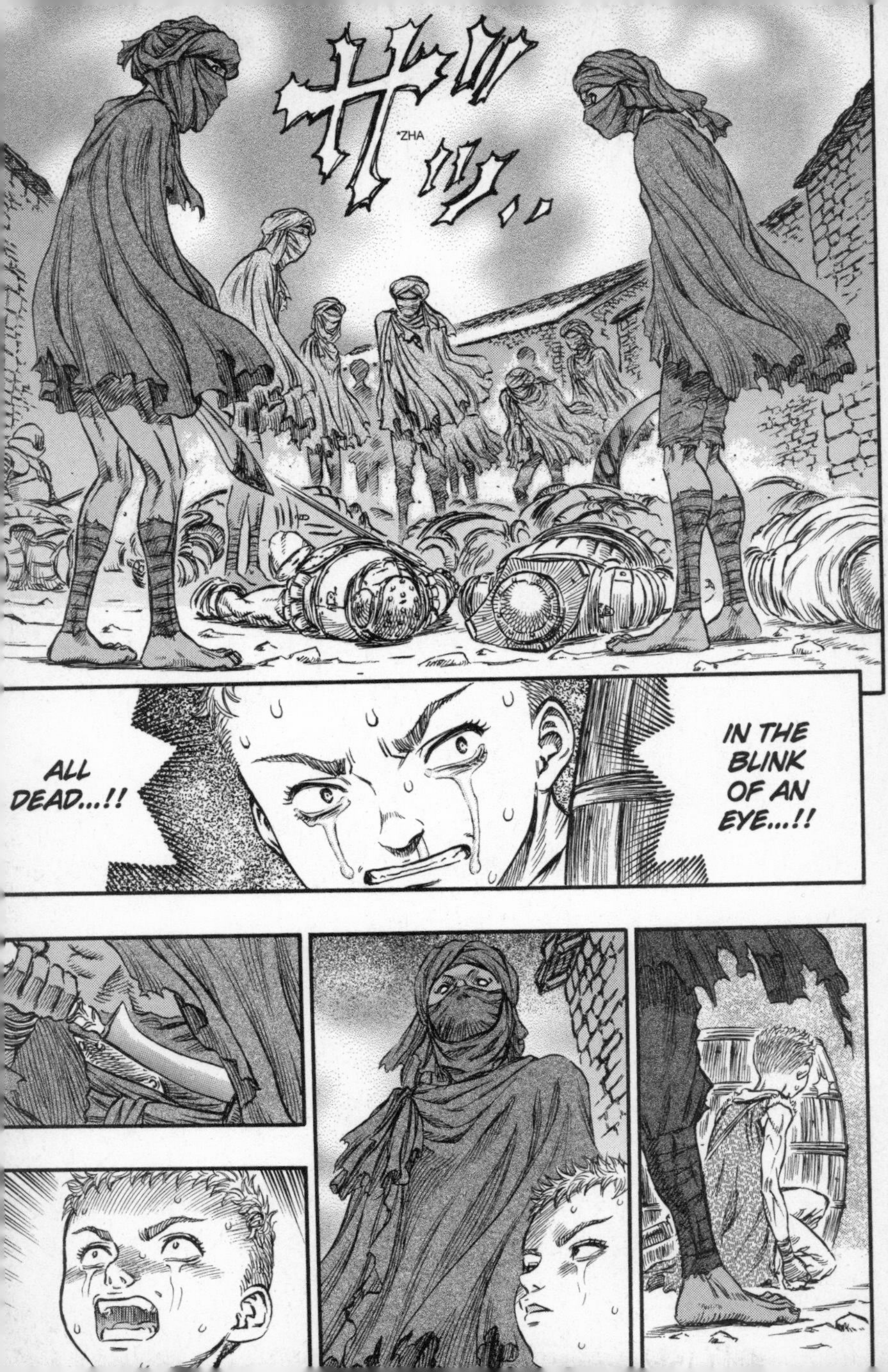
*ZHA
IN THE BLINK OF AN EYE...!!
ALL DEAD...!!

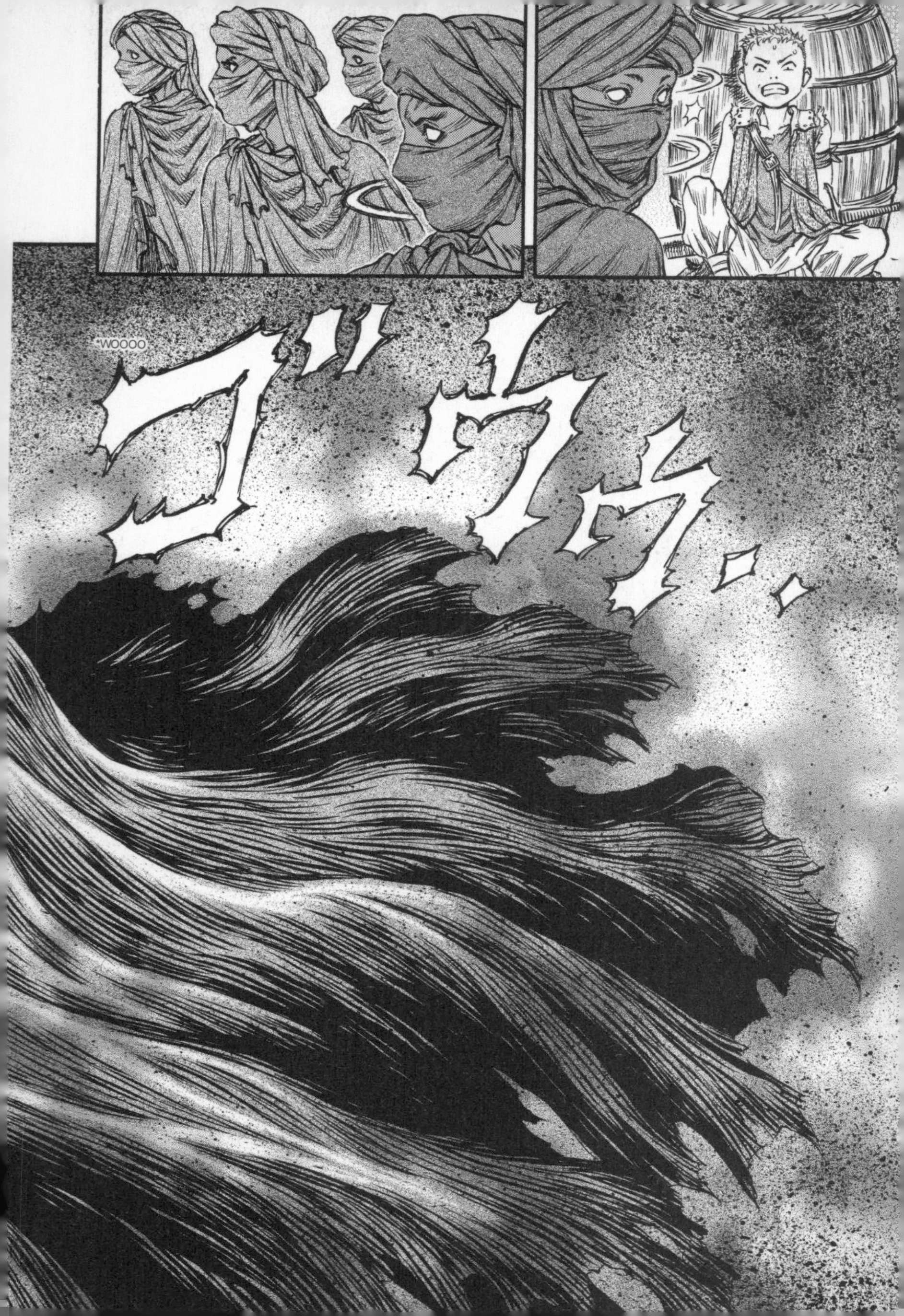

ゴウウ‥
*WOOOO

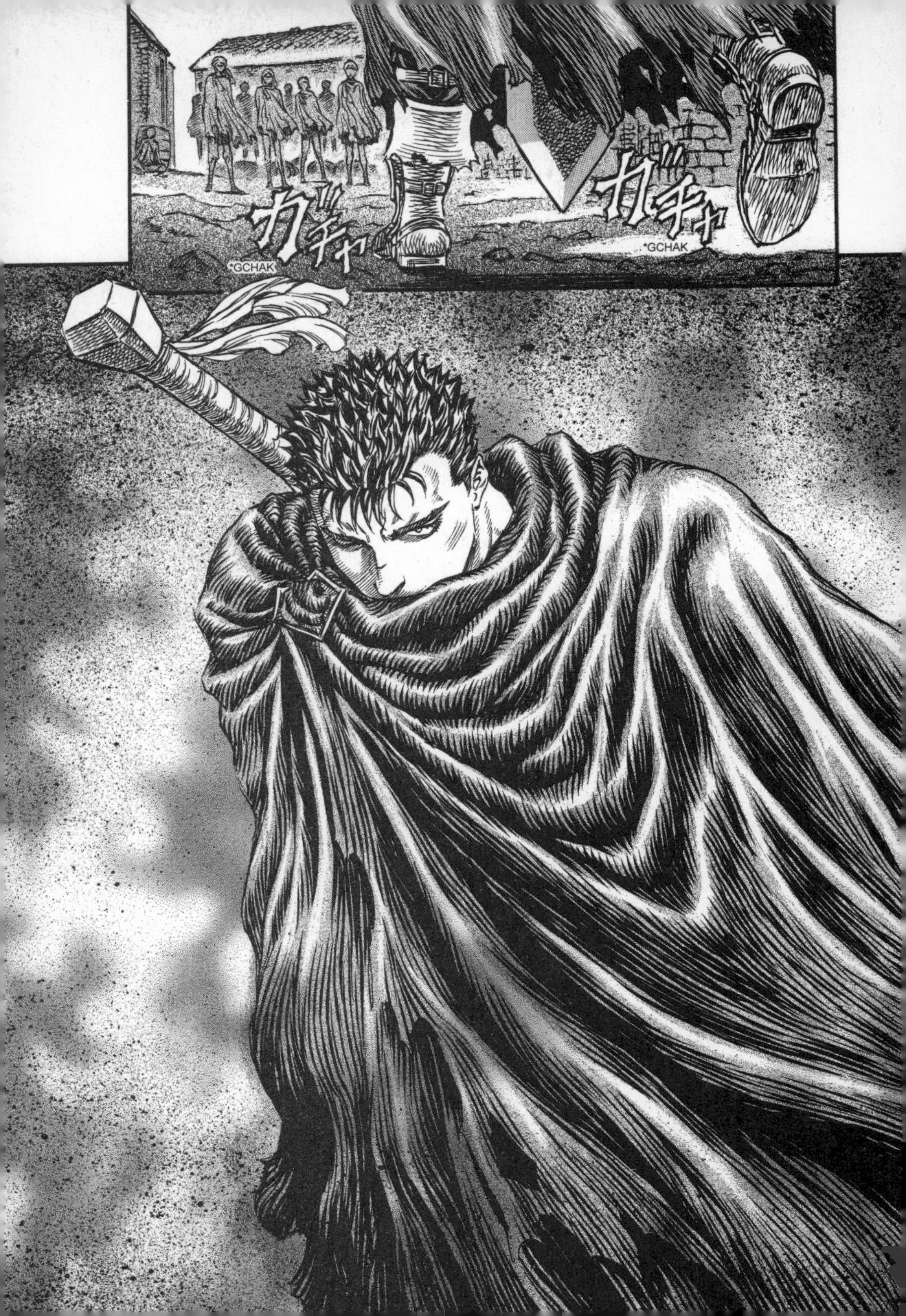
ガチャ
*GCHAK
ガチャ
*GCHAK

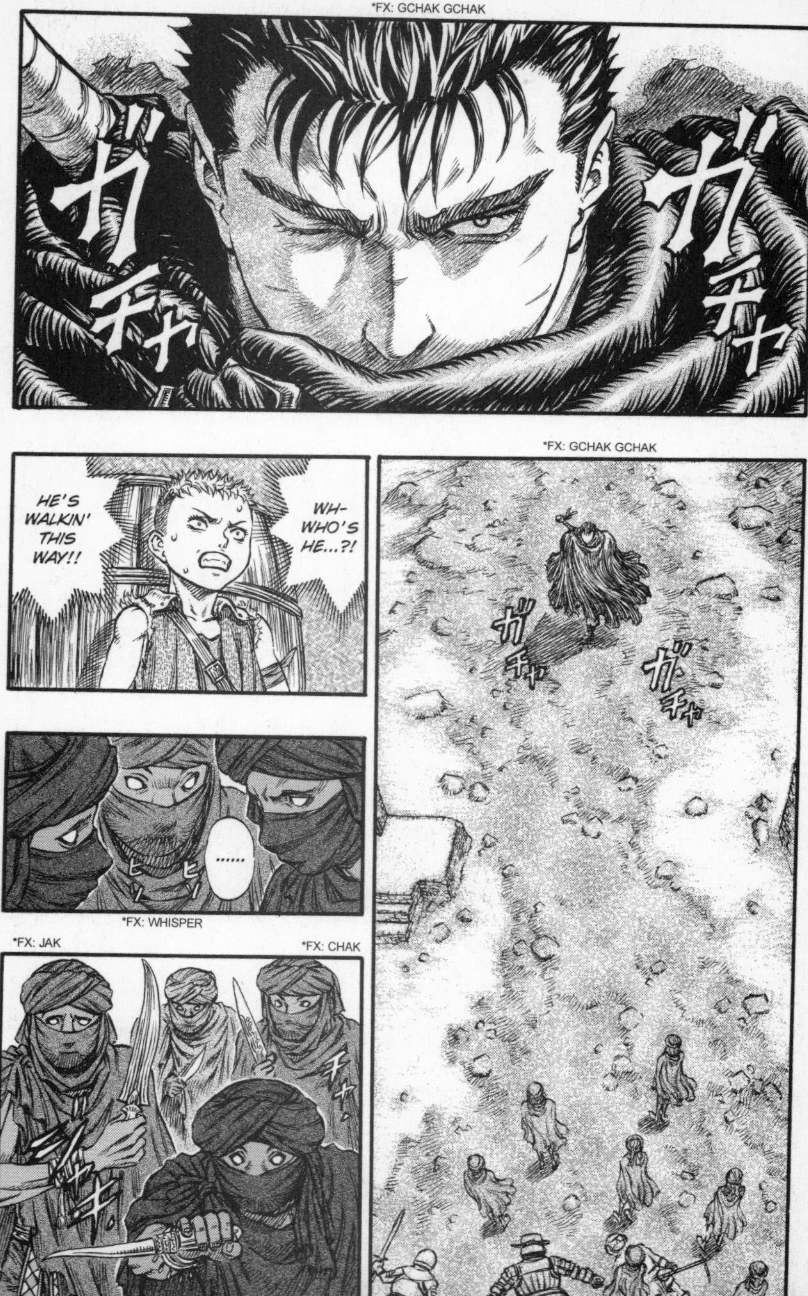
*FX: GCHAK GCHAK
*FX: GCHAK GCHAK
WH- WHO'S HE...?!
HE'S WALKIN' THIS WAY!!
......
*FX: WHISPER
*FX: CHAK
*FX: JAK

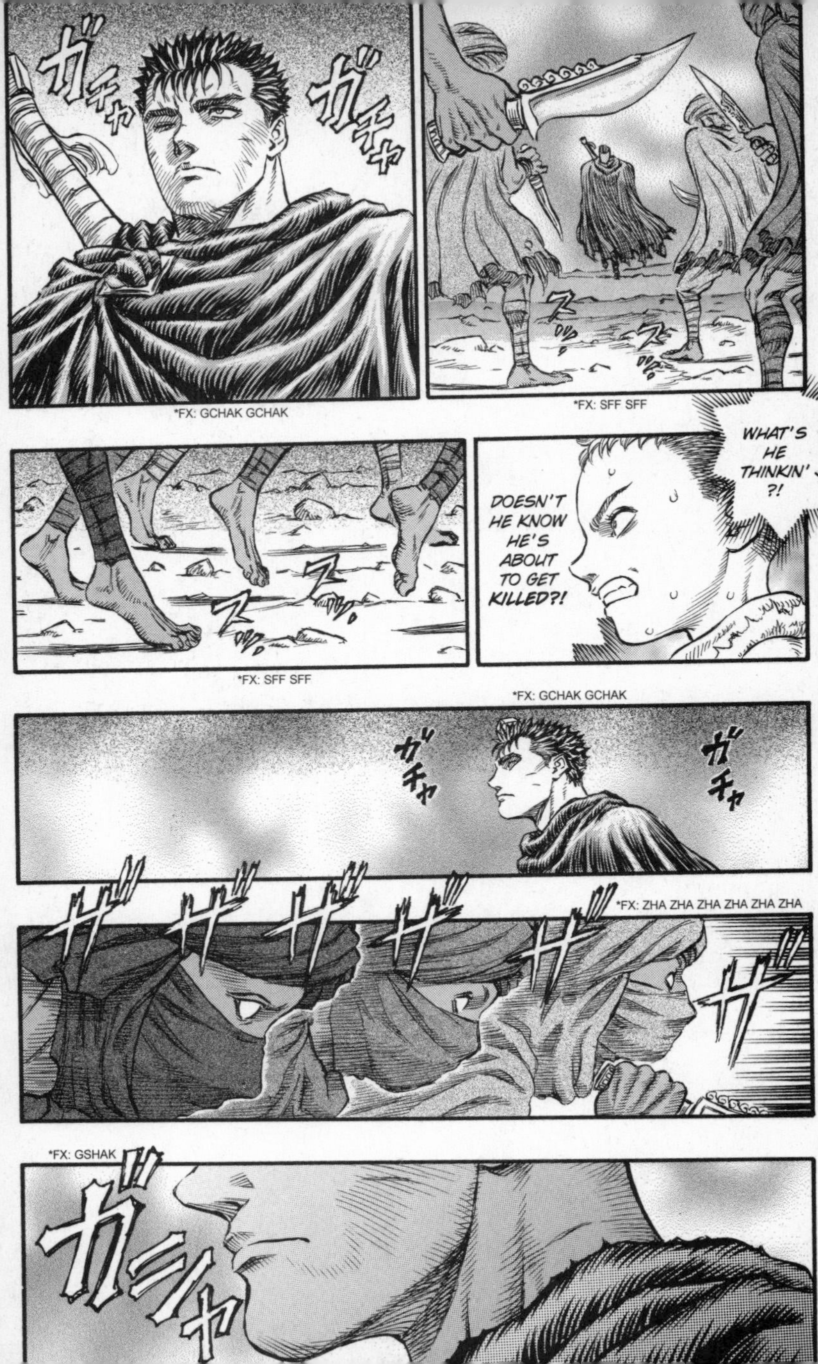
*FX: SFF SFF
*FX: GCHAK GCHAK
WHAT'S HE THINKIN'?!
DOESN'T HE KNOW HE'S ABOUT TO GET KILLED?!
*FX: SFF SFF
*FX: GCHAK GCHAK
*FX: ZHA ZHA ZHA ZHA ZHA ZHA
*FX: GSHAK

断罪篇
生誕祭の章　クシャーン斥候②

CONVICTION ARC
BIRTH CEREMONY CHAPTER

KUSHAN SCOUTS, PART 2

BERSERK

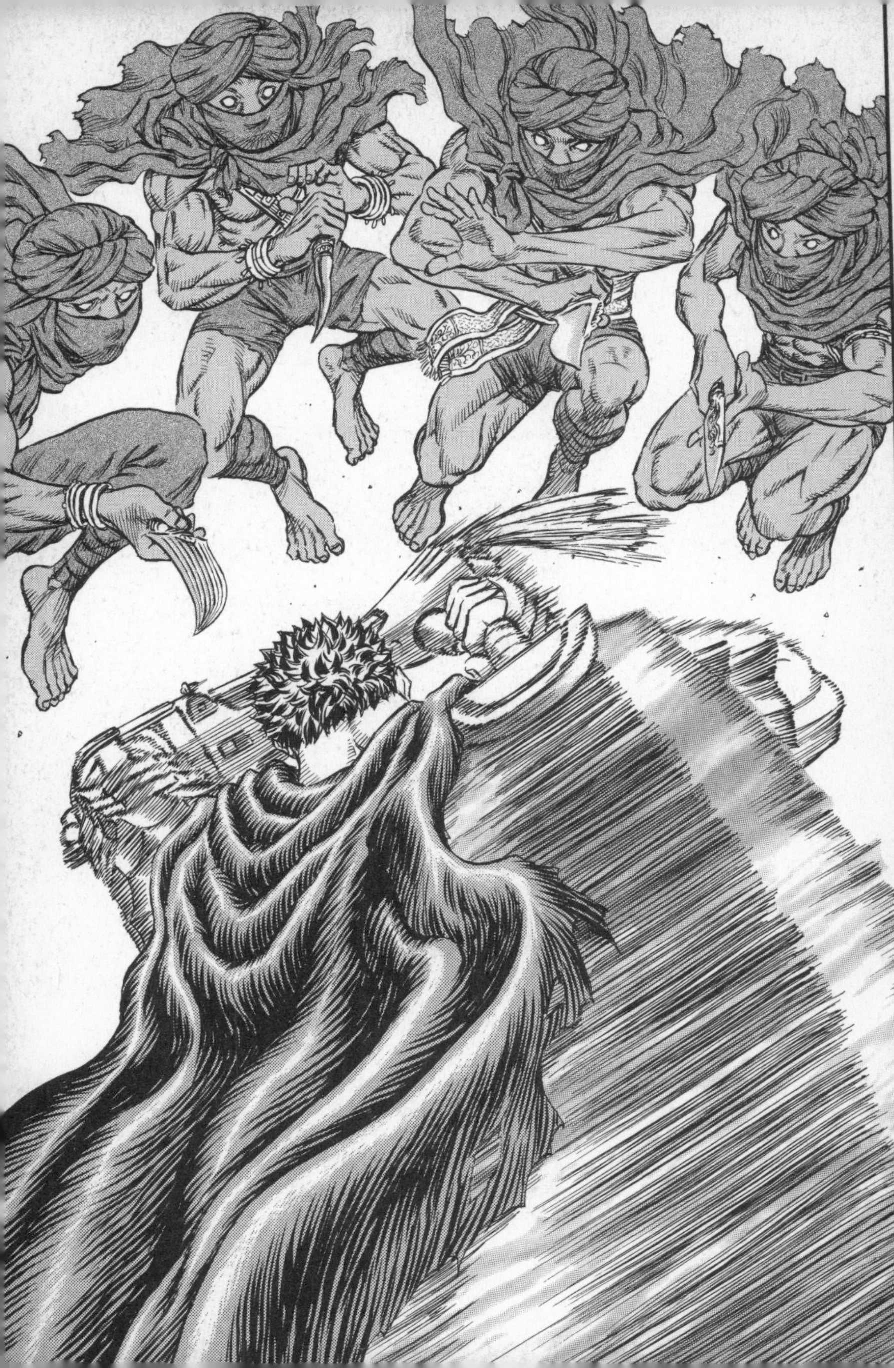

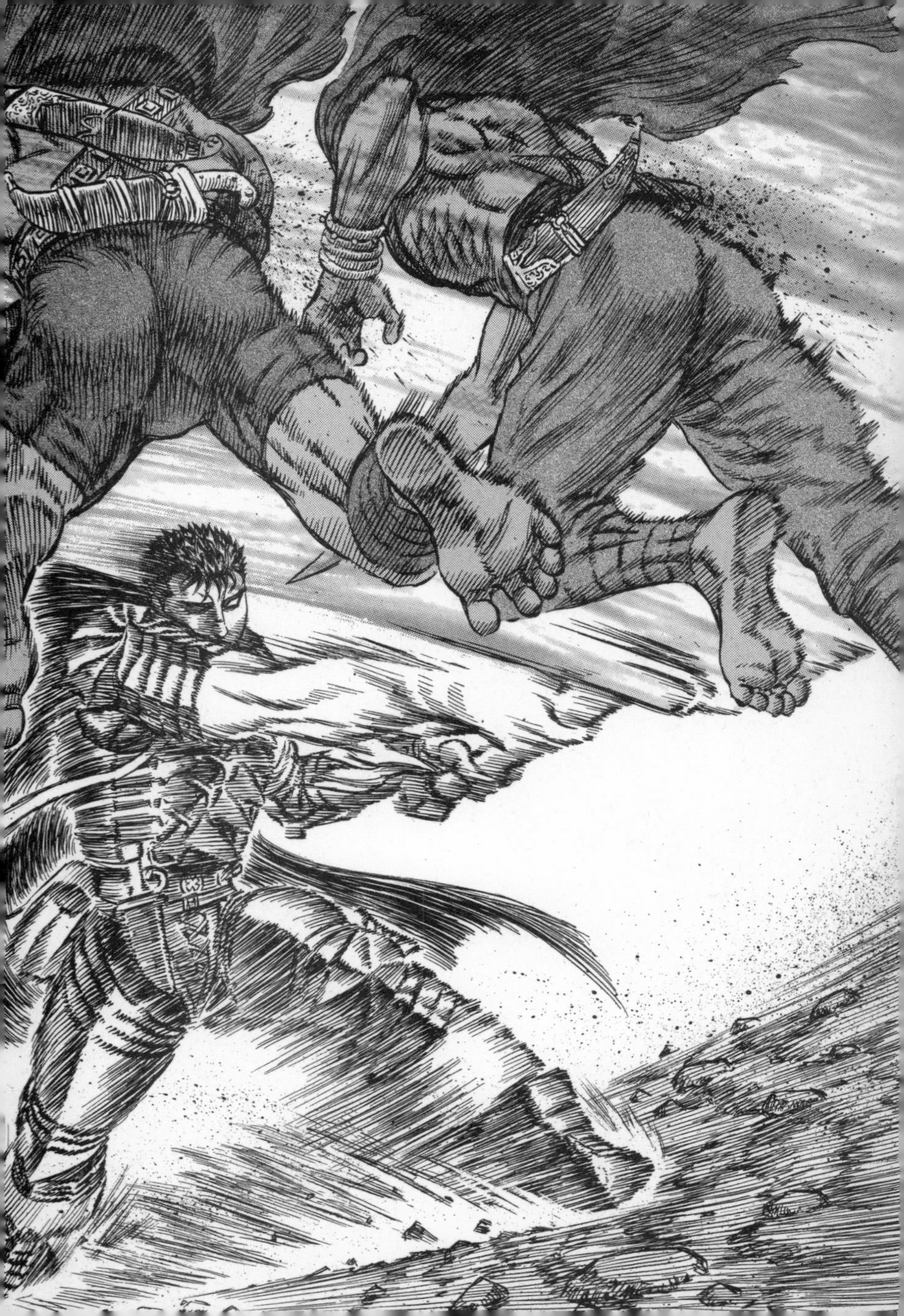

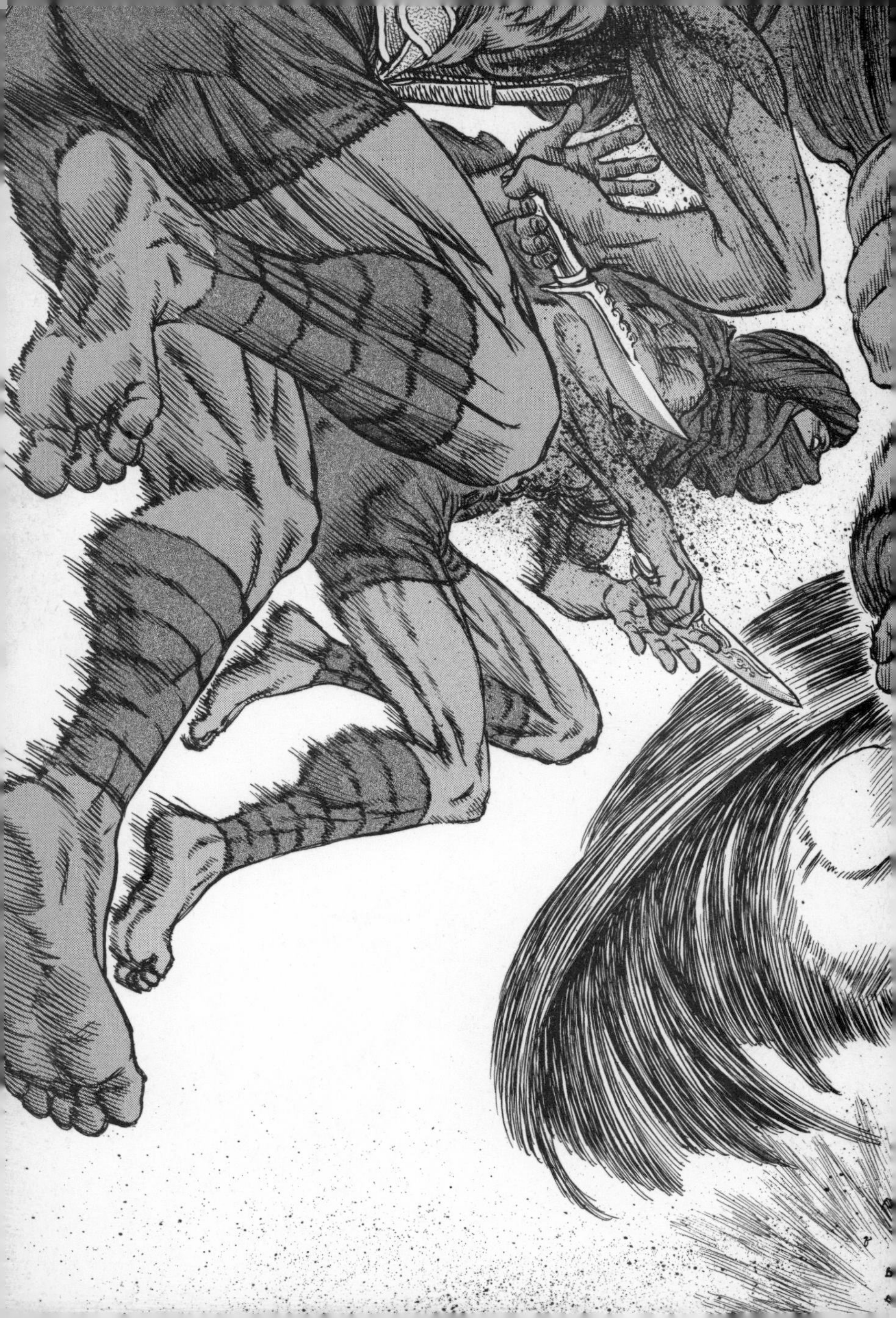

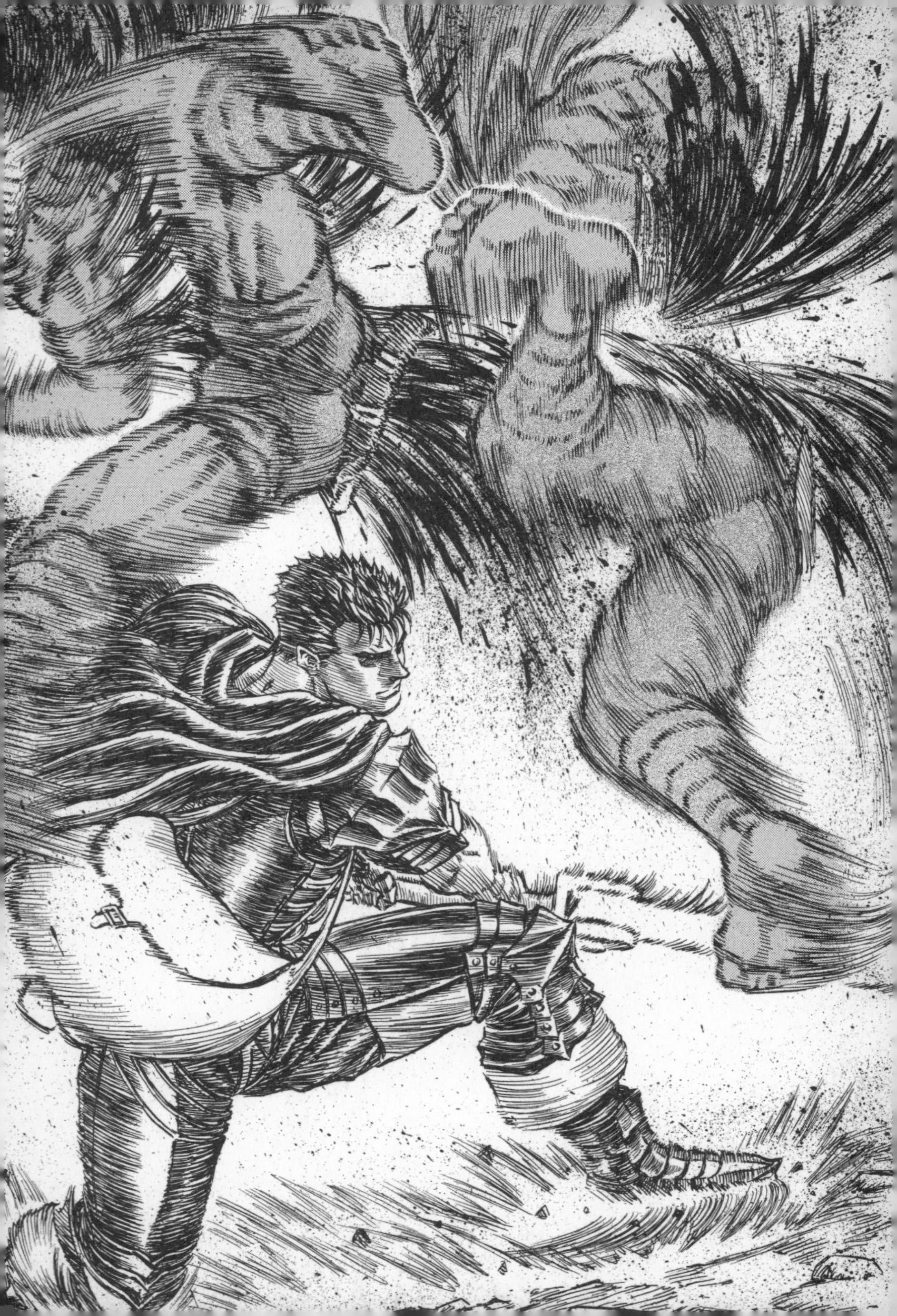

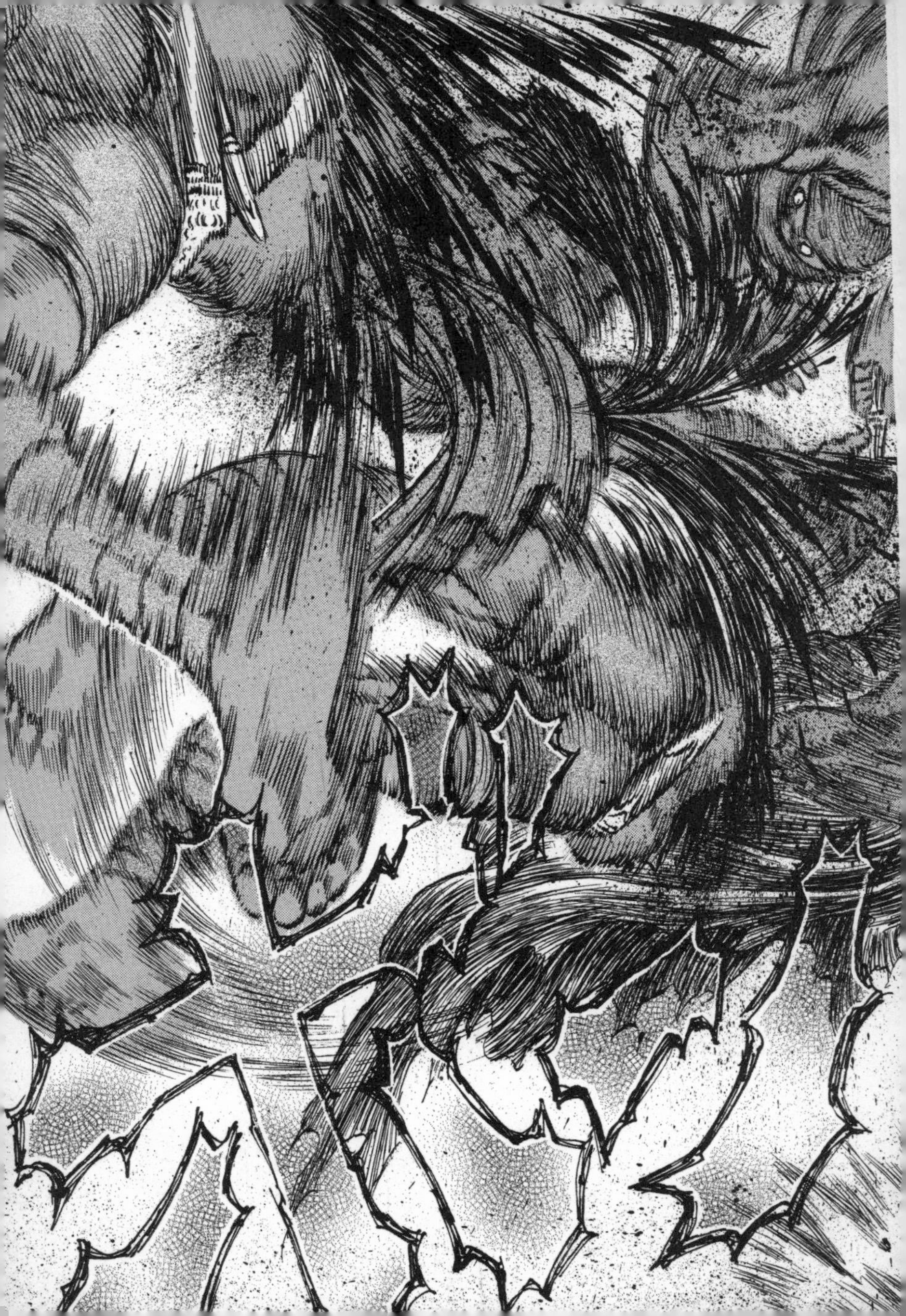

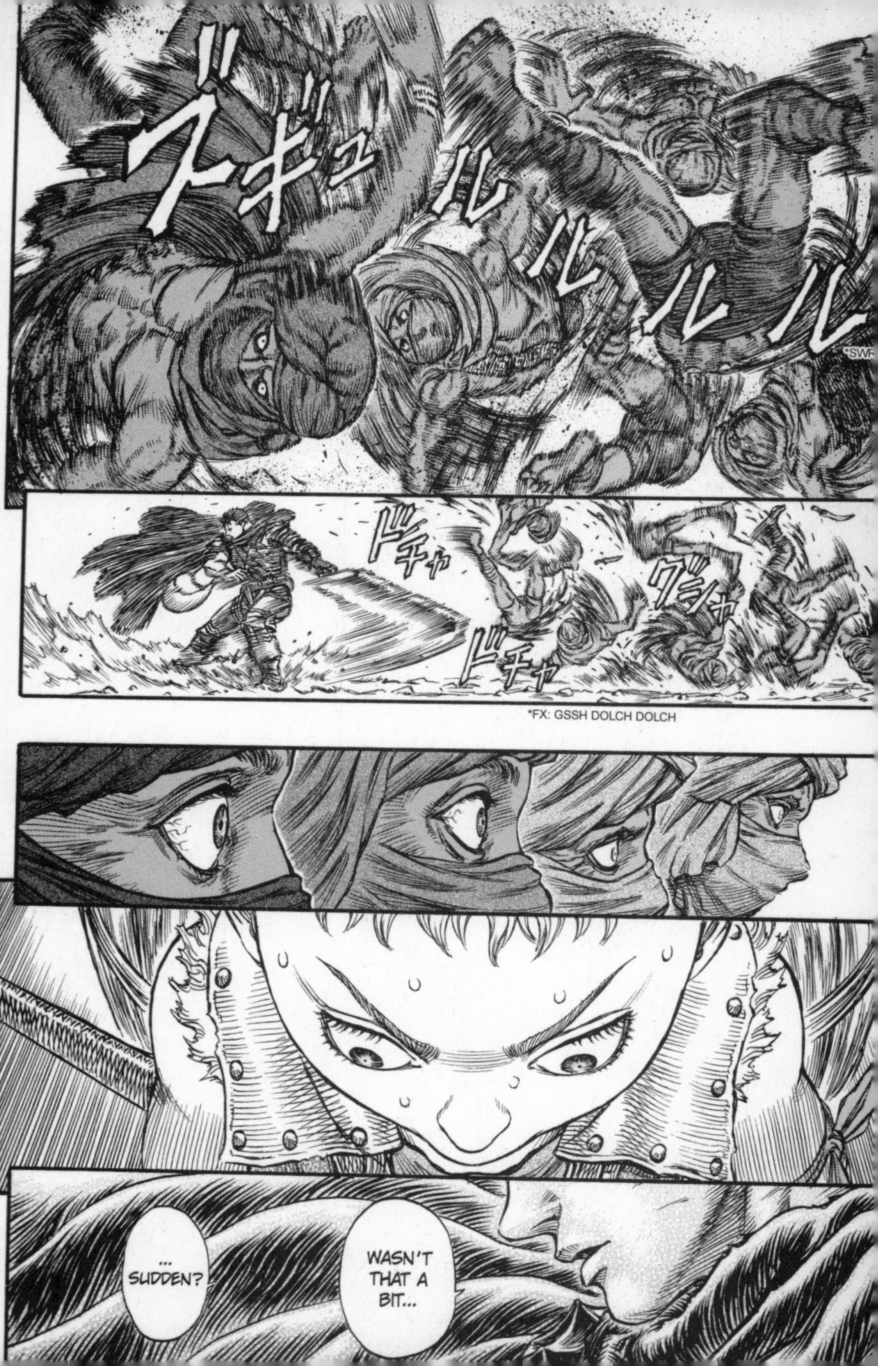
ズギュルルルルル
*SWR
グシャ
ドチャ
ドチャ
*FX: GSSH DOLCH DOLCH
WASN'T THAT A BIT...
... SUDDEN?

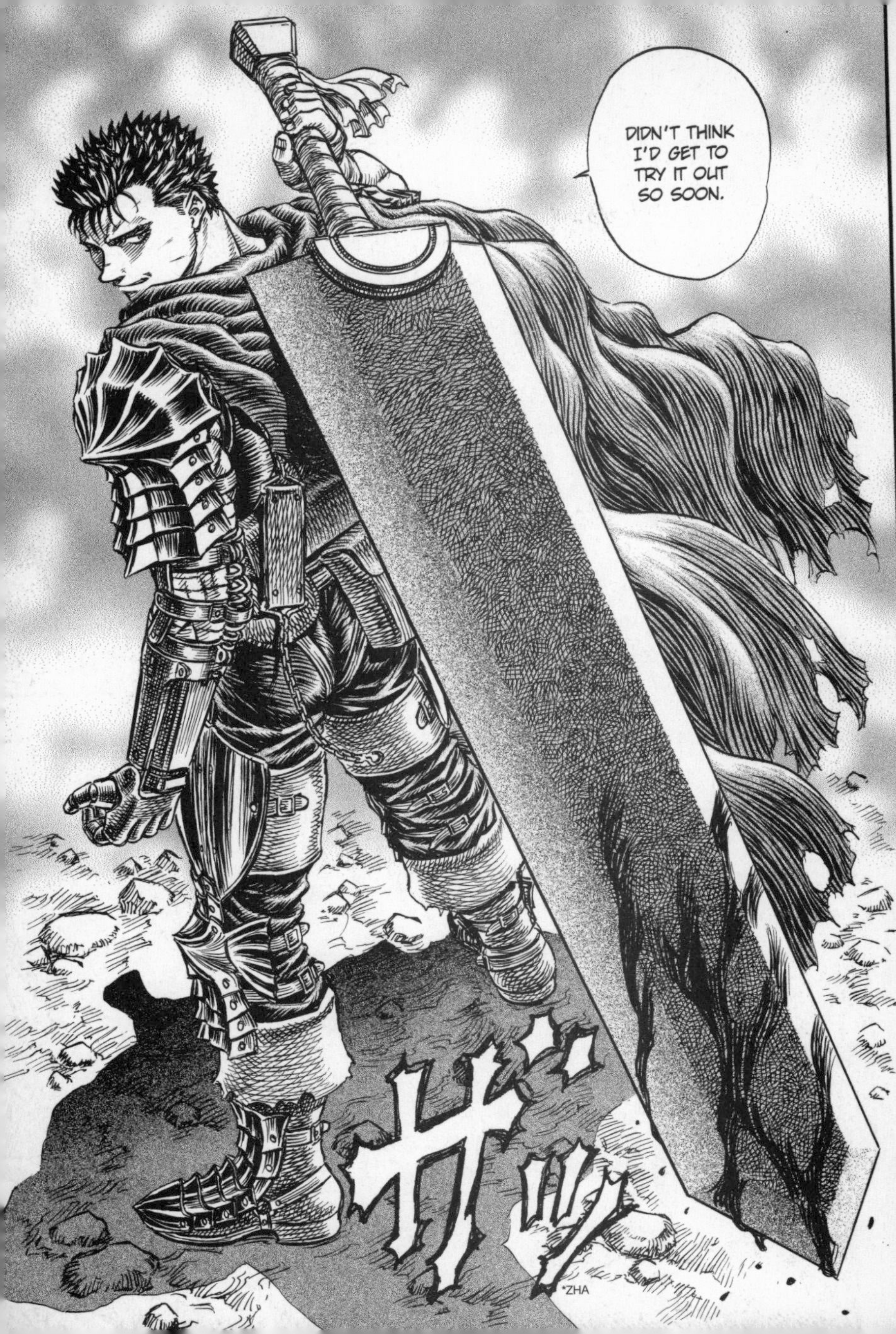
DIDN'T THINK I'D GET TO TRY IT OUT SO SOON.
*ZHA

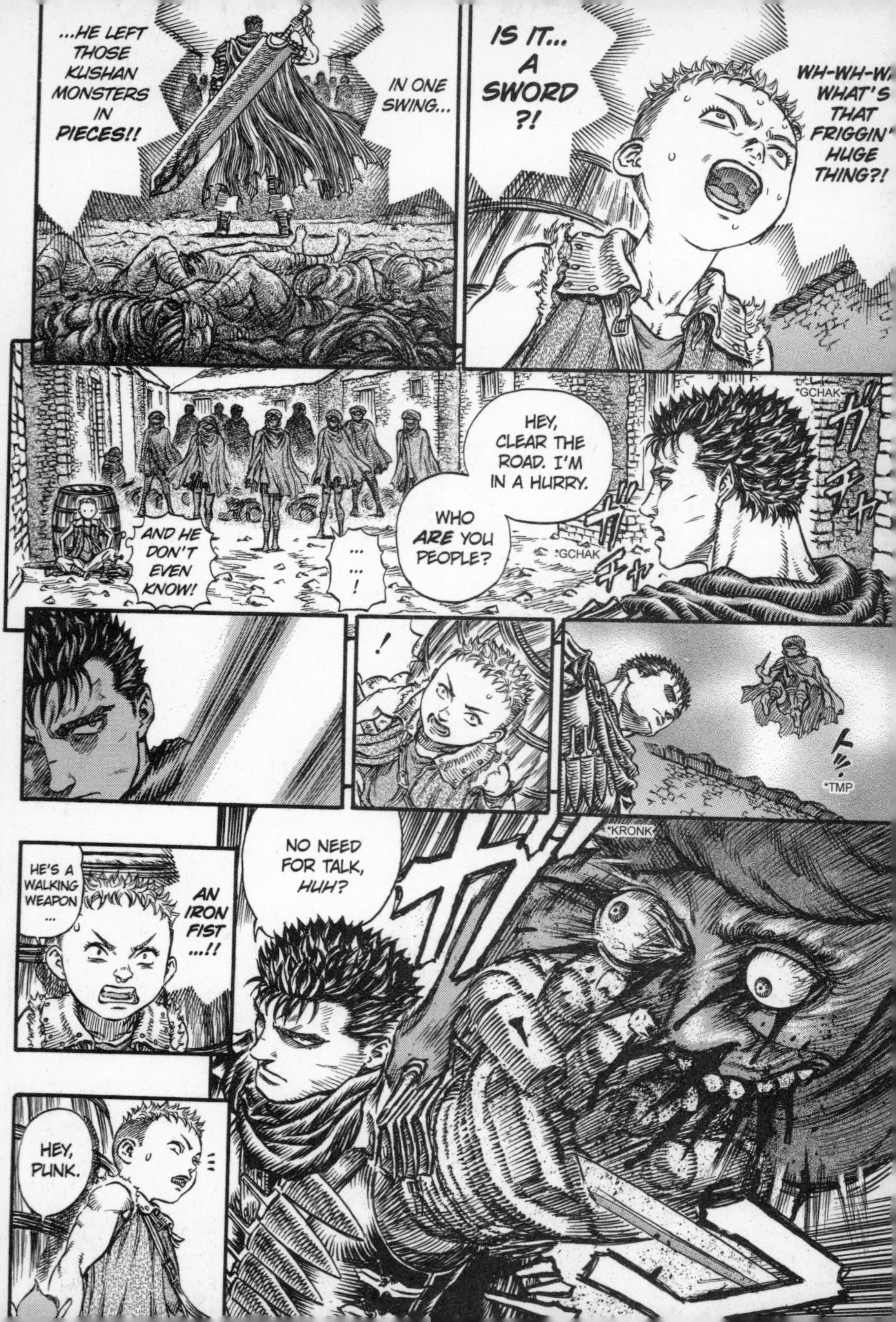
WH-WH-WH WHAT'S THAT FRIGGIN' HUGE THING?!
IS IT... A SWORD ?!
...HE LEFT THOSE KUSHAN MONSTERS IN PIECES!!
IN ONE SWING...
*GCHAK
HEY, CLEAR THE ROAD. I'M IN A HURRY.
*GCHAK
WHO ARE YOU PEOPLE?
......!
AND HE DON'T EVEN KNOW!
*TMP
!
*KRONK
NO NEED FOR TALK, HUH?
AN IRON FIST ...!!
HE'S A WALKING WEAPON ...
HEY, PUNK.

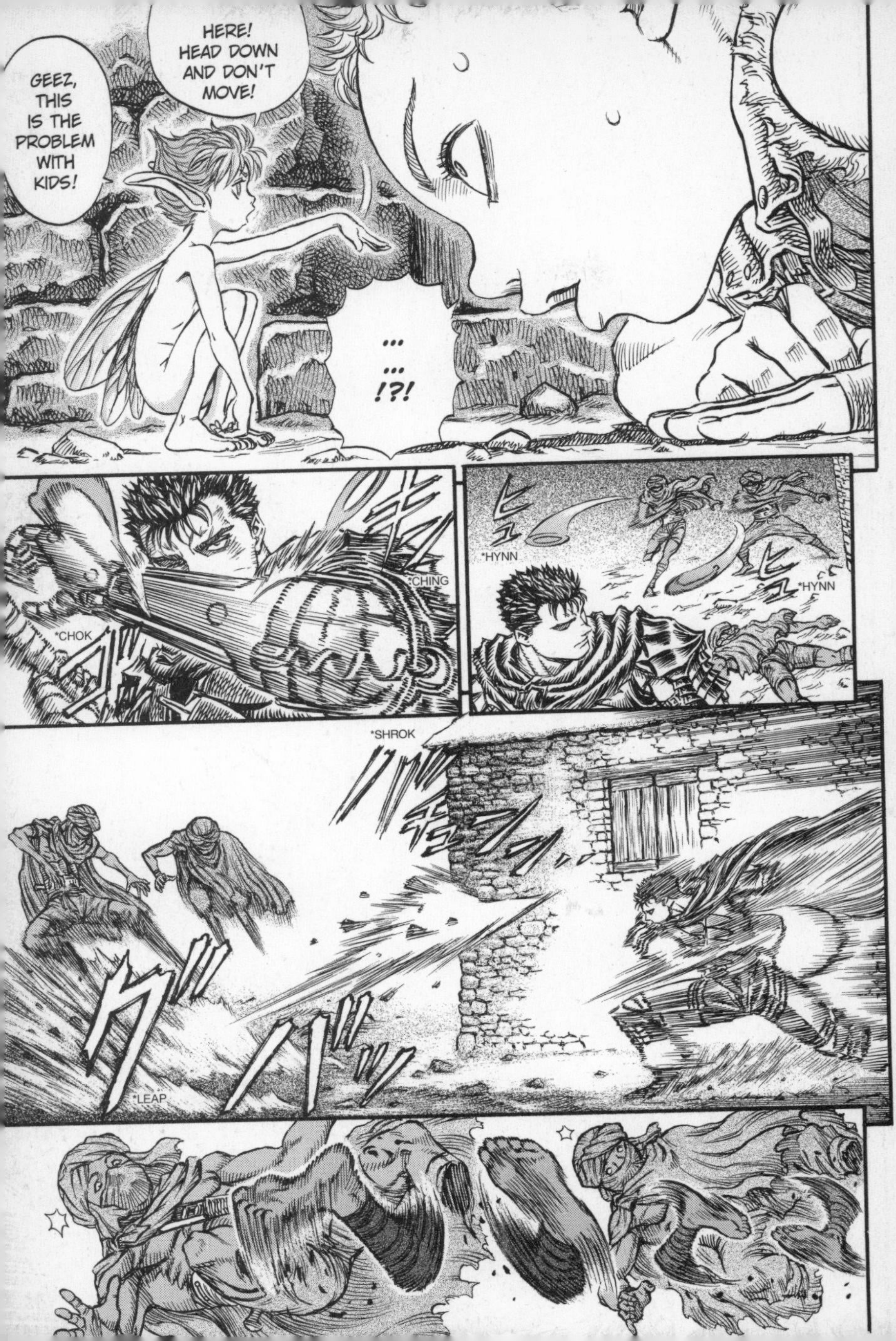
HERE! HEAD DOWN AND DON'T MOVE!
GEEZ, THIS IS THE PROBLEM WITH KIDS!
... ... !?!
*HYNN
*HYNN
*CHING
*CHOK
*SHROK
*LEAP

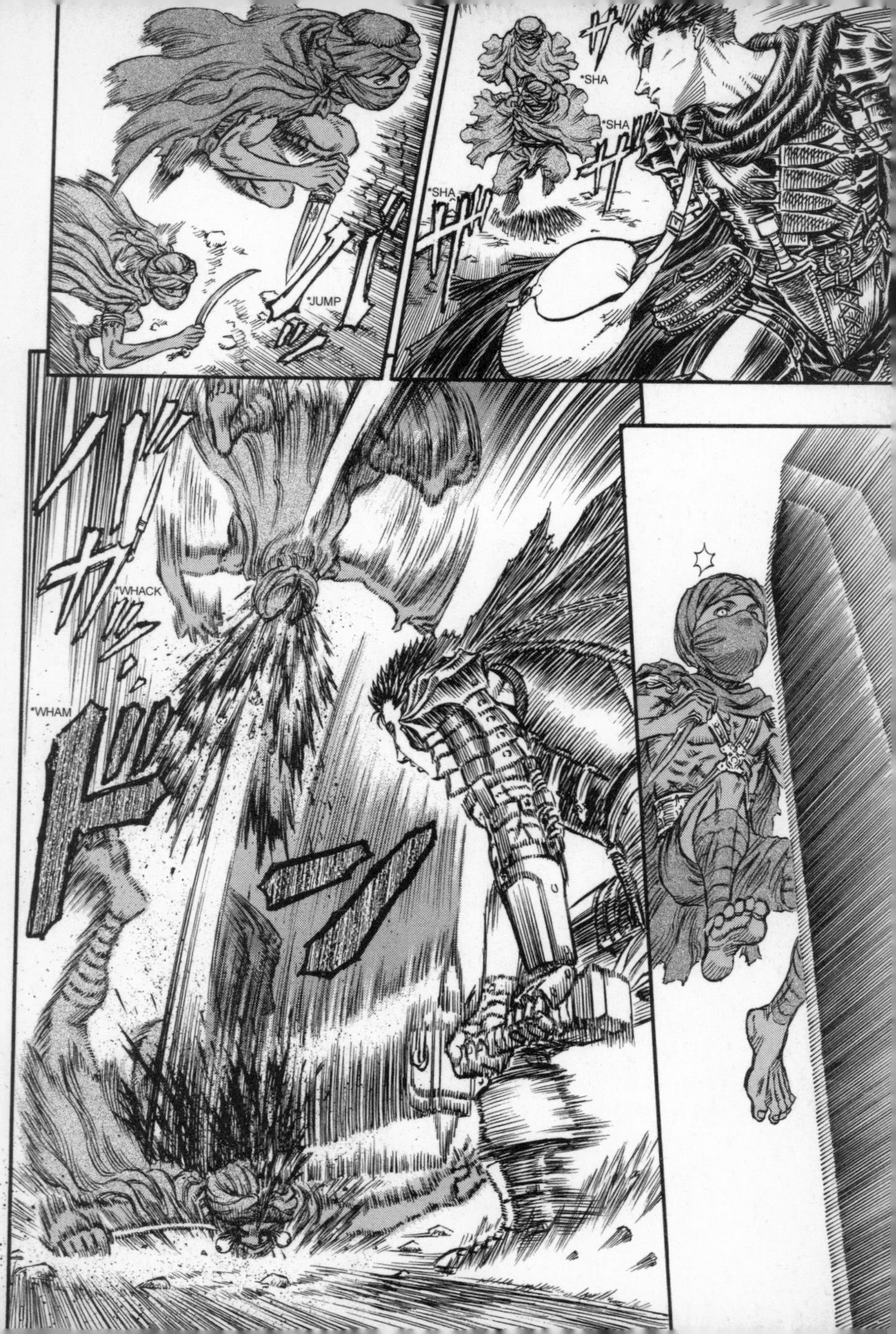
*SHA
*SHA
*SHA
*JUMP
*WHACK
*WHAM

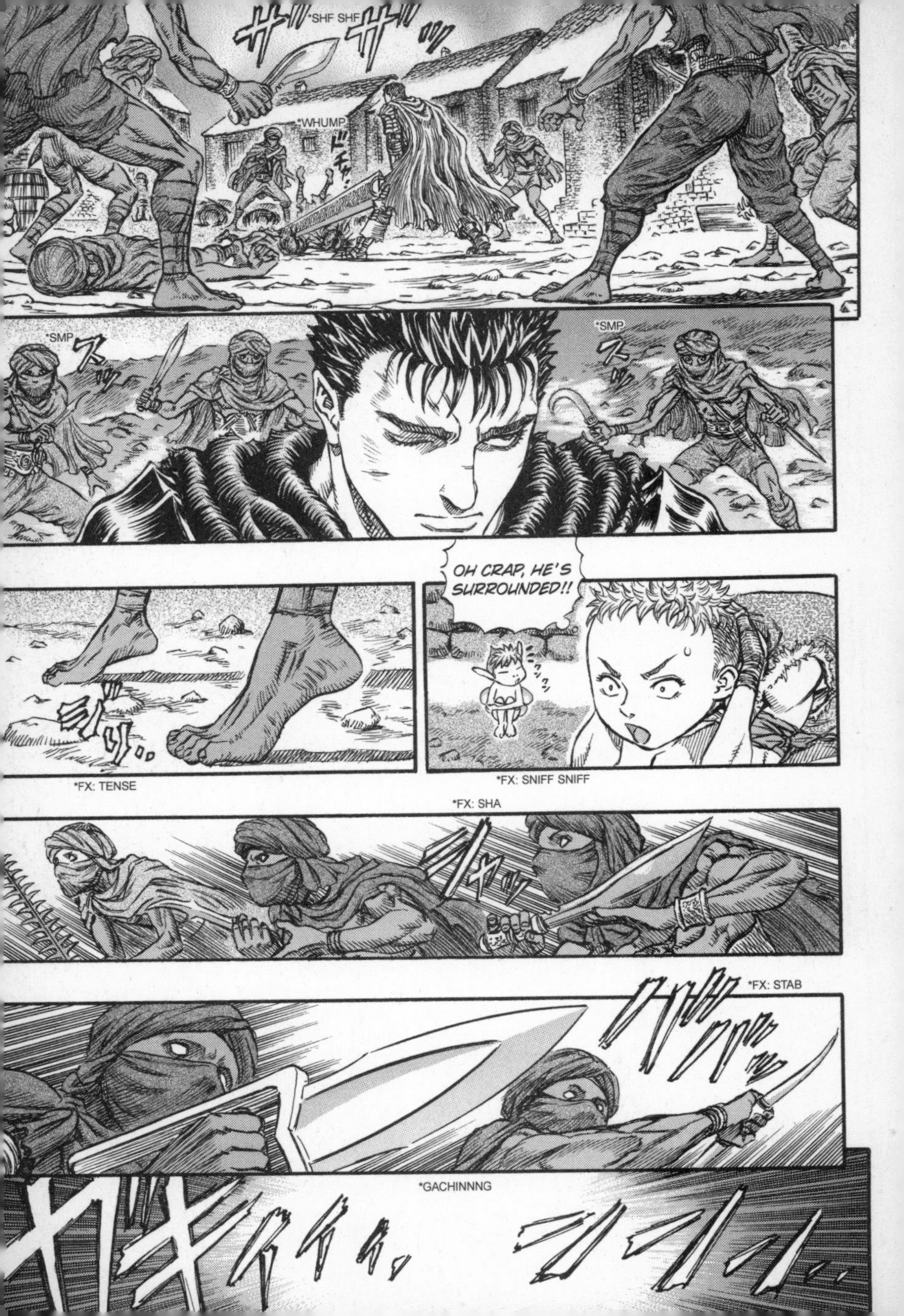
*SHF SHF
*WHUMP
*SMP
*SMP
OH CRAP, HE'S SURROUNDED!!
*FX: SNIFF SNIFF
*FX: TENSE
*FX: SHA
*FX: STAB
*GACHINNNG

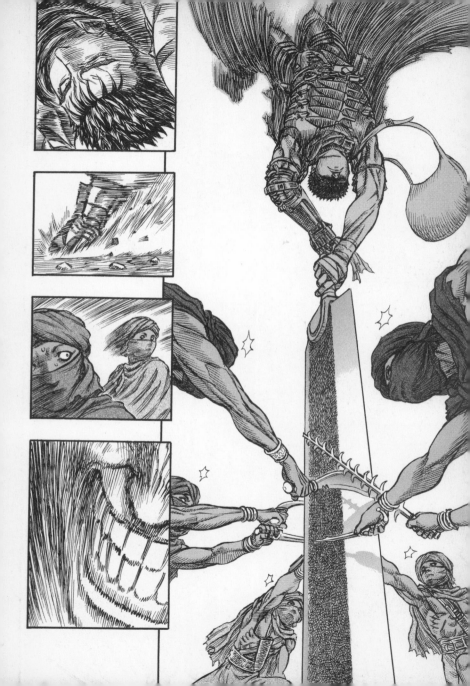

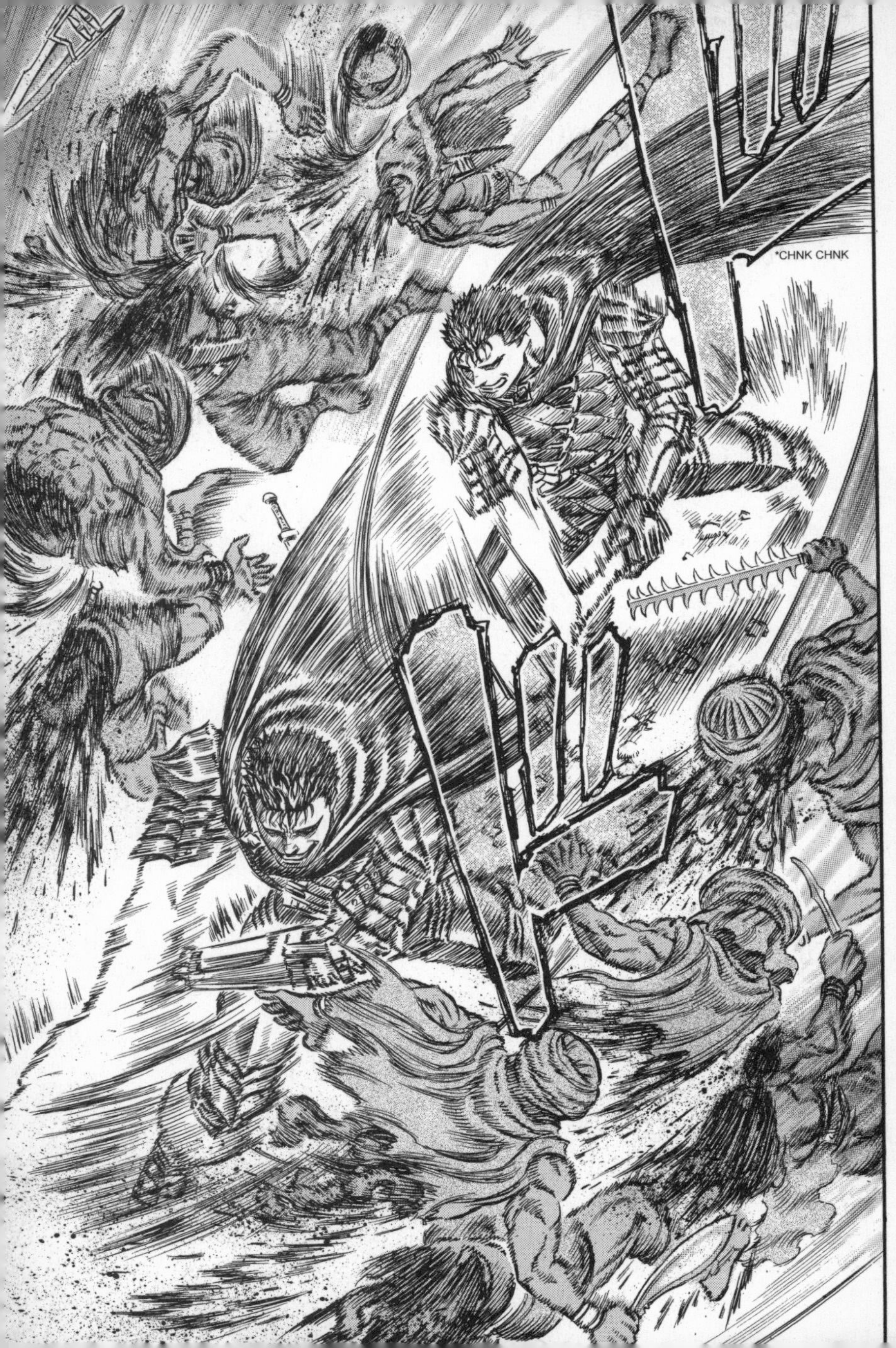
*CHNK CHNK

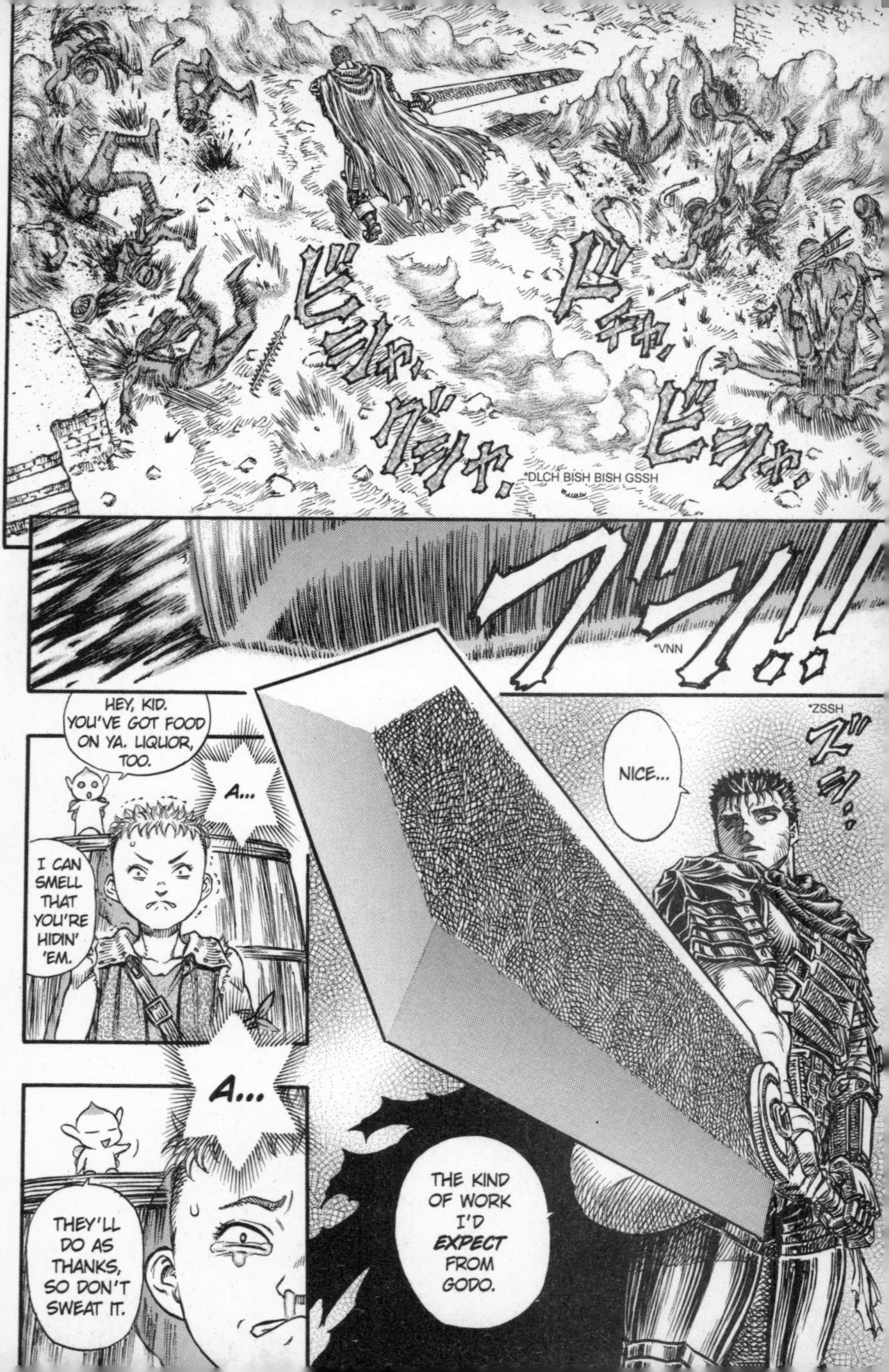
*DLCH BISH BISH GSSH
*VNN
*ZSSH
NICE...
THE KIND OF WORK I'D EXPECT FROM GODO.
HEY, KID. YOU'VE GOT FOOD ON YA. LIQUOR, TOO.
A...
I CAN SMELL THAT YOU'RE HIDIN' 'EM.
A...
THEY'LL DO AS THANKS, SO DON'T SWEAT IT.

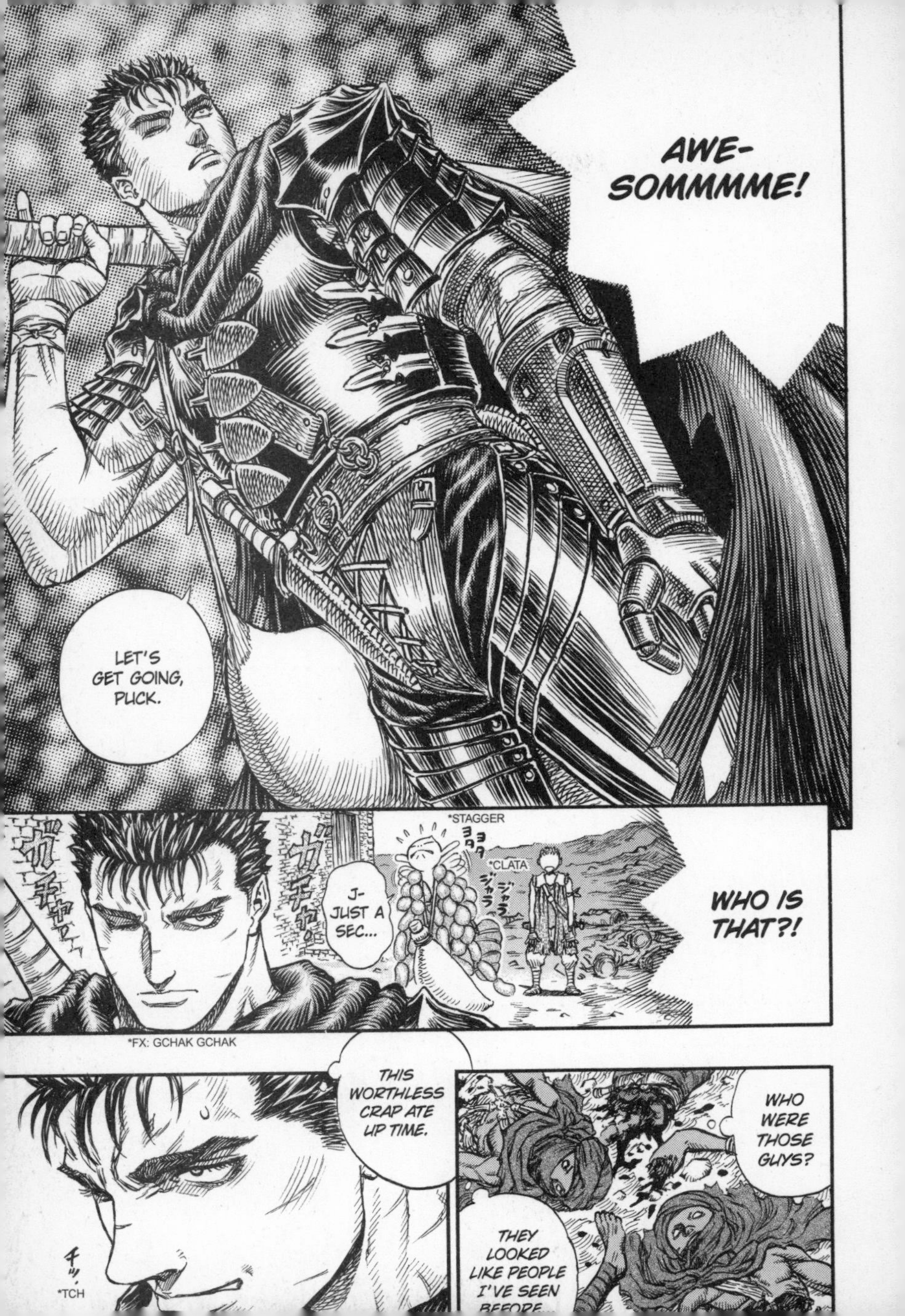
AWE-SOMMMME!
LET'S GET GOING, PUCK.
WHO IS THAT?!
*STAGGER
*CLATA
J-JUST A SEC...
*FX: GCHAK GCHAK
WHO WERE THOSE GUYS?
THEY LOOKED LIKE PEOPLE I'VE SEEN BEFORE...
THIS WORTHLESS CRAP ATE UP TIME.
*TCH

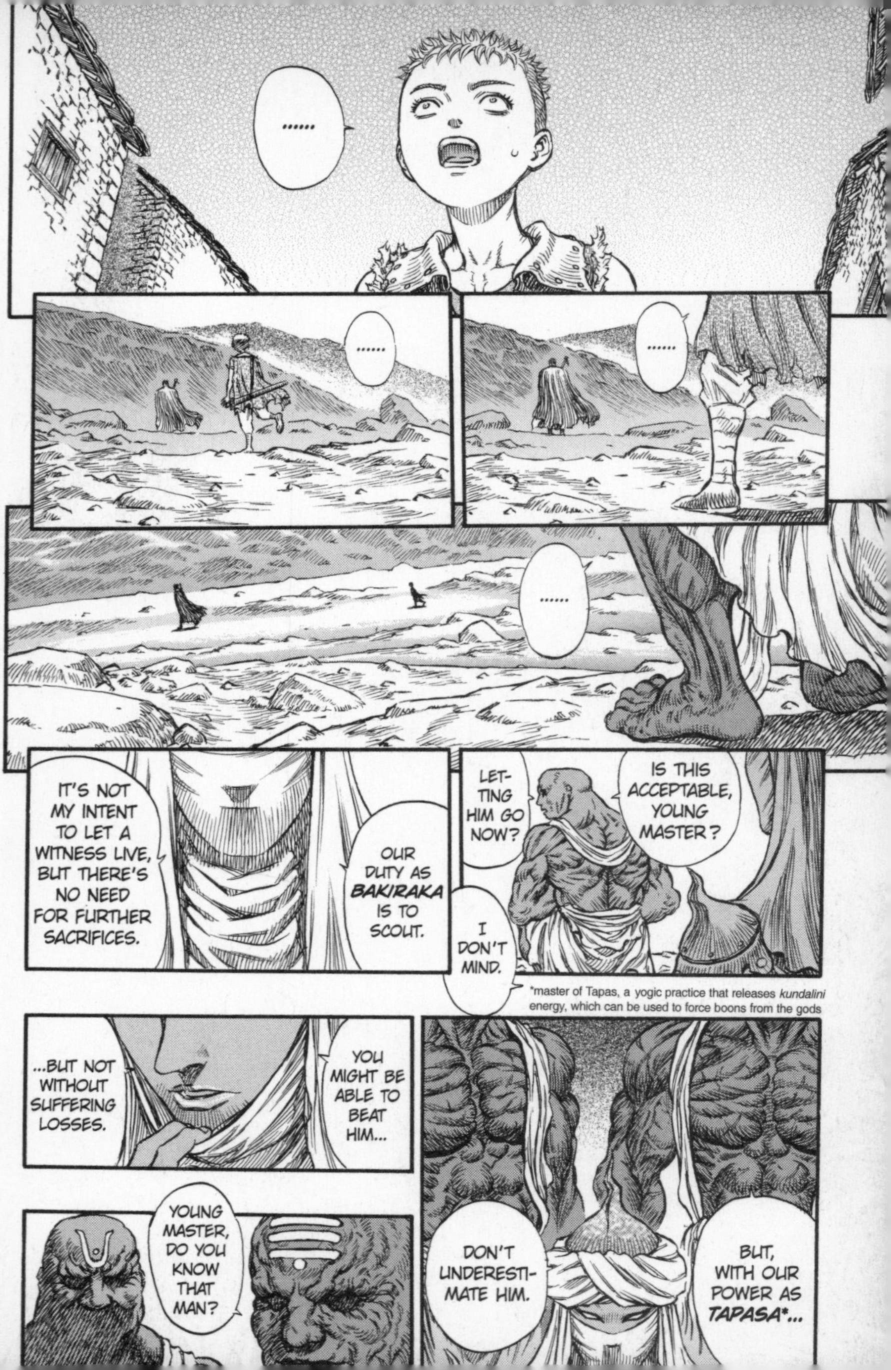
......
......
......
......
IS THIS ACCEPTABLE, YOUNG MASTER?
LETTING HIM GO NOW?
I DON'T MIND.
OUR DUTY AS **BAKIRAKA** IS TO SCOUT.
IT'S NOT MY INTENT TO LET A WITNESS LIVE, BUT THERE'S NO NEED FOR FURTHER SACRIFICES.
BUT, WITH OUR POWER AS **TAPASA***...
DON'T UNDERESTIMATE HIM.
YOU MIGHT BE ABLE TO BEAT HIM...
...BUT NOT WITHOUT SUFFERING LOSSES.
YOUNG MASTER, DO YOU KNOW THAT MAN?

*master of Tapas, a yogic practice that releases *kundalini* energy, which can be used to force boons from the gods

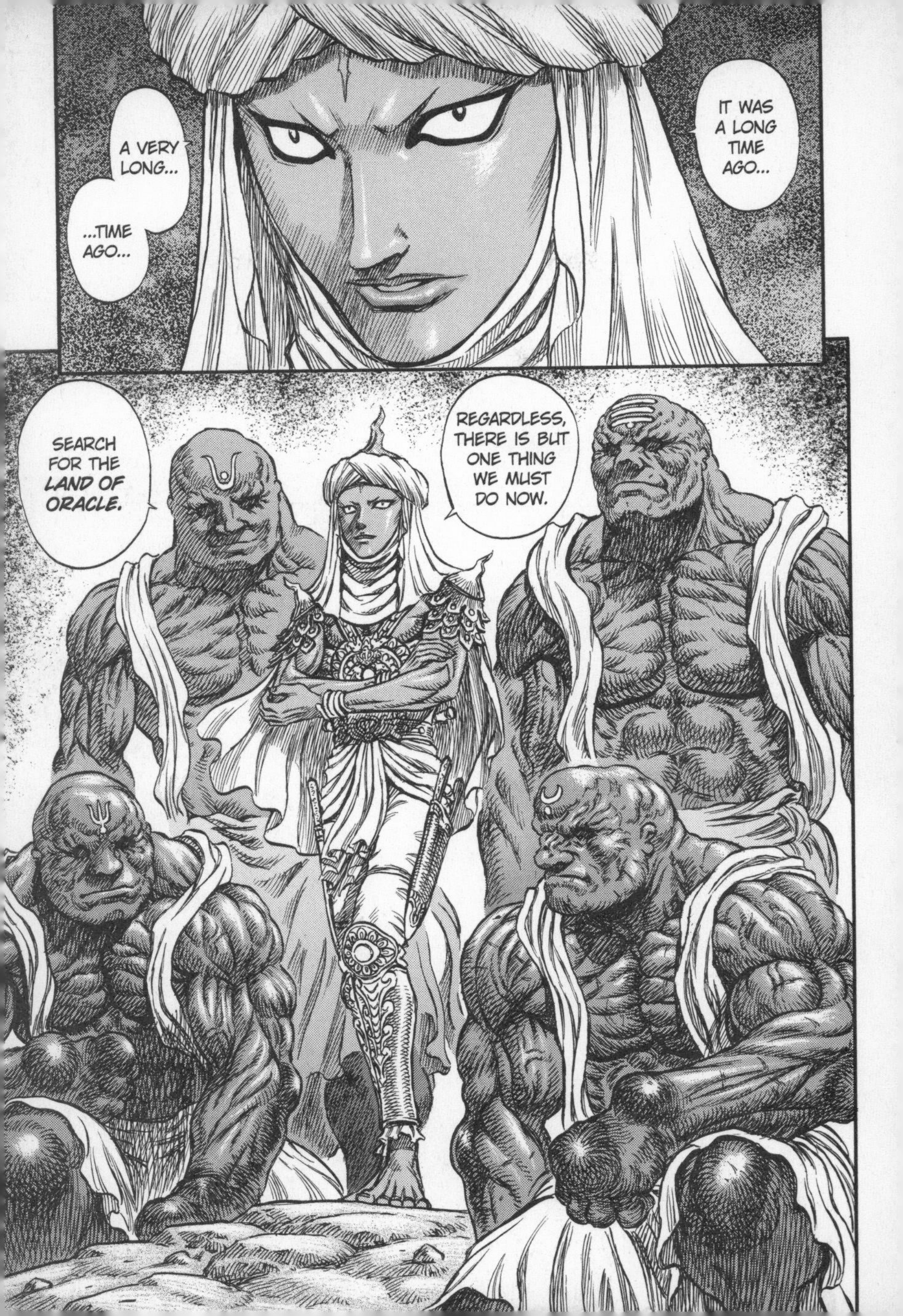
IT WAS A LONG TIME AGO...
A VERY LONG...
...TIME AGO...
REGARDLESS, THERE IS BUT ONE THING WE MUST DO NOW.
SEARCH FOR THE *LAND OF ORACLE.*

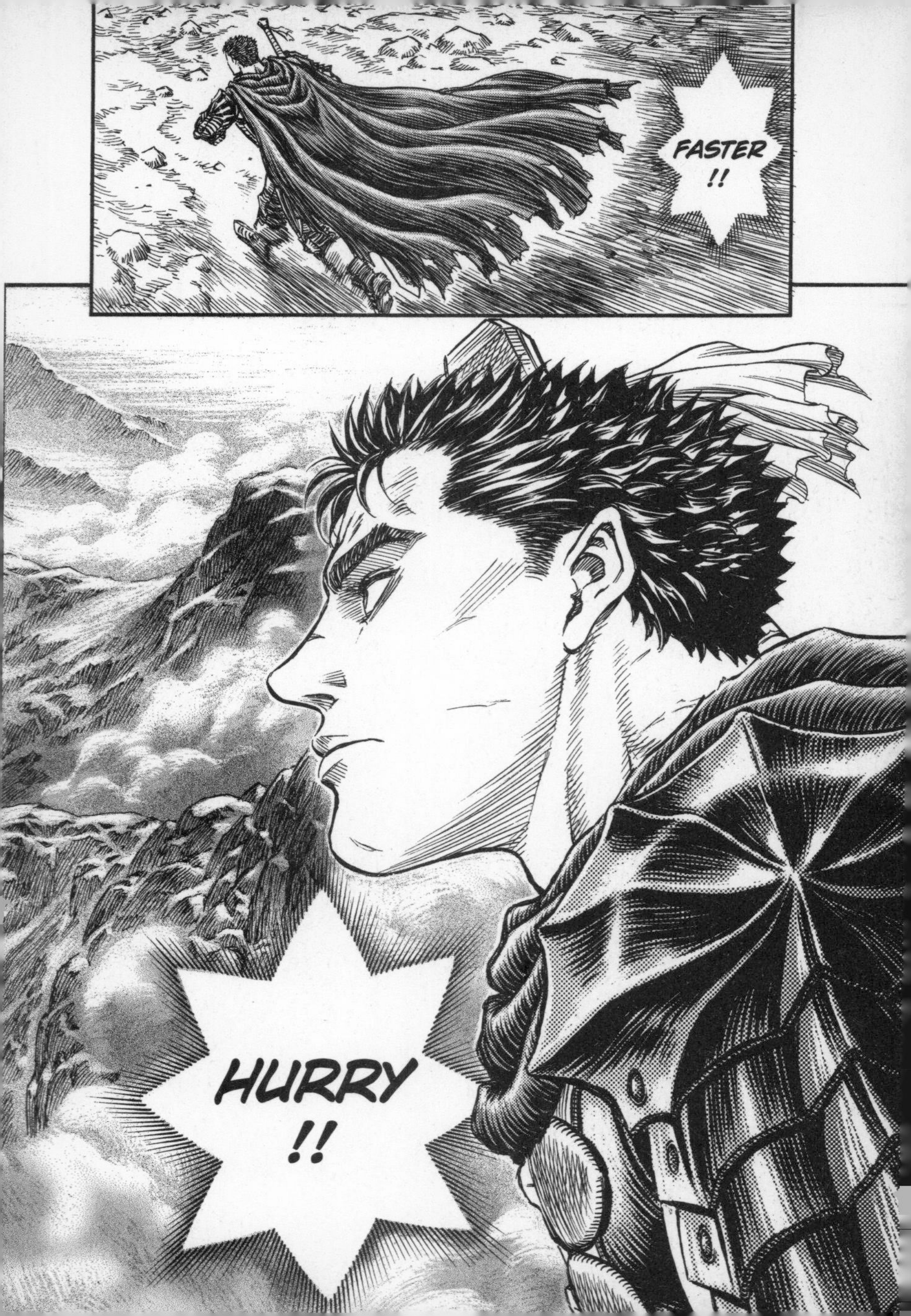
FASTER !!
HURRY !!

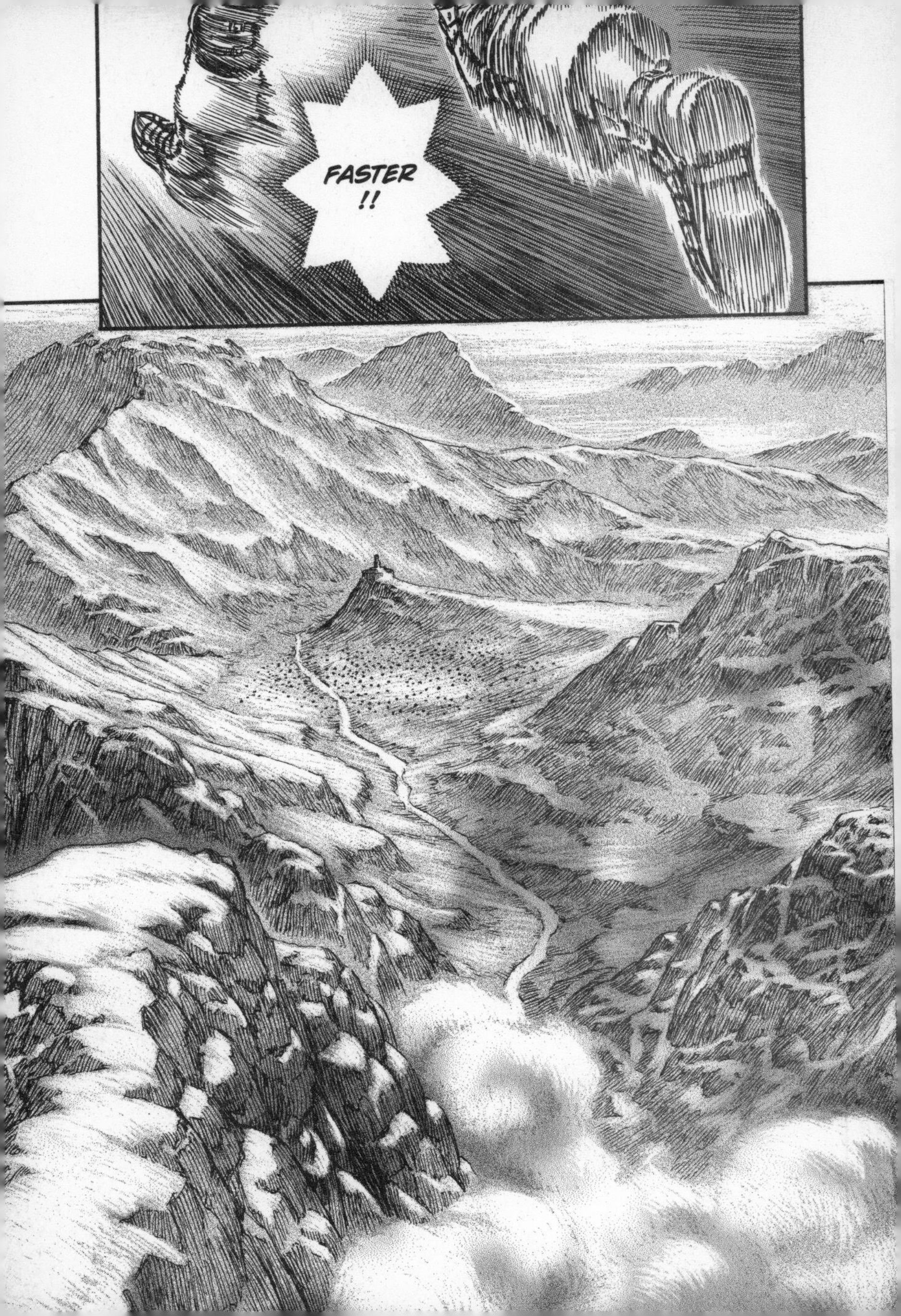
FASTER
!!

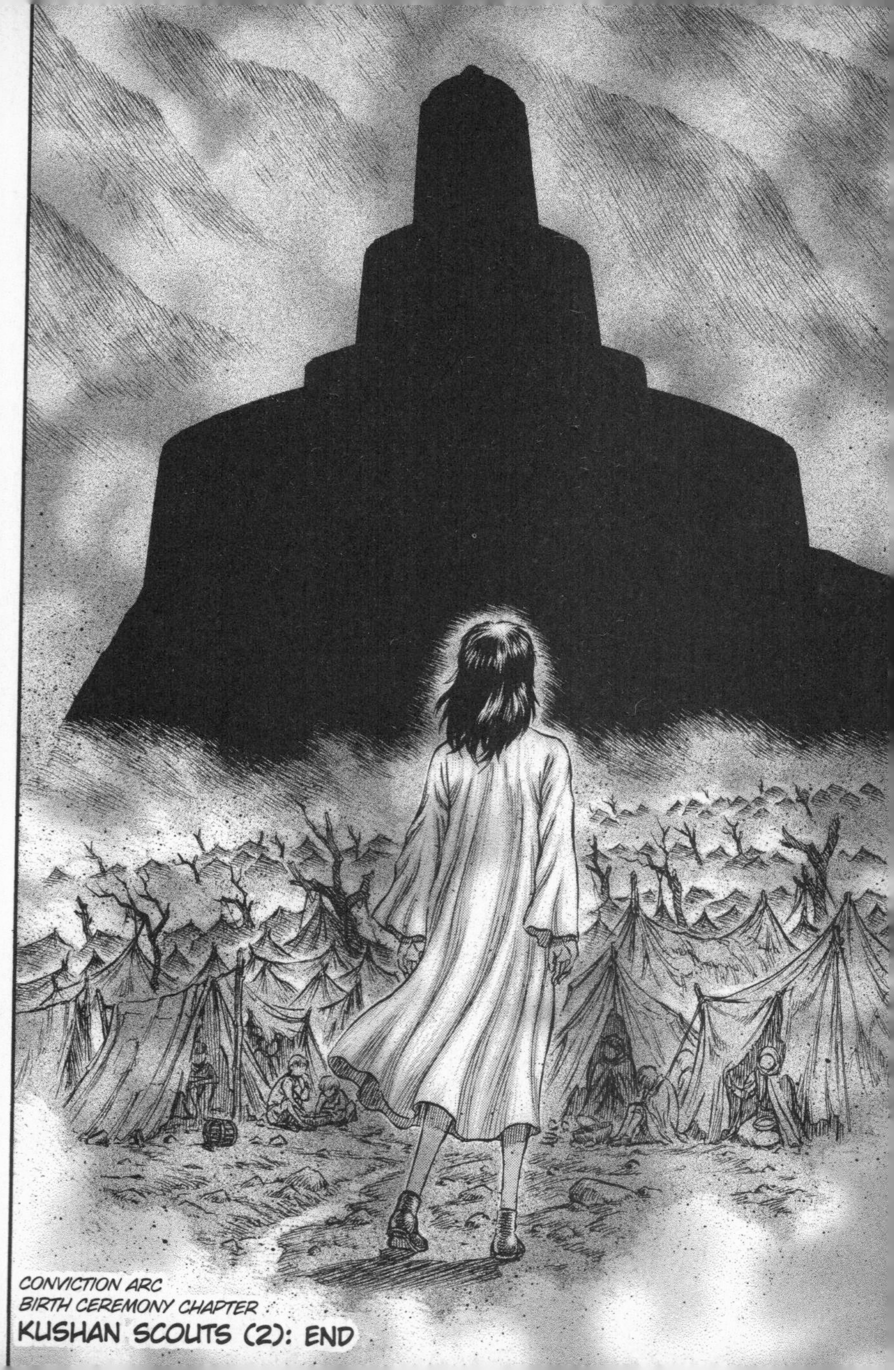
CONVICTION ARC
BIRTH CEREMONY CHAPTER
KUSHAN SCOUTS (2): END

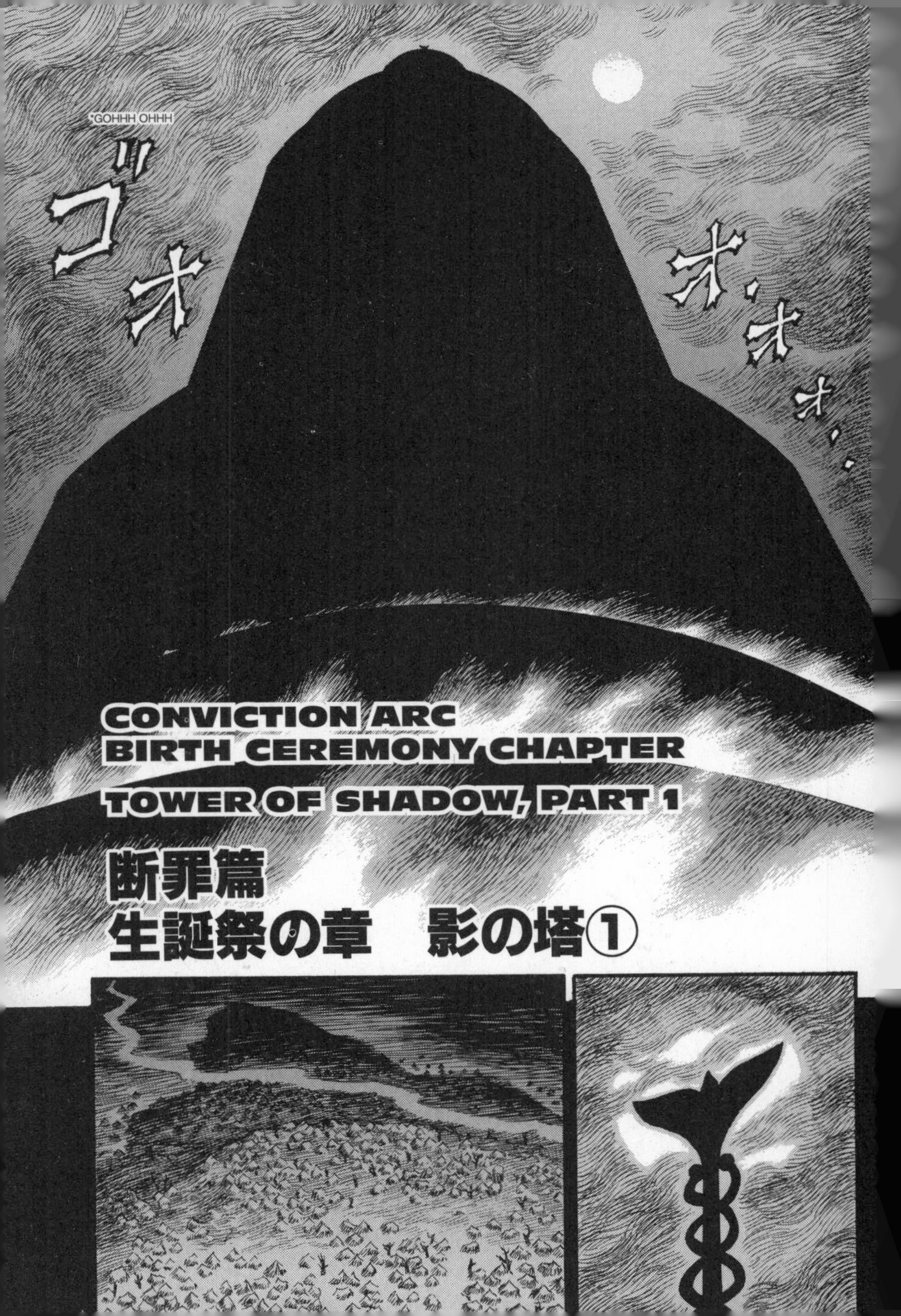
*GOHHH OHHH
ゴオ
オ・オオ・・
CONVICTION ARC
BIRTH CEREMONY CHAPTER
TOWER OF SHADOW, PART 1
断罪篇
生誕祭の章　影の塔①

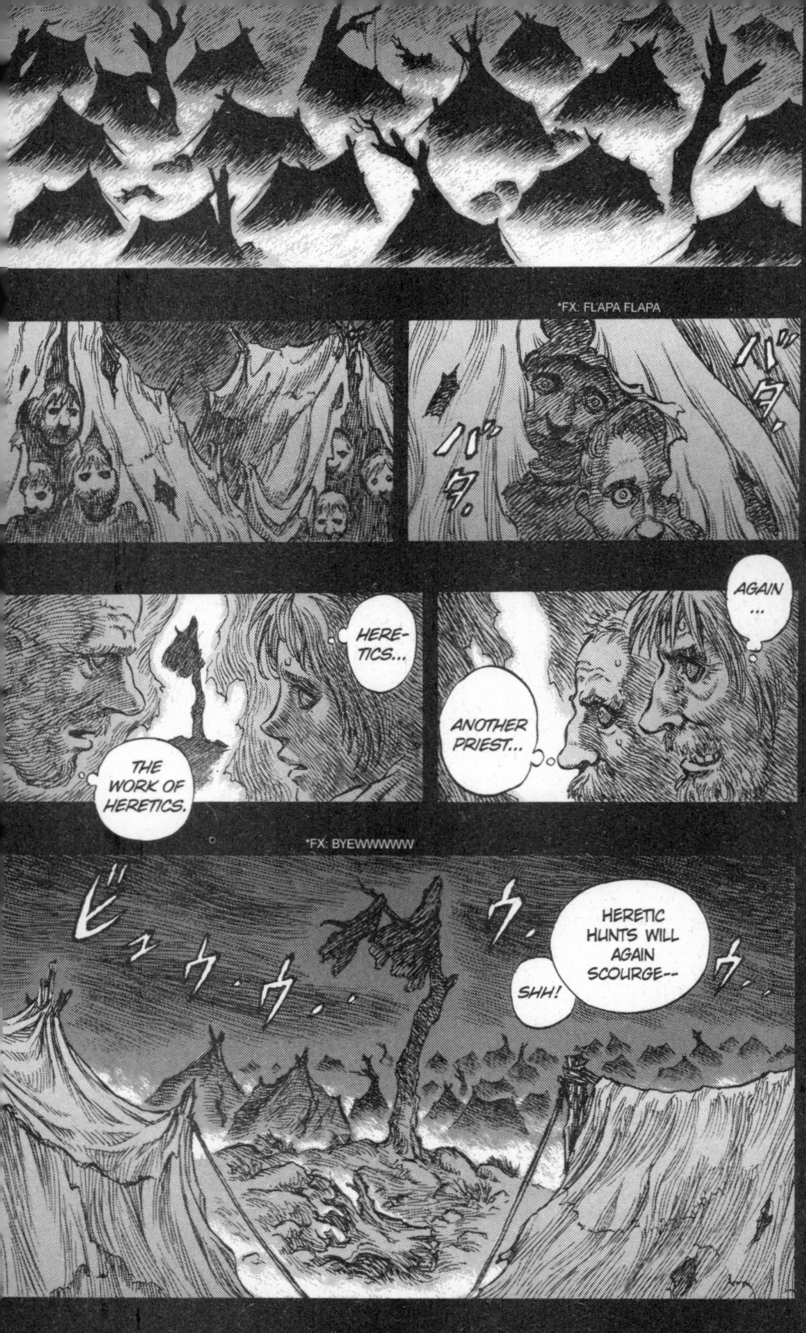
*FX: FLAPA FLAPA
AGAIN ...
ANOTHER PRIEST...
HERE-TICS...
THE WORK OF HERETICS.
*FX: BYEWWWWW
HERETIC HUNTS WILL AGAIN SCOURGE--
SHH!

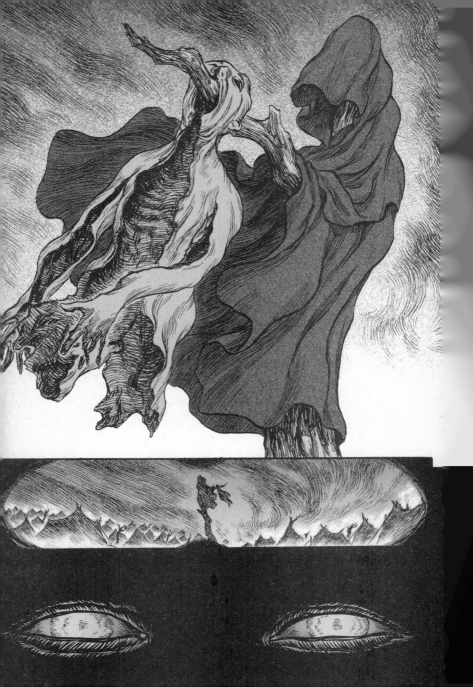

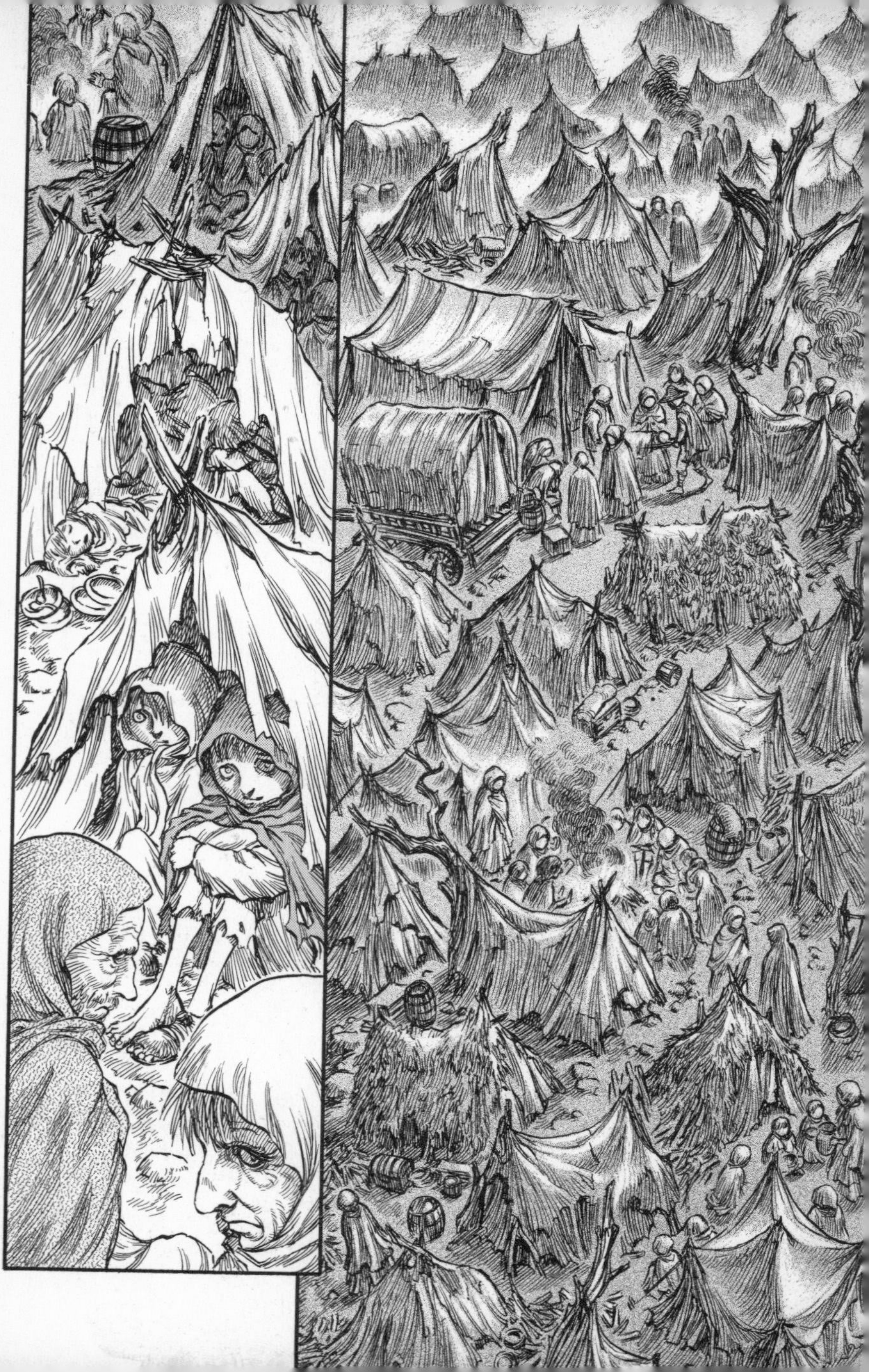

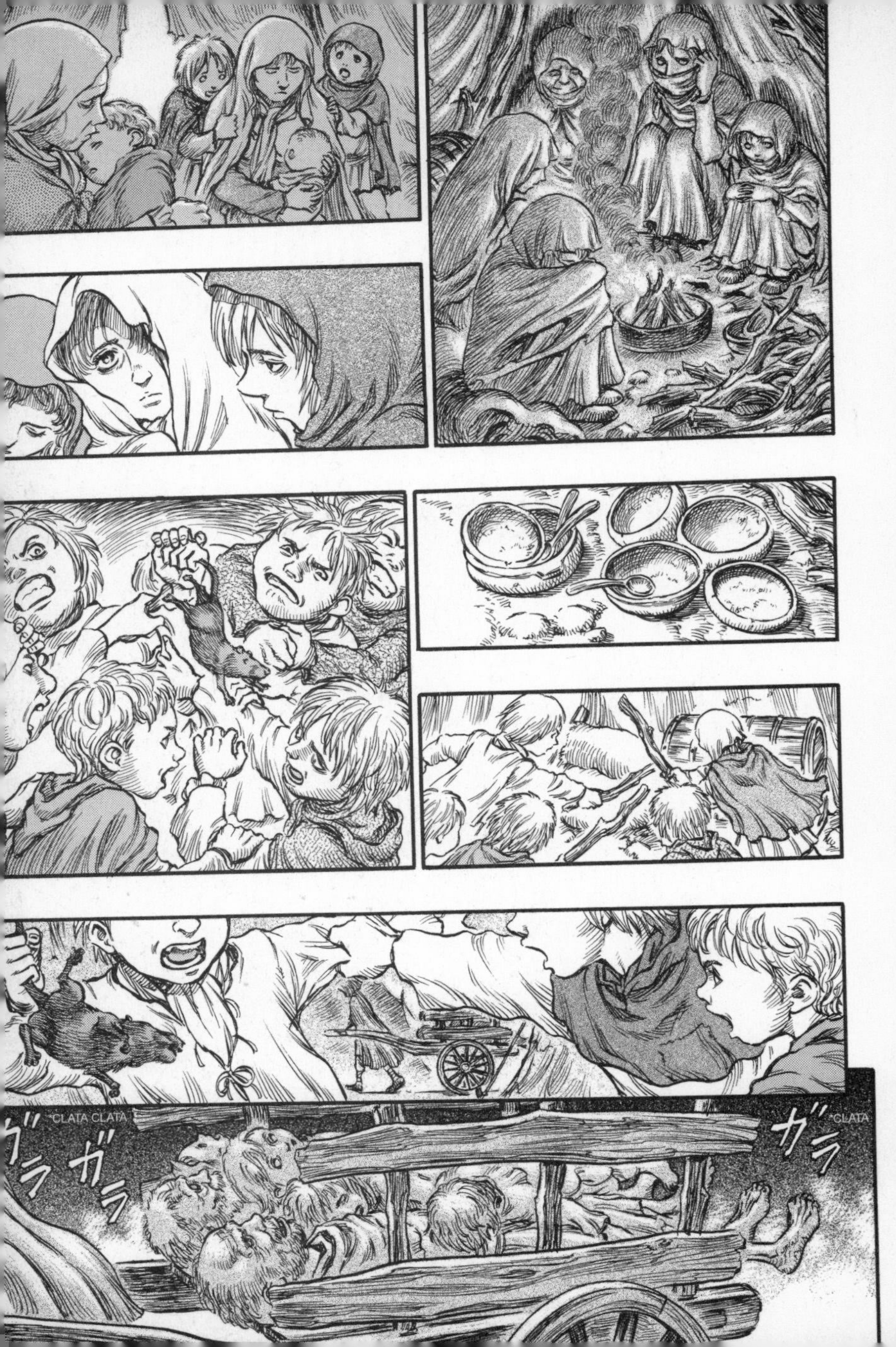
ガラ
CLATA
CLATA CLATA
ガラ
ガラ

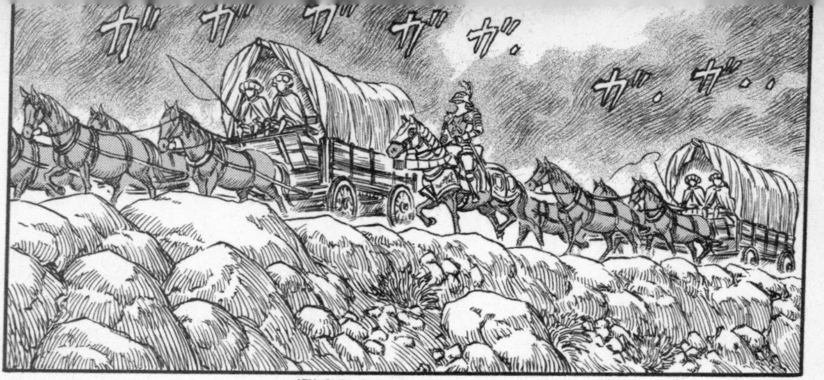
ガ ガ ガ ガ ガ。
ガ。ガ。。

*FX: CLOP CLOP CLOP CLOP CLOP CLOP CLOP

*FX: SHUFFLE

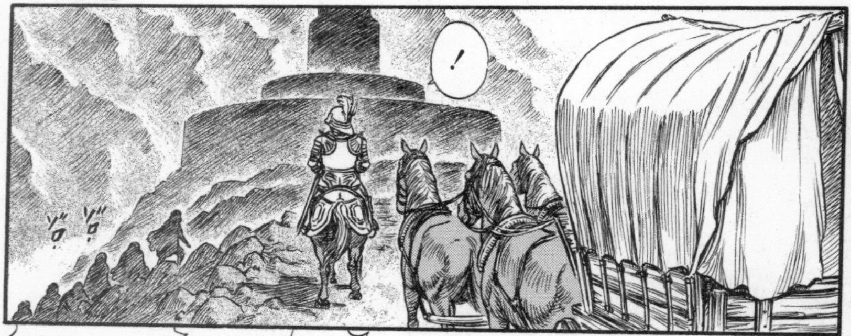
!
ゾロ ゾロ

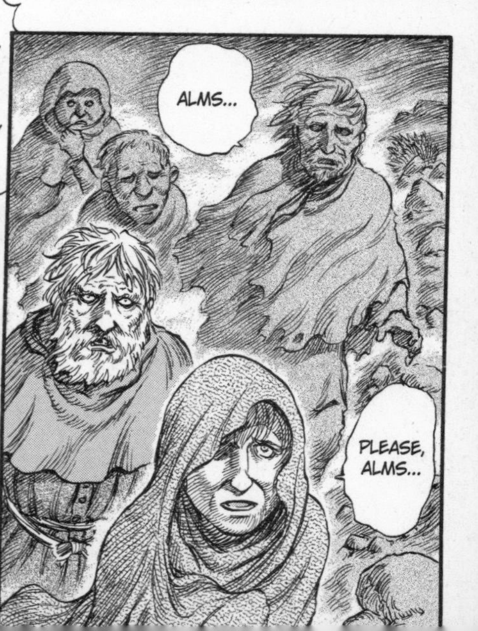
ALMS...
PLEASE, ALMS...

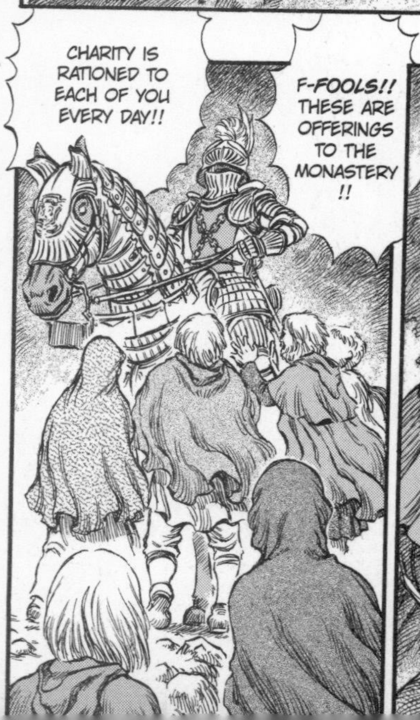
F-***FOOLS***!! THESE ARE OFFERINGS TO THE MONASTERY!!
CHARITY IS RATIONED TO EACH OF YOU EVERY DAY!!

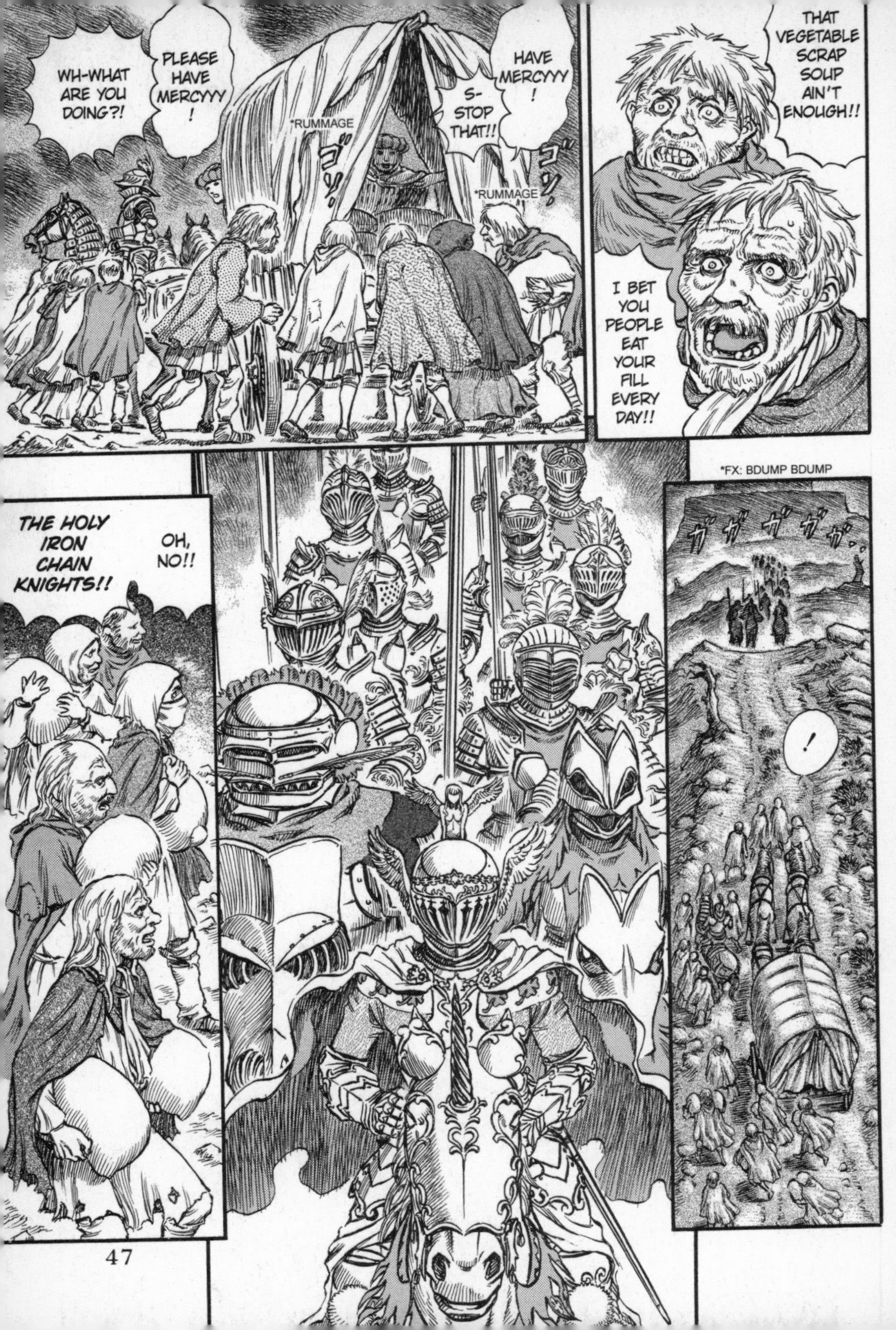
THAT VEGETABLE SCRAP SOUP AIN'T ENOUGH!!
I BET YOU PEOPLE EAT YOUR FILL EVERY DAY!!
HAVE MERCYYY!
S-STOP THAT!!
*RUMMAGE
PLEASE HAVE MERCYYY!
*RUMMAGE
WH-WHAT ARE YOU DOING?!
*FX: BDUMP BDUMP
!
OH, NO!!
THE HOLY IRON CHAIN KNIGHTS!!

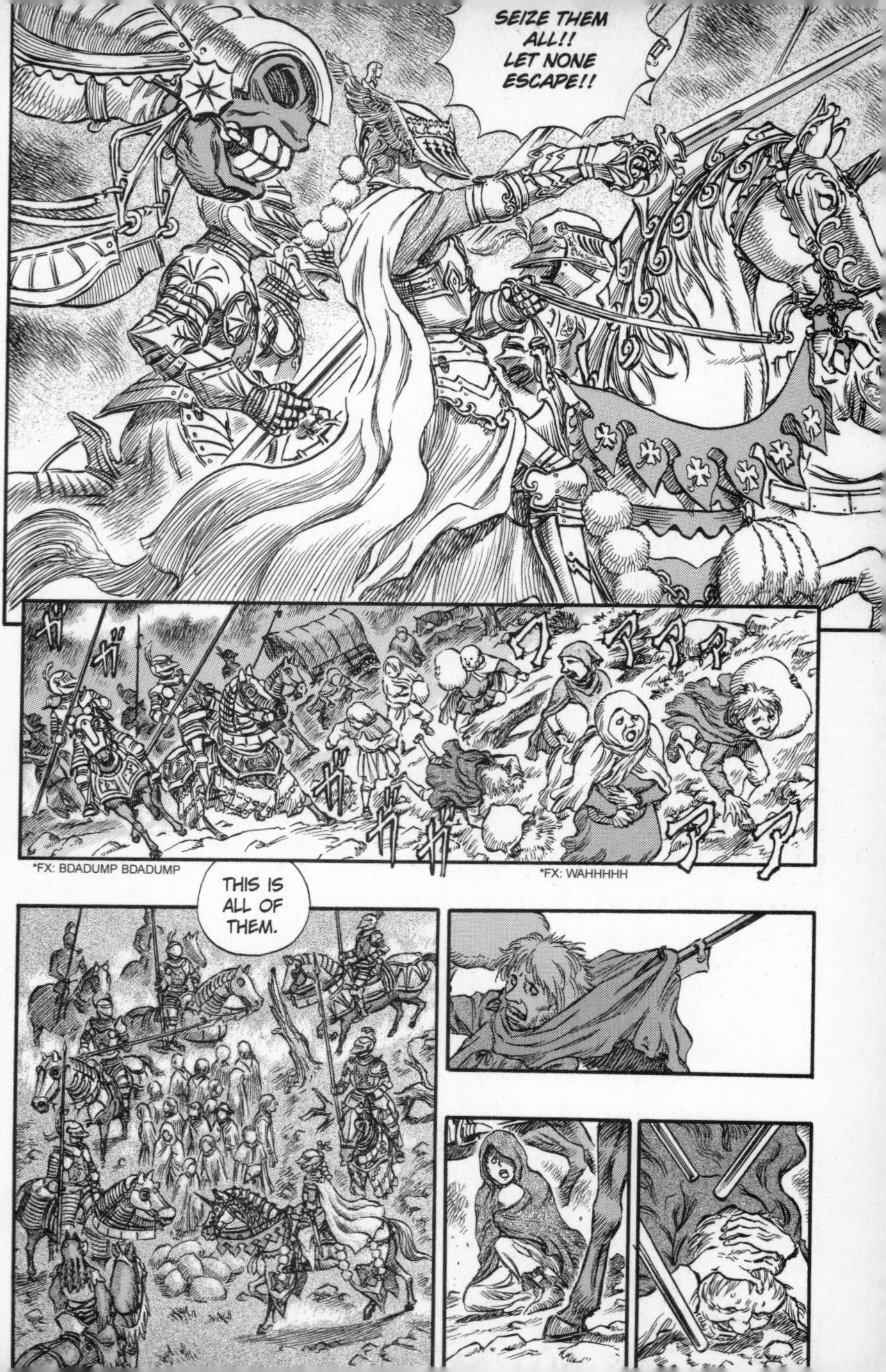
SEIZE THEM ALL!! LET NONE ESCAPE!!
*FX: WAHHHHH
*FX: BDADUMP BDADUMP
THIS IS ALL OF THEM.

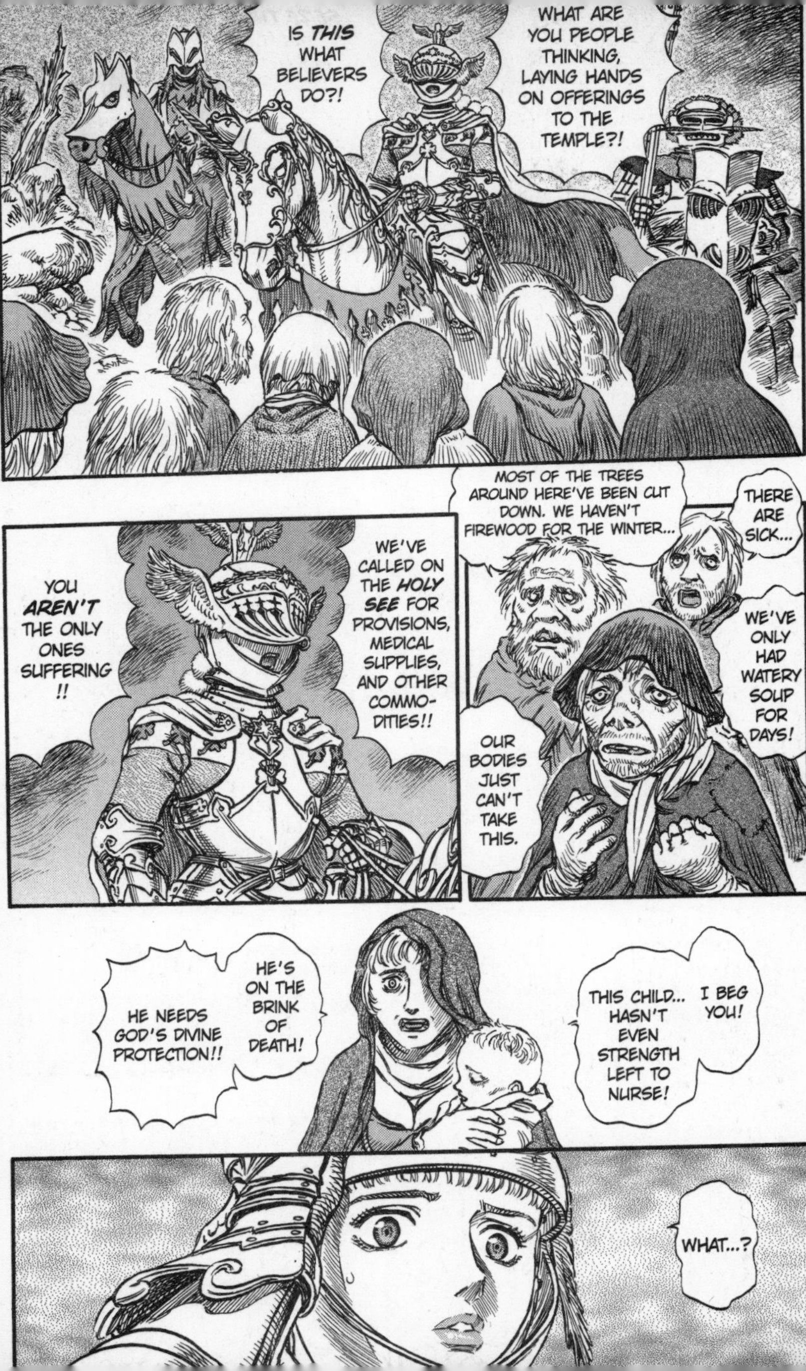
WHAT ARE YOU PEOPLE THINKING, LAYING HANDS ON OFFERINGS TO THE TEMPLE?!
IS THIS WHAT BELIEVERS DO?!
MOST OF THE TREES AROUND HERE'VE BEEN CUT DOWN. WE HAVEN'T FIREWOOD FOR THE WINTER...
THERE ARE SICK...
WE'VE ONLY HAD WATERY SOUP FOR DAYS!
OUR BODIES JUST CAN'T TAKE THIS.
WE'VE CALLED ON THE HOLY SEE FOR PROVISIONS, MEDICAL SUPPLIES, AND OTHER COMMODITIES!!
YOU AREN'T THE ONLY ONES SUFFERING!!
I BEG YOU!
THIS CHILD... HASN'T EVEN STRENGTH LEFT TO NURSE!
HE'S ON THE BRINK OF DEATH!
HE NEEDS GOD'S DIVINE PROTECTION!!
WHAT...?

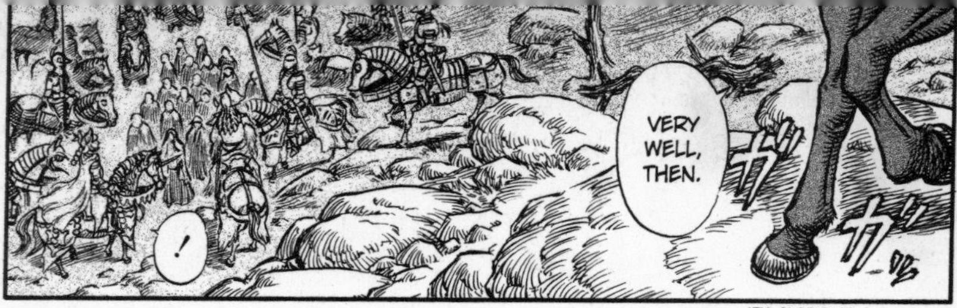
VERY WELL, THEN.
!
*FX: CLOP CLOP

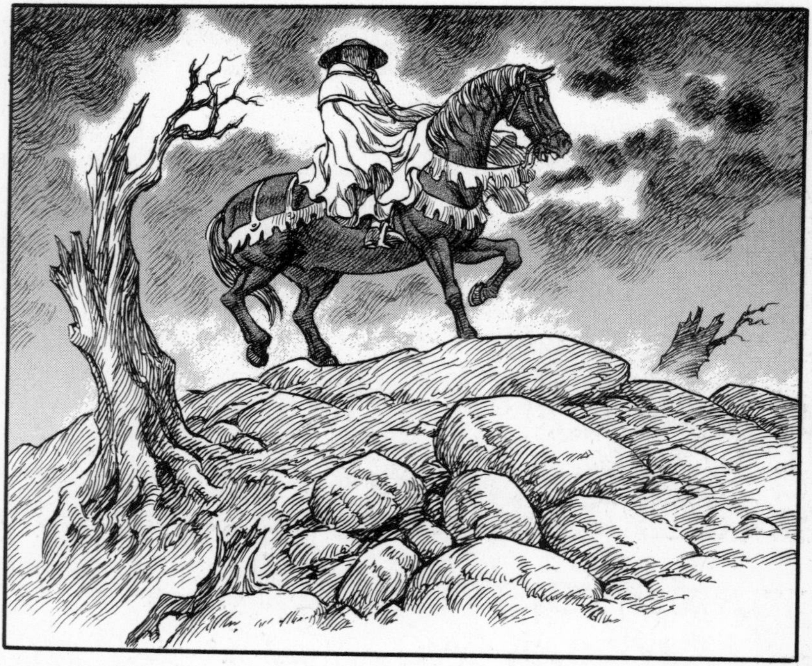

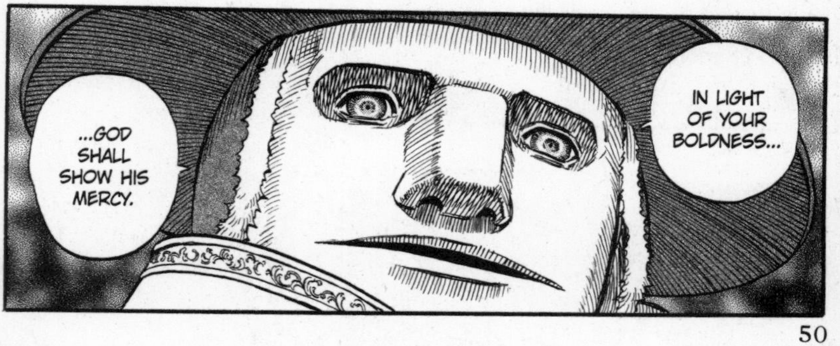
IN LIGHT OF YOUR BOLDNESS...
...GOD SHALL SHOW HIS MERCY.

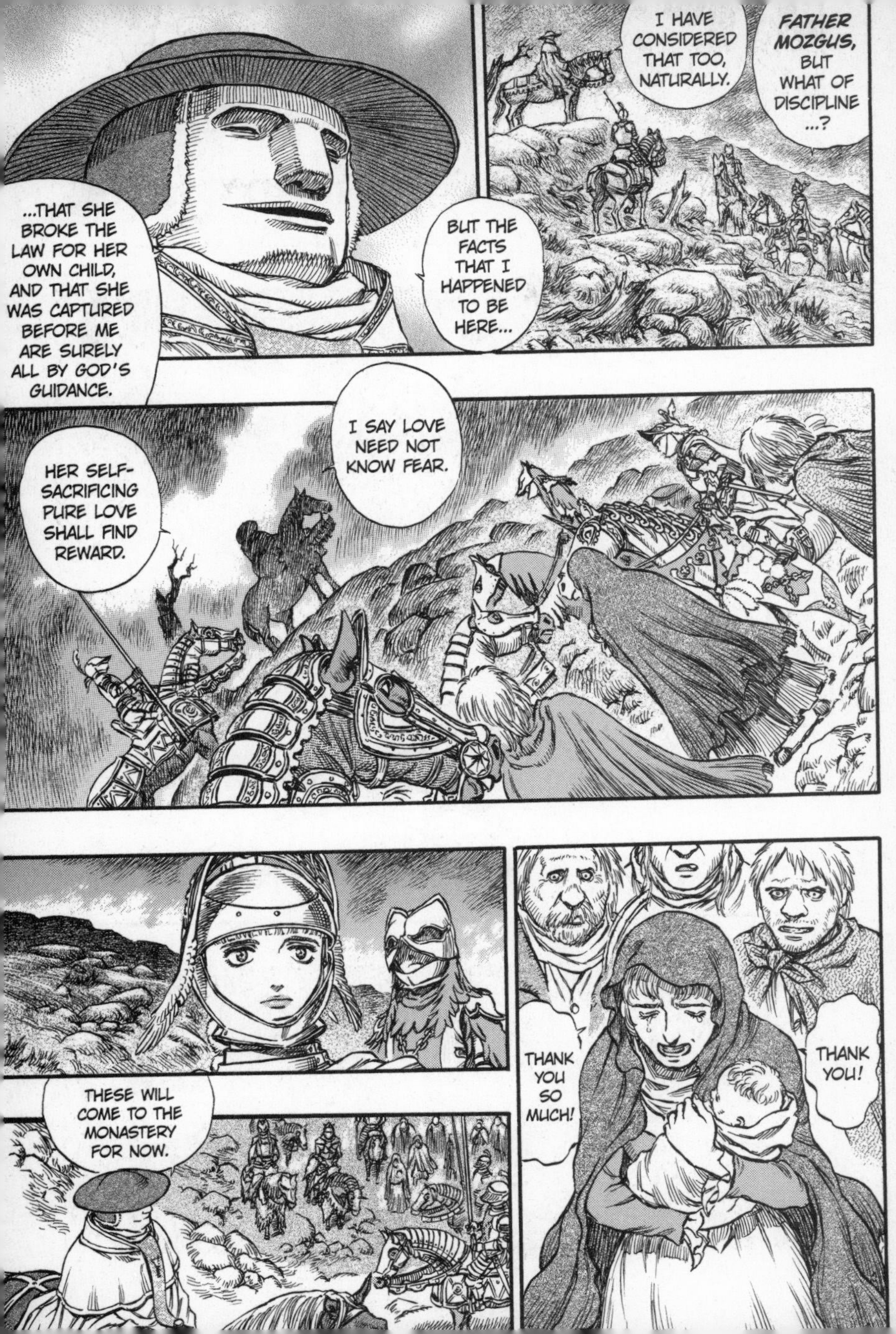
FATHER MOZGUS, BUT WHAT OF DISCIPLINE ...?
I HAVE CONSIDERED THAT TOO, NATURALLY.
BUT THE FACTS THAT I HAPPENED TO BE HERE...
...THAT SHE BROKE THE LAW FOR HER OWN CHILD, AND THAT SHE WAS CAPTURED BEFORE ME ARE SURELY ALL BY GOD'S GUIDANCE.
I SAY LOVE NEED NOT KNOW FEAR.
HER SELF-SACRIFICING PURE LOVE SHALL FIND REWARD.
THANK YOU!
THANK YOU SO MUCH!
THESE WILL COME TO THE MONASTERY FOR NOW.

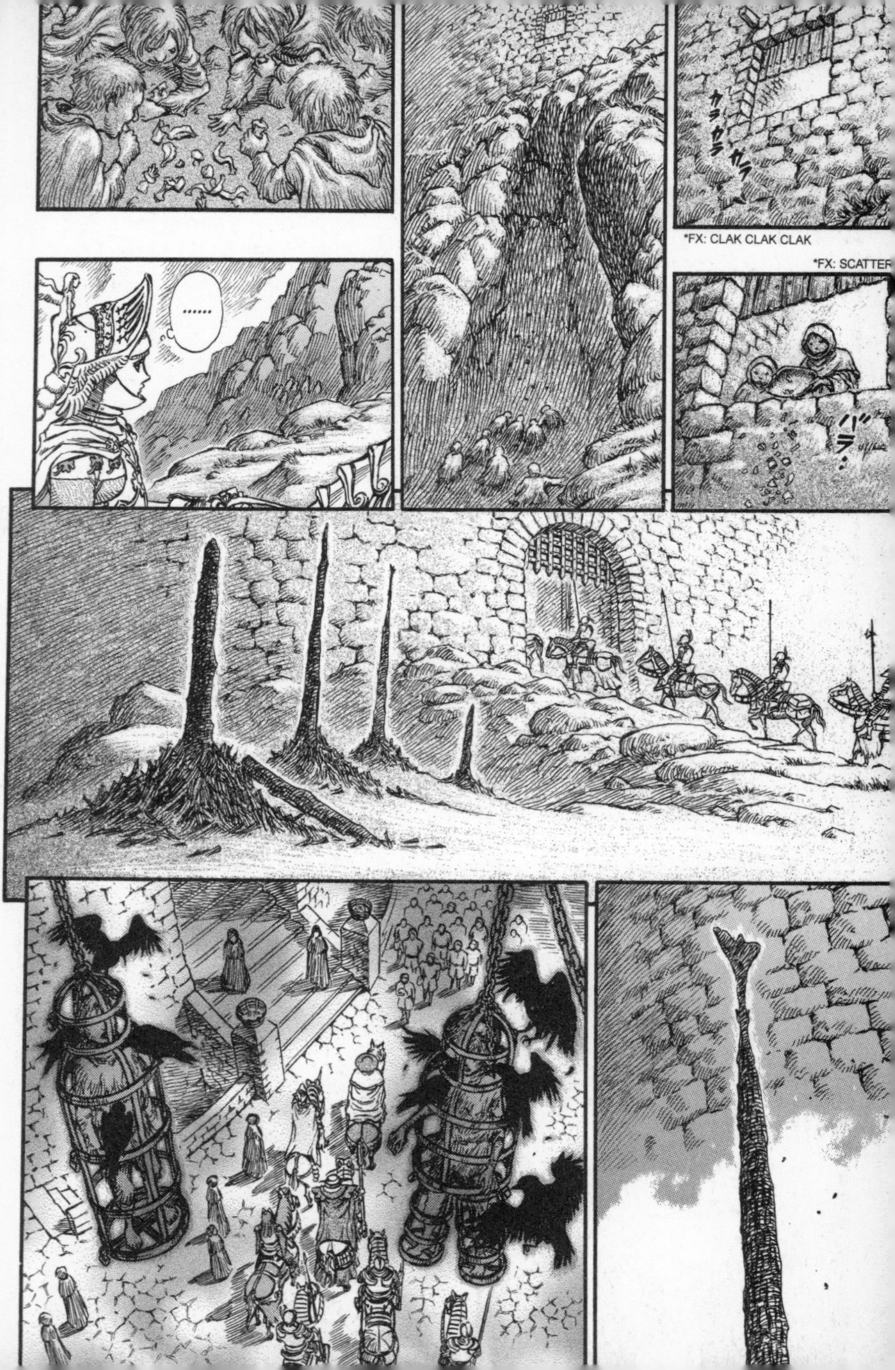
カラカラ
カラ
*FX: CLAK CLAK CLAK
*FX: SCATTER
バラ・
......

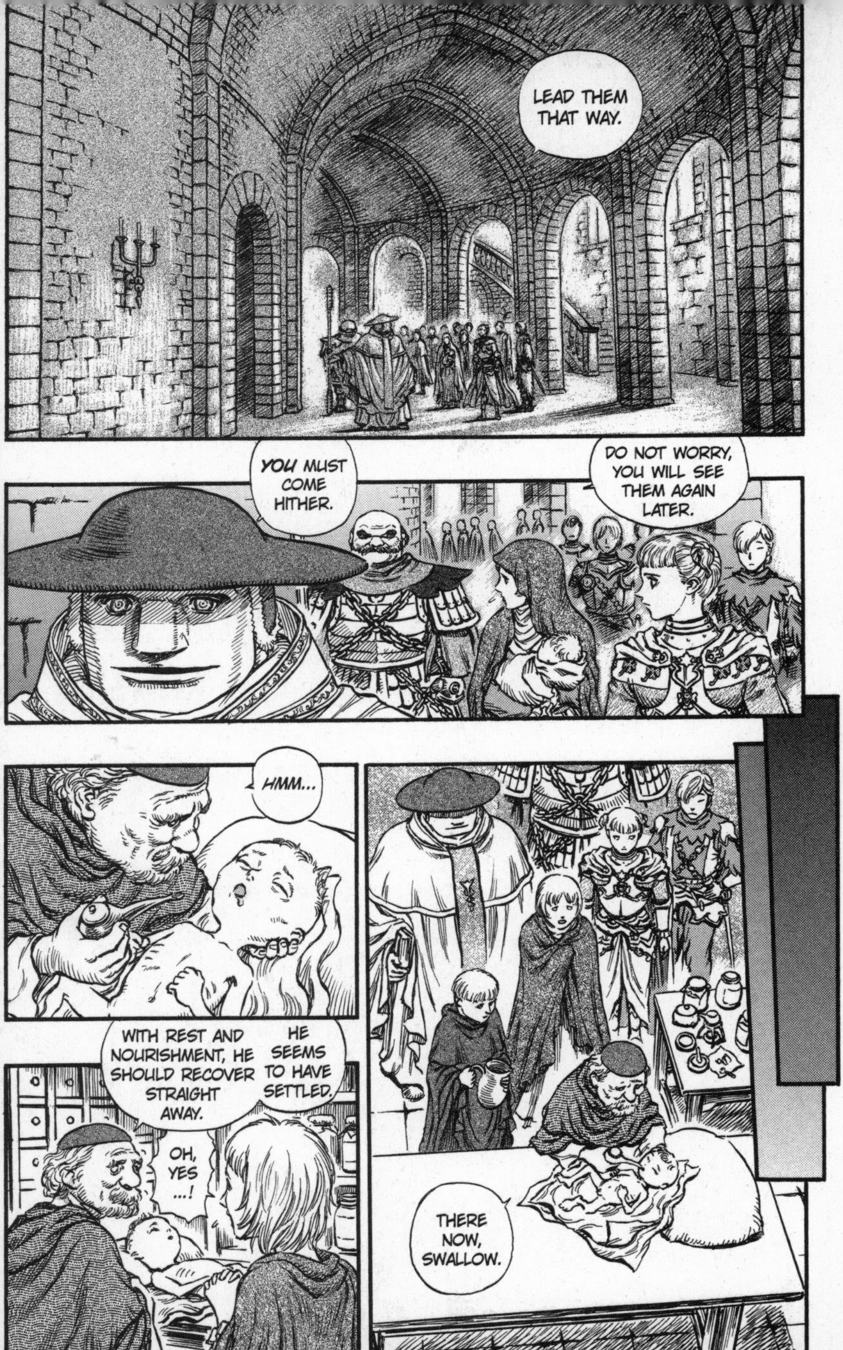
LEAD THEM THAT WAY.
DO NOT WORRY, YOU WILL SEE THEM AGAIN LATER.
YOU MUST COME HITHER.
THERE NOW, SWALLOW.
HMM...
HE SEEMS TO HAVE SETTLED.
WITH REST AND NOURISHMENT, HE SHOULD RECOVER STRAIGHT AWAY.
OH, YES ...!

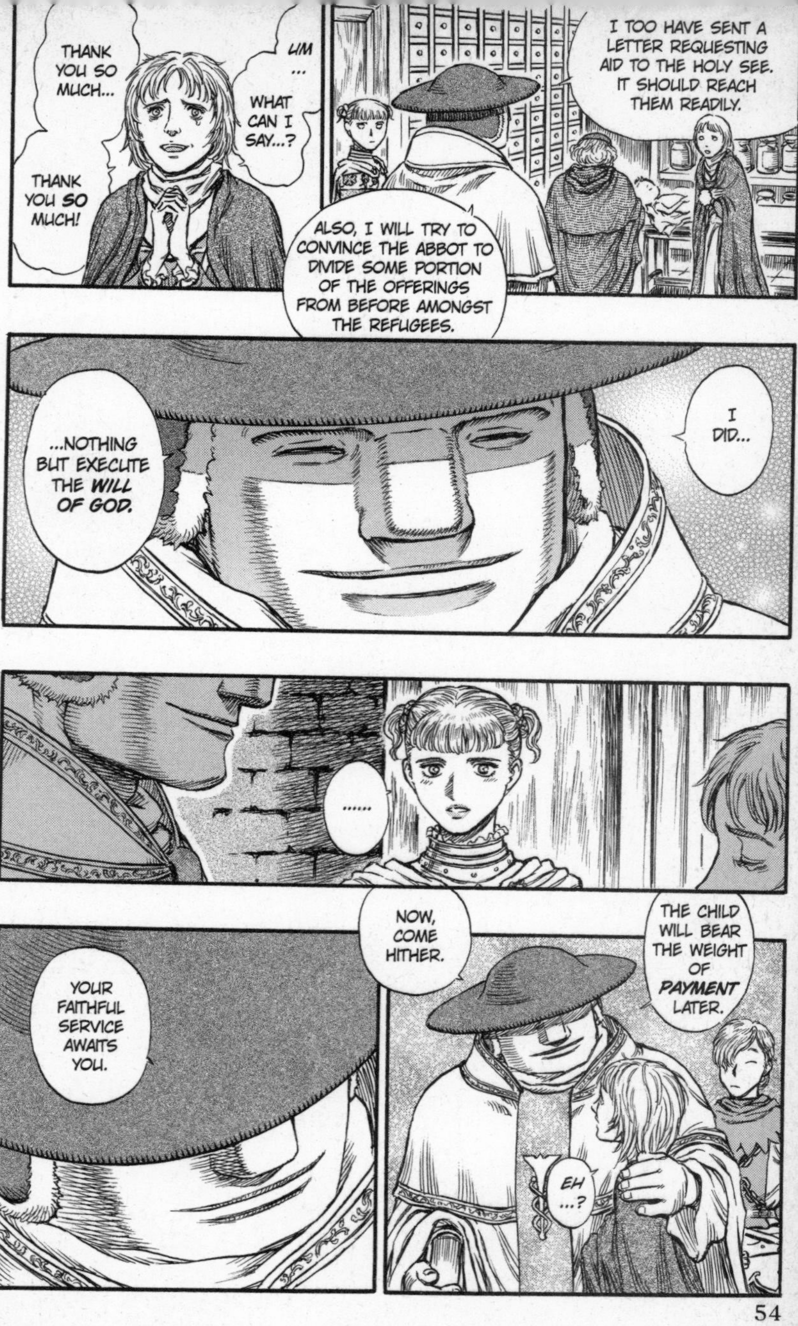
I TOO HAVE SENT A LETTER REQUESTING AID TO THE HOLY SEE. IT SHOULD REACH THEM READILY.
ALSO, I WILL TRY TO CONVINCE THE ABBOT TO DIVIDE SOME PORTION OF THE OFFERINGS FROM BEFORE AMONGST THE REFUGEES.
UM ...
WHAT CAN I SAY...?
THANK YOU SO MUCH...
THANK YOU *SO* MUCH!
I DID...
...NOTHING BUT EXECUTE THE *WILL OF GOD.*
......
THE CHILD WILL BEAR THE WEIGHT OF *PAYMENT* LATER.
NOW, COME HITHER.
EH ...?
YOUR FAITHFUL SERVICE AWAITS YOU.

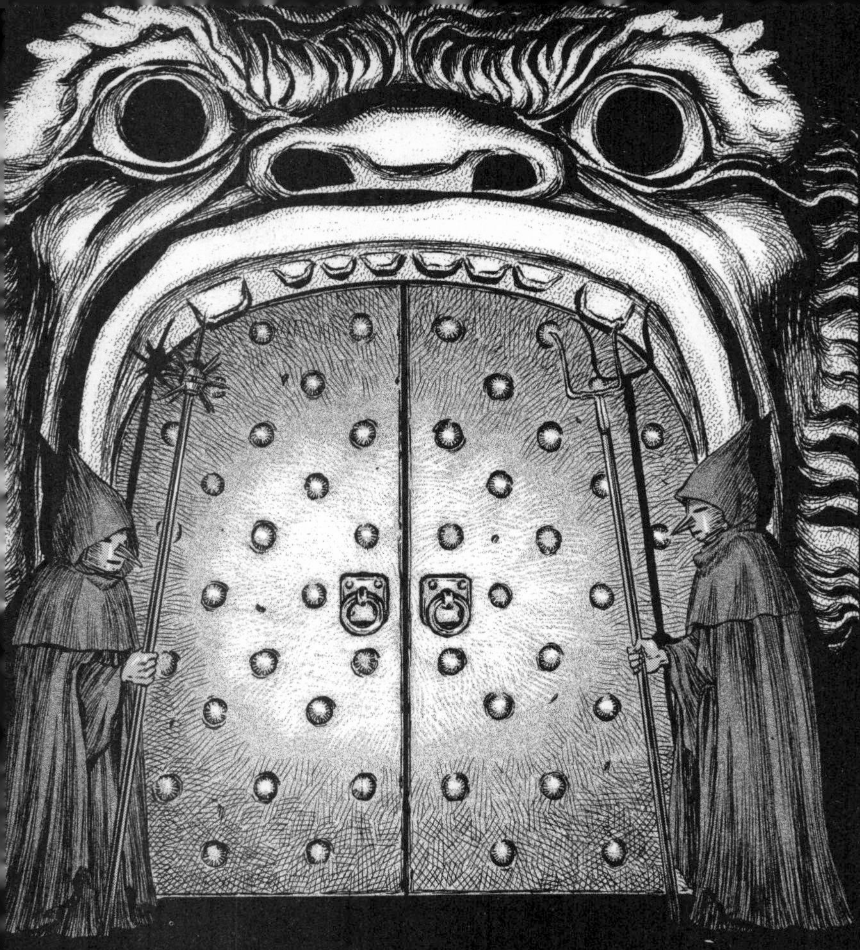

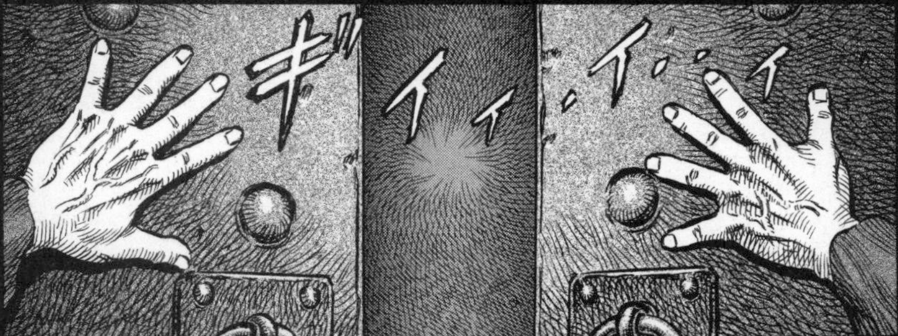
ギィィ・イ・イ

*FX: GREEEEE

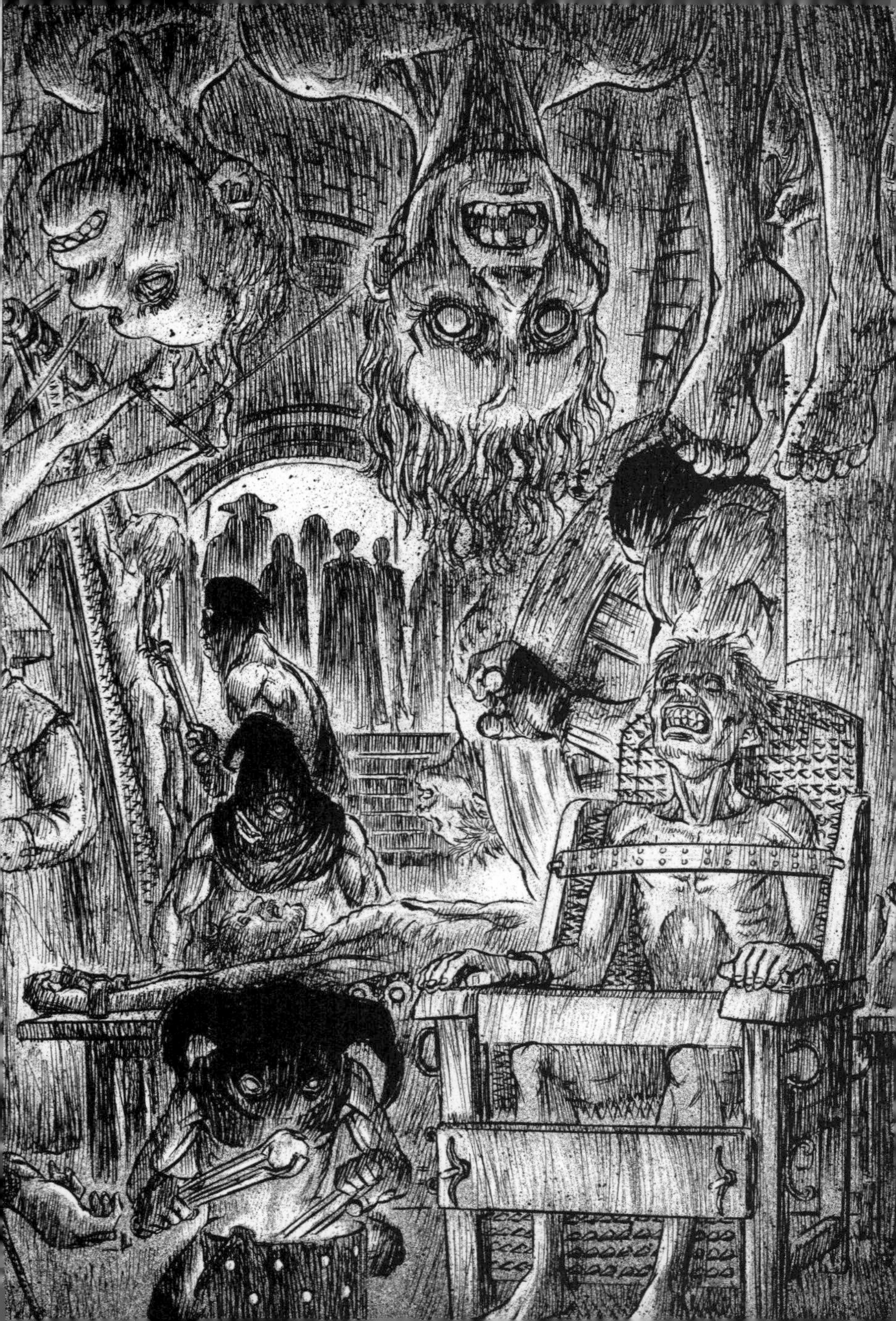

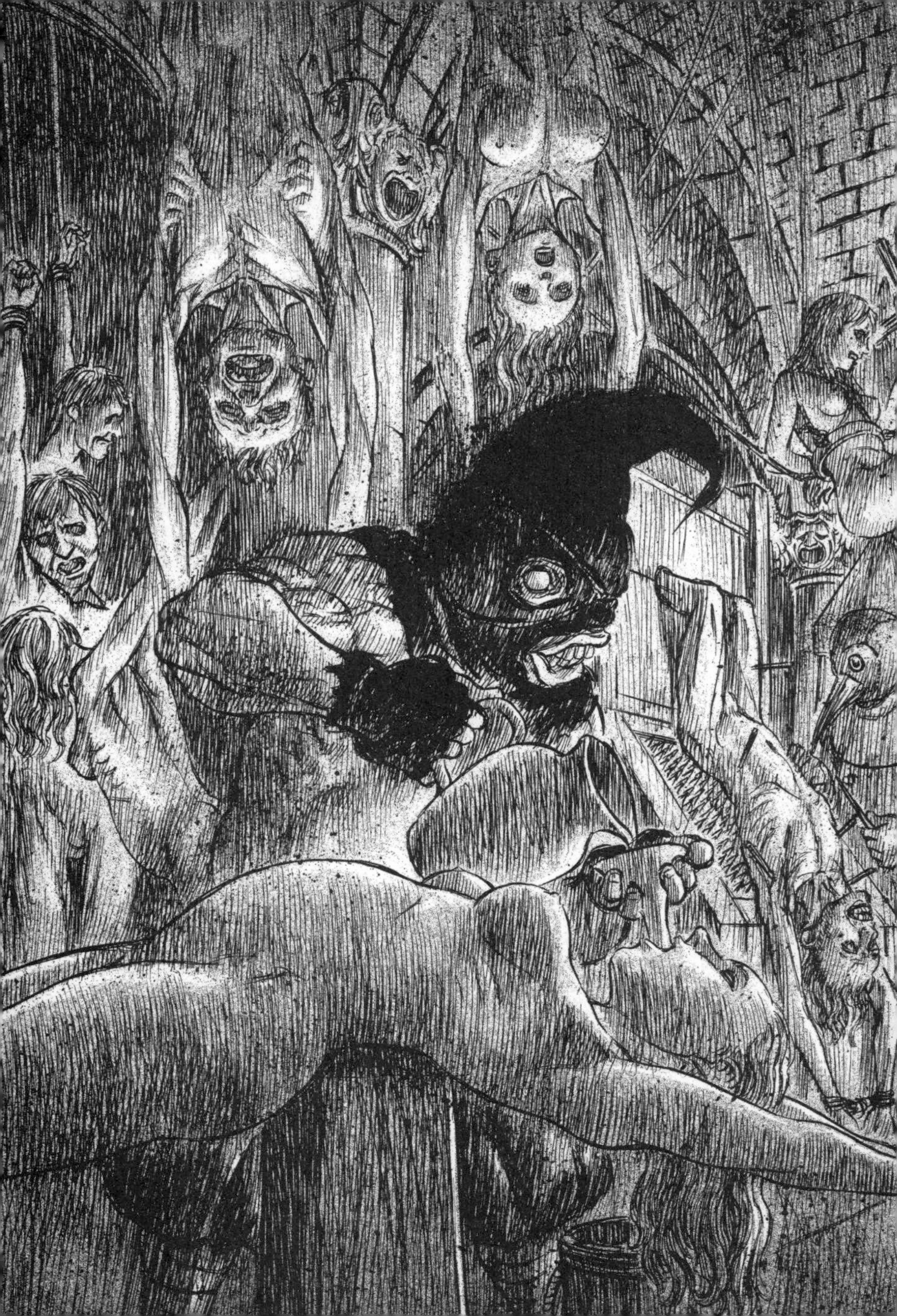

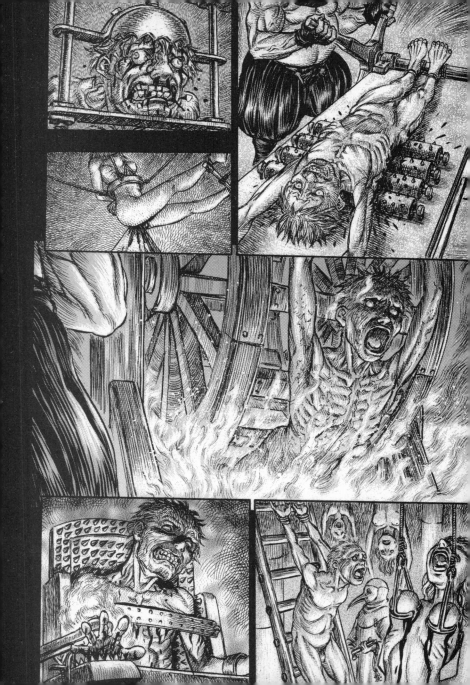

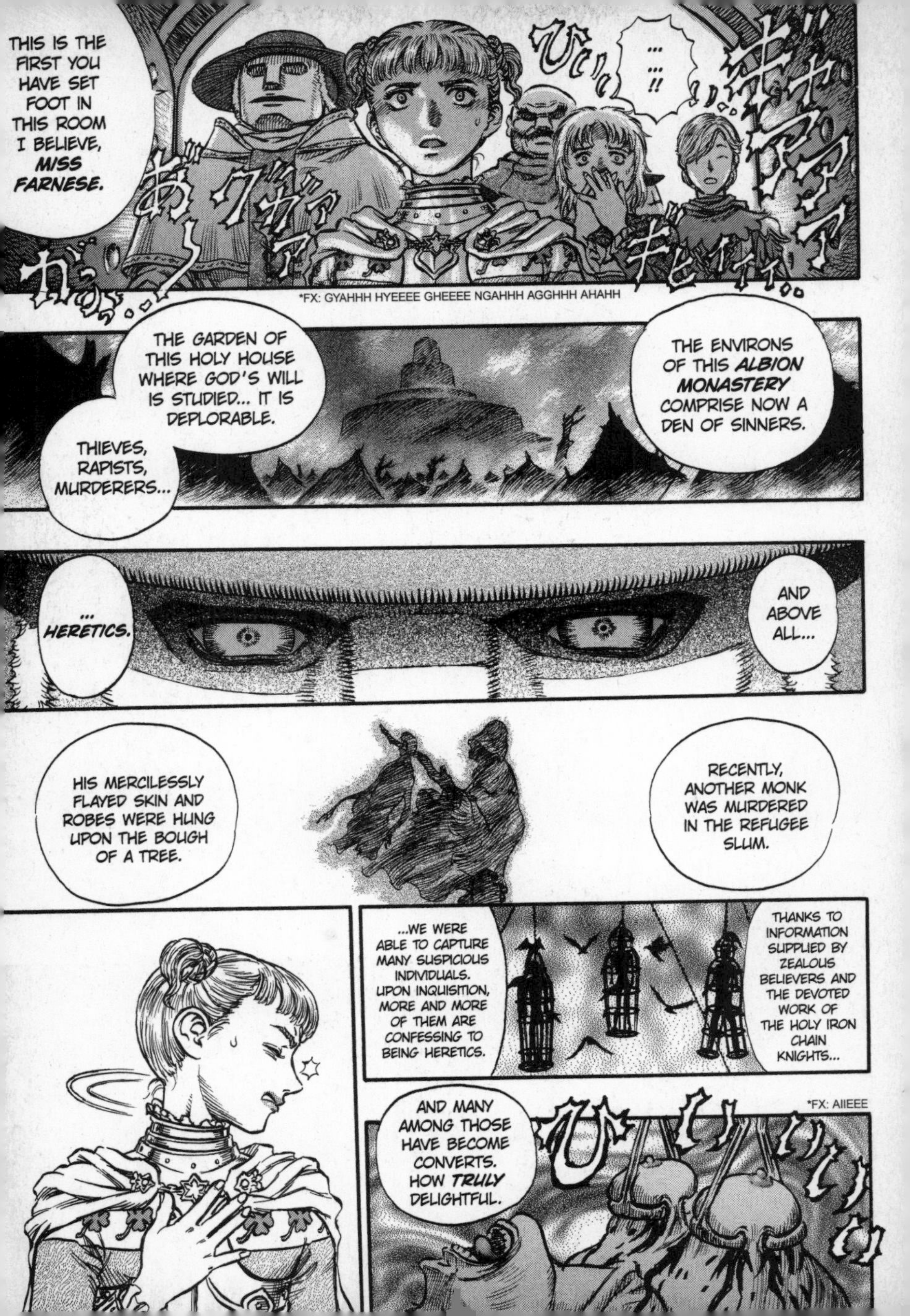
......!!
THIS IS THE FIRST YOU HAVE SET FOOT IN THIS ROOM I BELIEVE, *MISS FARNESE.*
*FX: GYAHHH HYEEEE GHEEEE NGAHHH AGGHHH AHAHH
THE ENVIRONS OF THIS *ALBION MONASTERY* COMPRISE NOW A DEN OF SINNERS.
THE GARDEN OF THIS HOLY HOUSE WHERE GOD'S WILL IS STUDIED... IT IS DEPLORABLE.
THIEVES, RAPISTS, MURDERERS...
AND ABOVE ALL...
... *HERETICS.*
RECENTLY, ANOTHER MONK WAS MURDERED IN THE REFUGEE SLUM.
HIS MERCILESSLY FLAYED SKIN AND ROBES WERE HUNG UPON THE BOUGH OF A TREE.
THANKS TO INFORMATION SUPPLIED BY ZEALOUS BELIEVERS AND THE DEVOTED WORK OF THE HOLY IRON CHAIN KNIGHTS...
...WE WERE ABLE TO CAPTURE MANY SUSPICIOUS INDIVIDUALS. UPON INQUISITION, MORE AND MORE OF THEM ARE CONFESSING TO BEING HERETICS.
*FX: AIIEEE
AND MANY AMONG THOSE HAVE BECOME CONVERTS. HOW *TRULY* DELIGHTFUL.

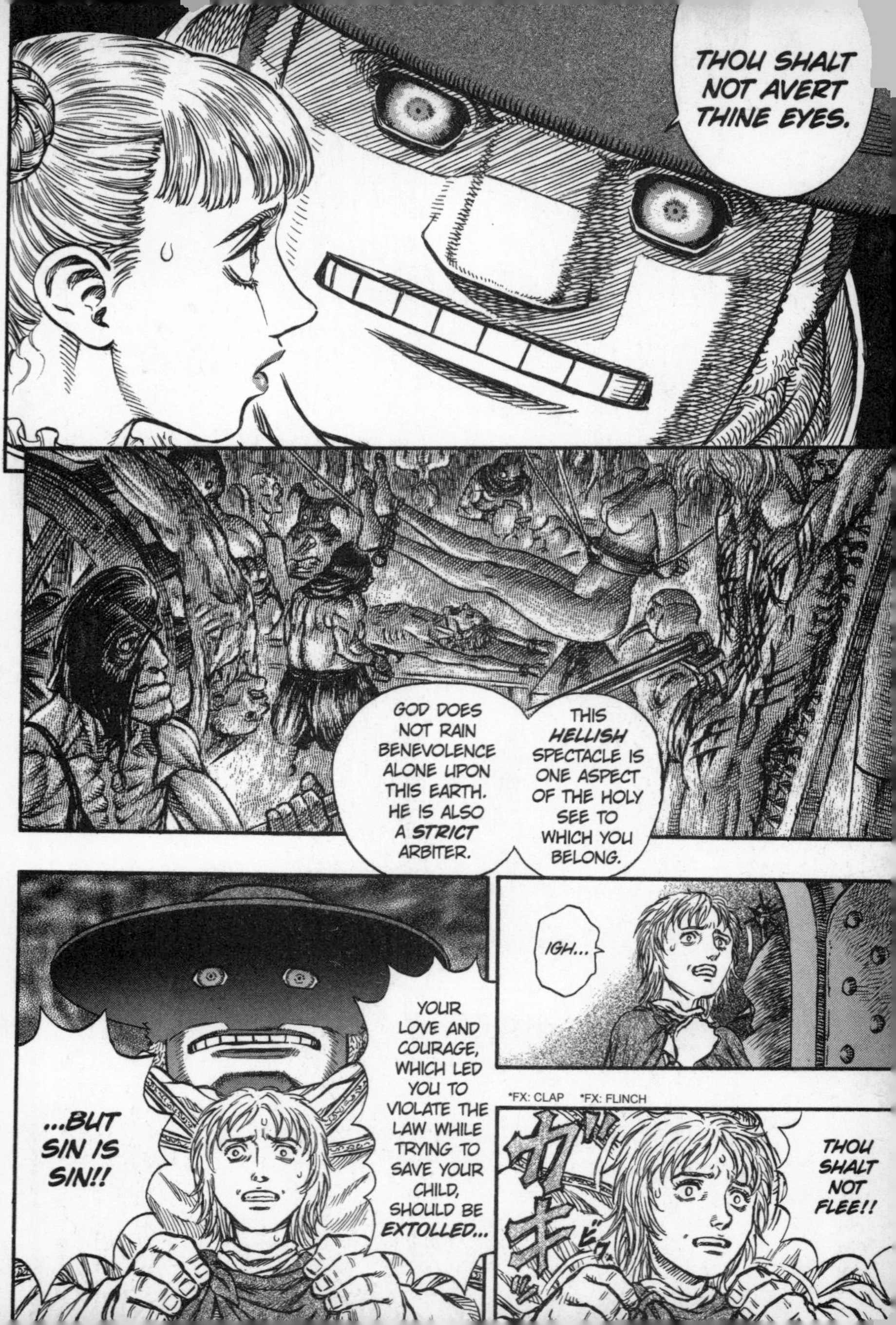
THOU SHALT NOT AVERT THINE EYES.
THIS HELLISH SPECTACLE IS ONE ASPECT OF THE HOLY SEE TO WHICH YOU BELONG.
GOD DOES NOT RAIN BENEVOLENCE ALONE UPON THIS EARTH. HE IS ALSO A STRICT ARBITER.
IGH...
*FX: CLAP *FX: FLINCH
THOU SHALT NOT FLEE!!
YOUR LOVE AND COURAGE, WHICH LED YOU TO VIOLATE THE LAW WHILE TRYING TO SAVE YOUR CHILD, SHOULD BE EXTOLLED...
...BUT SIN IS SIN!!

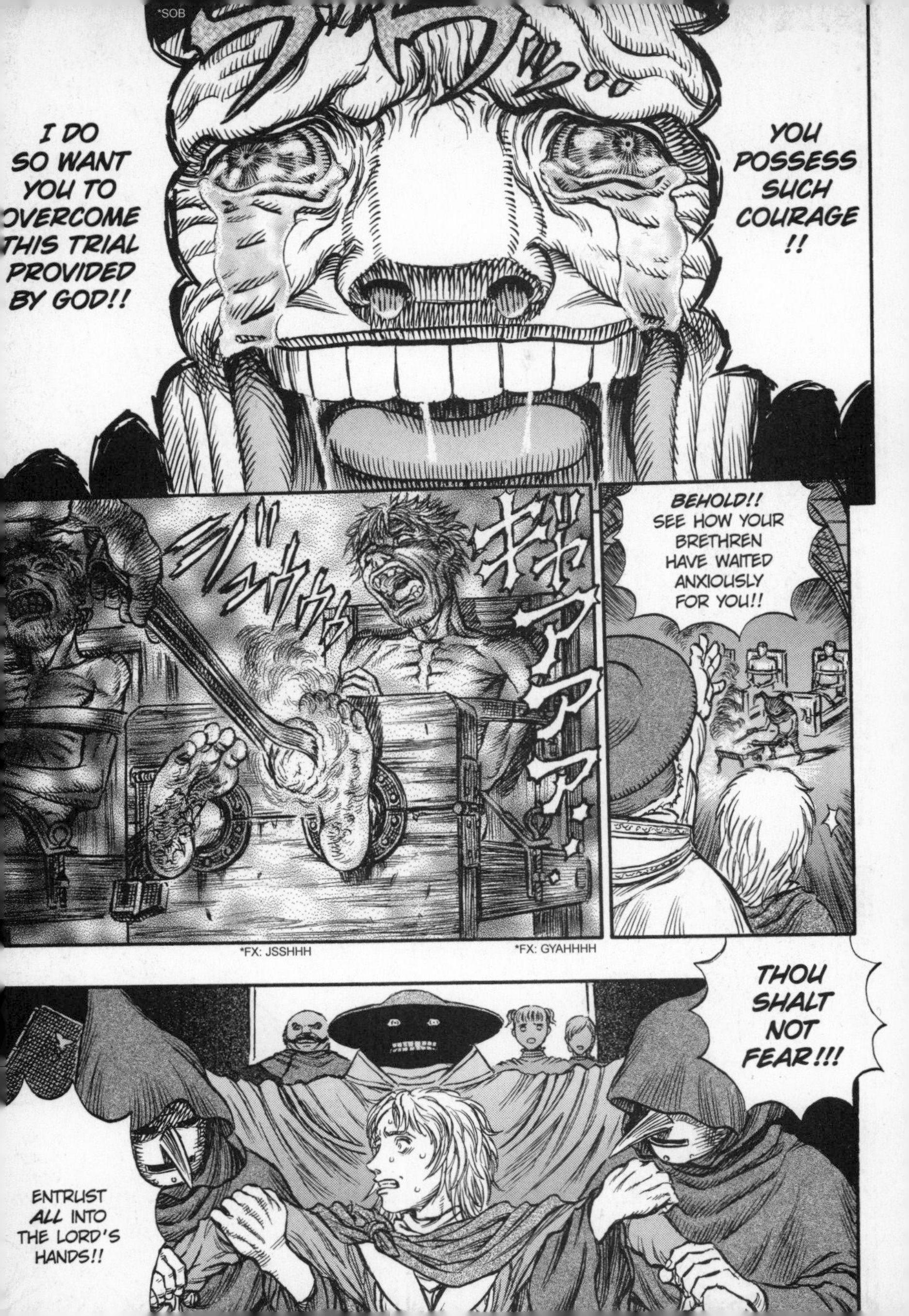
*SOB
YOU POSSESS SUCH COURAGE!!
I DO SO WANT YOU TO OVERCOME THIS TRIAL PROVIDED BY GOD!!
BEHOLD!! SEE HOW YOUR BRETHREN HAVE WAITED ANXIOUSLY FOR YOU!!
*FX: GYAHHHH
*FX: JSSHHH
THOU SHALT NOT FEAR!!!
ENTRUST ALL INTO THE LORD'S HANDS!!

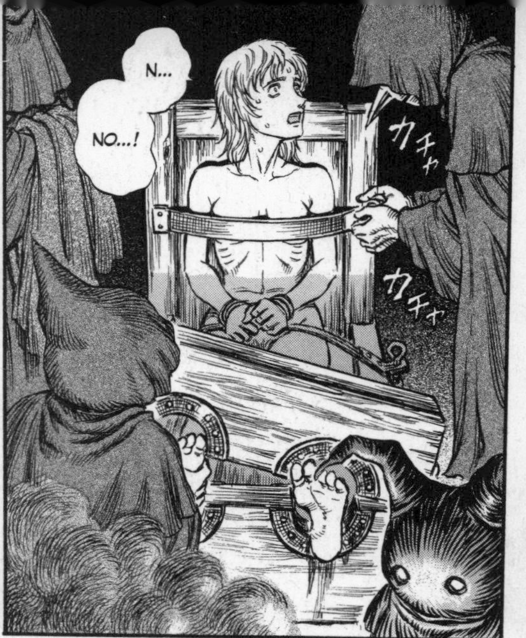
N...
NO...!
カチャ
カチャ
*FX: KCHAK KCHAK

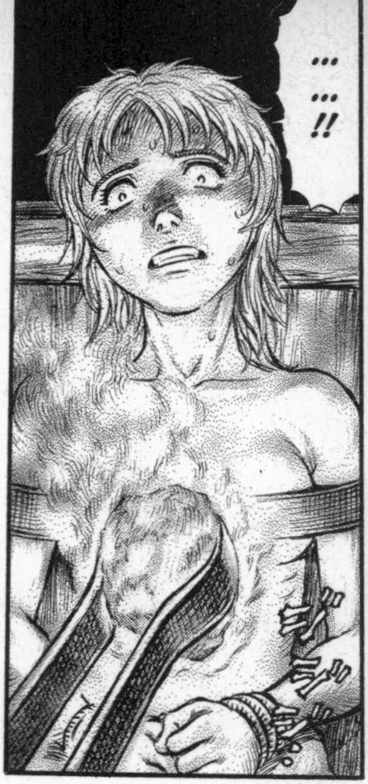
...
...
!!
*FX: SSSSS

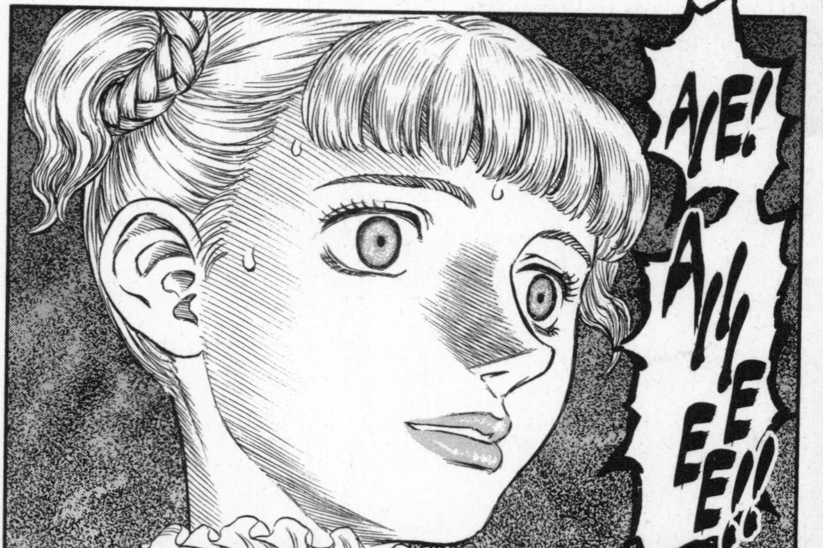
AIE!
AIIYEEEEE!!

CONVICTION ARC
BIRTH CEREMONY CHAPTER
TOWER OF SHADOW (1): END

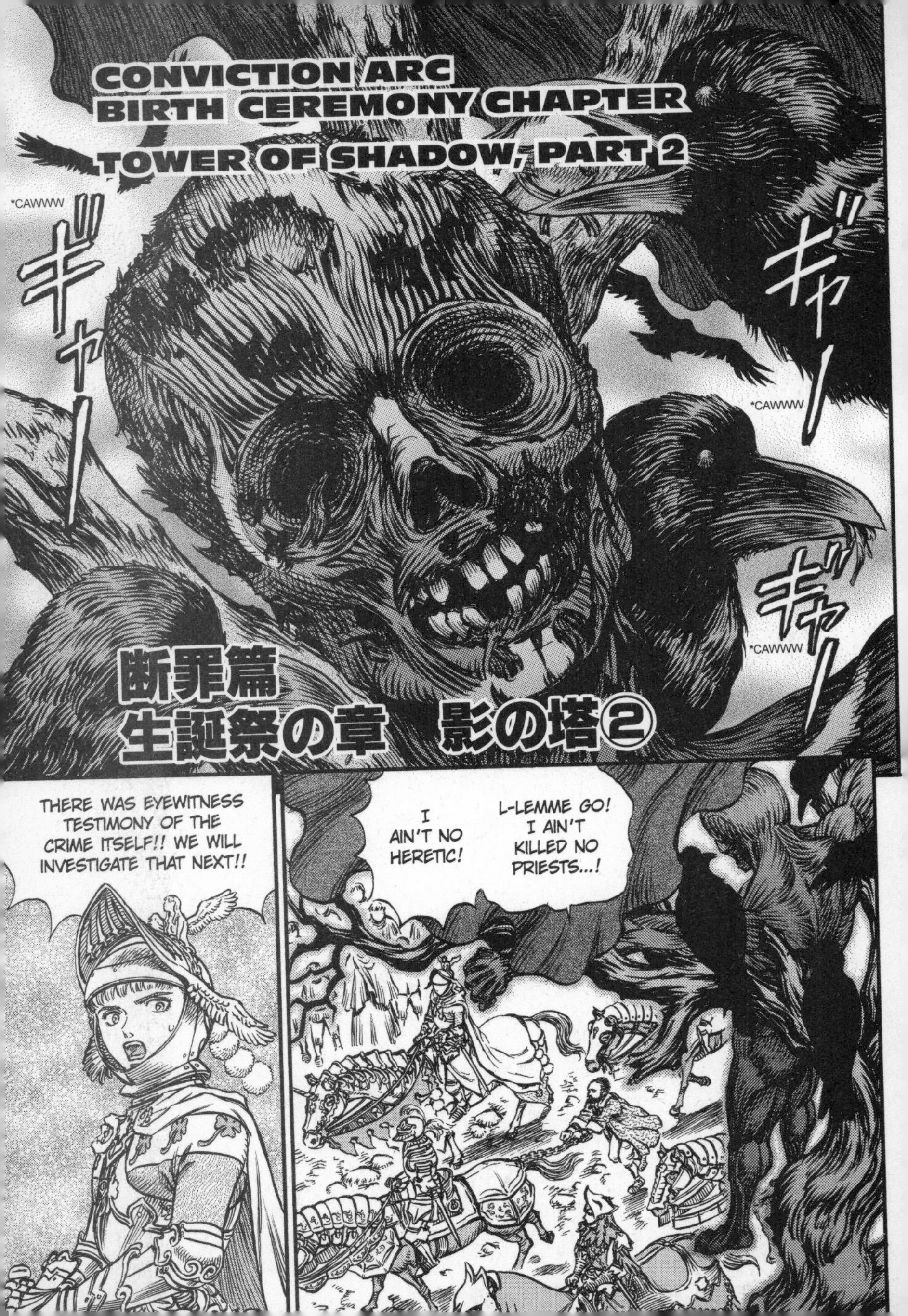
CONVICTION ARC
BIRTH CEREMONY CHAPTER
TOWER OF SHADOW, PART 2
ギャー
*CAWWW
ギャー
*CAWWW
ギャー
*CAWWW
断罪篇
生誕祭の章　影の塔②
L-LEMME GO! I AIN'T KILLED NO PRIESTS...!
I AIN'T NO HERETIC!
THERE WAS EYEWITNESS TESTIMONY OF THE CRIME ITSELF!! WE WILL INVESTIGATE THAT NEXT!!

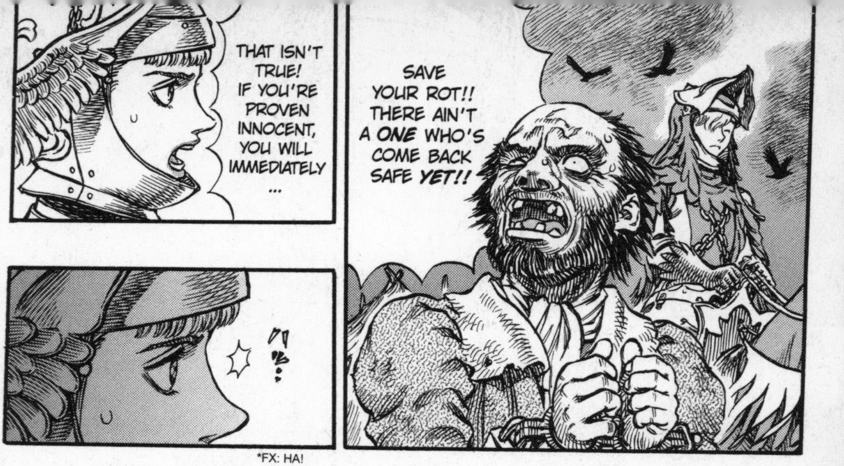
THAT ISN'T TRUE! IF YOU'RE PROVEN INNOCENT, YOU WILL IMMEDIATELY ...
SAVE YOUR ROT!! THERE AIN'T A ONE WHO'S COME BACK SAFE YET!!

*FX: HA!

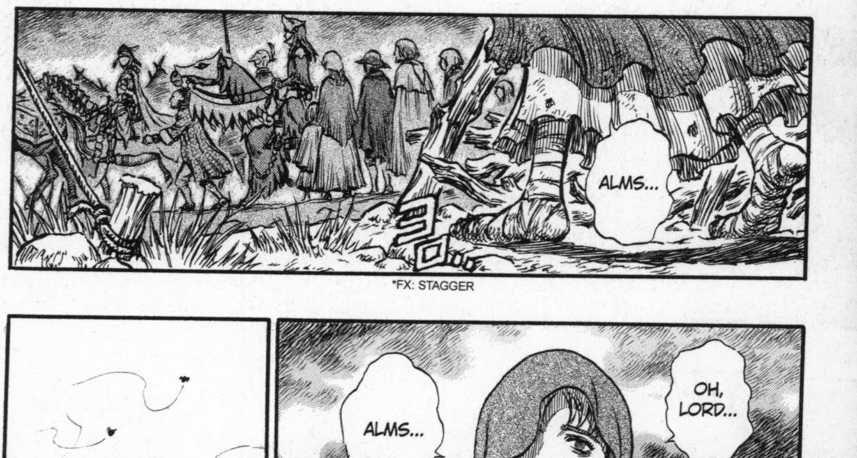
ALMS...

*FX: STAGGER

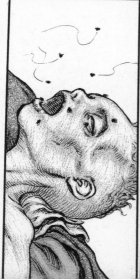

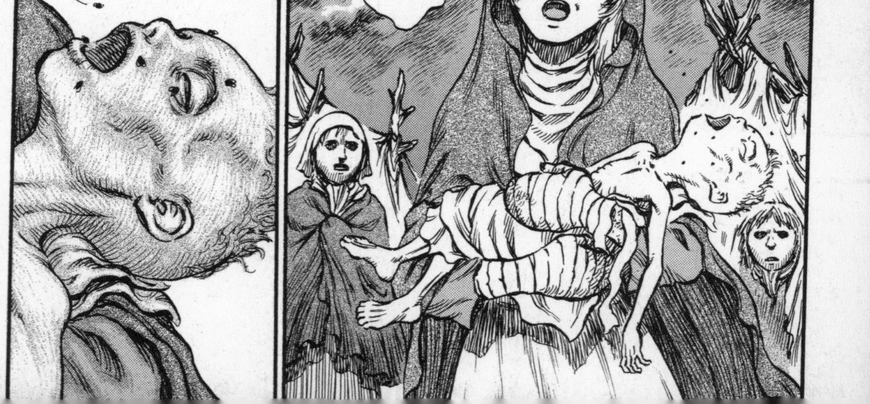
ALMS...
OH, LORD...

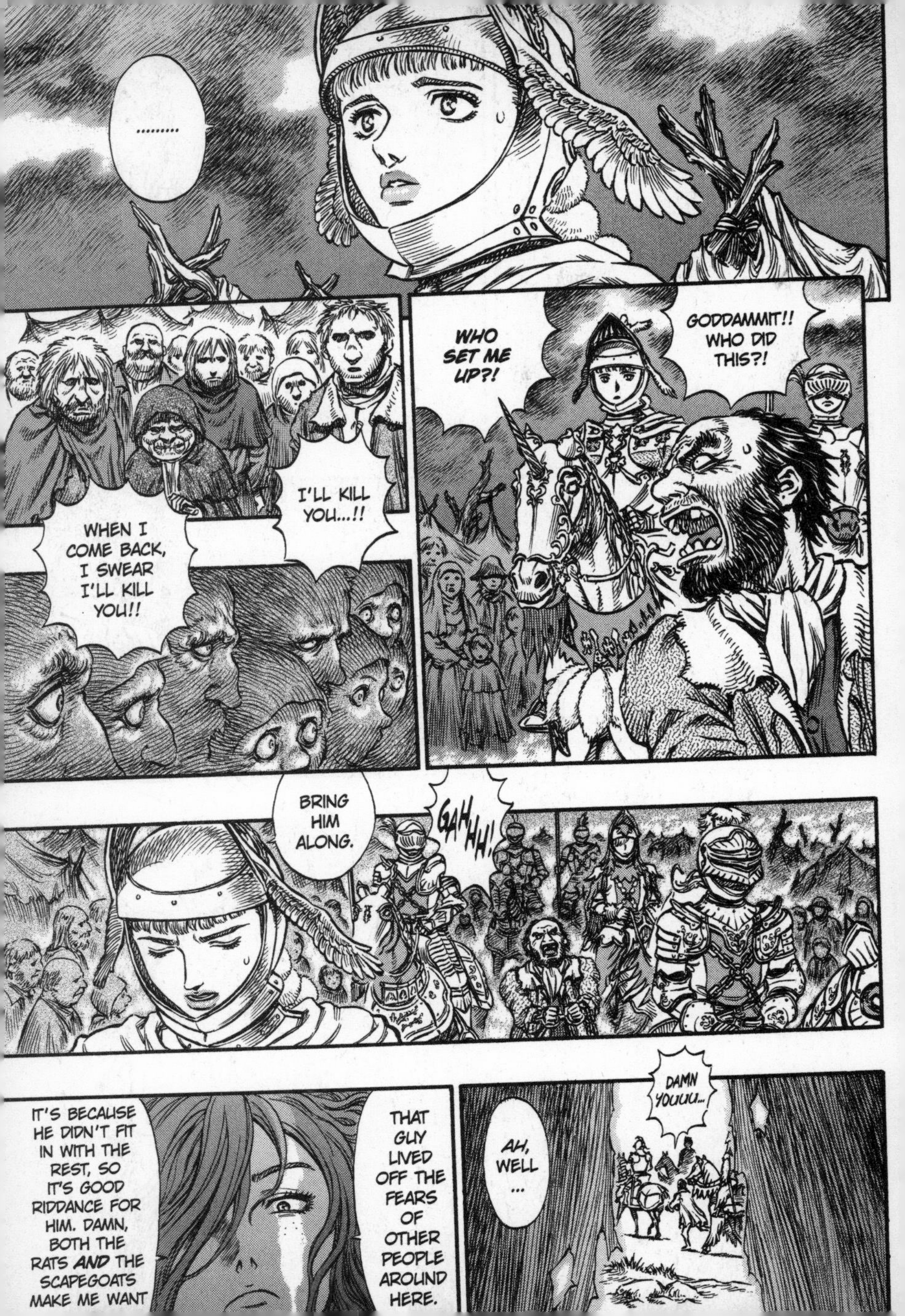
....
GODDAMMIT!! WHO DID THIS?!
WHO SET ME UP?!
I'LL KILL YOU...!!
WHEN I COME BACK, I SWEAR I'LL KILL YOU!!
GAHHH!
BRING HIM ALONG.
DAMN YOUUU...
AH, WELL ...
THAT GUY LIVED OFF THE FEARS OF OTHER PEOPLE AROUND HERE.
IT'S BECAUSE HE DIDN'T FIT IN WITH THE REST, SO IT'S GOOD RIDDANCE FOR HIM. DAMN, BOTH THE RATS *AND* THE SCAPEGOATS MAKE ME WANT

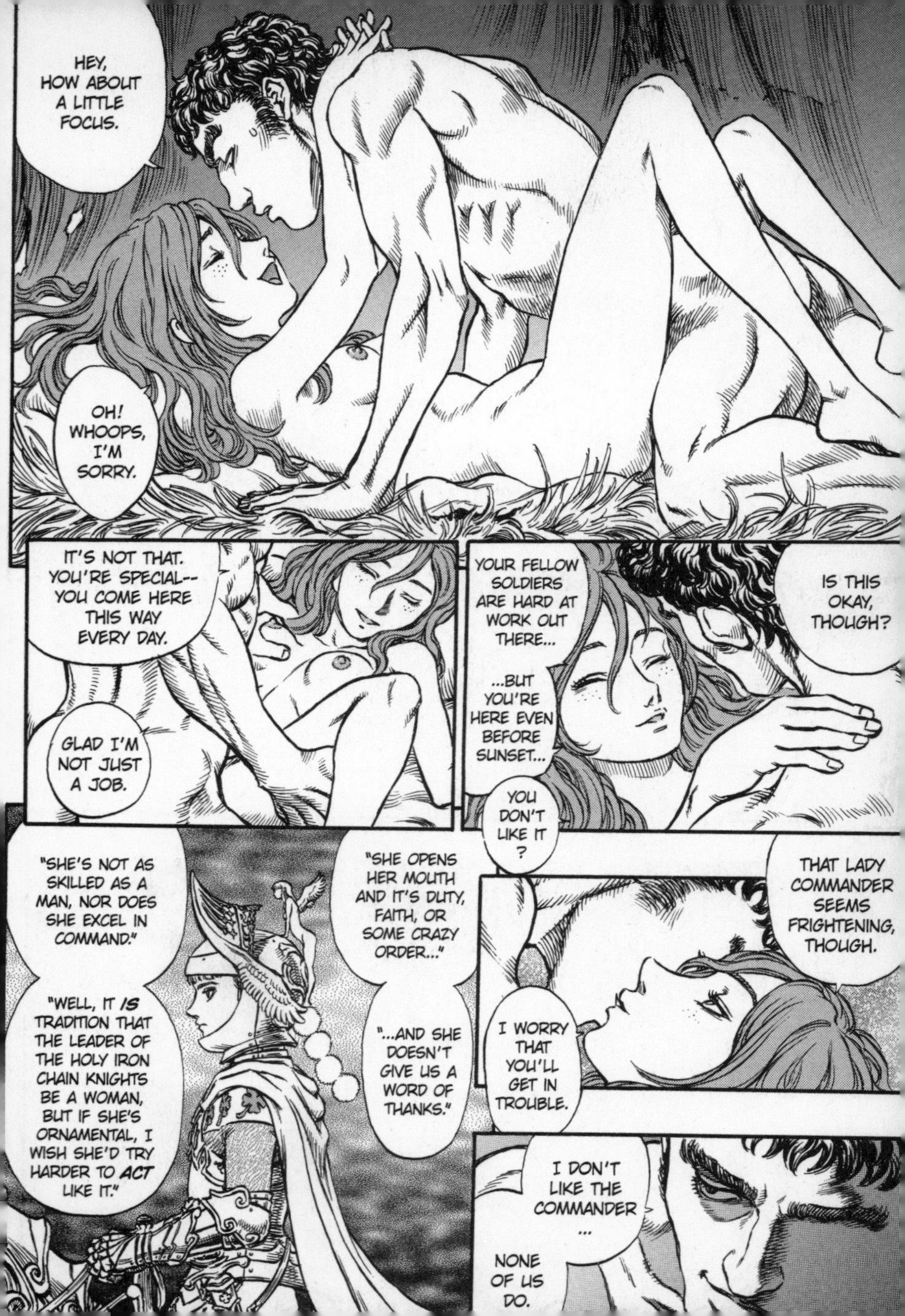
HEY, HOW ABOUT A LITTLE FOCUS.
OH! WHOOPS, I'M SORRY.
IS THIS OKAY, THOUGH?
YOUR FELLOW SOLDIERS ARE HARD AT WORK OUT THERE...
...BUT YOU'RE HERE EVEN BEFORE SUNSET...
YOU DON'T LIKE IT ?
IT'S NOT THAT. YOU'RE SPECIAL-- YOU COME HERE THIS WAY EVERY DAY.
GLAD I'M NOT JUST A JOB.
THAT LADY COMMANDER SEEMS FRIGHTENING, THOUGH.
I WORRY THAT YOU'LL GET IN TROUBLE.
I DON'T LIKE THE COMMANDER ...
NONE OF US DO.
"SHE OPENS HER MOUTH AND IT'S DUTY, FAITH, OR SOME CRAZY ORDER..."
"...AND SHE DOESN'T GIVE US A WORD OF THANKS."
"SHE'S NOT AS SKILLED AS A MAN, NOR DOES SHE EXCEL IN COMMAND."
"WELL, IT *IS* TRADITION THAT THE LEADER OF THE HOLY IRON CHAIN KNIGHTS BE A WOMAN, BUT IF SHE'S ORNAMENTAL, I WISH SHE'D TRY HARDER TO *ACT* LIKE IT."

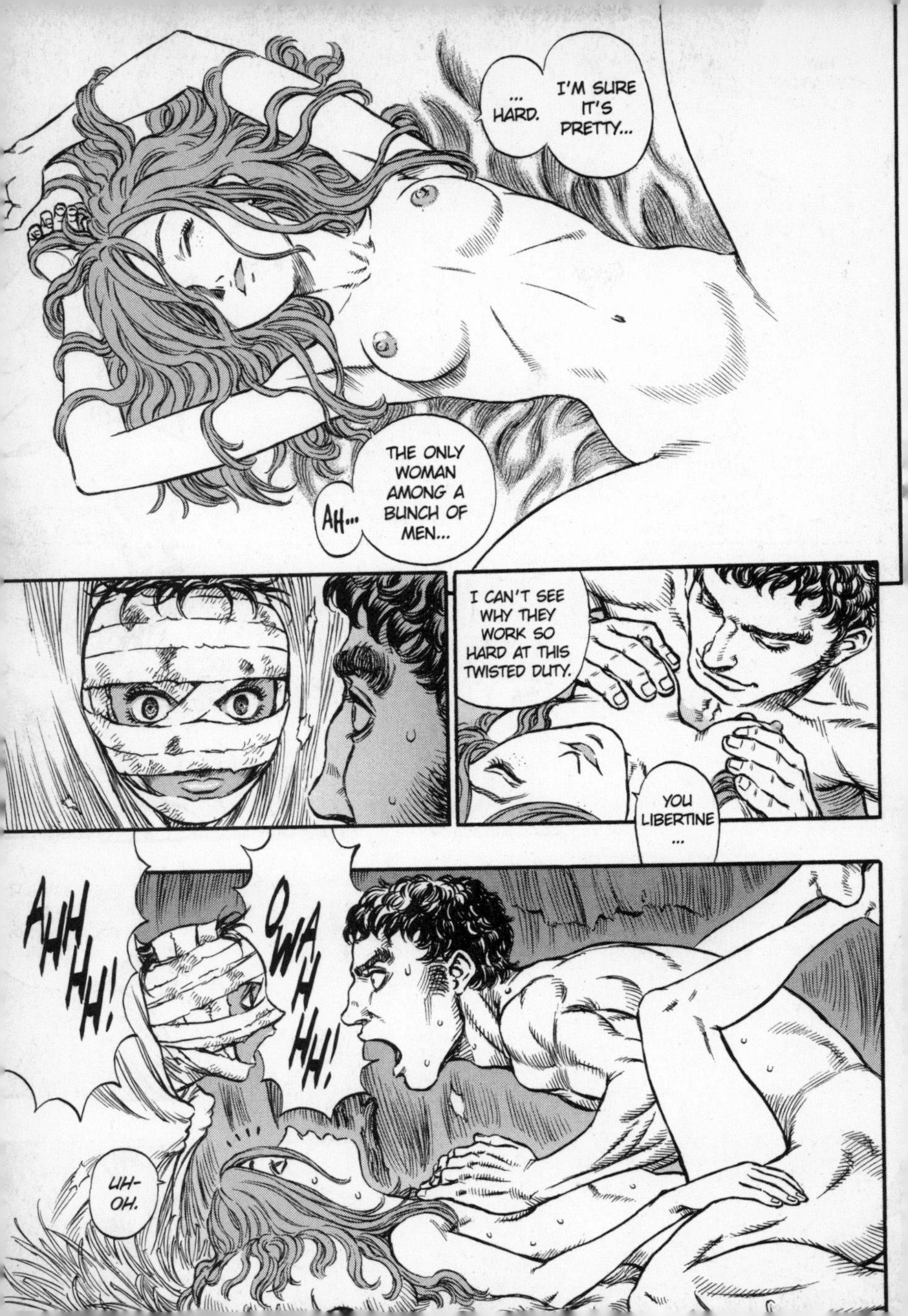
I'M SURE IT'S PRETTY...
... HARD.
THE ONLY WOMAN AMONG A BUNCH OF MEN...
AH...
I CAN'T SEE WHY THEY WORK SO HARD AT THIS TWISTED DUTY.
YOU LIBERTINE ...
OWAHHHHH!
AHHHHH!
UH-OH.

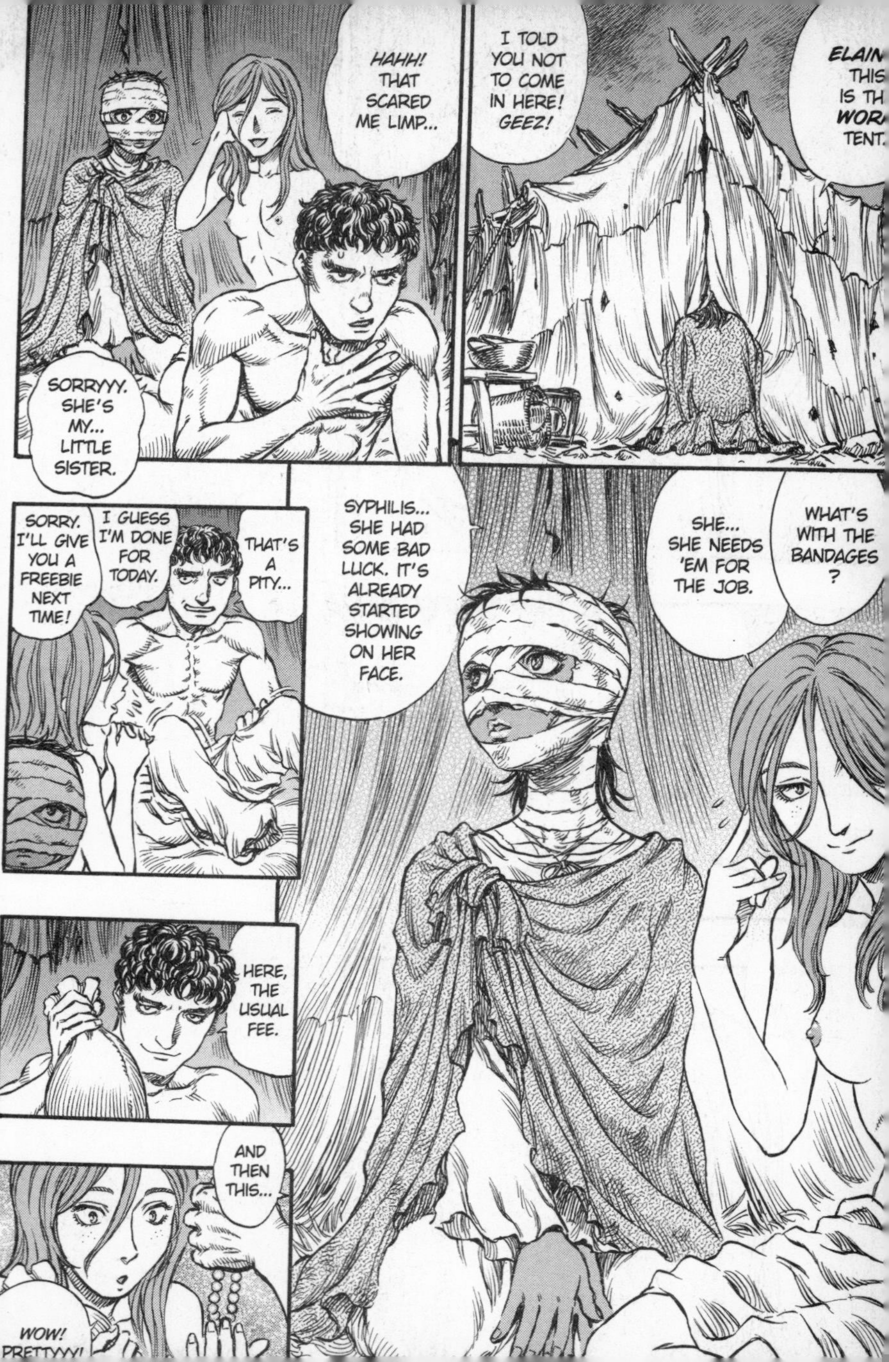

ELAIN
THIS
IS TH
WOR
TENT.
I TOLD YOU NOT TO COME IN HERE! GEEZ!
HAHH! THAT SCARED ME LIMP...
SORRYYY. SHE'S MY... LITTLE SISTER.
WHAT'S WITH THE BANDAGES?
SHE... SHE NEEDS 'EM FOR THE JOB.
SYPHILIS... SHE HAD SOME BAD LUCK. IT'S ALREADY STARTED SHOWING ON HER FACE.
THAT'S A PITY...
I GUESS I'M DONE FOR TODAY.
SORRY. I'LL GIVE YOU A FREEBIE NEXT TIME!
HERE, THE USUAL FEE.
AND THEN THIS...
WOW! PRETTYYY!

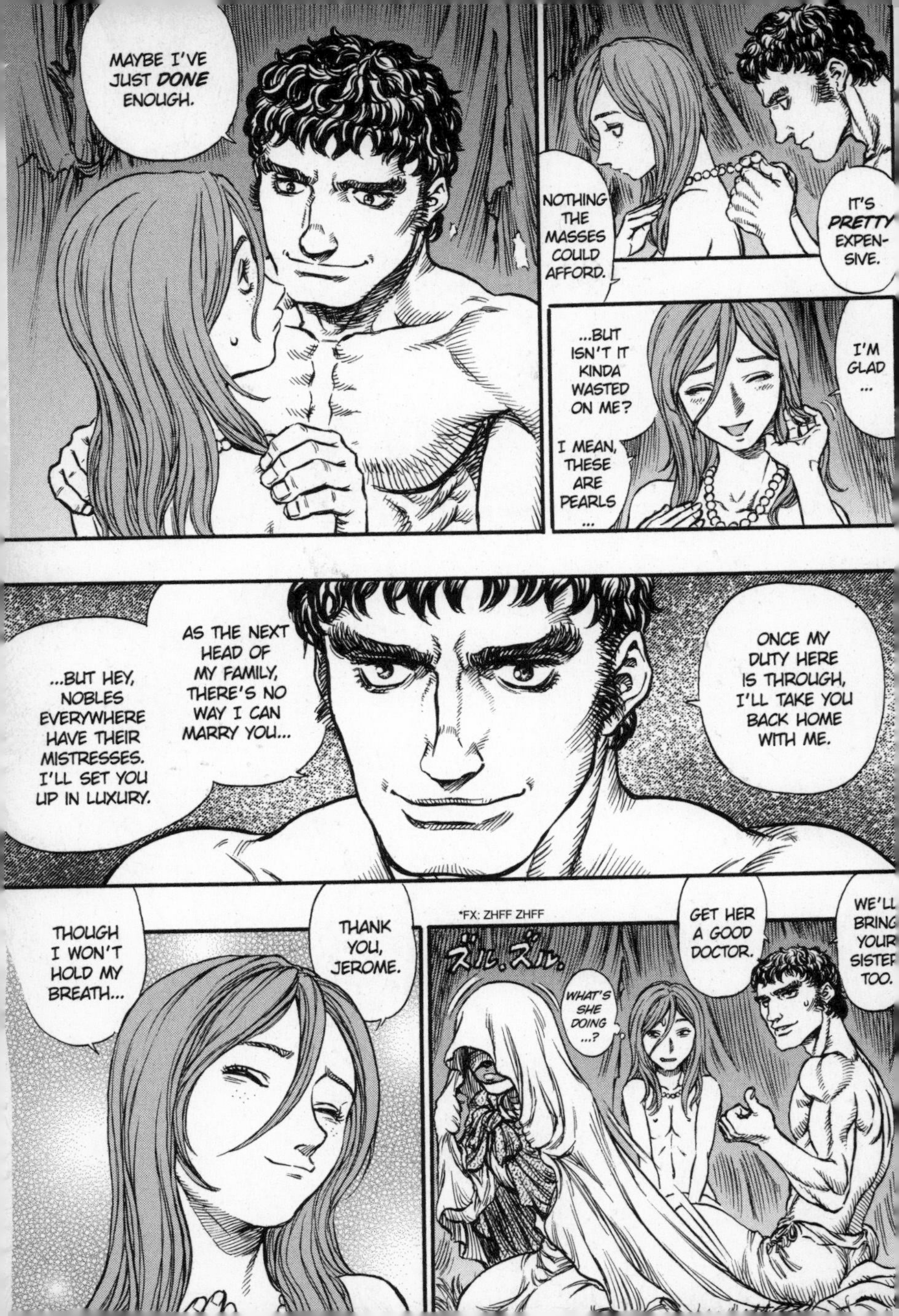
IT'S *PRETTY* EXPEN-SIVE.
NOTHING THE MASSES COULD AFFORD.
I'M GLAD...
...BUT ISN'T IT KINDA WASTED ON ME? I MEAN, THESE ARE PEARLS...
MAYBE I'VE JUST *DONE* ENOUGH.
ONCE MY DUTY HERE IS THROUGH, I'LL TAKE YOU BACK HOME WITH ME.
AS THE NEXT HEAD OF MY FAMILY, THERE'S NO WAY I CAN MARRY YOU...
...BUT HEY, NOBLES EVERYWHERE HAVE THEIR MISTRESSES. I'LL SET YOU UP IN LUXURY.
WE'LL BRING YOUR SISTER TOO.
GET HER A GOOD DOCTOR.
WHAT'S SHE DOING...?
ズル.ズル.
*FX: ZHFF ZHFF
THANK YOU, JEROME.
THOUGH I WON'T HOLD MY BREATH...

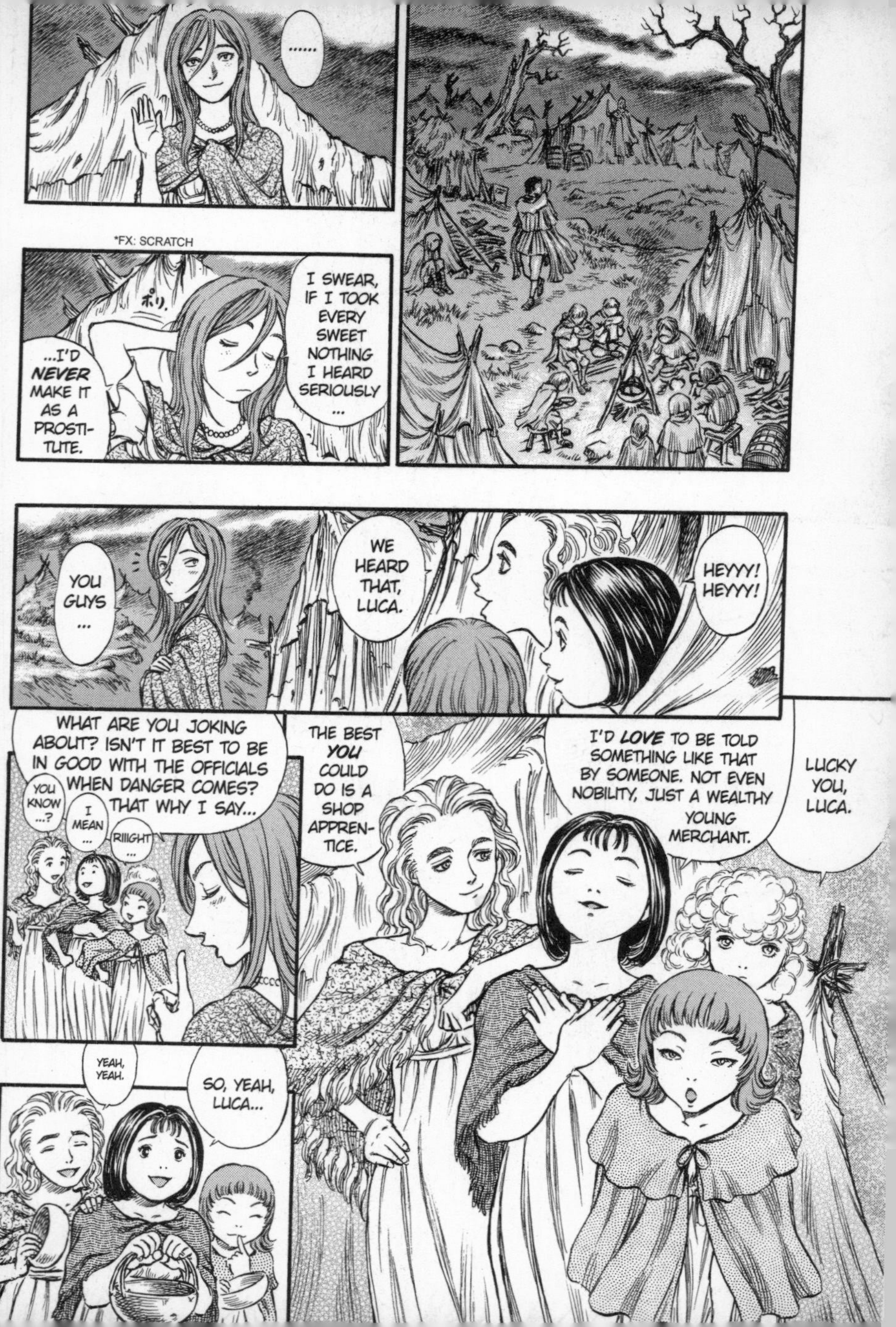
......
*FX: SCRATCH
ポリ.
I SWEAR, IF I TOOK EVERY SWEET NOTHING I HEARD SERIOUSLY ...
...I'D **NEVER** MAKE IT AS A PROSTI-TUTE.
HEYYY! HEYYY!
WE HEARD THAT, LUCA.
YOU GUYS ...
LUCKY YOU, LUCA.
I'D **LOVE** TO BE TOLD SOMETHING LIKE THAT BY SOMEONE. NOT EVEN NOBILITY, JUST A WEALTHY YOUNG MERCHANT.
THE BEST **YOU** COULD DO IS A SHOP APPREN-TICE.
WHAT ARE YOU JOKING ABOUT? ISN'T IT BEST TO BE IN GOOD WITH THE OFFICIALS WHEN DANGER COMES? THAT WHY I SAY...
YOU KNOW ...?
I MEAN ...
RIIIGHT ...
SO, YEAH, LUCA...
YEAH, YEAH.

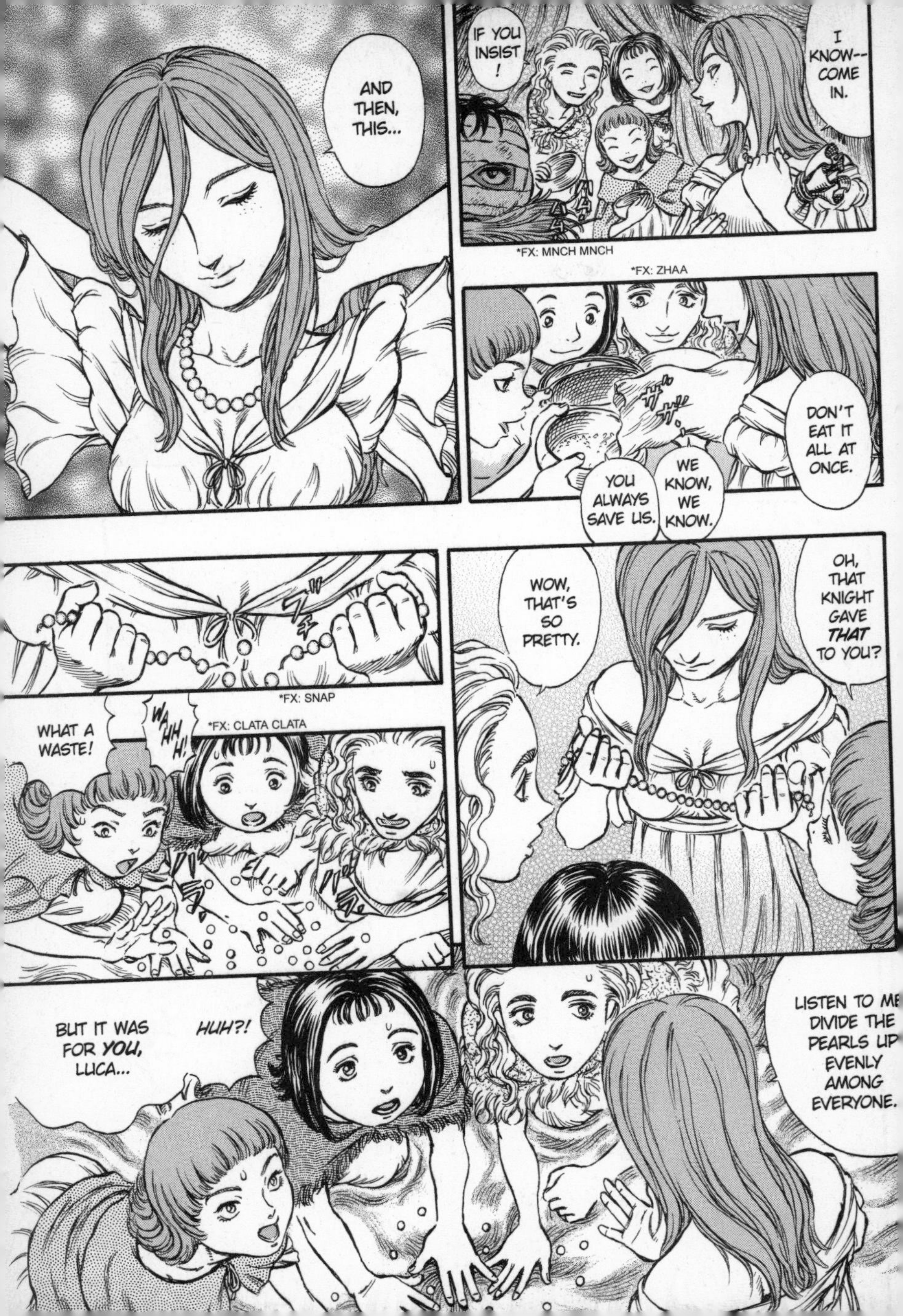
I KNOW--COME IN.
IF YOU INSIST!
*FX: MNCH MNCH
*FX: ZHAA
DON'T EAT IT ALL AT ONCE.
WE KNOW, WE KNOW.
YOU ALWAYS SAVE US.
AND THEN, THIS...
OH, THAT KNIGHT GAVE *THAT* TO YOU?
WOW, THAT'S SO PRETTY.
*FX: SNAP
WAHH!
*FX: CLATA CLATA
WHAT A WASTE!
LISTEN TO ME. DIVIDE THE PEARLS UP EVENLY AMONG EVERYONE.
HUH?!
BUT IT WAS FOR *YOU*, LUCA...

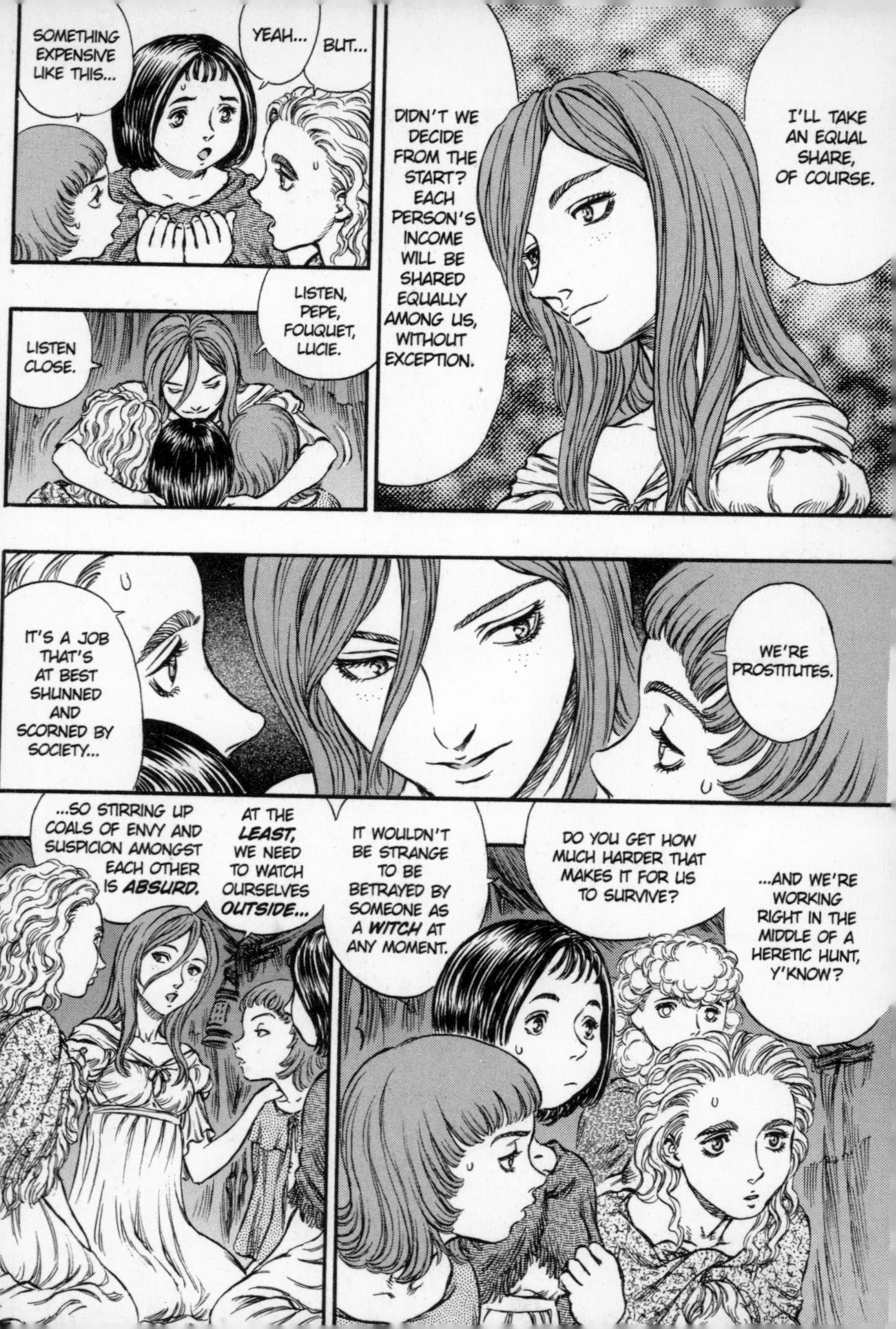

I'LL TAKE AN EQUAL SHARE, OF COURSE.
DIDN'T WE DECIDE FROM THE START? EACH PERSON'S INCOME WILL BE SHARED EQUALLY AMONG US, WITHOUT EXCEPTION.
YEAH...
BUT...
SOMETHING EXPENSIVE LIKE THIS...
LISTEN, PEPE, FOUQUET, LUCIE.
LISTEN CLOSE.
WE'RE PROSTITUTES.
IT'S A JOB THAT'S AT BEST SHUNNED AND SCORNED BY SOCIETY...
...AND WE'RE WORKING RIGHT IN THE MIDDLE OF A HERETIC HUNT, Y'KNOW?
DO YOU GET HOW MUCH HARDER THAT MAKES IT FOR US TO SURVIVE?
IT WOULDN'T BE STRANGE TO BE BETRAYED BY SOMEONE AS A *WITCH* AT ANY MOMENT.
AT THE *LEAST,* WE NEED TO WATCH OURSELVES *OUTSIDE...*
...SO STIRRING UP COALS OF ENVY AND SUSPICION AMONGST EACH OTHER IS *ABSURD.*

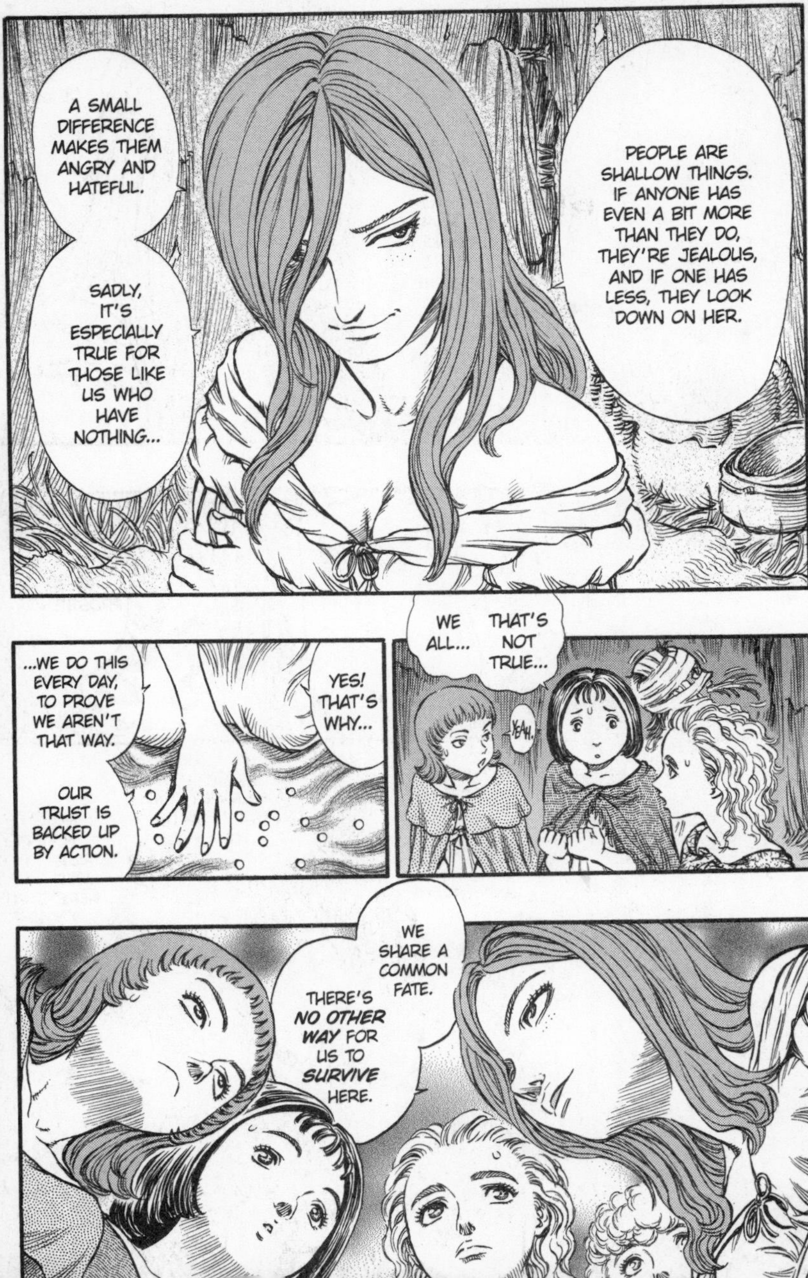
PEOPLE ARE SHALLOW THINGS. IF ANYONE HAS EVEN A BIT MORE THAN THEY DO, THEY'RE JEALOUS, AND IF ONE HAS LESS, THEY LOOK DOWN ON HER.
A SMALL DIFFERENCE MAKES THEM ANGRY AND HATEFUL.
SADLY, IT'S ESPECIALLY TRUE FOR THOSE LIKE US WHO HAVE NOTHING...
THAT'S NOT TRUE...
WE ALL...
YEAH.
YES! THAT'S WHY...
...WE DO THIS EVERY DAY, TO PROVE WE AREN'T THAT WAY.
OUR TRUST IS BACKED UP BY ACTION.
WE SHARE A COMMON FATE.
THERE'S ***NO OTHER WAY*** FOR US TO ***SURVIVE*** HERE.

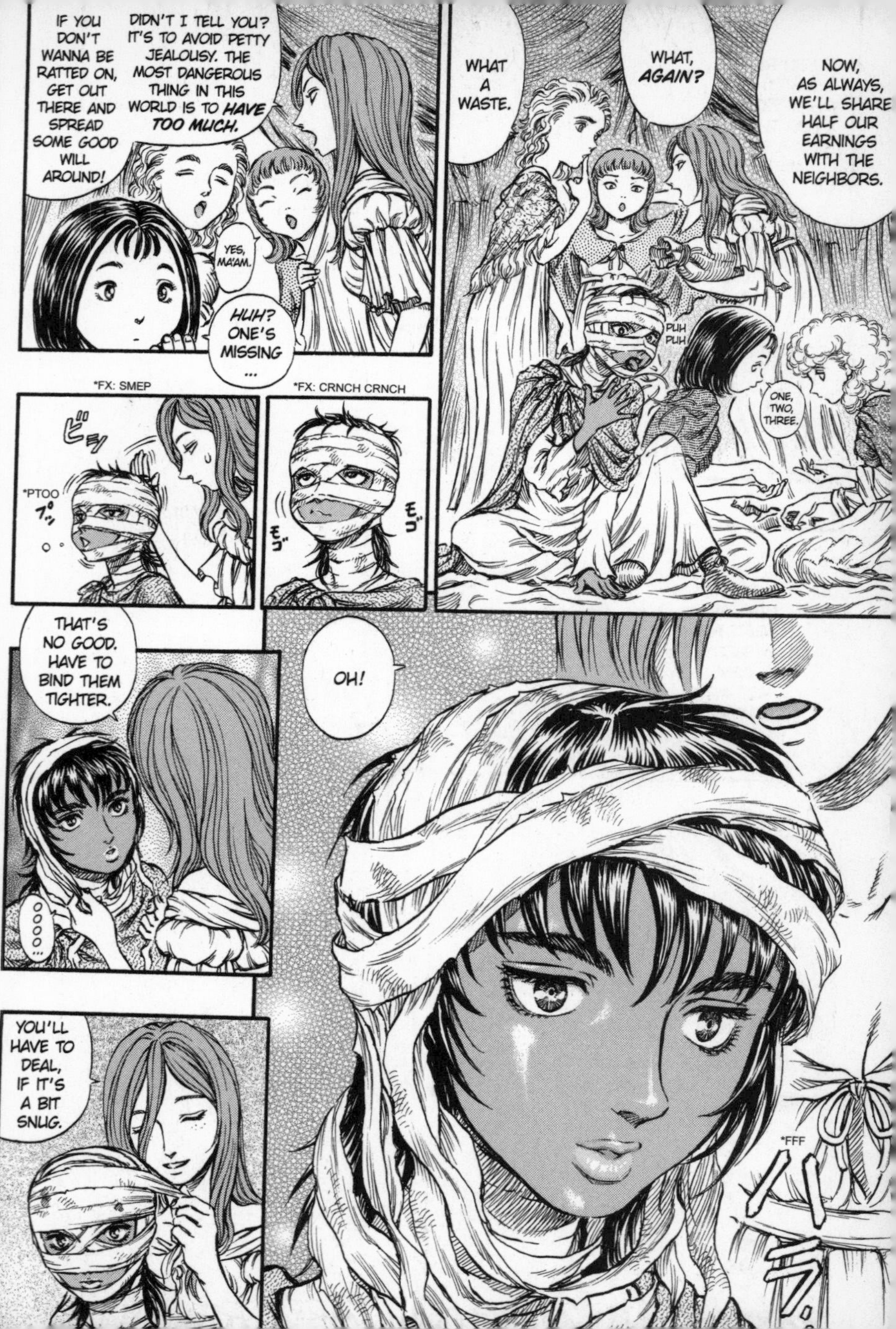
NOW, AS ALWAYS, WE'LL SHARE HALF OUR EARNINGS WITH THE NEIGHBORS.
WHAT, AGAIN?
WHAT A WASTE.
PUH PUH
ONE, TWO, THREE.
DIDN'T I TELL YOU? IT'S TO AVOID PETTY JEALOUSY. THE MOST DANGEROUS THING IN THIS WORLD IS TO HAVE TOO MUCH.
IF YOU DON'T WANNA BE RATTED ON, GET OUT THERE AND SPREAD SOME GOOD WILL AROUND!
YES, MA'AM.
HUH? ONE'S MISSING...
*FX: CRNCH CRNCH
*FX: SMEP
*PTOO
OH!
*FFF
THAT'S NO GOOD. HAVE TO BIND THEM TIGHTER.
OOOO...
YOU'LL HAVE TO DEAL, IF IT'S A BIT SNUG.

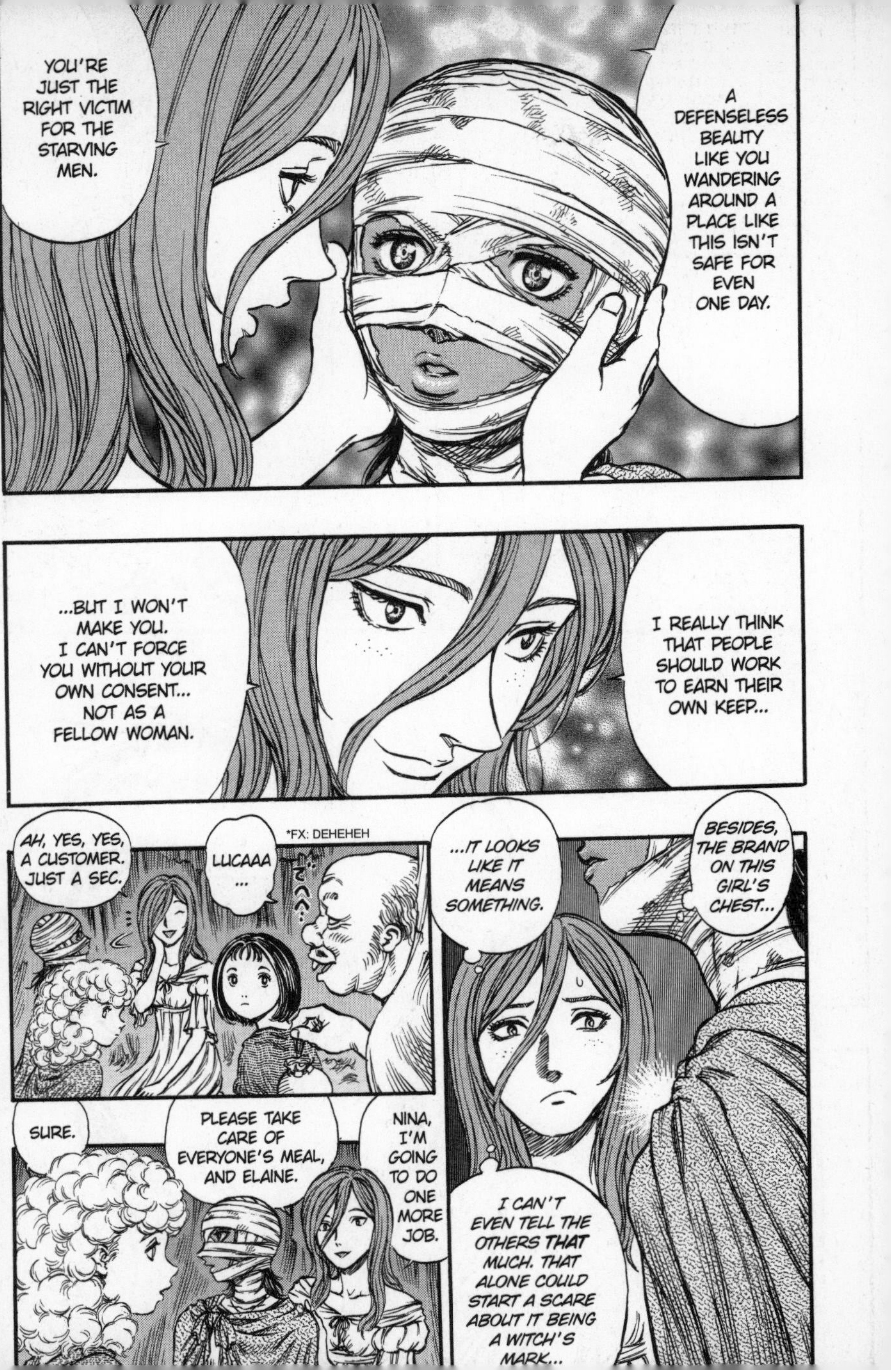
A DEFENSELESS BEAUTY LIKE YOU WANDERING AROUND A PLACE LIKE THIS ISN'T SAFE FOR EVEN ONE DAY.
YOU'RE JUST THE RIGHT VICTIM FOR THE STARVING MEN.
I REALLY THINK THAT PEOPLE SHOULD WORK TO EARN THEIR OWN KEEP...
...BUT I WON'T MAKE YOU. I CAN'T FORCE YOU WITHOUT YOUR OWN CONSENT... NOT AS A FELLOW WOMAN.
BESIDES, THE BRAND ON THIS GIRL'S CHEST...
...IT LOOKS LIKE IT MEANS SOMETHING.
I CAN'T EVEN TELL THE OTHERS THAT MUCH. THAT ALONE COULD START A SCARE ABOUT IT BEING A WITCH'S MARK...
*FX: DEHEHEH
LUCAAA ...
AH, YES, YES, A CUSTOMER. JUST A SEC.
NINA, I'M GOING TO DO ONE MORE JOB.
PLEASE TAKE CARE OF EVERYONE'S MEAL, AND ELAINE.
SURE.

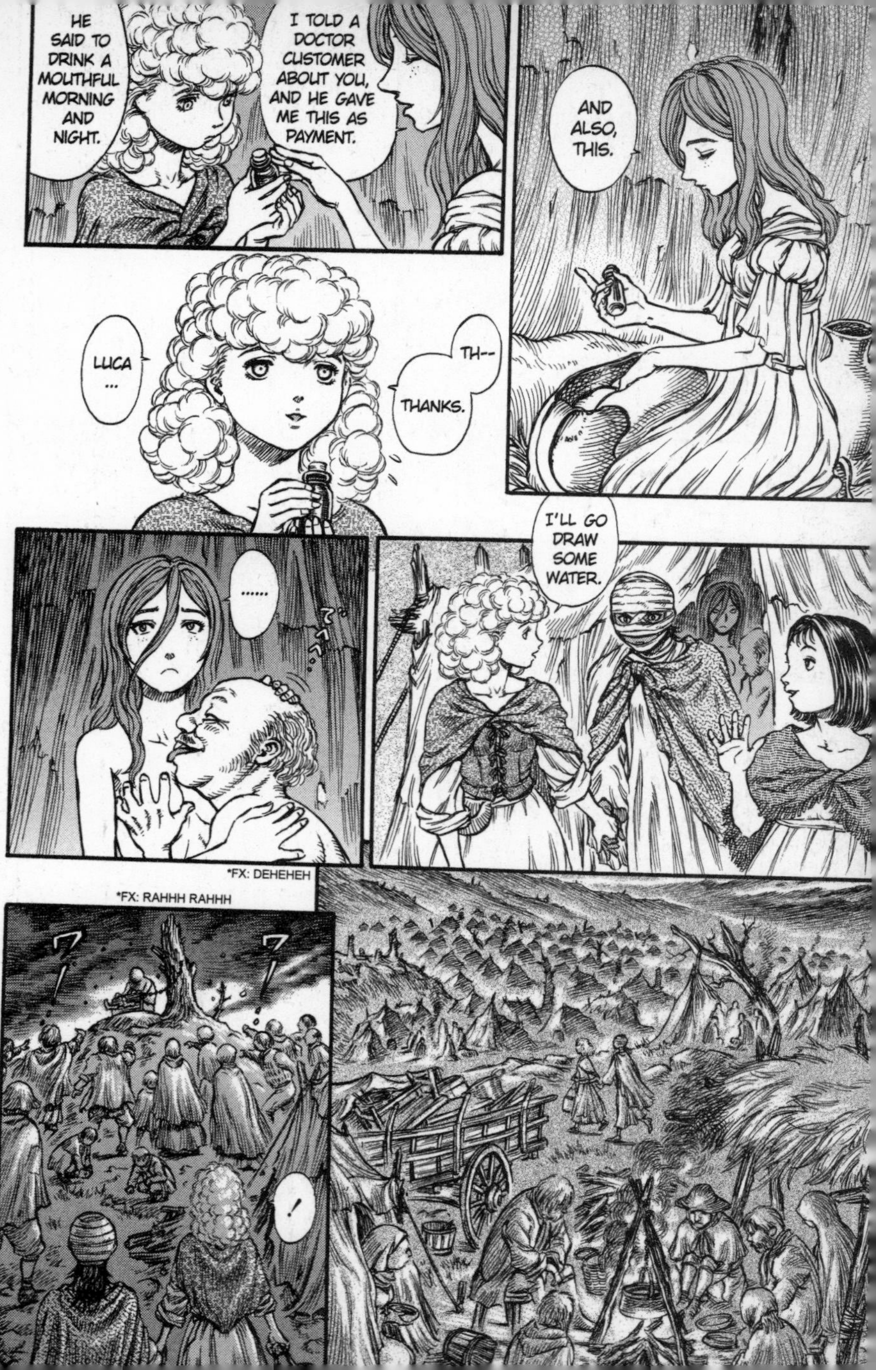
AND ALSO, THIS.
I TOLD A DOCTOR CUSTOMER ABOUT YOU, AND HE GAVE ME THIS AS PAYMENT.
HE SAID TO DRINK A MOUTHFUL MORNING AND NIGHT.
TH--
THANKS.
LUCA ...
I'LL GO DRAW SOME WATER.
......
*FX: DEHEHEH
*FX: RAHHH RAHHH
!

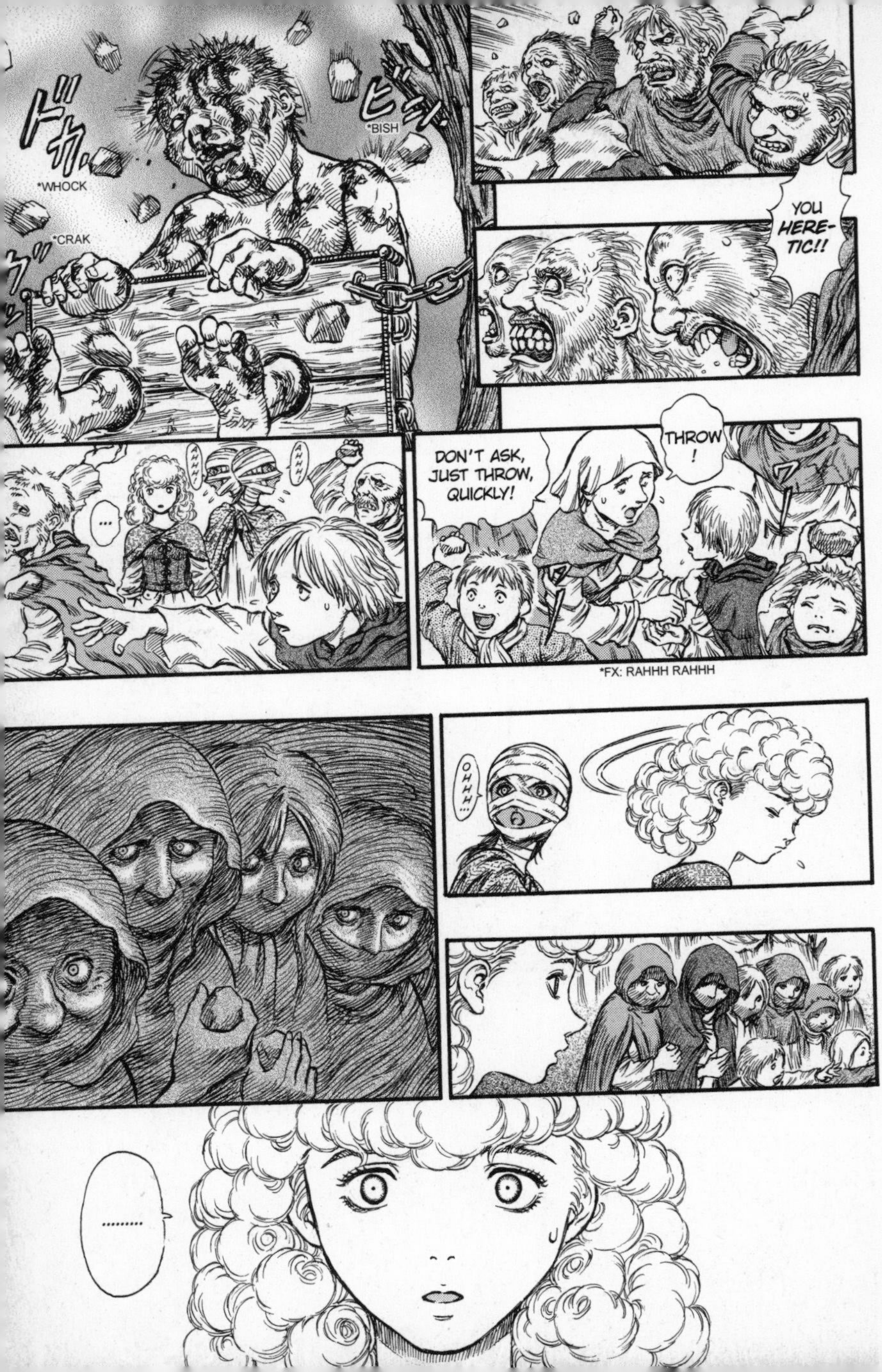
YOU HERETIC!!
*BISH
*WHOCK
*CRAK
THROW!
DON'T ASK, JUST THROW, QUICKLY!
*FX: RAHHH RAHHH
...
OHHH...
....

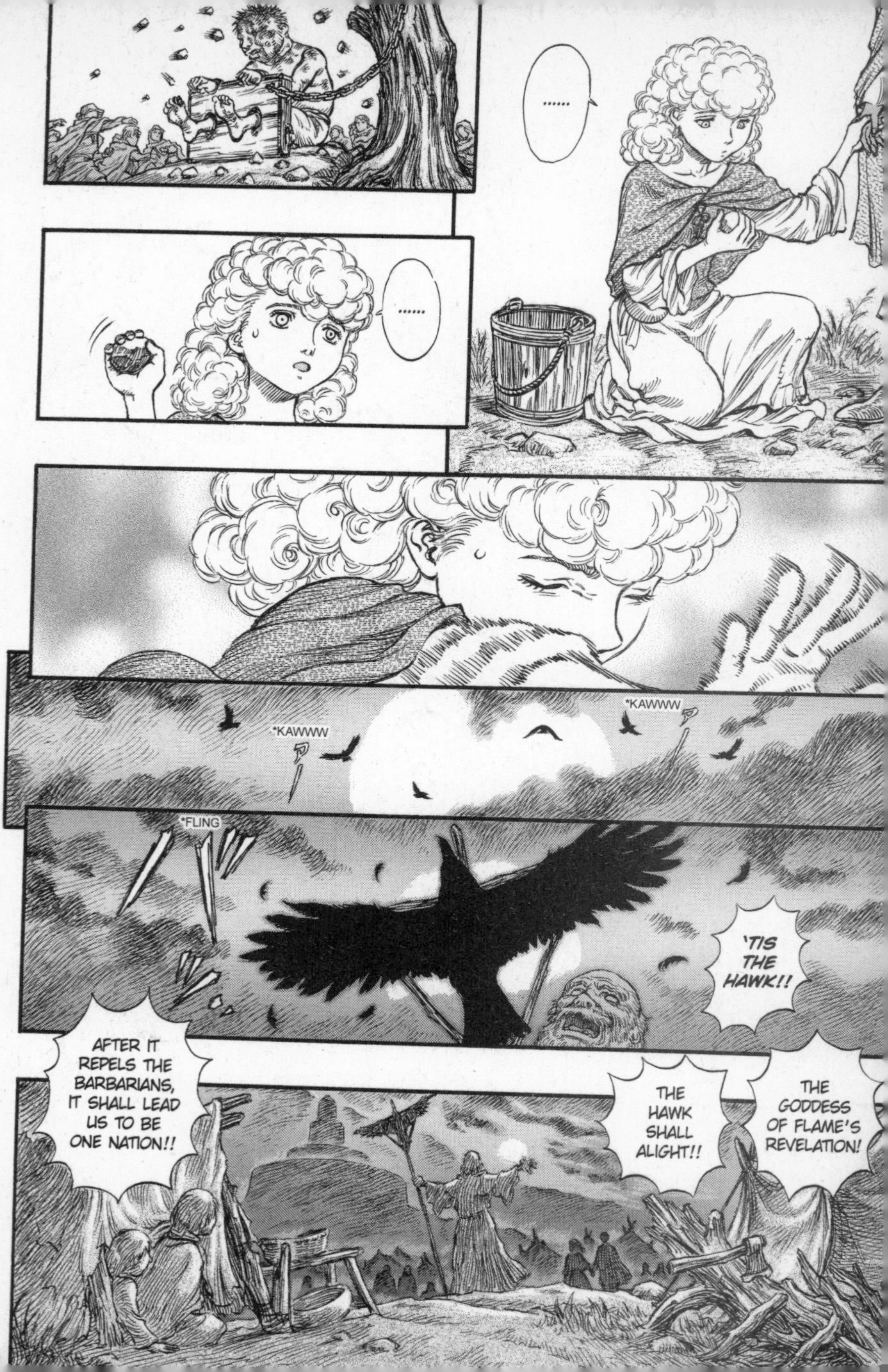
......
......
*KAWWW
*KAWWW
'TIS THE HAWK!!
*FLING
THE GODDESS OF FLAME'S REVELATION!
THE HAWK SHALL ALIGHT!!
AFTER IT REPELS THE BARBARIANS, IT SHALL LEAD US TO BE ONE NATION!!

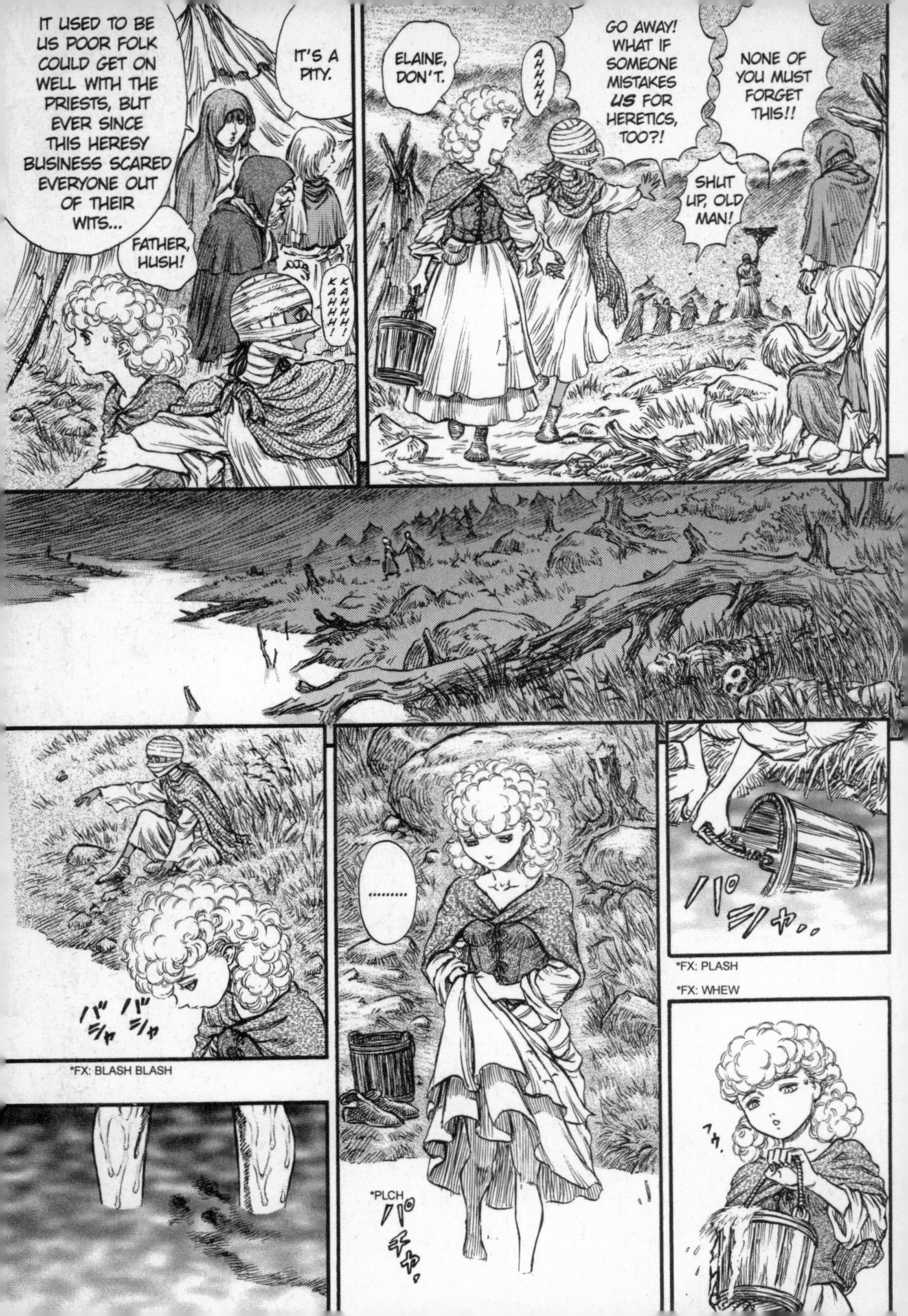
NONE OF YOU MUST FORGET THIS!!
SHUT UP, OLD MAN!
GO AWAY! WHAT IF SOMEONE MISTAKES US FOR HERETICS, TOO?!
AHHHH!
ELAINE, DON'T.
IT'S A PITY.
IT USED TO BE US POOR FOLK COULD GET ON WELL WITH THE PRIESTS, BUT EVER SINCE THIS HERESY BUSINESS SCARED EVERYONE OUT OF THEIR WITS...
FATHER, HUSH!
KAHHHH!
*FX: PLASH
*FX: WHEW
....
*PLCH
*FX: BLASH BLASH

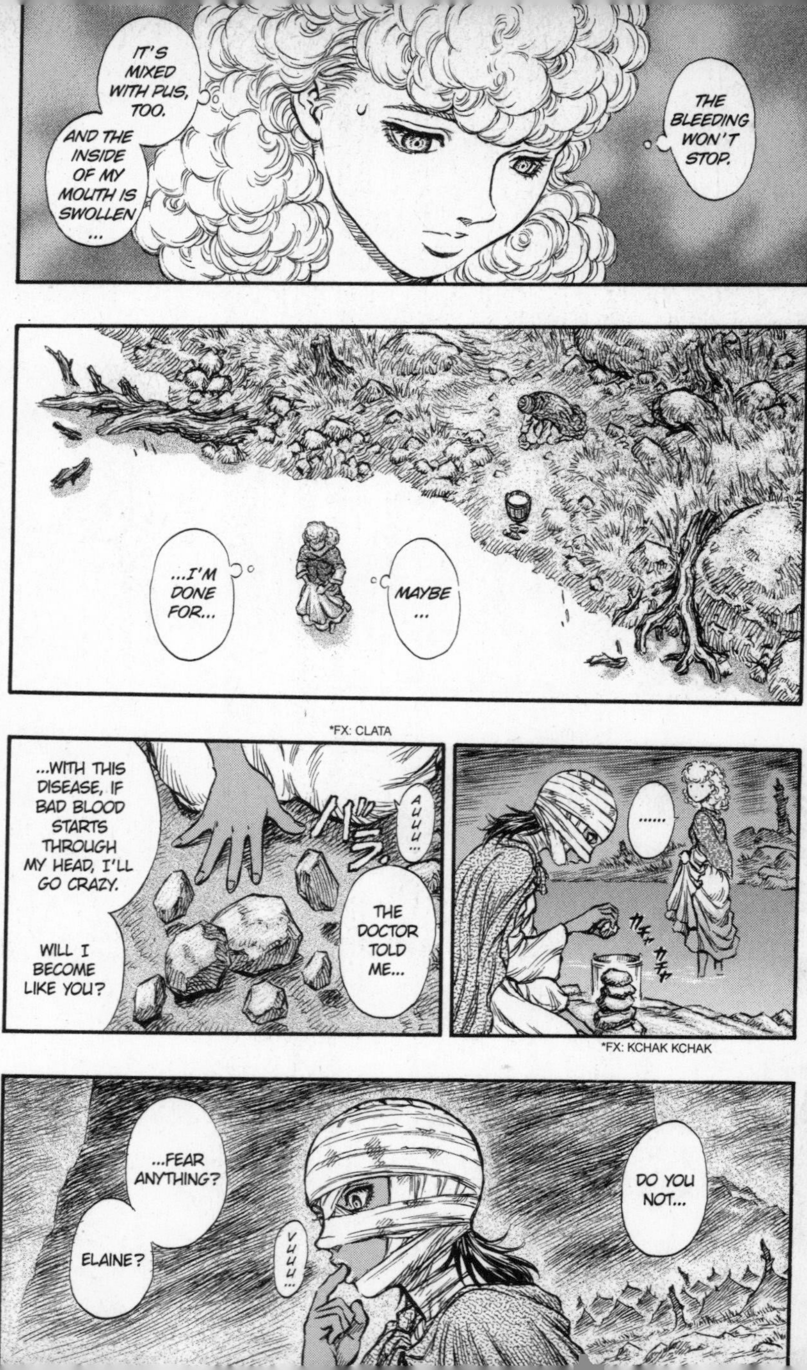
THE BLEEDING WON'T STOP.
IT'S MIXED WITH PUS, TOO.
AND THE INSIDE OF MY MOUTH IS SWOLLEN ...
MAYBE ...
...I'M DONE FOR...
......
*FX: KCHAK KCHAK
AUUU...
THE DOCTOR TOLD ME...
...WITH THIS DISEASE, IF BAD BLOOD STARTS THROUGH MY HEAD, I'LL GO CRAZY.
WILL I BECOME LIKE YOU?
*FX: CLATA
DO YOU NOT...
...FEAR ANYTHING?
VUUU...
ELAINE?

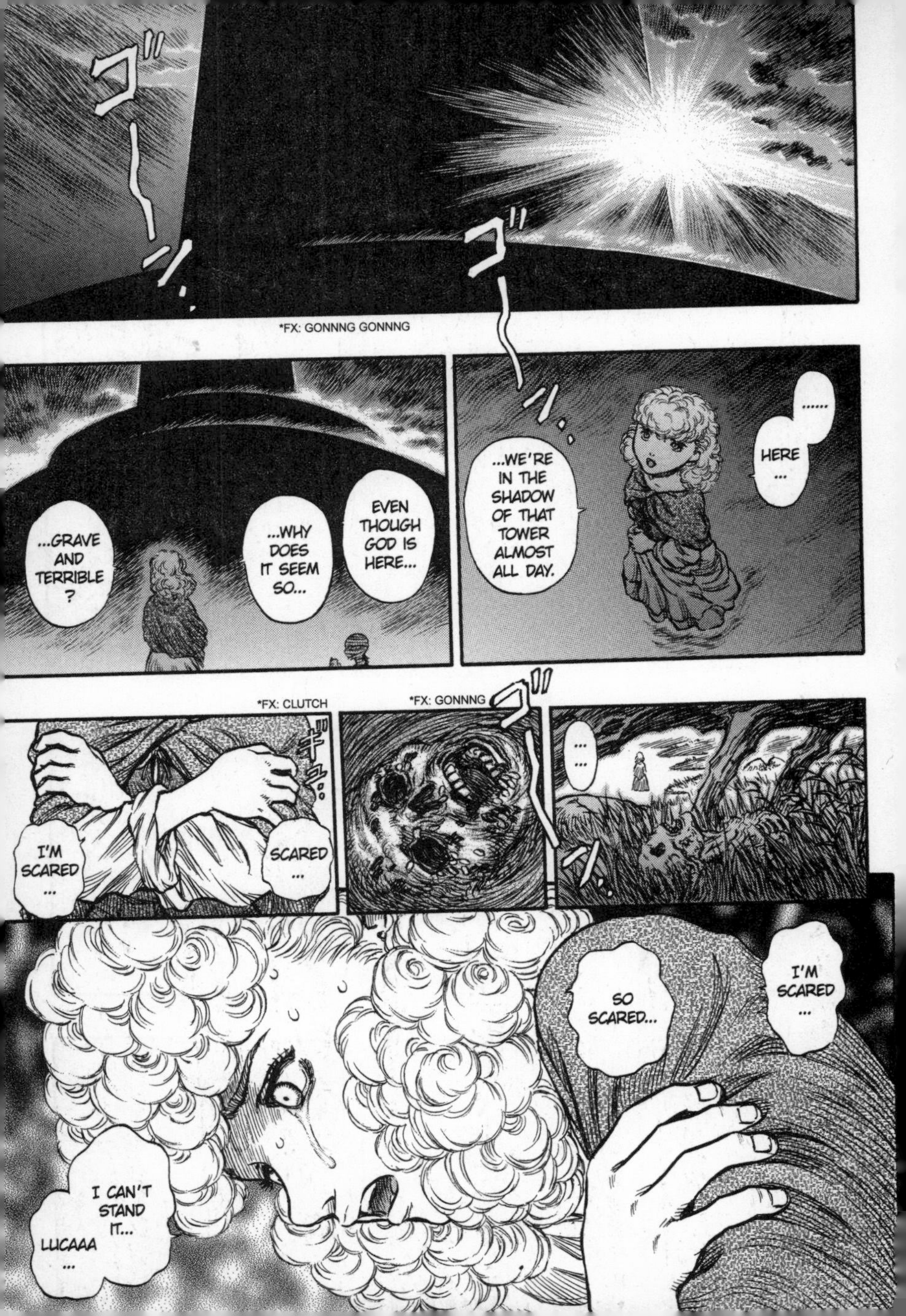
*FX: GONNNG GONNNG
......
HERE ...
...WE'RE IN THE SHADOW OF THAT TOWER ALMOST ALL DAY.
EVEN THOUGH GOD IS HERE...
...WHY DOES IT SEEM SO...
...GRAVE AND TERRIBLE ?
*FX: GONNNG
... ...
*FX: CLUTCH
SCARED ...
I'M SCARED ...
I'M SCARED ...
SO SCARED...
I CAN'T STAND IT...
LUCAAA ...

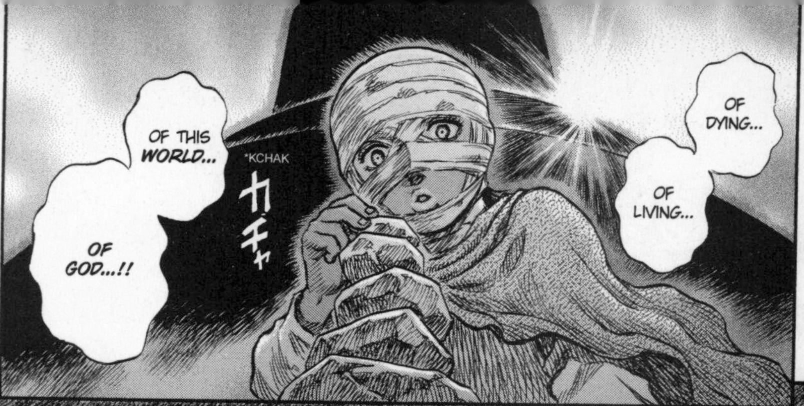
OF DYING...
OF LIVING...
*KCHAK
カチャ
OF THIS WORLD...
OF GOD...!!
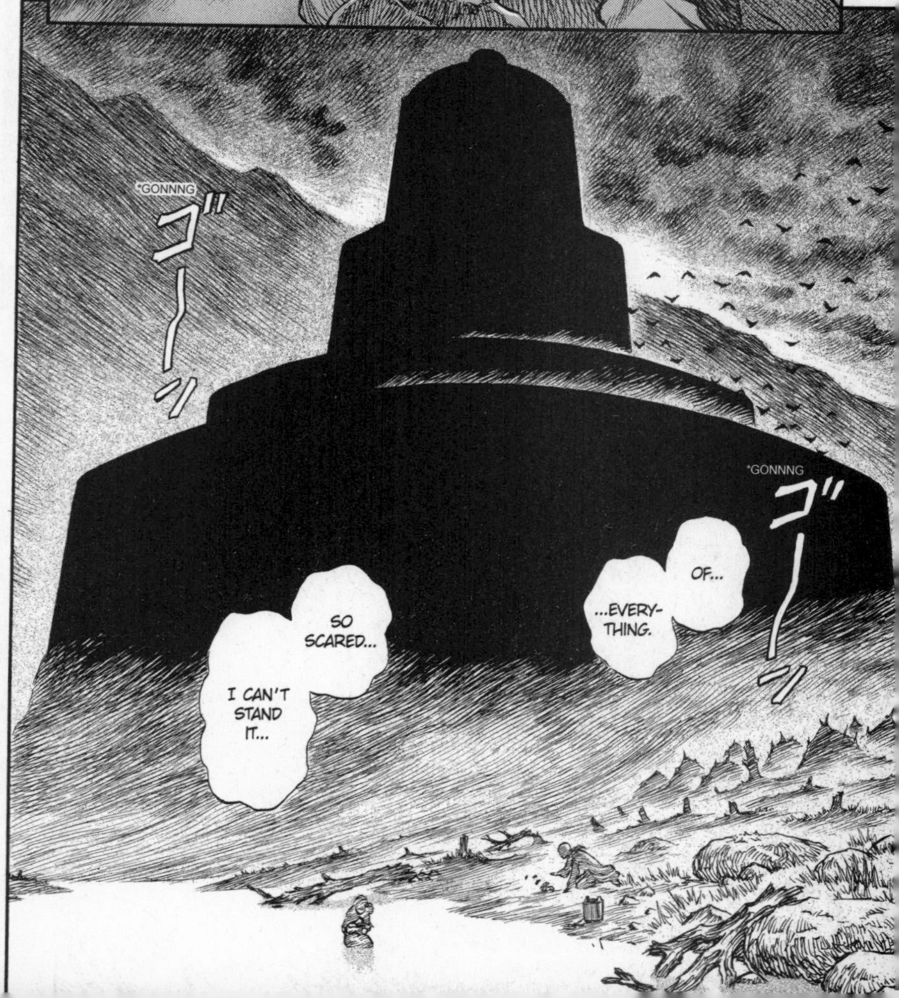
*GONNNG
ゴ〜〜ッ
OF...
...EVERY-THING.
SO SCARED...
I CAN'T STAND IT...
*GONNNG
ゴ〜〜ッ

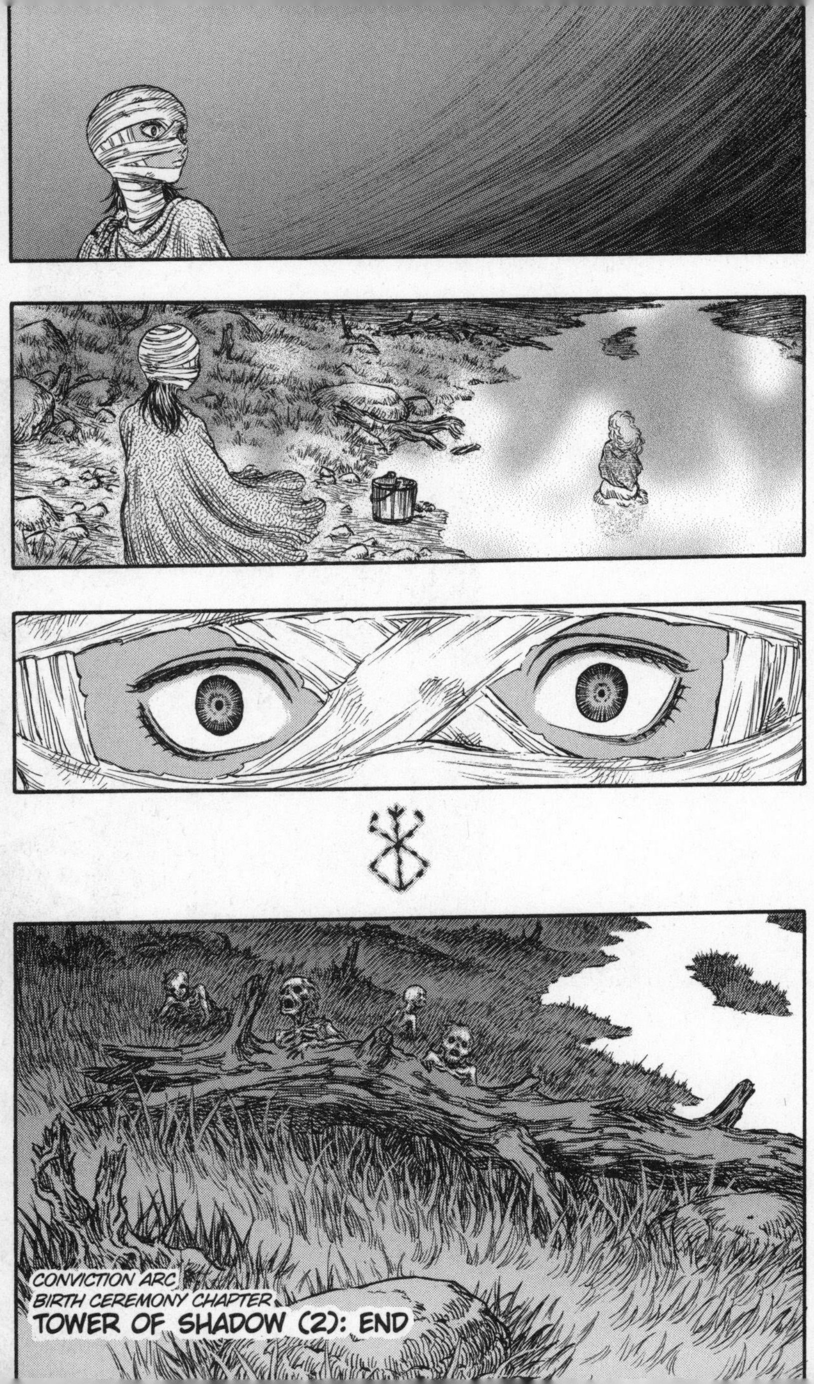
CONVICTION ARC
BIRTH CEREMONY CHAPTER
TOWER OF SHADOW (2): END

BERSERK

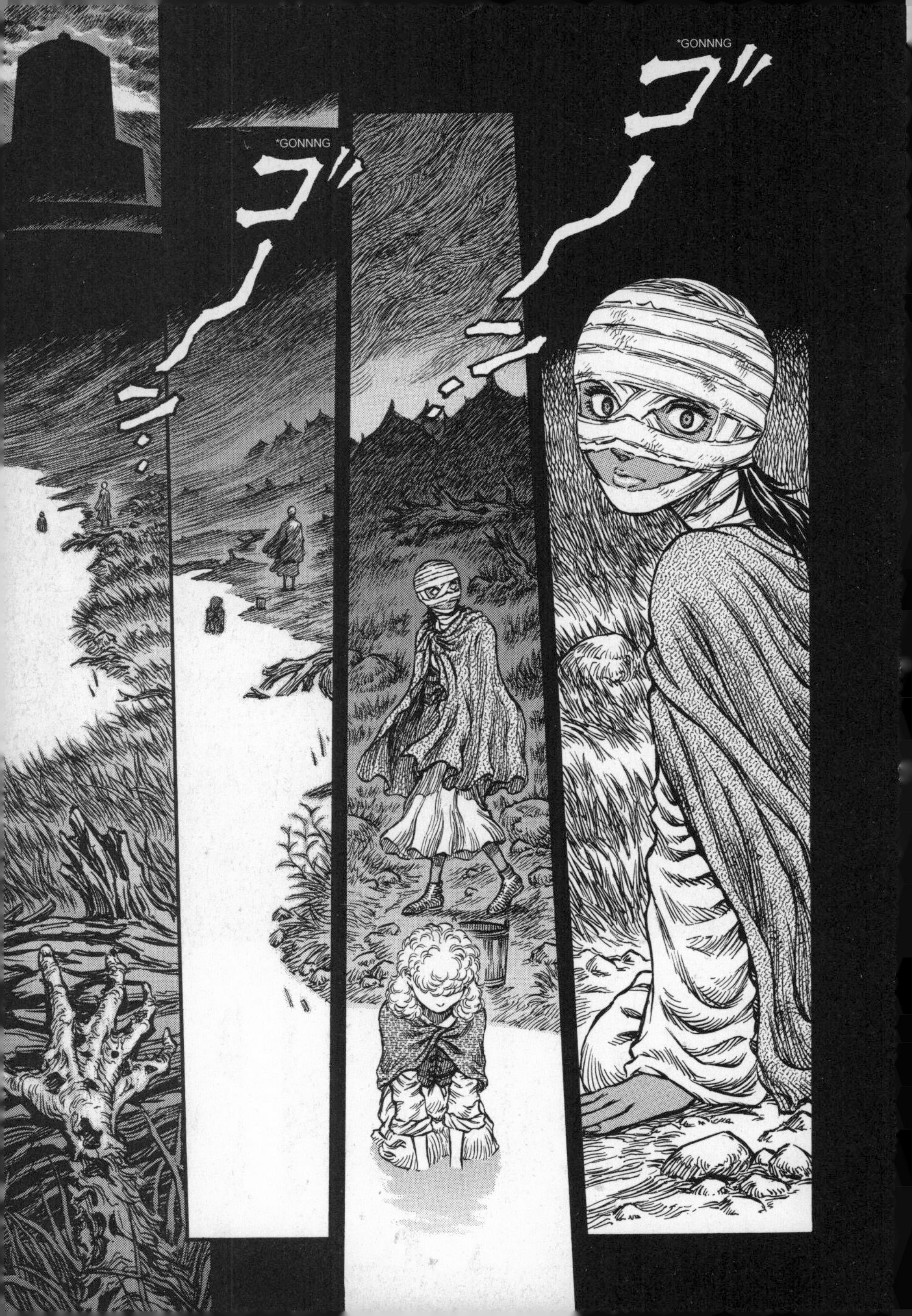
*GONNNG
*GONNNG

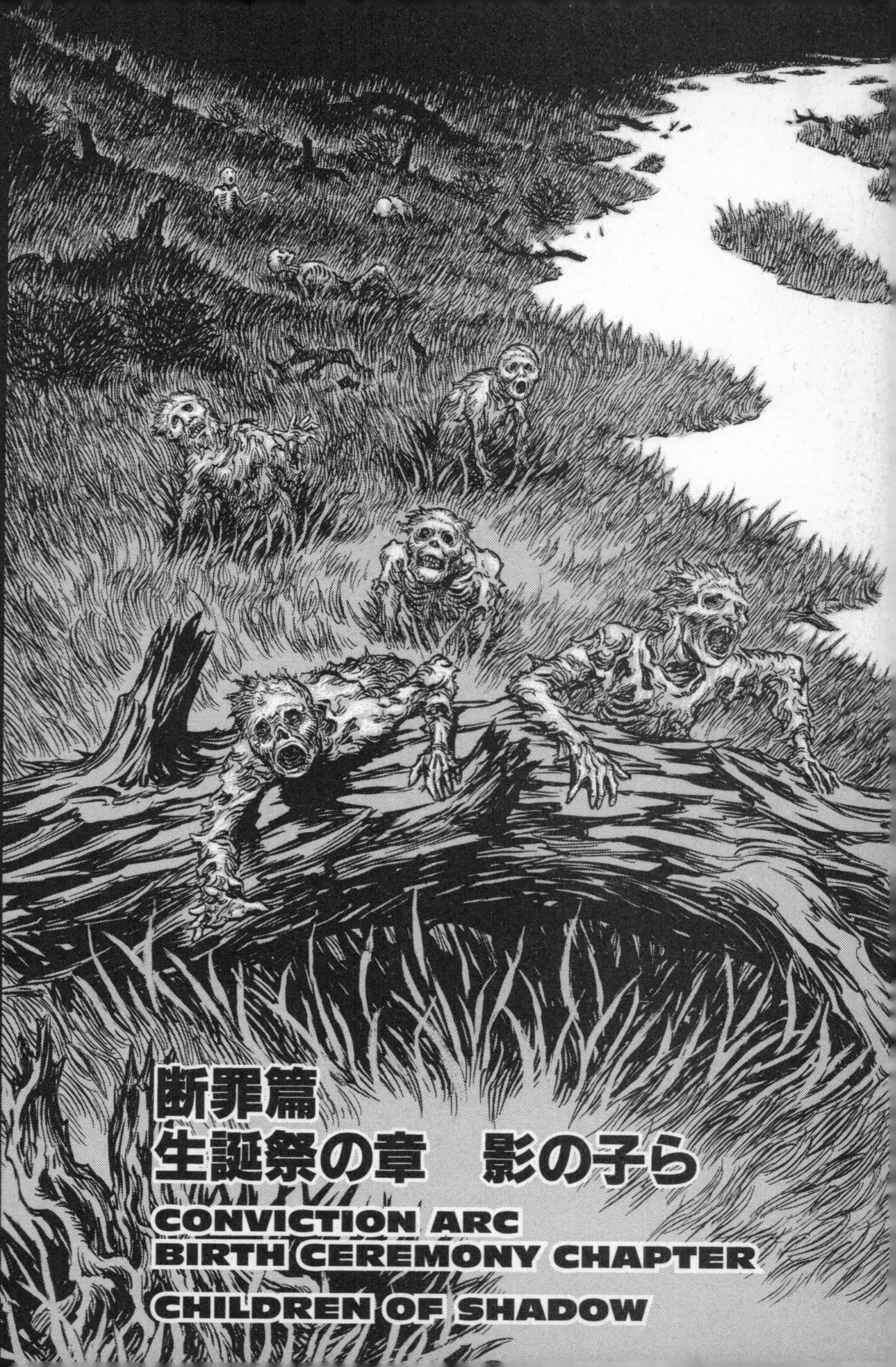
断罪篇
生誕祭の章　影の子ら
CONVICTION ARC
BIRTH CEREMONY CHAPTER
CHILDREN OF SHADOW

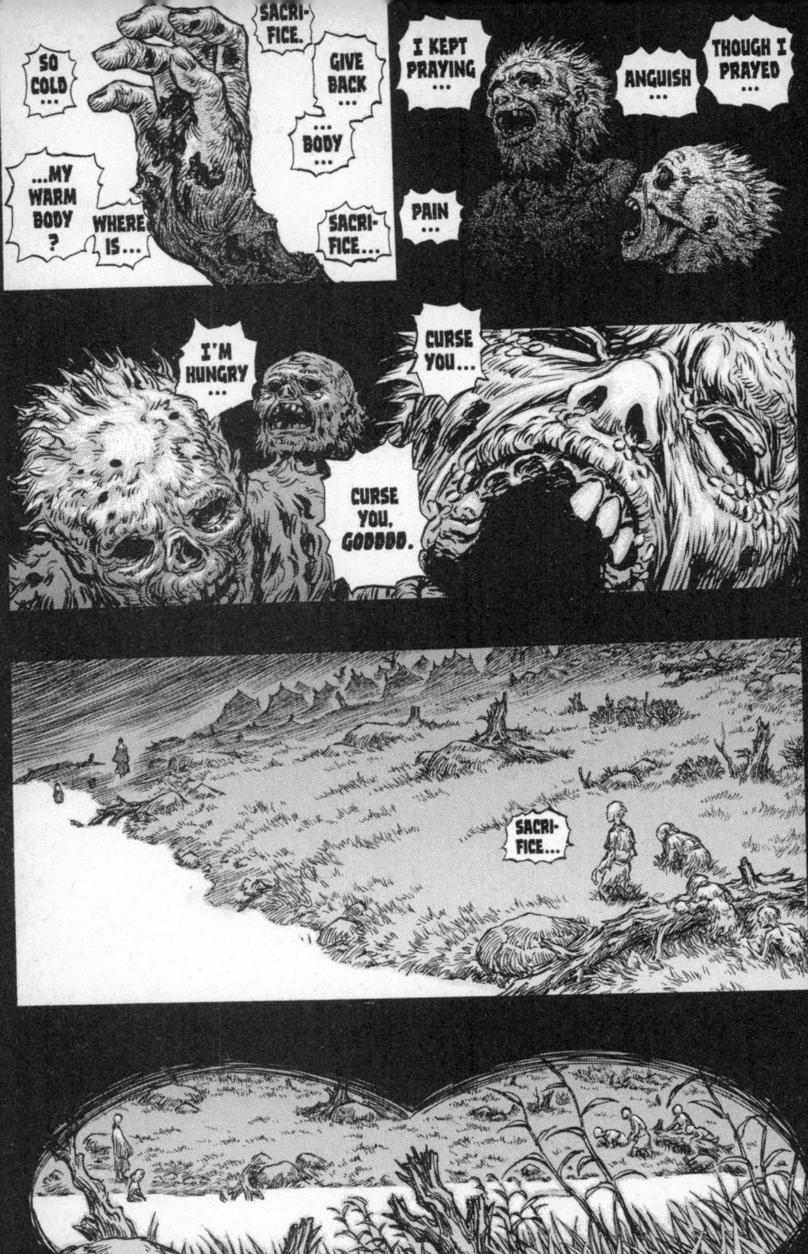
THOUGH I PRAYED...
ANGUISH...
I KEPT PRAYING...
PAIN...
SACRIFICE.
GIVE BACK...
...BODY...
SO COLD...
SACRIFICE...
WHERE IS...
...MY WARM BODY?
CURSE YOU...
CURSE YOU, GODDDD.
I'M HUNGRY...
SACRIFICE...

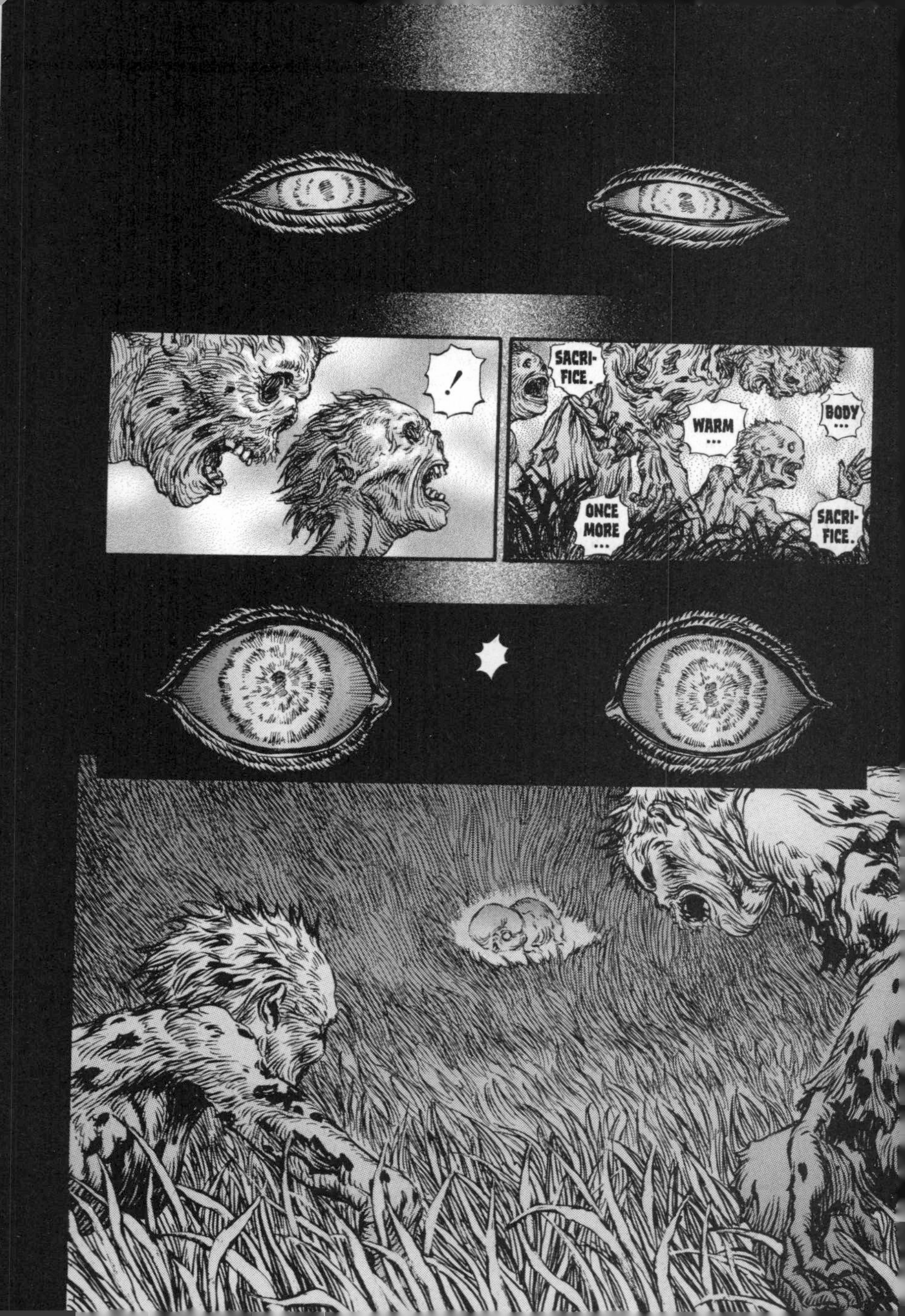
BODY...
WARM...
SACRI-FICE.
SACRI-FICE.
ONCE MORE...
!

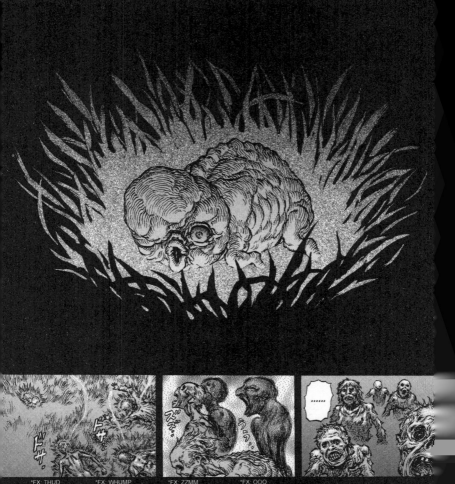

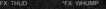

*FX: THUD   *FX: WHUMP   *FX: ZZMM   *FX: OOO

*WHFF

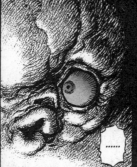

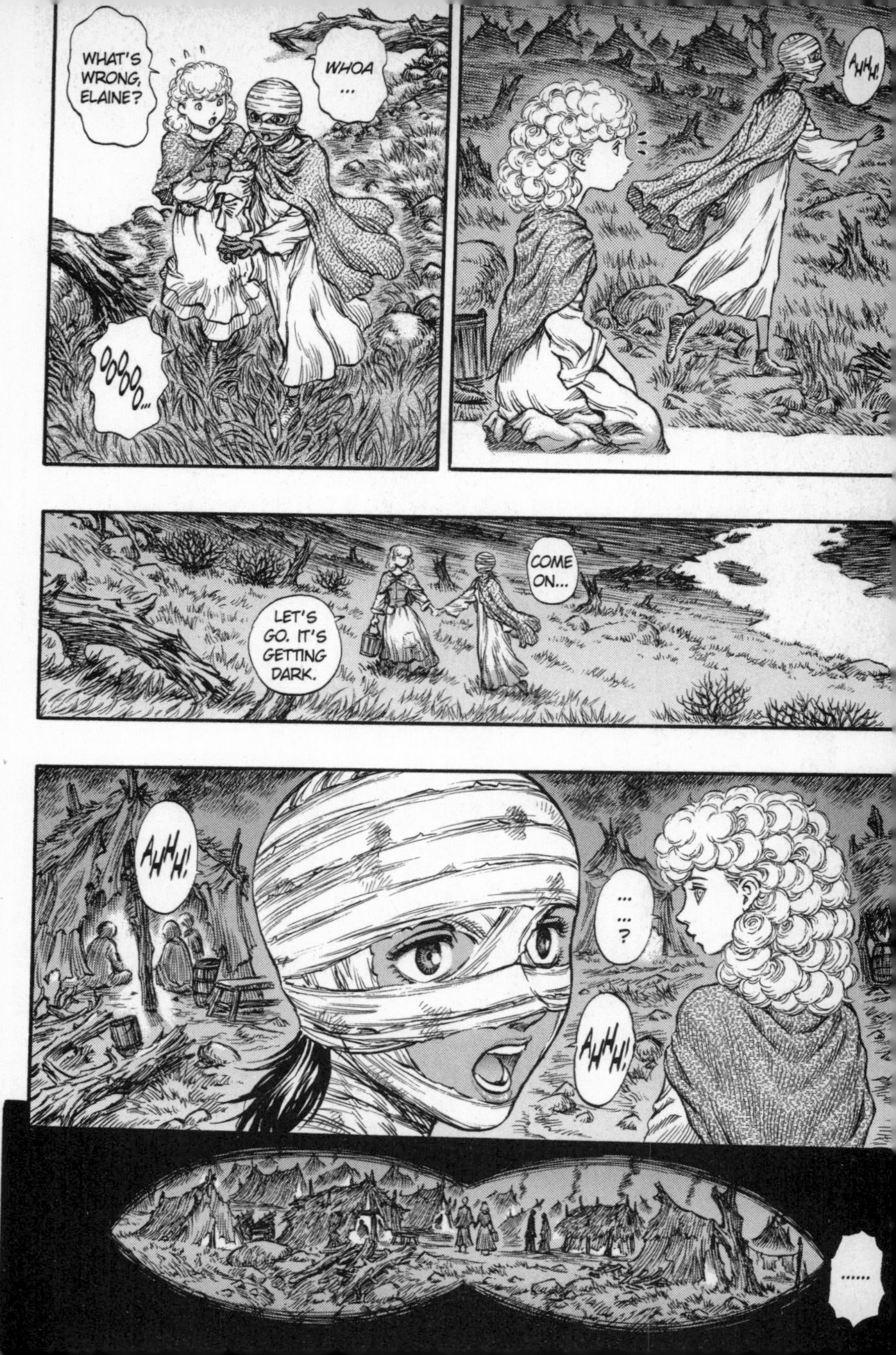
AHHH!
WHOA ...
WHAT'S WRONG, ELAINE?
OOOOO...
COME ON...
LET'S GO. IT'S GETTING DARK.
... ... ?
AHHH!
AHHH!
......

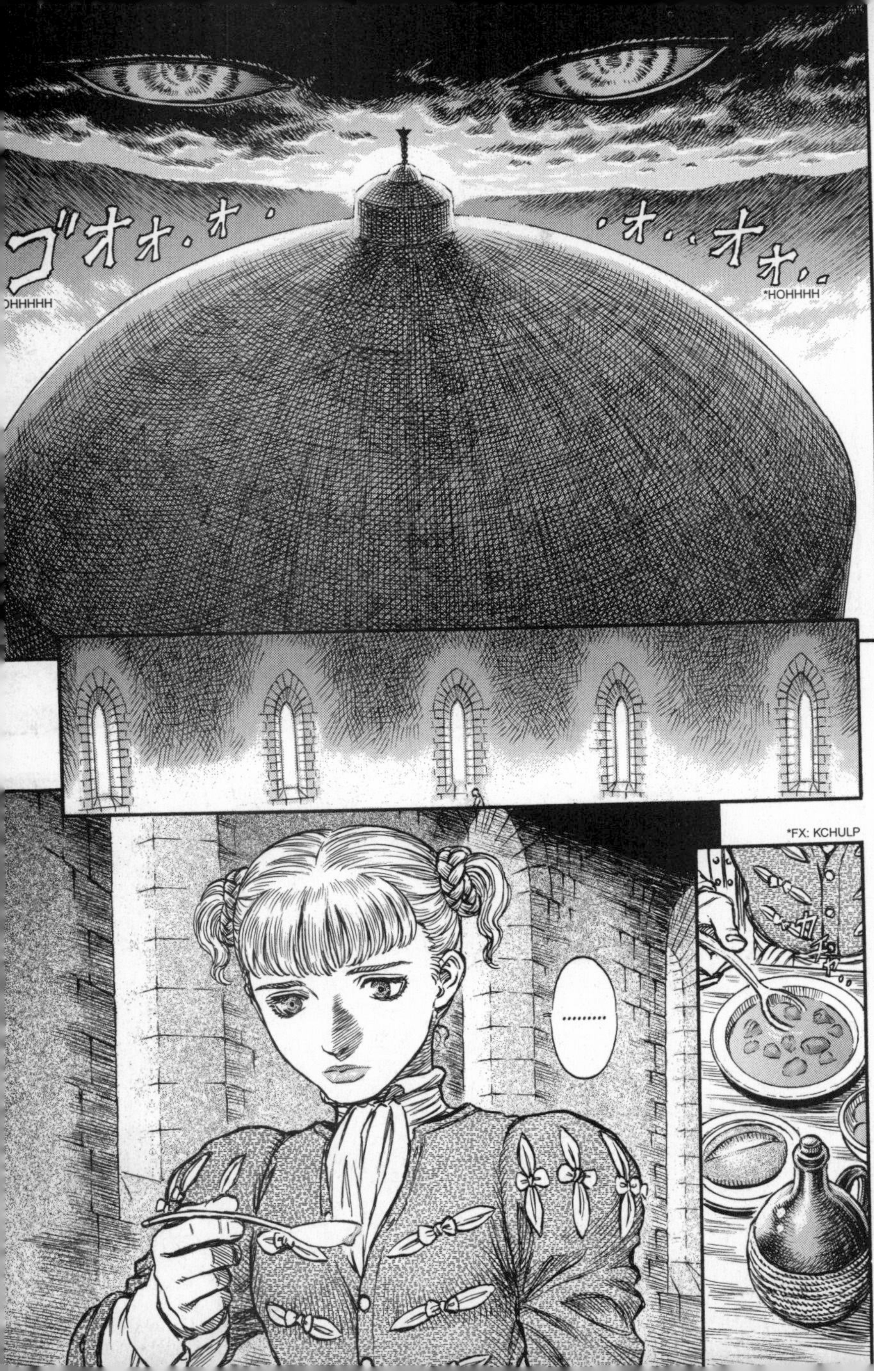
ゴオォ・オ・
OHHHHH
・オ・・オォ・・
*HOHHHH
*FX: KCHULP
....

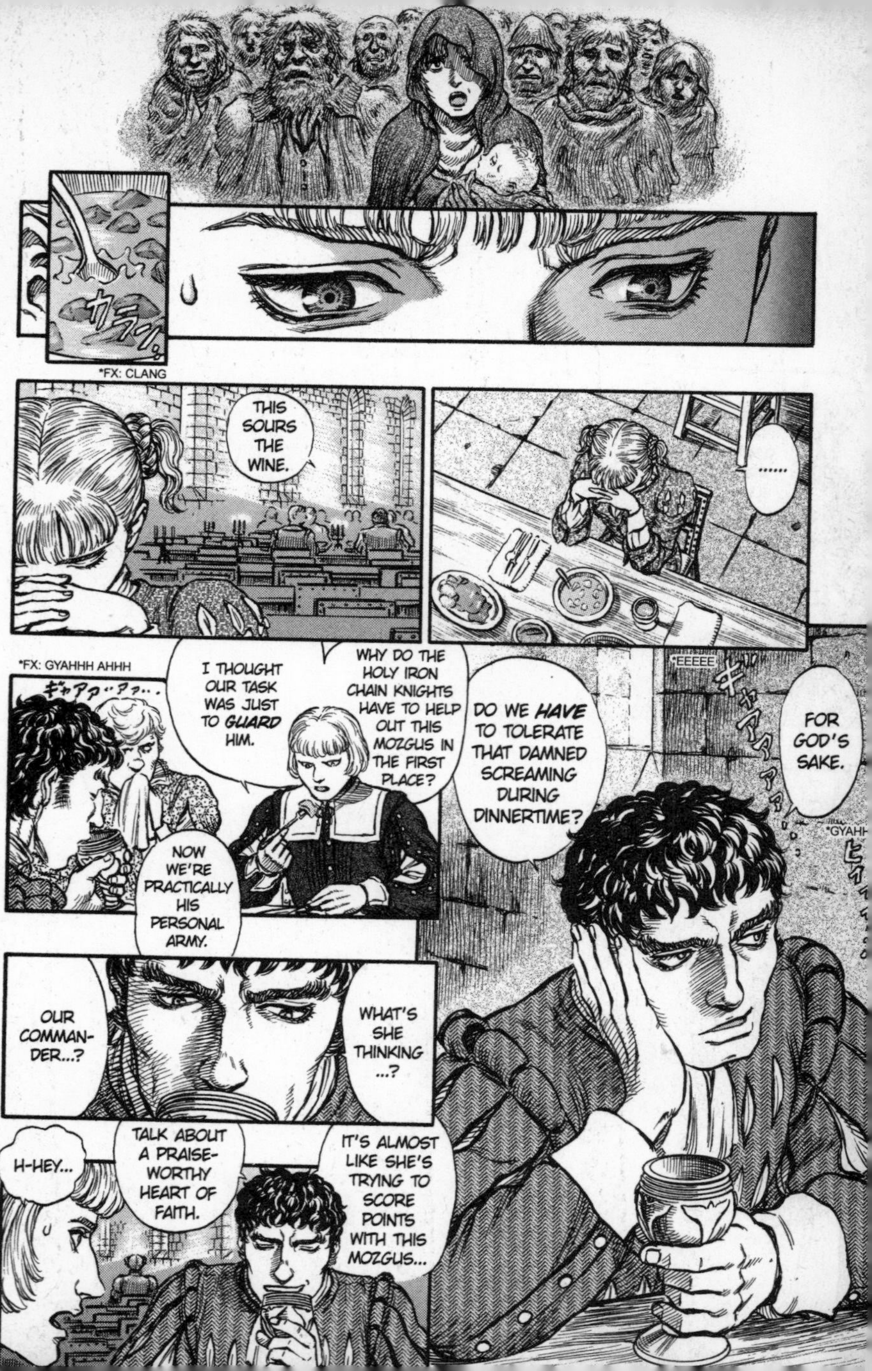
カラン
*FX: CLANG
......
THIS SOURS THE WINE.
*EEEEE
FOR GOD'S SAKE.
DO WE *HAVE* TO TOLERATE THAT DAMNED SCREAMING DURING DINNERTIME?
*GYAHH
WHY DO THE HOLY IRON CHAIN KNIGHTS HAVE TO HELP OUT THIS MOZGUS IN THE FIRST PLACE?
I THOUGHT OUR TASK WAS JUST TO *GUARD* HIM.
NOW WE'RE PRACTICALLY HIS PERSONAL ARMY.
*FX: GYAHHH AHHH
WHAT'S SHE THINKING ...?
OUR COMMANDER...?
IT'S ALMOST LIKE SHE'S TRYING TO SCORE POINTS WITH THIS MOZGUS...
TALK ABOUT A PRAISE-WORTHY HEART OF FAITH.
H-HEY...

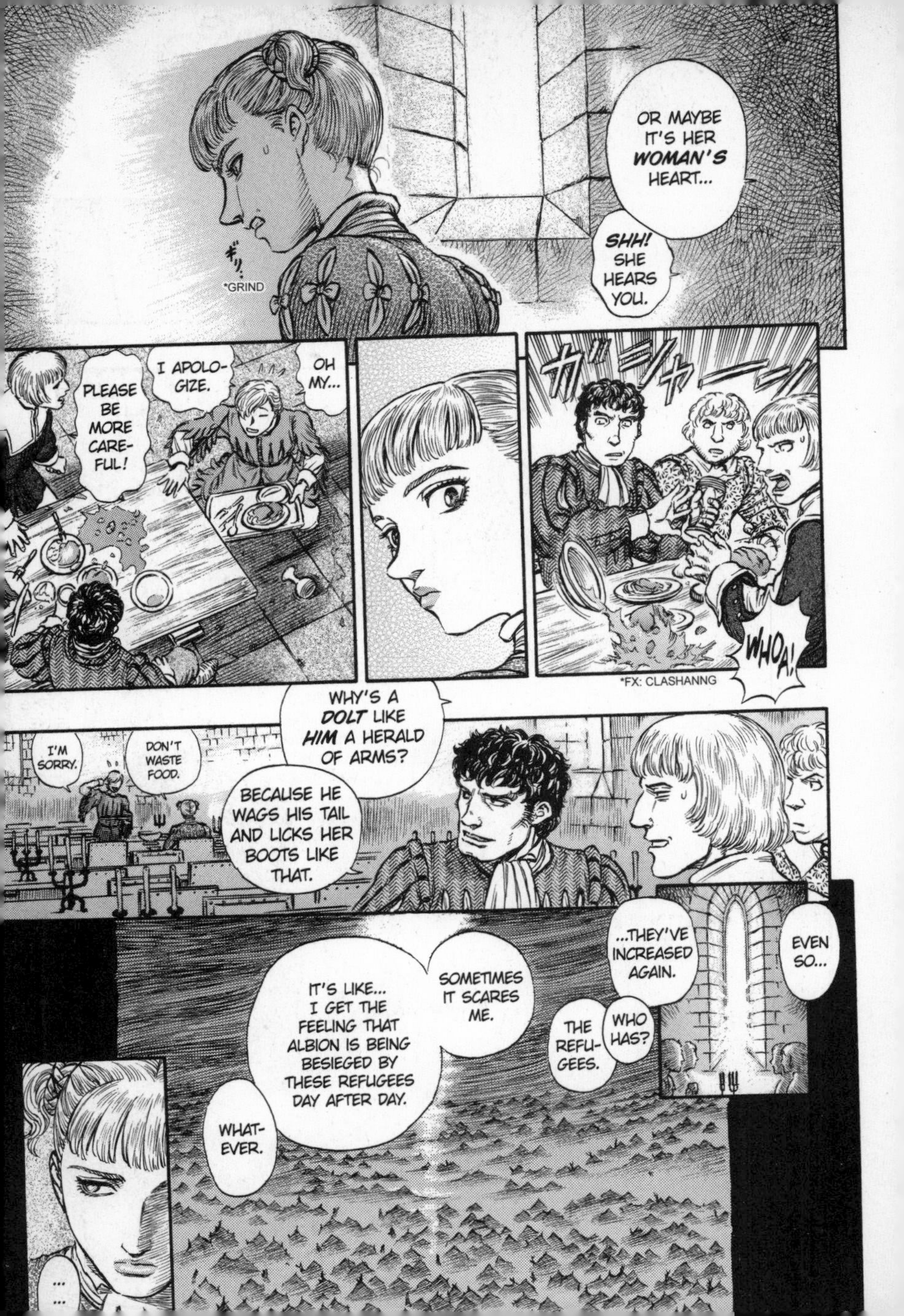
OR MAYBE IT'S HER WOMAN'S HEART...
SHH! SHE HEARS YOU.
ギリ
*GRIND
*FX: CLASHANNG
WHOA!
OH MY...
I APOLOGIZE.
PLEASE BE MORE CAREFUL!
WHY'S A DOLT LIKE HIM A HERALD OF ARMS?
BECAUSE HE WAGS HIS TAIL AND LICKS HER BOOTS LIKE THAT.
DON'T WASTE FOOD.
I'M SORRY.
EVEN SO...
...THEY'VE INCREASED AGAIN.
WHO HAS?
THE REFUGEES.
SOMETIMES IT SCARES ME.
IT'S LIKE... I GET THE FEELING THAT ALBION IS BEING BESIEGED BY THESE REFUGEES DAY AFTER DAY.
WHATEVER.
...
...

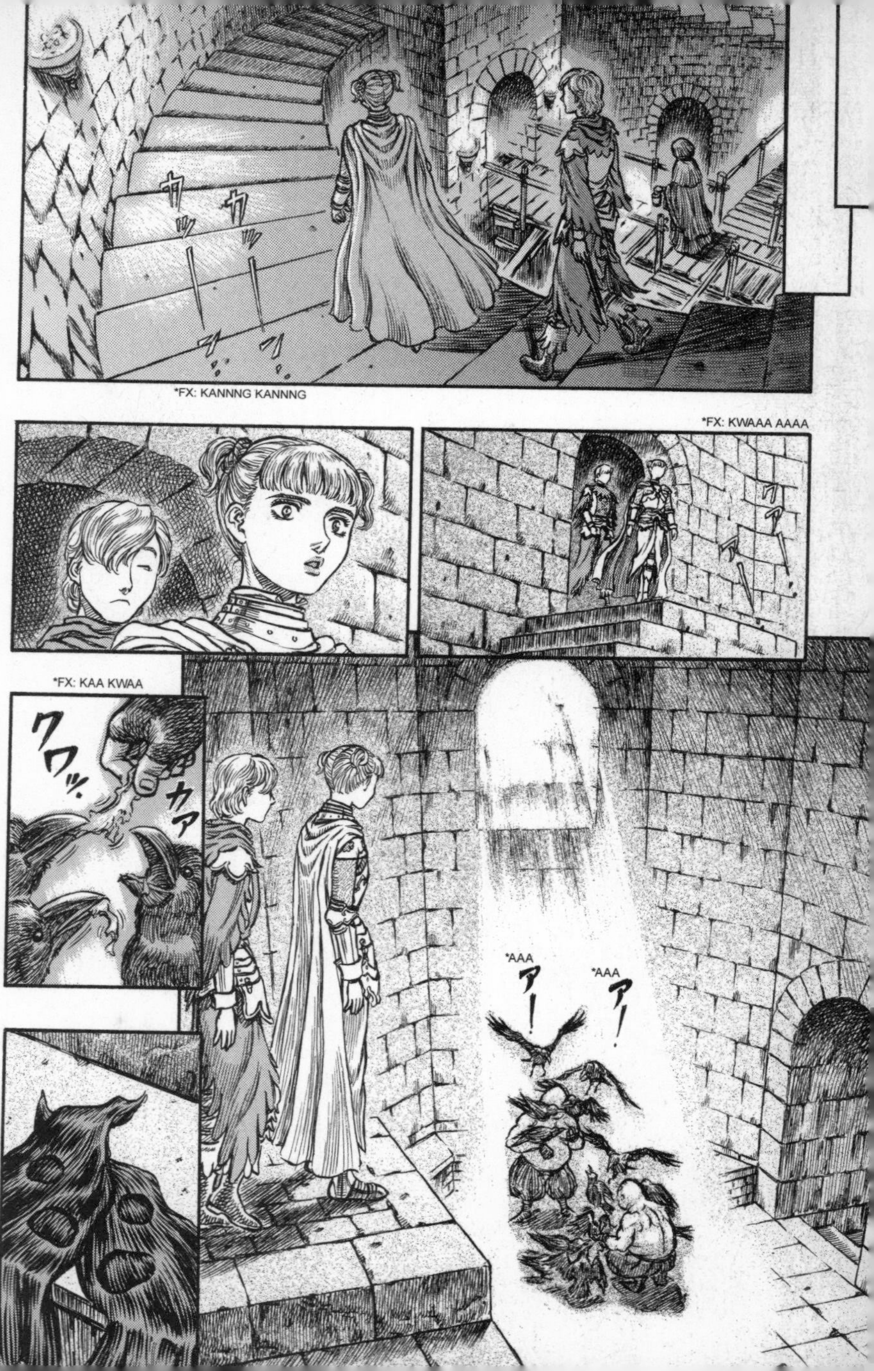
*FX: KANNNG KANNNG
*FX: KWAAA AAAA
*AAA
*AAA
*FX: KAA KWAA

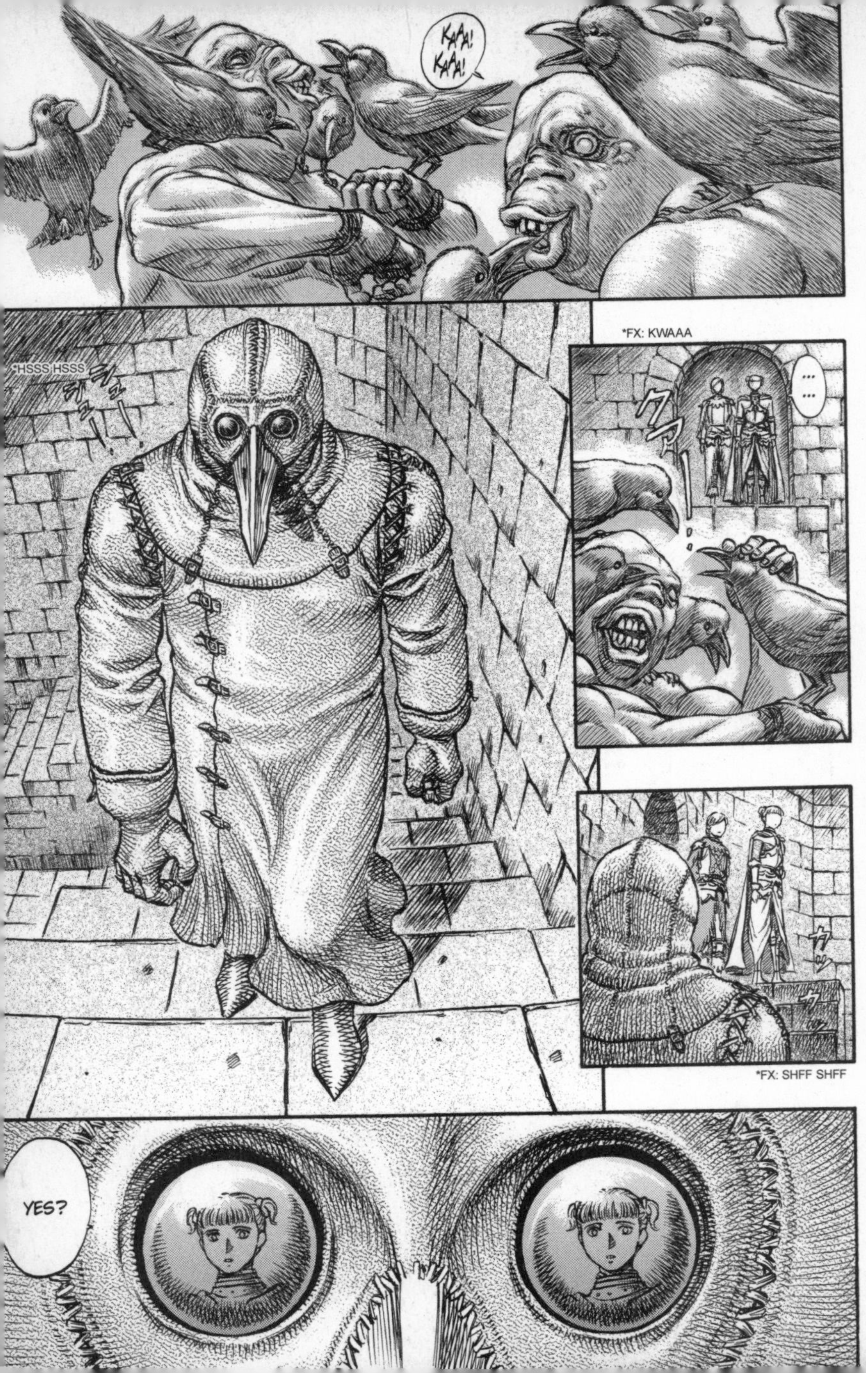
KAAA! KAAA!
*FX: KWAAA
... ...
*FX: SHFF SHFF
*HSSS HSSS
YES?

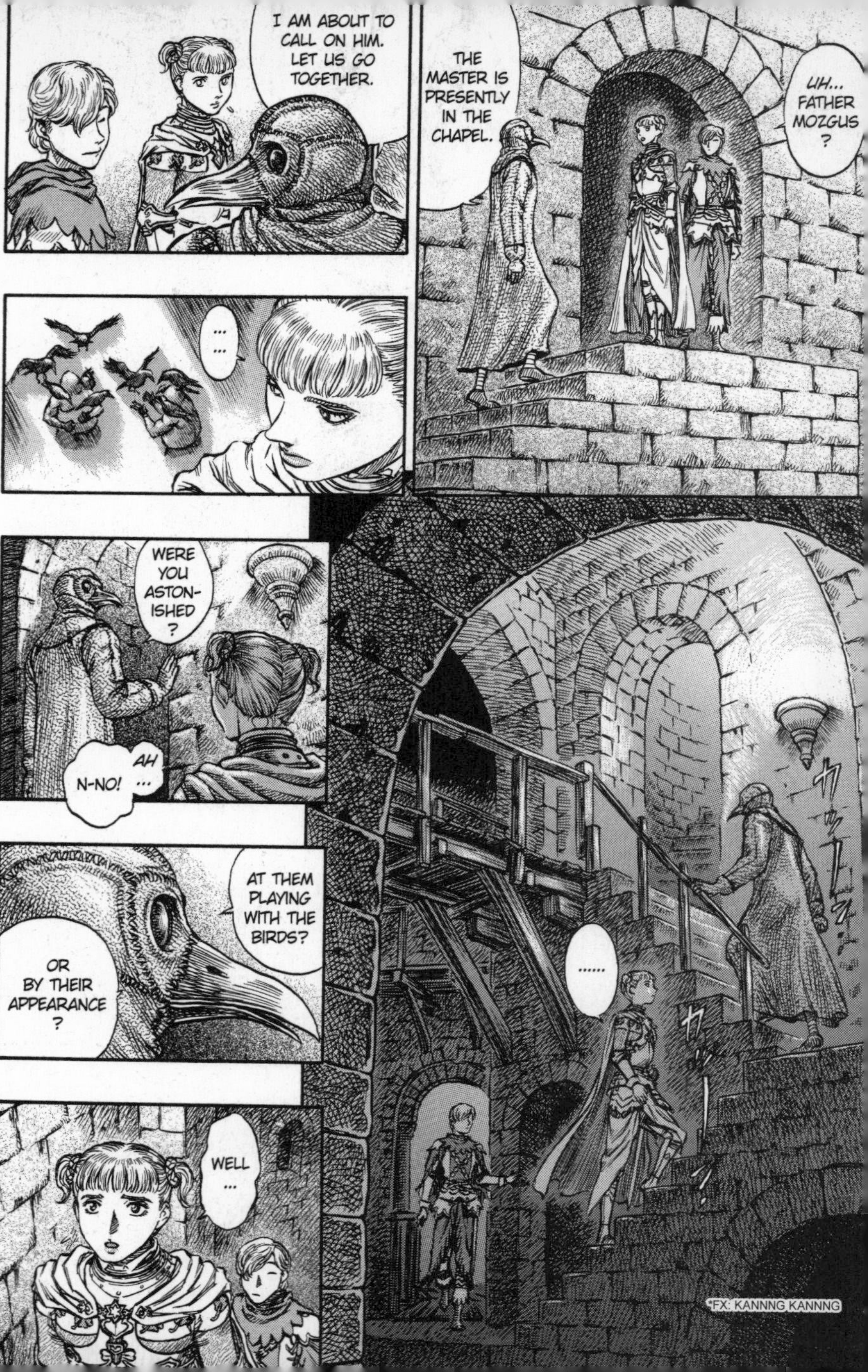
UH... FATHER MOZGUS ?
THE MASTER IS PRESENTLY IN THE CHAPEL.
I AM ABOUT TO CALL ON HIM. LET US GO TOGETHER.
... ...
......
*FX: KANNNG KANNNG
WERE YOU ASTON-ISHED ?
AH ...
N-NO!
AT THEM PLAYING WITH THE BIRDS?
OR BY THEIR APPEARANCE ?
WELL ...

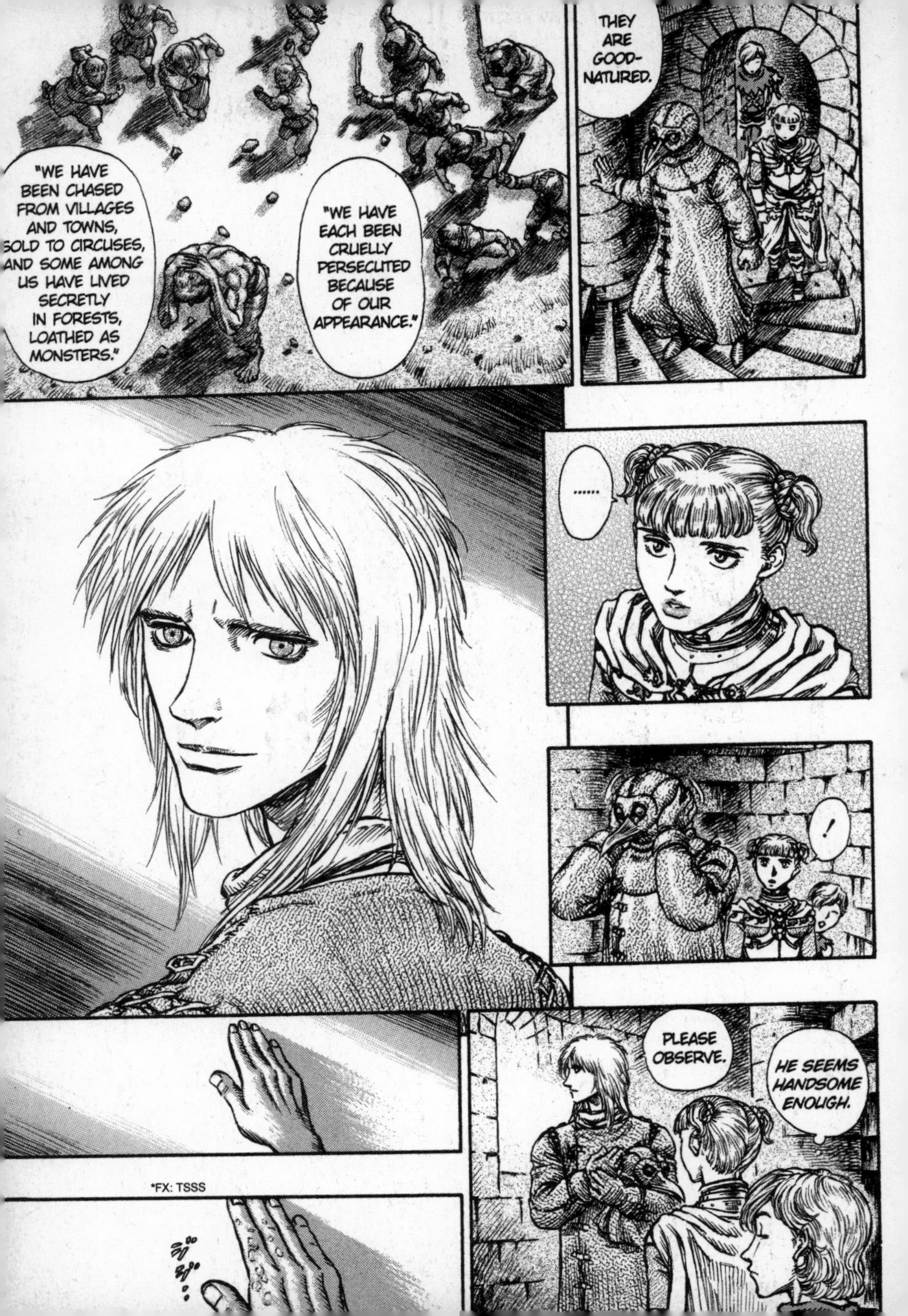
THEY ARE GOOD-NATURED.
"WE HAVE EACH BEEN CRUELLY PERSECUTED BECAUSE OF OUR APPEARANCE."
"WE HAVE BEEN CHASED FROM VILLAGES AND TOWNS, SOLD TO CIRCUSES, AND SOME AMONG US HAVE LIVED SECRETLY IN FORESTS, LOATHED AS MONSTERS."
......
!
PLEASE OBSERVE.
HE SEEMS HANDSOME ENOUGH.
*FX: TSSS

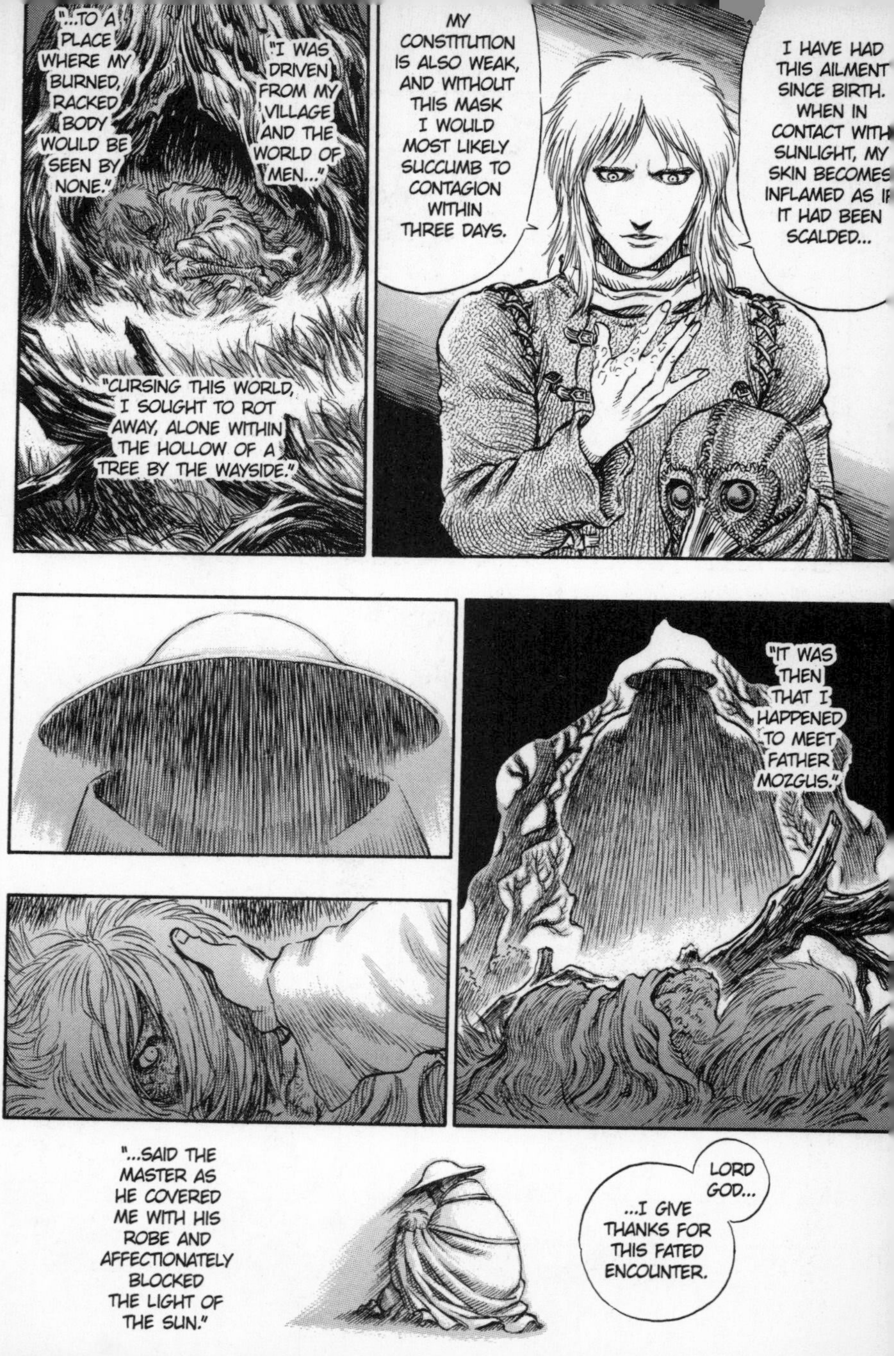
I HAVE HAD THIS AILMENT SINCE BIRTH. WHEN IN CONTACT WITH SUNLIGHT, MY SKIN BECOMES INFLAMED AS IF IT HAD BEEN SCALDED...
MY CONSTITUTION IS ALSO WEAK, AND WITHOUT THIS MASK I WOULD MOST LIKELY SUCCUMB TO CONTAGION WITHIN THREE DAYS.
"I WAS DRIVEN FROM MY VILLAGE AND THE WORLD OF MEN..."
"...TO A PLACE WHERE MY BURNED, RACKED BODY WOULD BE SEEN BY NONE."
"CURSING THIS WORLD, I SOUGHT TO ROT AWAY, ALONE WITHIN THE HOLLOW OF A TREE BY THE WAYSIDE."
"IT WAS THEN THAT I HAPPENED TO MEET FATHER MOZGUS."
LORD GOD...
...I GIVE THANKS FOR THIS FATED ENCOUNTER.
"...SAID THE MASTER AS HE COVERED ME WITH HIS ROBE AND AFFECTIONATELY BLOCKED THE LIGHT OF THE SUN."

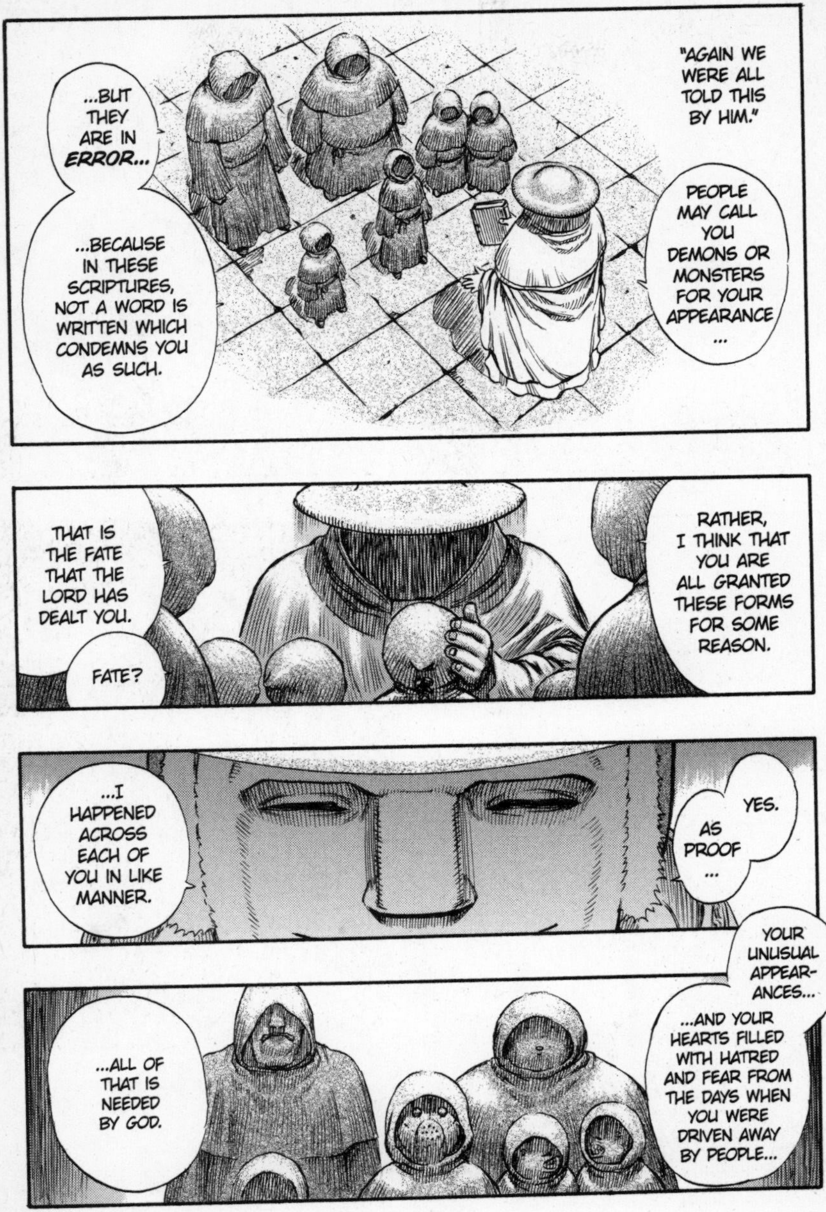
"AGAIN WE WERE ALL TOLD THIS BY HIM."
PEOPLE MAY CALL YOU DEMONS OR MONSTERS FOR YOUR APPEARANCE...
...BUT THEY ARE IN ERROR...
...BECAUSE IN THESE SCRIPTURES, NOT A WORD IS WRITTEN WHICH CONDEMNS YOU AS SUCH.
RATHER, I THINK THAT YOU ARE ALL GRANTED THESE FORMS FOR SOME REASON.
THAT IS THE FATE THAT THE LORD HAS DEALT YOU.
FATE?
YES. AS PROOF...
...I HAPPENED ACROSS EACH OF YOU IN LIKE MANNER.
YOUR UNUSUAL APPEARANCES...
...AND YOUR HEARTS FILLED WITH HATRED AND FEAR FROM THE DAYS WHEN YOU WERE DRIVEN AWAY BY PEOPLE...
...ALL OF THAT IS NEEDED BY GOD.

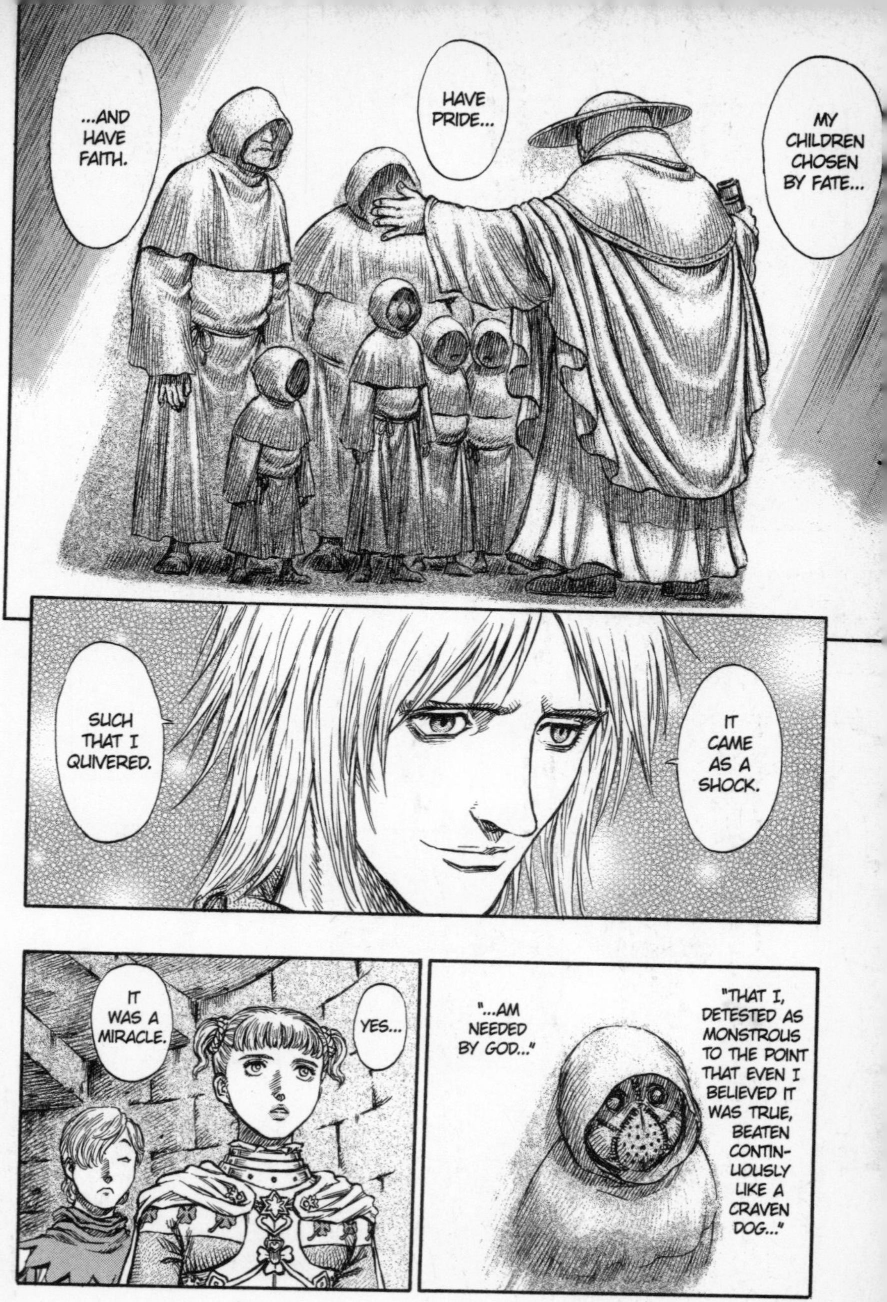
MY CHILDREN CHOSEN BY FATE...
HAVE PRIDE...
...AND HAVE FAITH.
IT CAME AS A SHOCK.
SUCH THAT I QUIVERED.
"THAT I, DETESTED AS MONSTROUS TO THE POINT THAT EVEN I BELIEVED IT WAS TRUE, BEATEN CONTIN-UOUSLY LIKE A CRAVEN DOG..."
"...AM NEEDED BY GOD..."
YES...
IT WAS A MIRACLE.

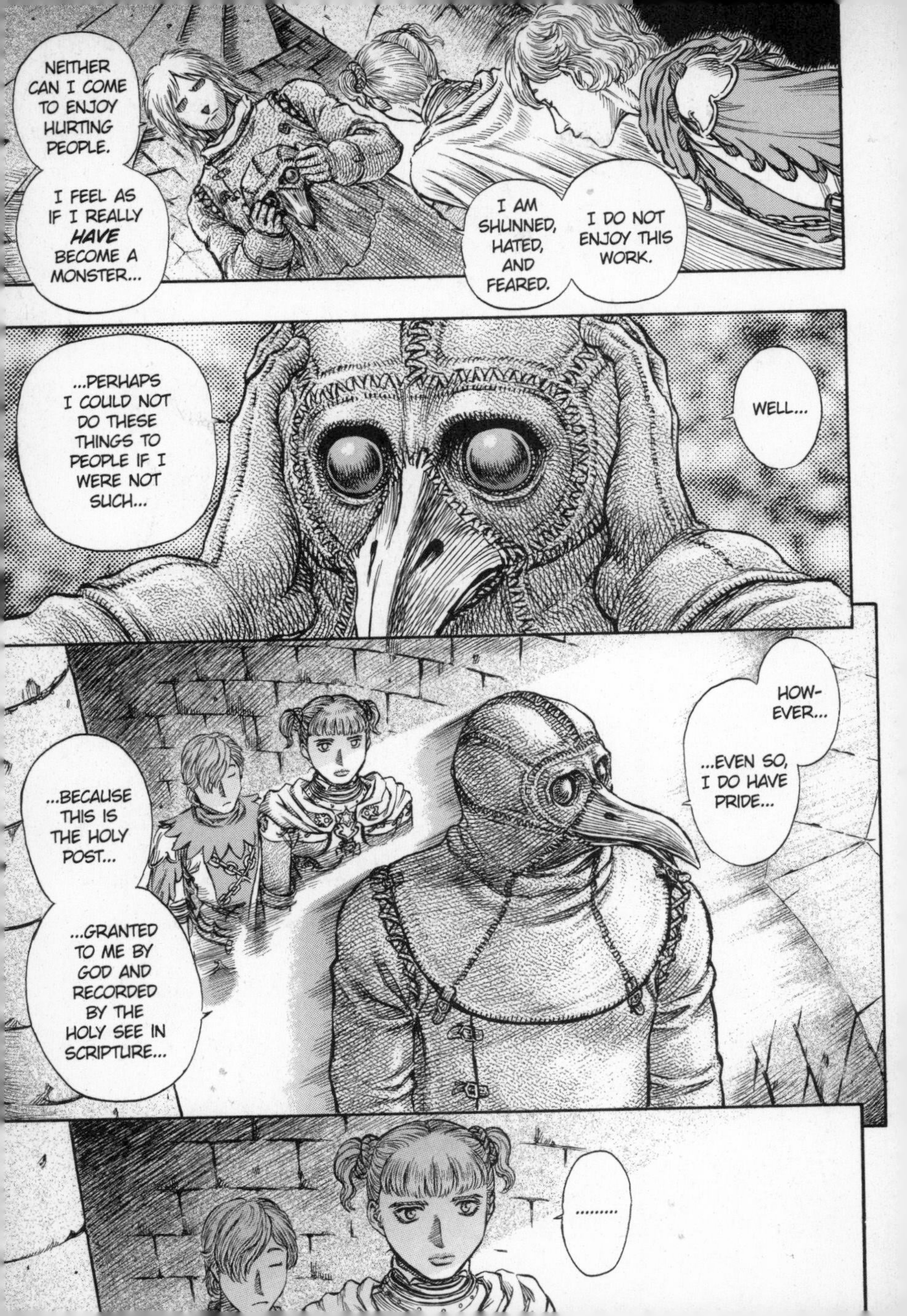
I DO NOT ENJOY THIS WORK.
I AM SHUNNED, HATED, AND FEARED.
NEITHER CAN I COME TO ENJOY HURTING PEOPLE.
I FEEL AS IF I REALLY *HAVE* BECOME A MONSTER...
WELL...
...PERHAPS I COULD NOT DO THESE THINGS TO PEOPLE IF I WERE NOT SUCH...
HOW-EVER...
...EVEN SO, I DO HAVE PRIDE...
...BECAUSE THIS IS THE HOLY POST...
...GRANTED TO ME BY GOD AND RECORDED BY THE HOLY SEE IN SCRIPTURE...
....

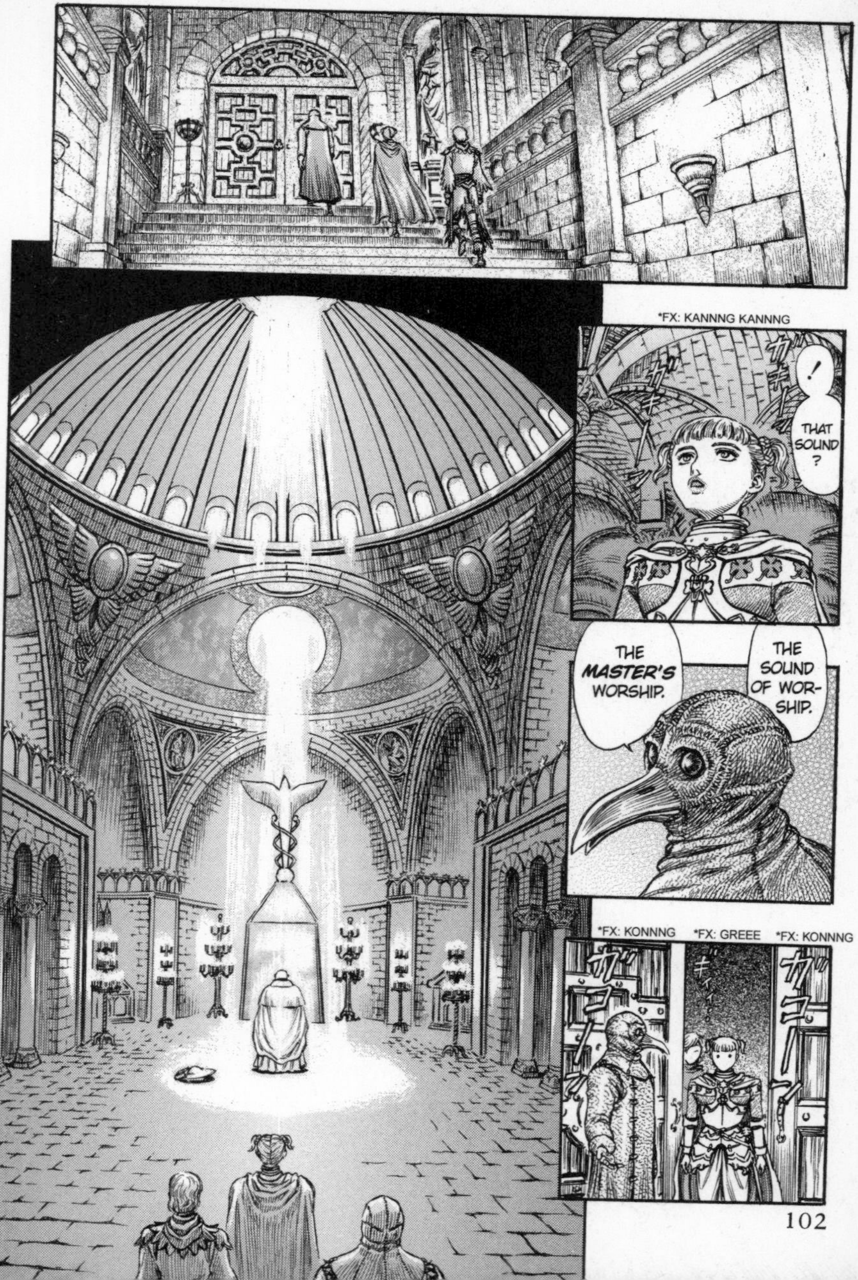
*FX: KANNNG KANNNG
!
THAT SOUND?
THE SOUND OF WOR-SHIP.
THE *MASTER'S* WORSHIP.
*FX: KONNNG
*FX: GREEE
*FX: KONNNG

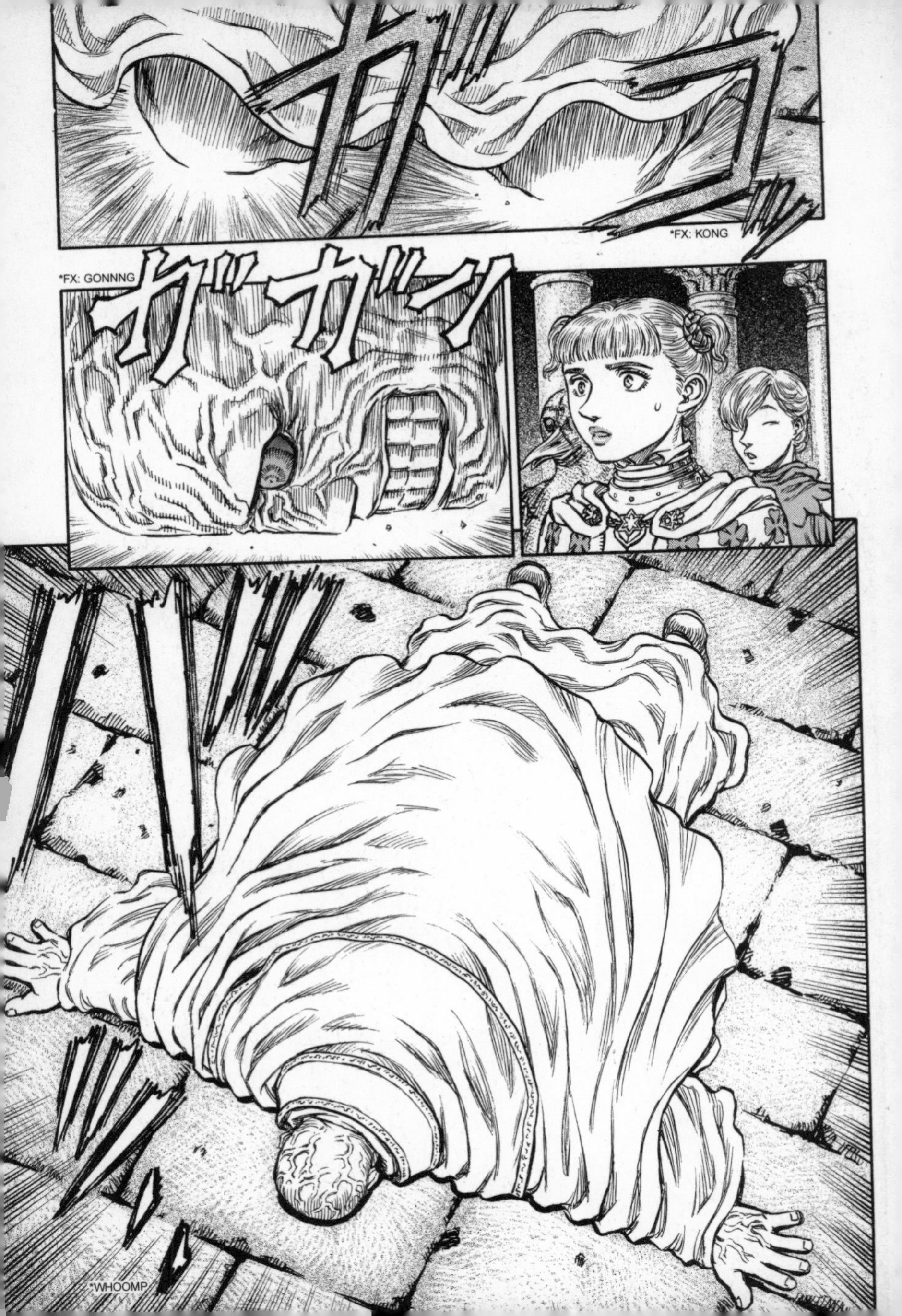
*FX: KONG
*FX: GONNNG
*WHOOMP

BERSERK

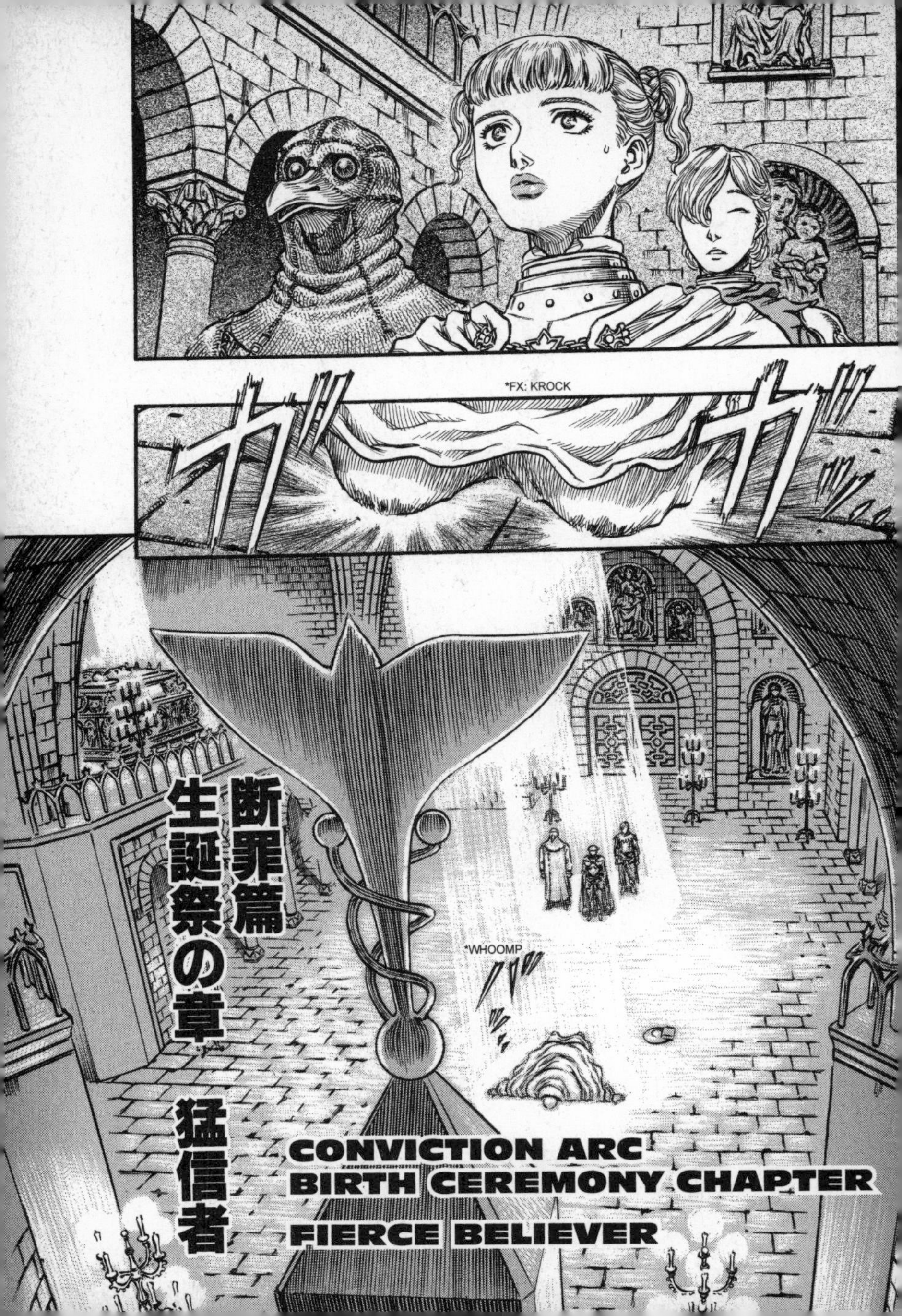
*FX: KROCK
*WHOOMP
断罪篇
生誕祭の章
猛信者
CONVICTION ARC
BIRTH CEREMONY CHAPTER
FIERCE BELIEVER

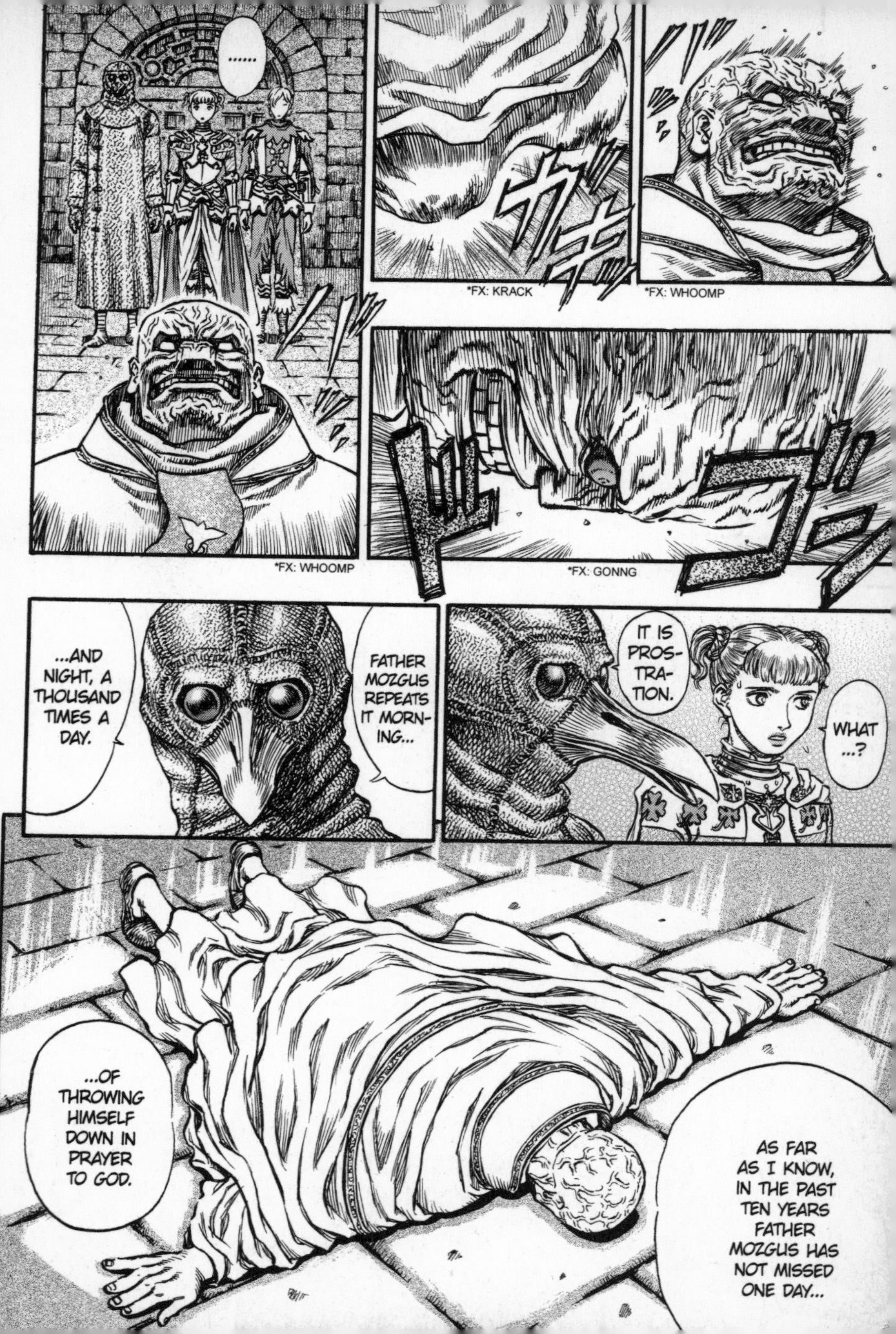
*FX: WHOOMP
*FX: KRACK
*FX: GONNG
......
*FX: WHOOMP
WHAT ...?
IT IS PROS-TRA-TION.
FATHER MOZGUS REPEATS IT MORNING-ING...
...AND NIGHT, A THOUSAND TIMES A DAY.
AS FAR AS I KNOW, IN THE PAST TEN YEARS FATHER MOZGUS HAS NOT MISSED ONE DAY...
...OF THROWING HIMSELF DOWN IN PRAYER TO GOD.

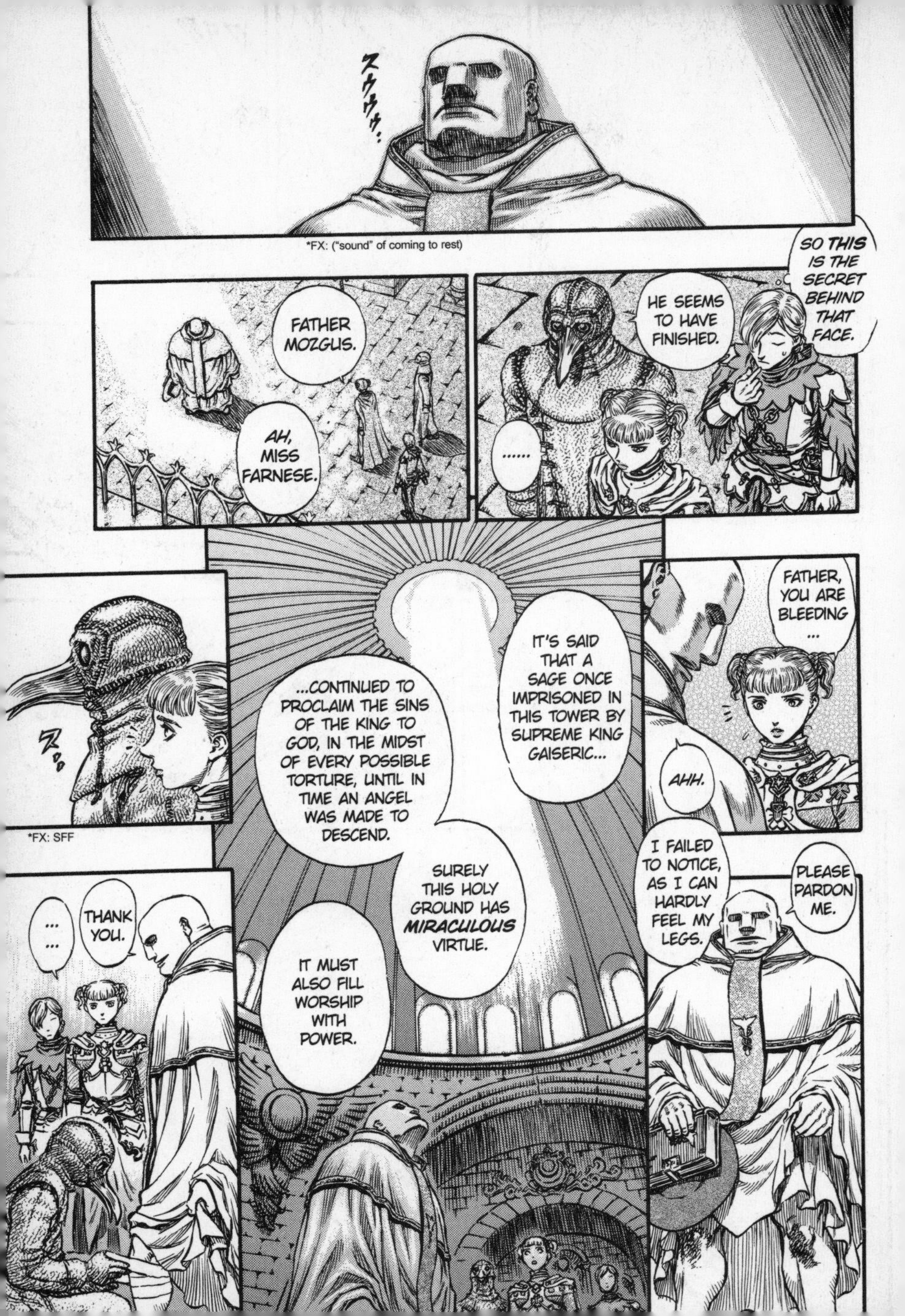
スゥゥゥ…
*FX: ("sound" of coming to rest)
SO THIS IS THE SECRET BEHIND THAT FACE.
HE SEEMS TO HAVE FINISHED.
......
FATHER MOZGUS.
AH, MISS FARNESE.
FATHER, YOU ARE BLEEDING ...
AHH.
IT'S SAID THAT A SAGE ONCE IMPRISONED IN THIS TOWER BY SUPREME KING GAISERIC...
...CONTINUED TO PROCLAIM THE SINS OF THE KING TO GOD, IN THE MIDST OF EVERY POSSIBLE TORTURE, UNTIL IN TIME AN ANGEL WAS MADE TO DESCEND.
SURELY THIS HOLY GROUND HAS MIRACULOUS VIRTUE.
IT MUST ALSO FILL WORSHIP WITH POWER.
ズ
*FX: SFF
PLEASE PARDON ME.
I FAILED TO NOTICE, AS I CAN HARDLY FEEL MY LEGS.
THANK YOU.
... ...

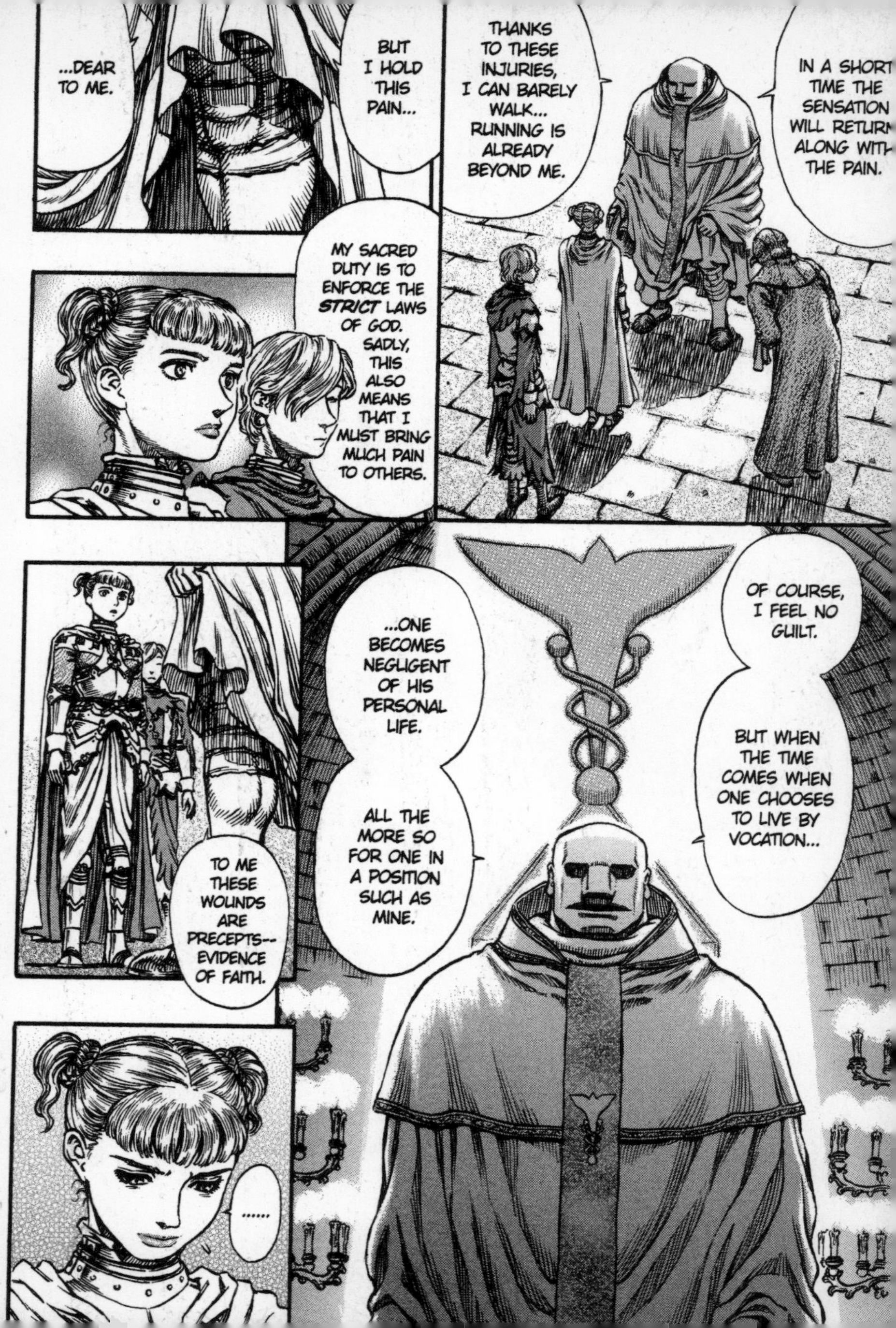
IN A SHORT TIME THE SENSATION WILL RETURN ALONG WITH THE PAIN.
THANKS TO THESE INJURIES, I CAN BARELY WALK... RUNNING IS ALREADY BEYOND ME.
BUT I HOLD THIS PAIN...
...DEAR TO ME.
MY SACRED DUTY IS TO ENFORCE THE *STRICT* LAWS OF GOD. SADLY, THIS ALSO MEANS THAT I MUST BRING MUCH PAIN TO OTHERS.
OF COURSE, I FEEL NO GUILT.
BUT WHEN THE TIME COMES WHEN ONE CHOOSES TO LIVE BY VOCATION...
...ONE BECOMES NEGLIGENT OF HIS PERSONAL LIFE.
ALL THE MORE SO FOR ONE IN A POSITION SUCH AS MINE.
TO ME THESE WOUNDS ARE PRECEPTS-- EVIDENCE OF FAITH.
......

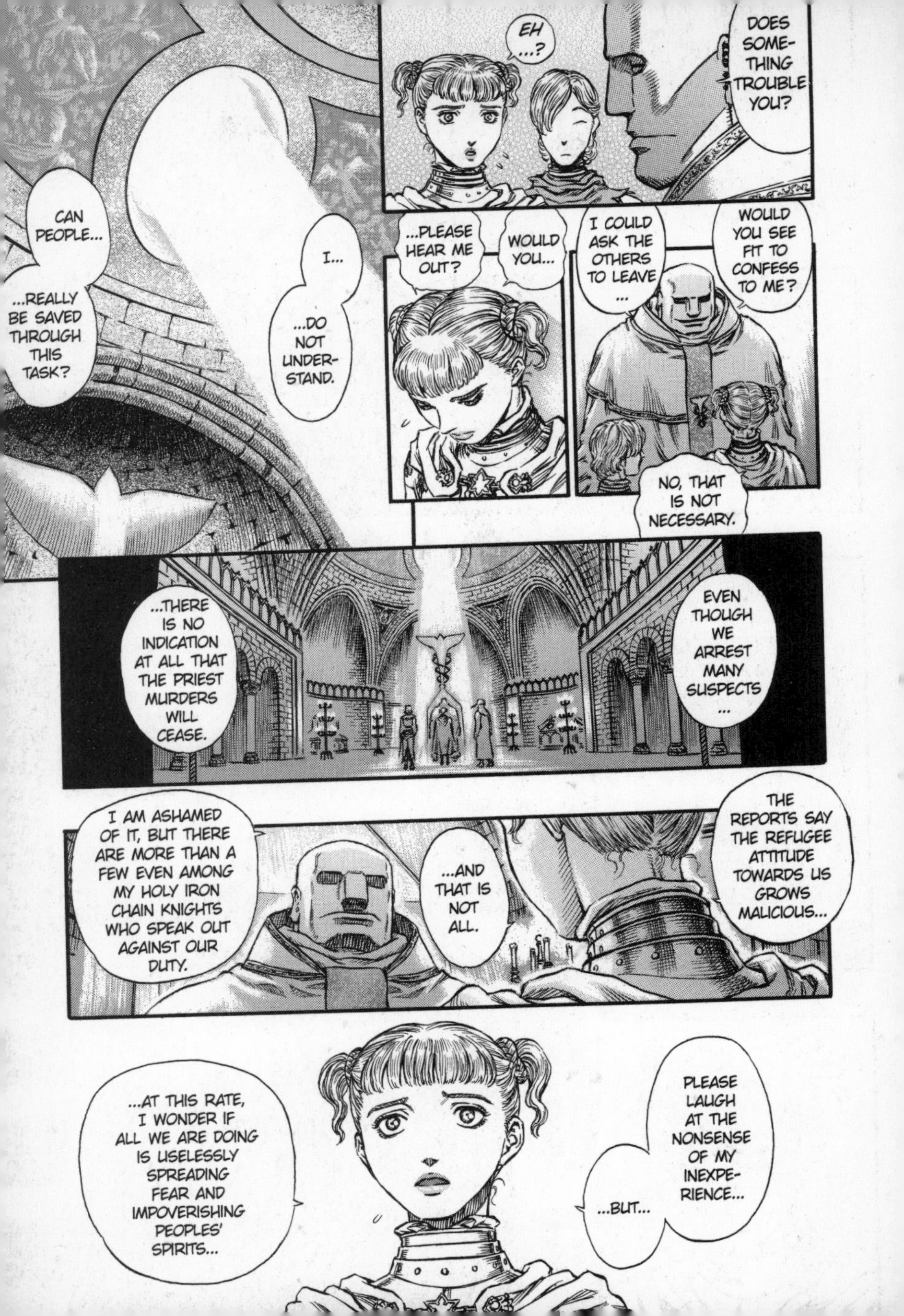
DOES SOMETHING TROUBLE YOU?
EH ...?
WOULD YOU SEE FIT TO CONFESS TO ME?
I COULD ASK THE OTHERS TO LEAVE ...
NO, THAT IS NOT NECESSARY.
WOULD YOU...
...PLEASE HEAR ME OUT?
I...
...DO NOT UNDERSTAND.
CAN PEOPLE...
...REALLY BE SAVED THROUGH THIS TASK?
EVEN THOUGH WE ARREST MANY SUSPECTS ...
...THERE IS NO INDICATION AT ALL THAT THE PRIEST MURDERS WILL CEASE.
THE REPORTS SAY THE REFUGEE ATTITUDE TOWARDS US GROWS MALICIOUS...
...AND THAT IS NOT ALL.
I AM ASHAMED OF IT, BUT THERE ARE MORE THAN A FEW EVEN AMONG MY HOLY IRON CHAIN KNIGHTS WHO SPEAK OUT AGAINST OUR DUTY.
PLEASE LAUGH AT THE NONSENSE OF MY INEXPERIENCE...
...BUT...
...AT THIS RATE, I WONDER IF ALL WE ARE DOING IS USELESSLY SPREADING FEAR AND IMPOVERISHING PEOPLES' SPIRITS...

I SHALL TELL YOU A STORY.

....

"IN ANCIENT TIMES THERE WAS A HOLY WOMAN WHO PRACTICED POVERTY AND DEVOTED HER ENTIRE LIFE TO THE AID OF OTHERS."

"IT IS SAID THAT SHE WOULD SEEK OUT THOSE DYING, ABANDONED BY THE WORLD OF MAN WITHOUT EVEN A SECOND GLANCE DUE TO POVERTY, DISEASE, AND THE LIKE. SHE WOULD COVER THEM WITH BLANKETS, EMBRACE THEM, AND HOLD THEIR HAND LIKE A MOTHER, SO THEY COULD AT LEAST HAVE PEACE WHEN GOD CALLED FOR THEM."

"ONE TIME, SHE DISCOVERED, FALLEN BY THE WAYSIDE, AN EMACIATED OLD MAN WHO WAS DYING."

"AS ALWAYS, SHE EMBRACED THE MAN AND GRASPED HIS HAND."

"BUT THIS IS WHAT HE SAID: 'THE FACT THAT I AM LYING HERE ROTTING BY THE WAYSIDE IS PROOF THAT I HAVE LIVED A PROUD LIFE OF SOLITUDE AND INDEPENDENCE.'"

"'PLEASE DO NOT DISGRACE MY SUBLIME MOMENT OF DEATH WITH YOUR WARMTH.'"

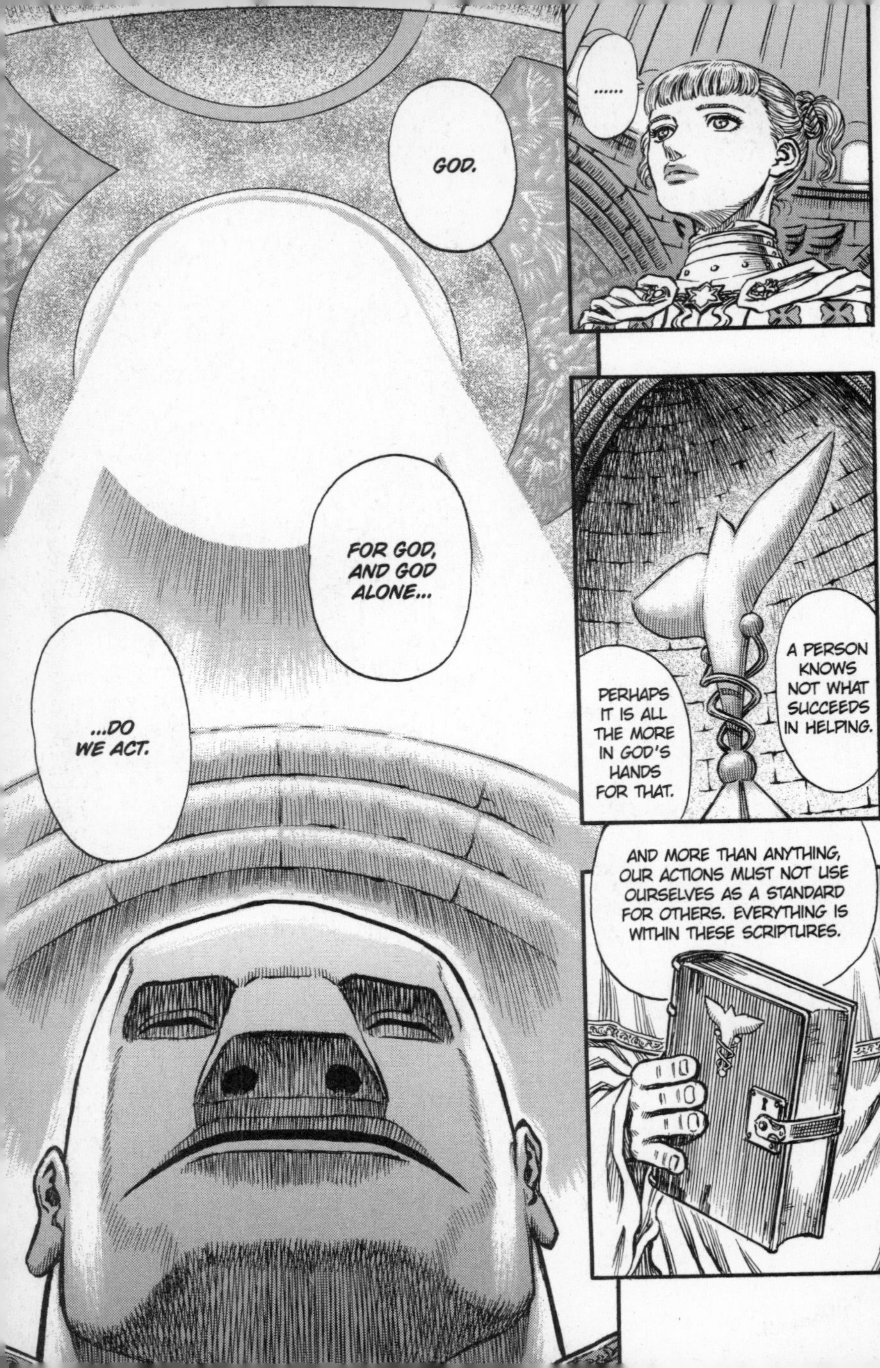
......
A PERSON KNOWS NOT WHAT SUCCEEDS IN HELPING.
PERHAPS IT IS ALL THE MORE IN GOD'S HANDS FOR THAT.
AND MORE THAN ANYTHING, OUR ACTIONS MUST NOT USE OURSELVES AS A STANDARD FOR OTHERS. EVERYTHING IS WITHIN THESE SCRIPTURES.
GOD.
FOR GOD, AND GOD ALONE...
...DO WE ACT.

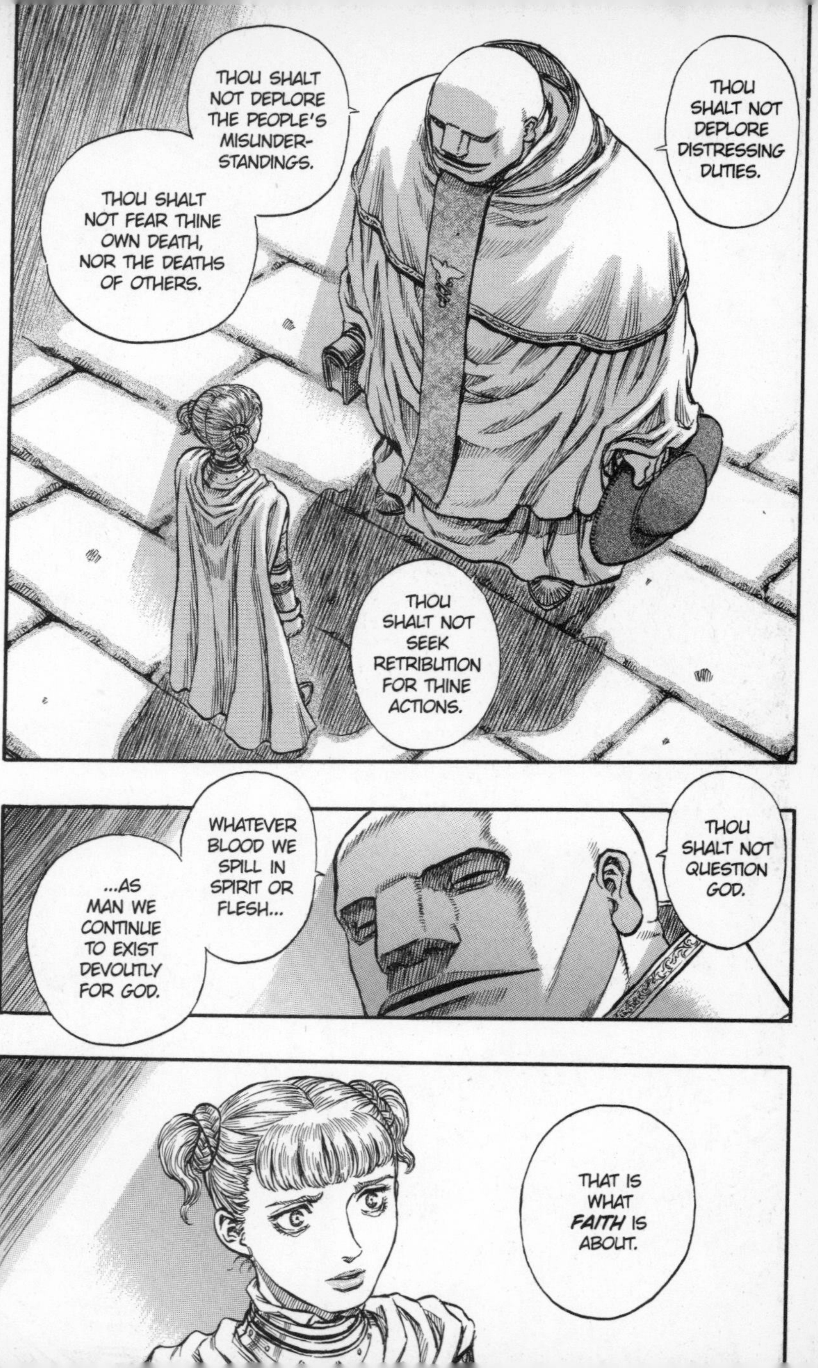
THOU SHALT NOT DEPLORE DISTRESSING DUTIES.
THOU SHALT NOT DEPLORE THE PEOPLE'S MISUNDER-STANDINGS.
THOU SHALT NOT FEAR THINE OWN DEATH, NOR THE DEATHS OF OTHERS.
THOU SHALT NOT SEEK RETRIBUTION FOR THINE ACTIONS.
THOU SHALT NOT QUESTION GOD.
WHATEVER BLOOD WE SPILL IN SPIRIT OR FLESH...
...AS MAN WE CONTINUE TO EXIST DEVOUTLY FOR GOD.
THAT IS WHAT *FAITH* IS ABOUT.

MAY THE LORD BE WITH YOU.

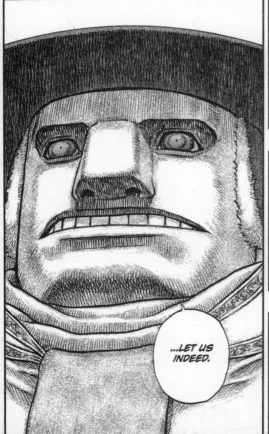

...LET US INDEED.

......

*FX: SKITCH

YES.

MASTER, PLEASE LET US RETURN.

THEN...

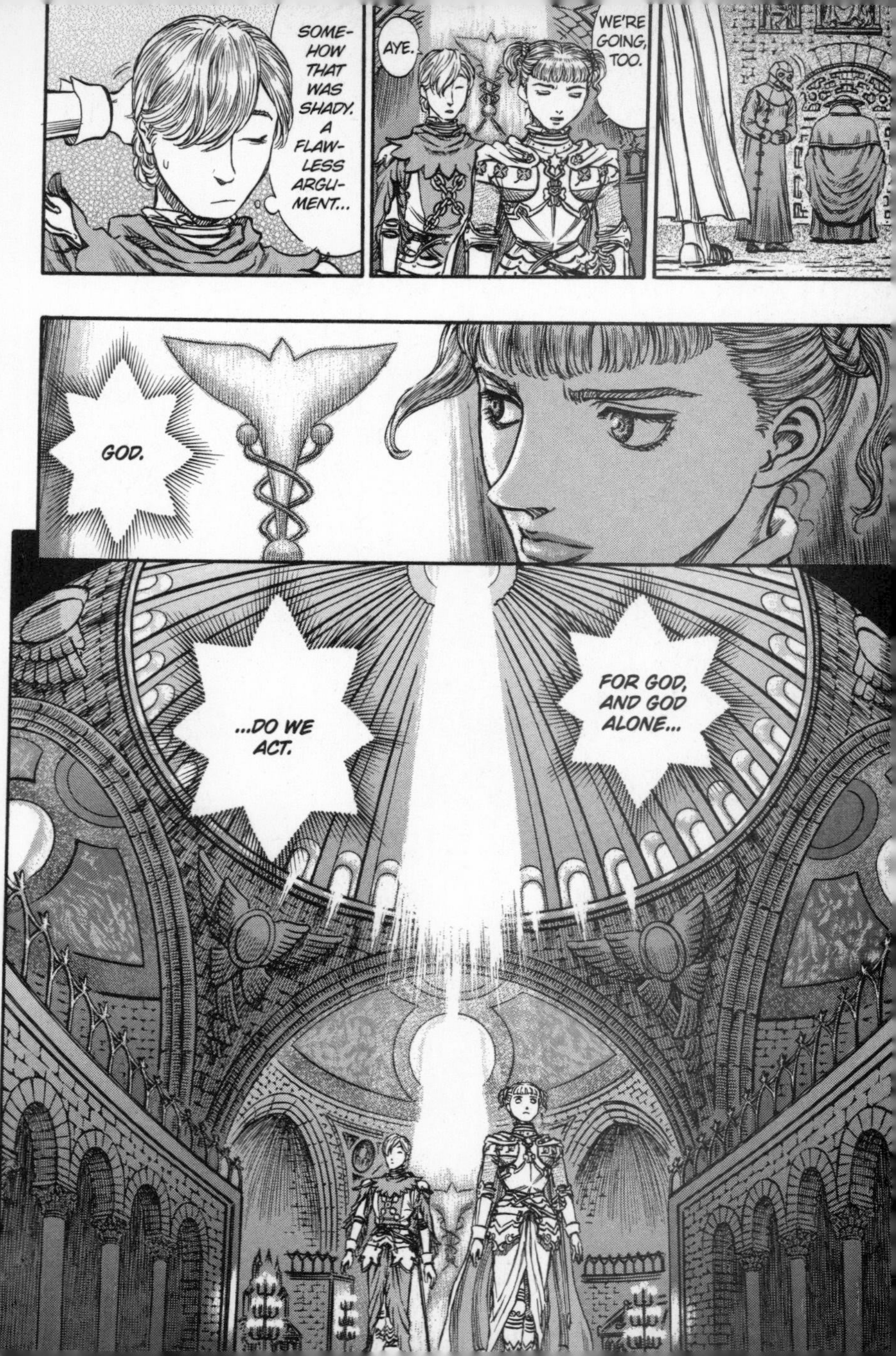
WE'RE GOING, TOO.
AYE.
SOMEHOW THAT WAS SHADY. A FLAWLESS ARGUMENT...
GOD.
FOR GOD, AND GOD ALONE...
...DO WE ACT.

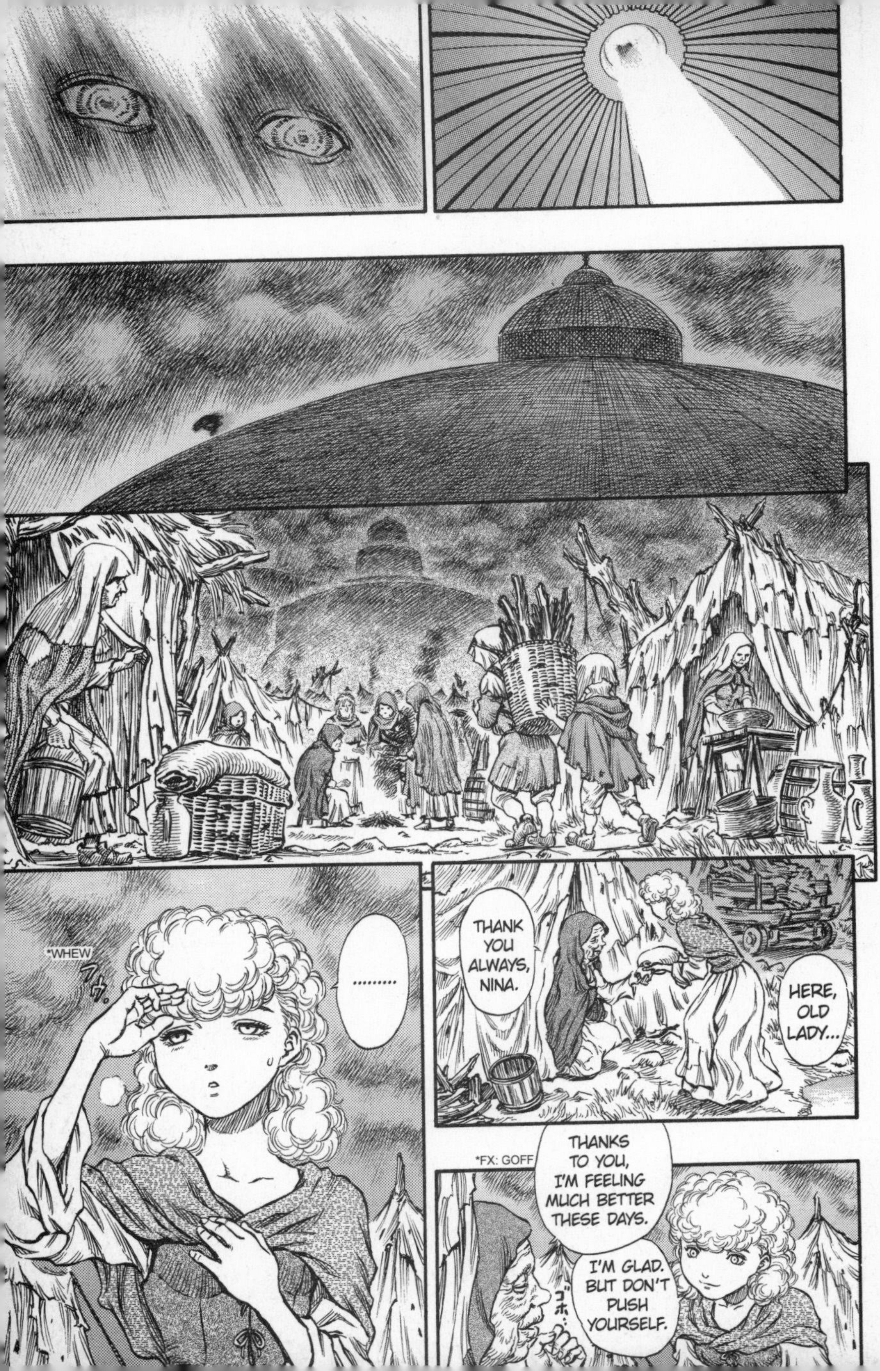
HERE, OLD LADY...
THANK YOU ALWAYS, NINA.
*FX: GOFF
THANKS TO YOU, I'M FEELING MUCH BETTER THESE DAYS.
I'M GLAD. BUT DON'T PUSH YOURSELF.
ゴホ…
*WHEW
フゥ。
....

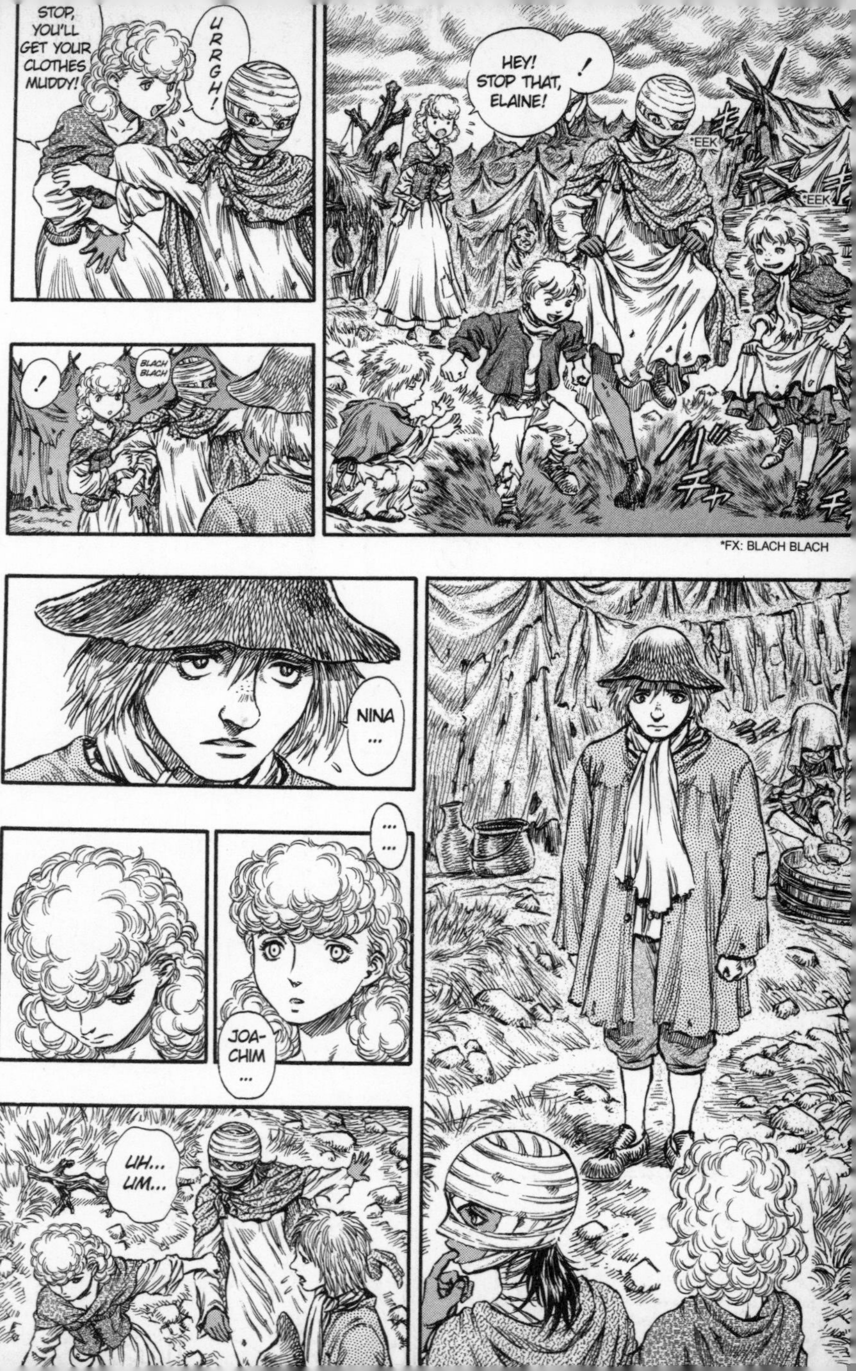
HEY! STOP THAT, ELAINE!
!
*EEK
*EEK
STOP, YOU'LL GET YOUR CLOTHES MUDDY!
URRGH!
!
BLACH BLACH
NINA ...
... ...
JOA-CHIM ...
UH... UM...
*FX: BLACH BLACH

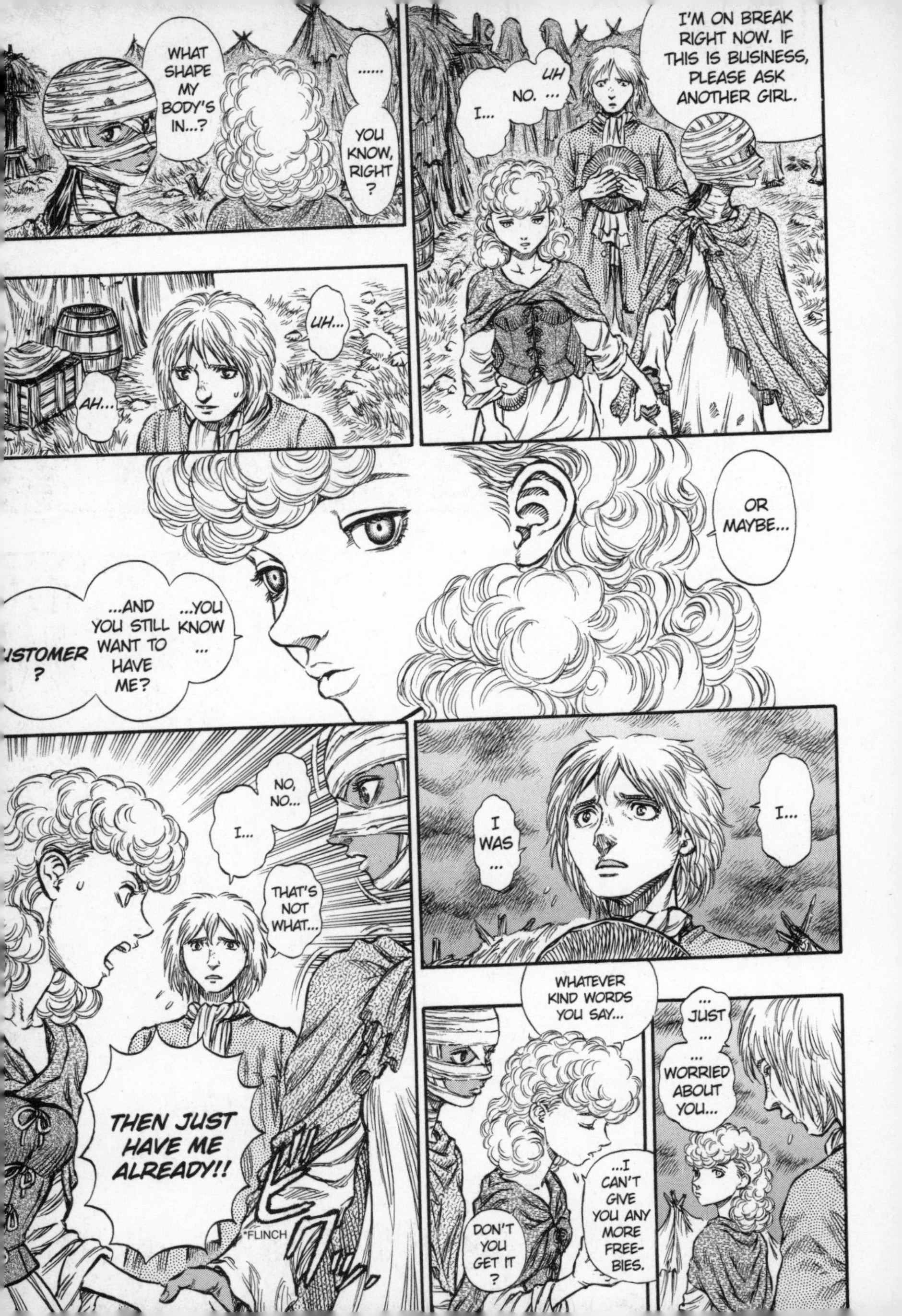

I'M ON BREAK RIGHT NOW. IF THIS IS BUSINESS, PLEASE ASK ANOTHER GIRL.
UH ... NO. ...
I...
......
YOU KNOW, RIGHT ?
WHAT SHAPE MY BODY'S IN...?
UH...
AH...
OR MAYBE...
...YOU KNOW ...
...AND YOU STILL WANT TO HAVE ME?
USTOMER ?
I...
I WAS ...
WHATEVER KIND WORDS YOU SAY...
... JUST ... ... WORRIED ABOUT YOU...
...I CAN'T GIVE YOU ANY MORE FREE-BIES.
DON'T YOU GET IT ?
NO, NO... I...
THAT'S NOT WHAT...
THEN JUST HAVE ME ALREADY!!
*FLINCH

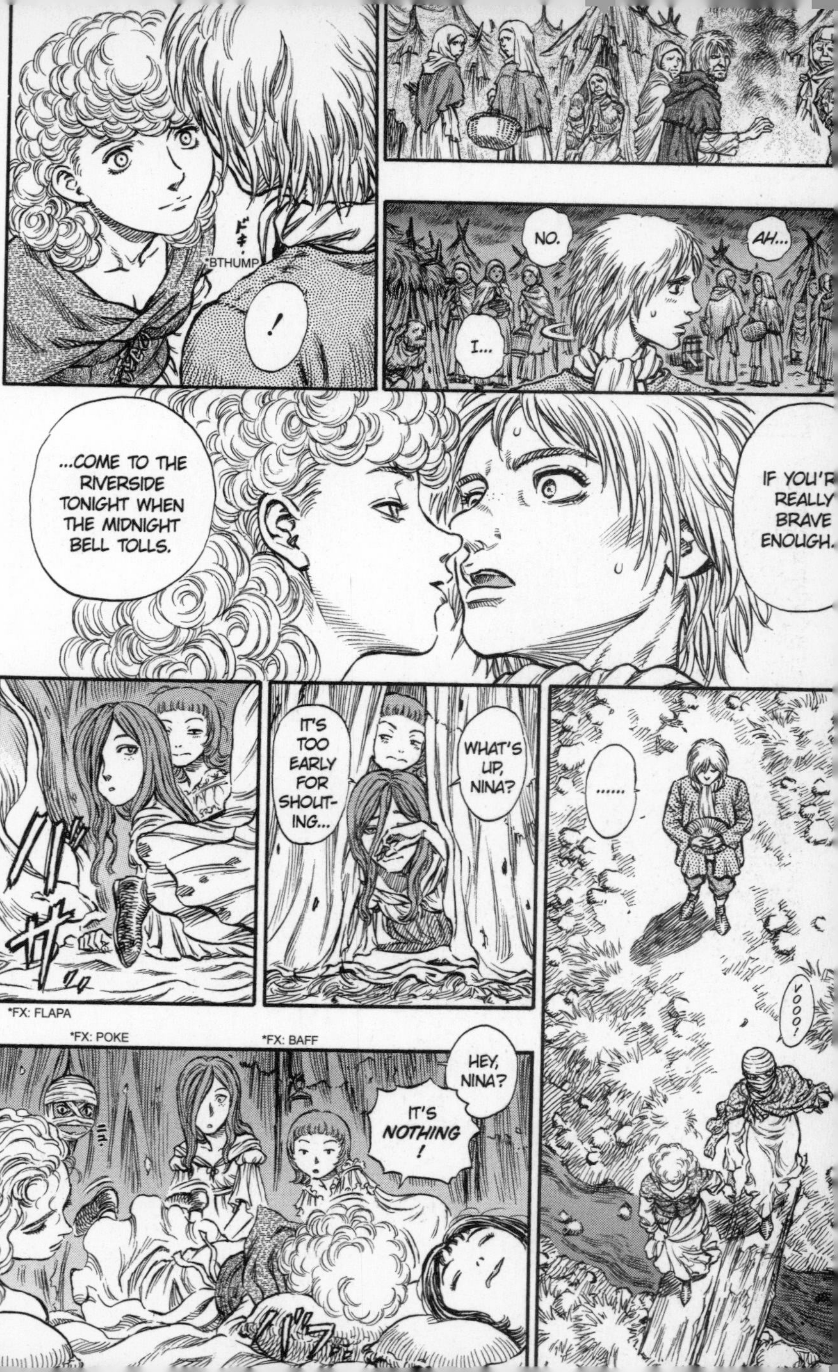
AH...
NO.
I...
*BTHUMP
!
IF YOU'R
REALLY
BRAVE
ENOUGH...
...COME TO THE RIVERSIDE TONIGHT WHEN THE MIDNIGHT BELL TOLLS.
......
VOOO!
WHAT'S UP, NINA?
IT'S TOO EARLY FOR SHOUT-ING...
*FX: FLAPA
HEY, NINA?
IT'S NOTHING!
*FX: BAFF
*FX: POKE

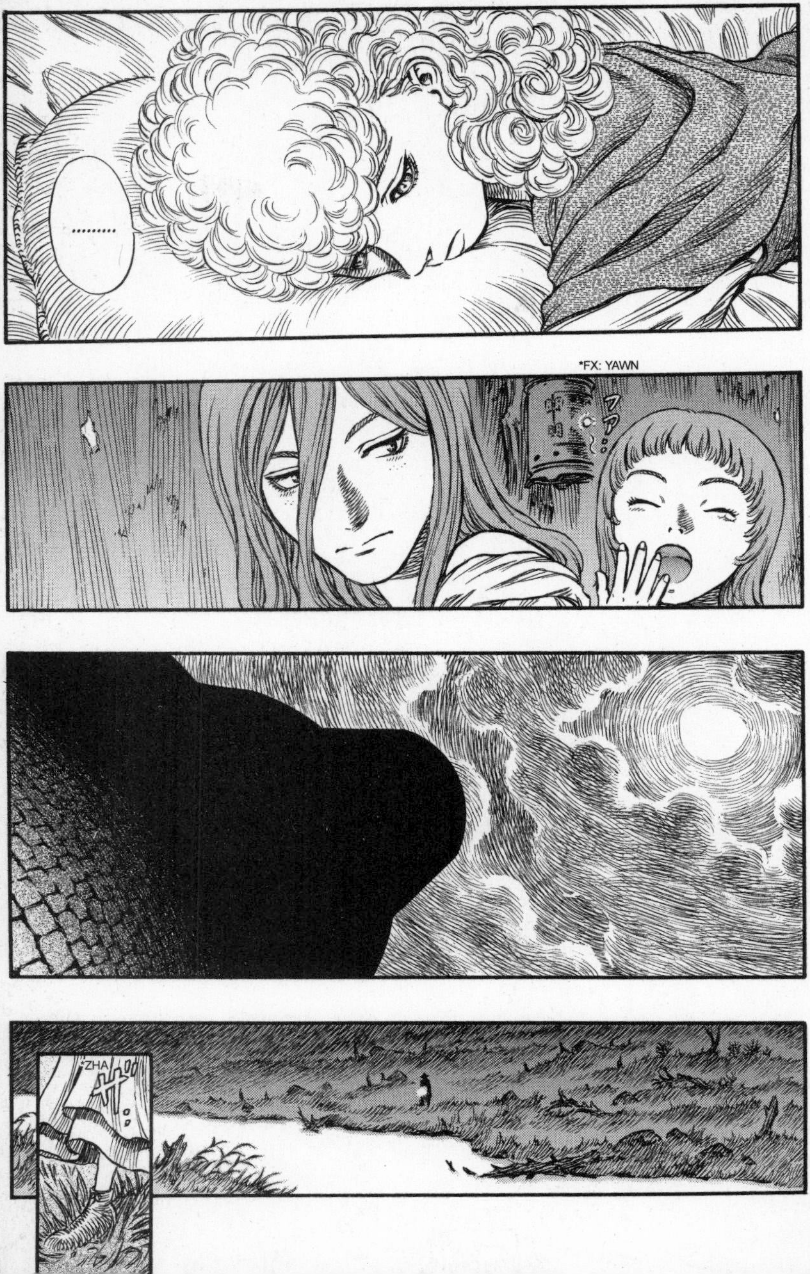

....
*FX: YAWN
*ZHA

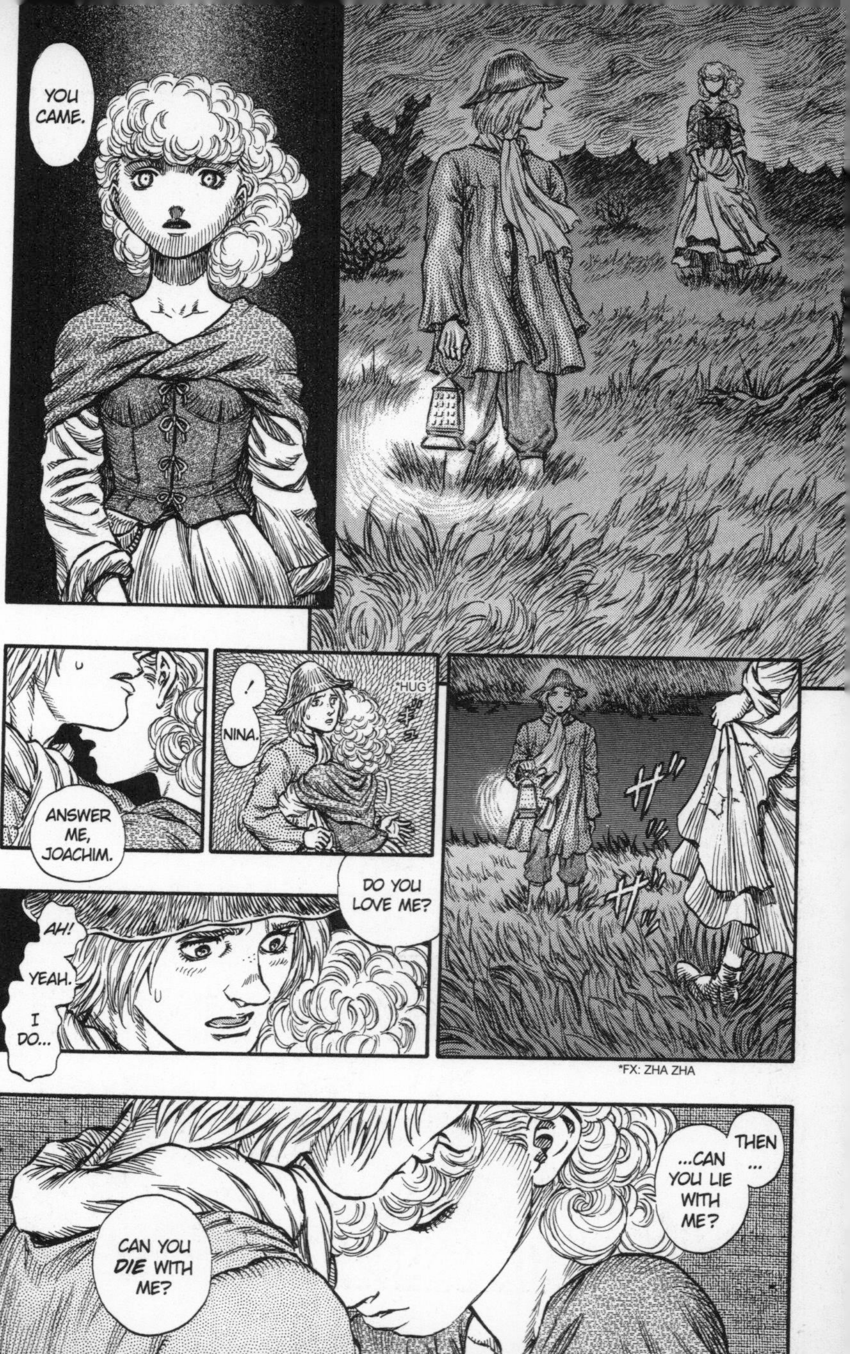
YOU CAME.
*FX: ZHA ZHA
*HUG
!
NINA.
ANSWER ME, JOACHIM.
DO YOU LOVE ME?
AH!
YEAH.
I DO...
THEN...
...CAN YOU LIE WITH ME?
CAN YOU *DIE* WITH ME?

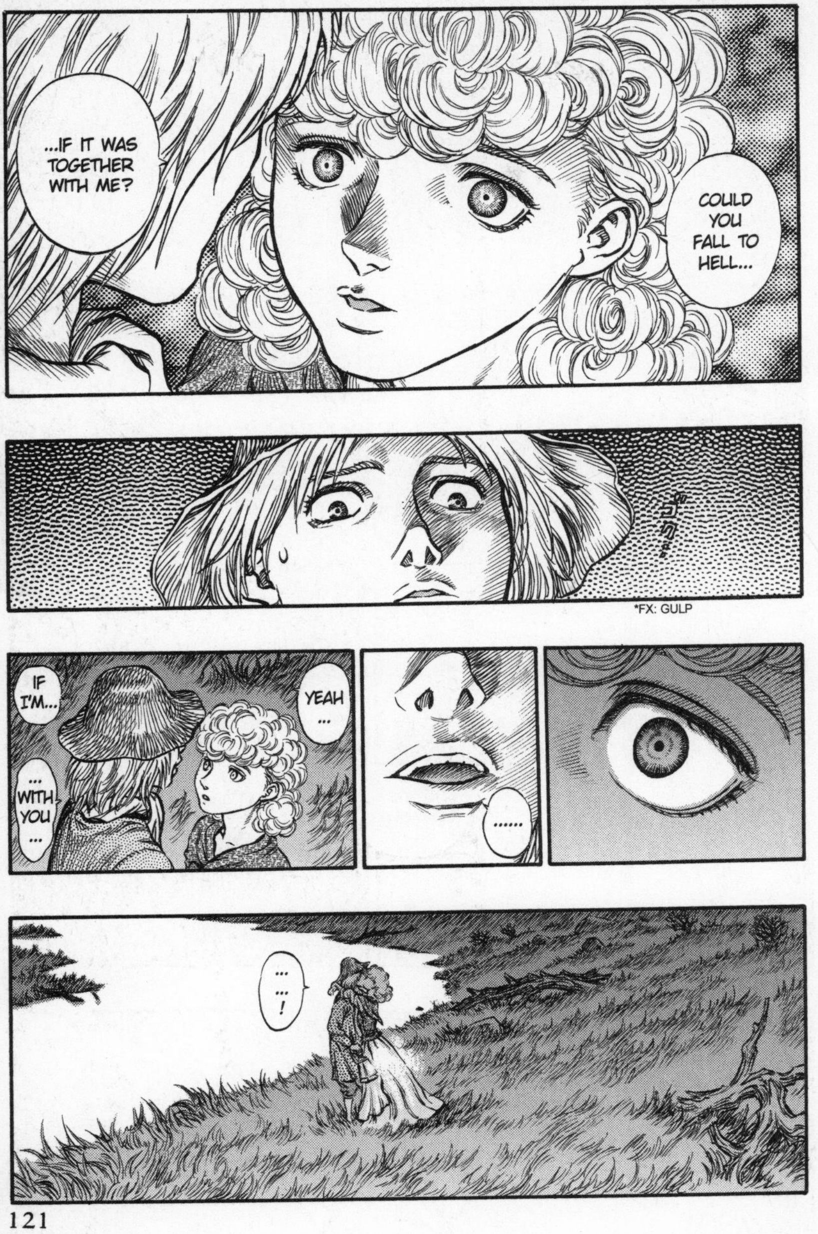
COULD YOU FALL TO HELL...
...IF IT WAS TOGETHER WITH ME?
*FX: GULP
......
YEAH ...
IF I'M...
... WITH YOU ...
... ... !

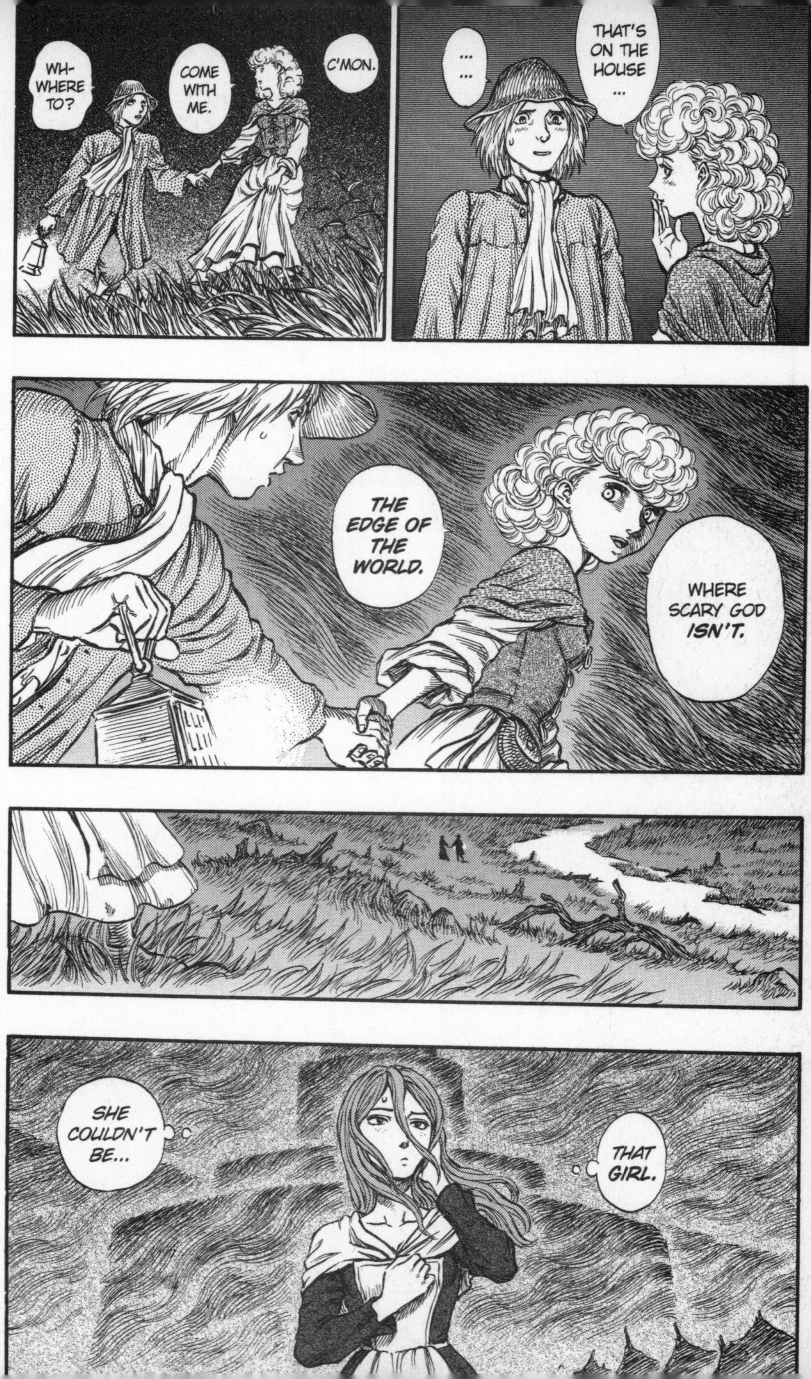
THAT'S ON THE HOUSE ...
... ...
C'MON.
COME WITH ME.
WH-WHERE TO?
THE EDGE OF THE WORLD.
WHERE SCARY GOD ISN'T.
SHE COULDN'T BE...
THAT GIRL.

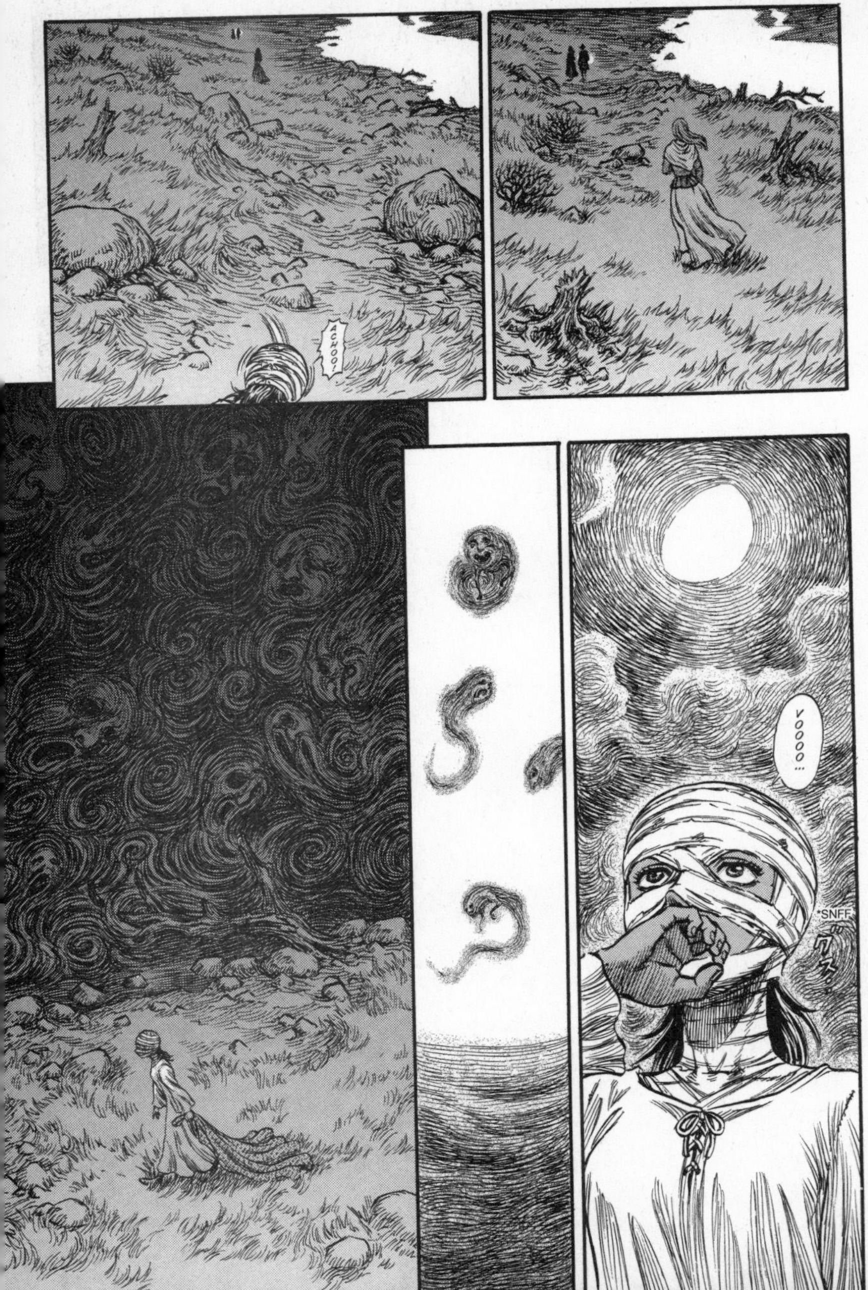
ACHOO!
VOOOO...
*SNFF
グス

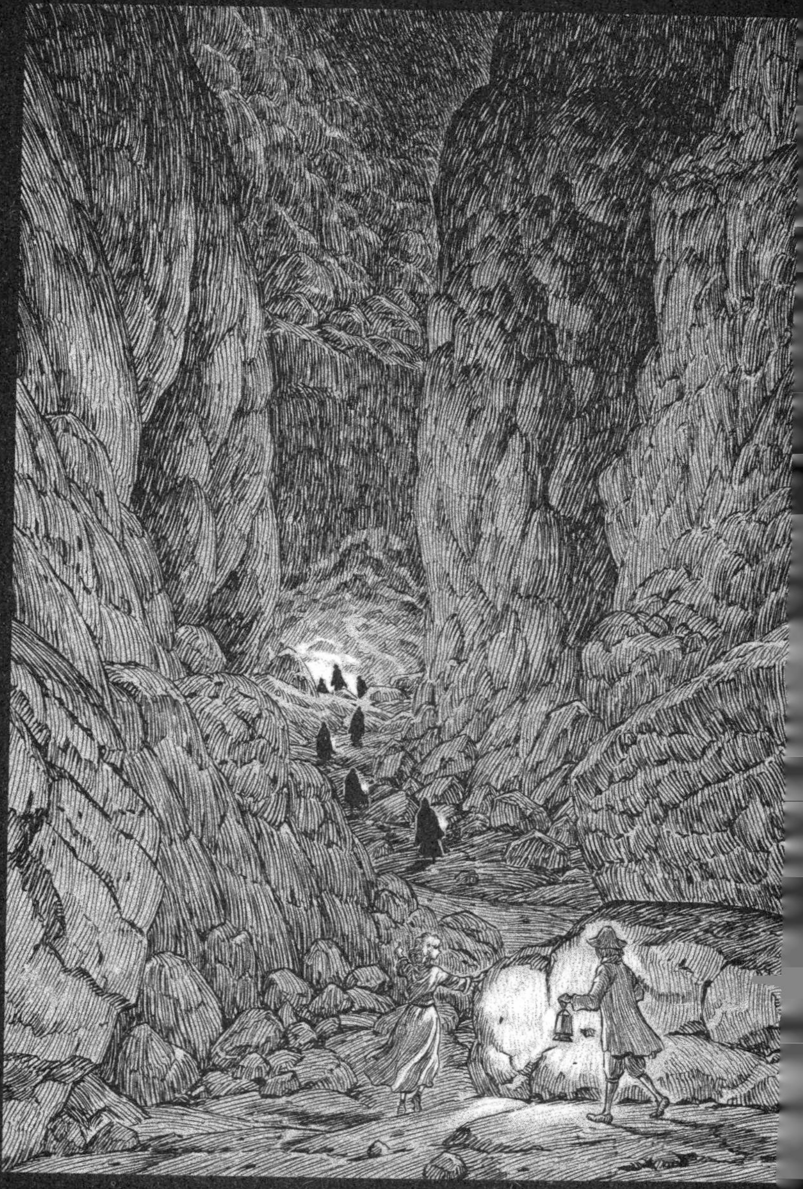

CONVICTION ARC
BIRTH CEREMONY CHAPTER
FIERCE BELIEVER: END

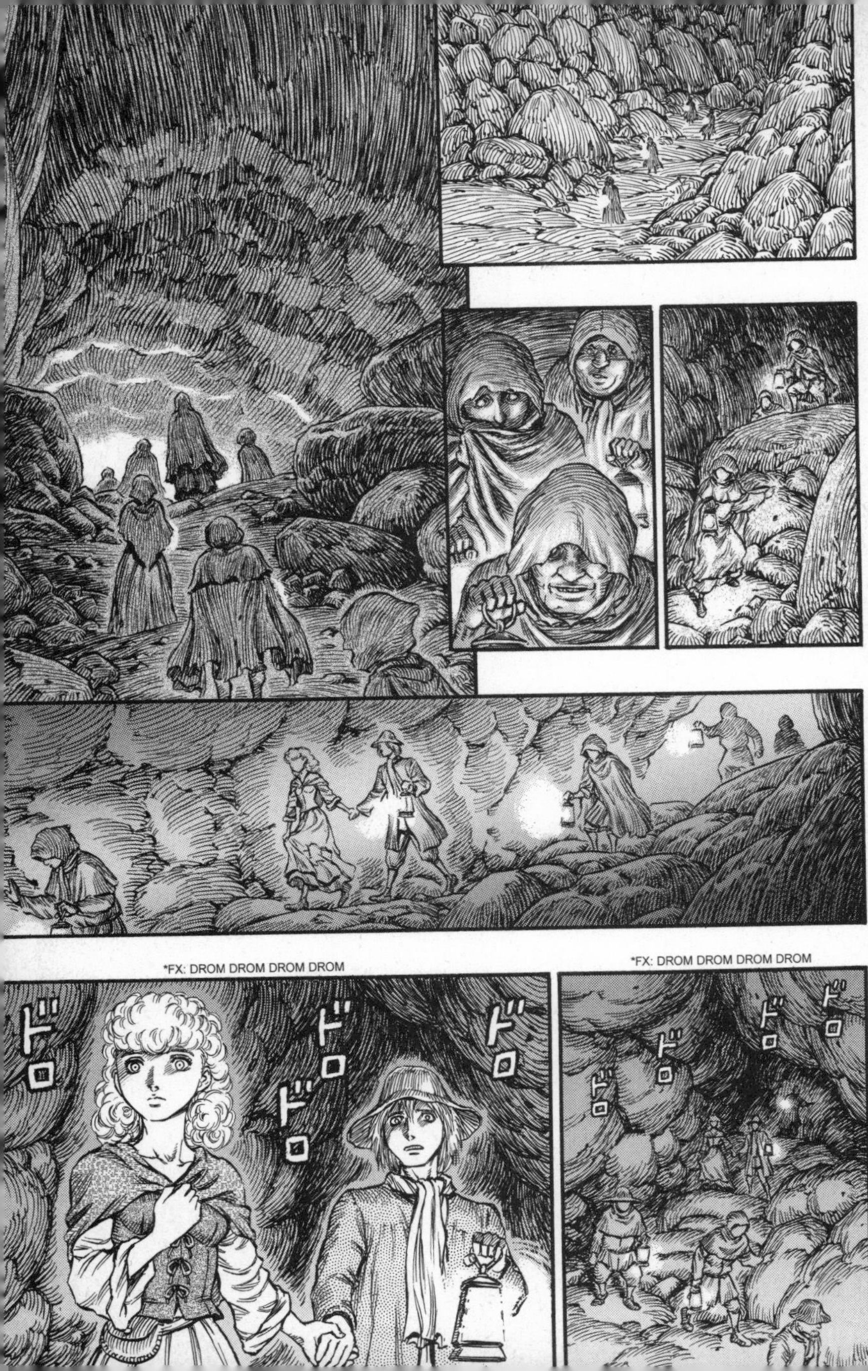
*FX: DROM DROM DROM DROM
ドロ
ドロ
ドロ
ドロ
*FX: DROM DROM DROM DROM
ドロ
ドロ
ドロ
ドロ

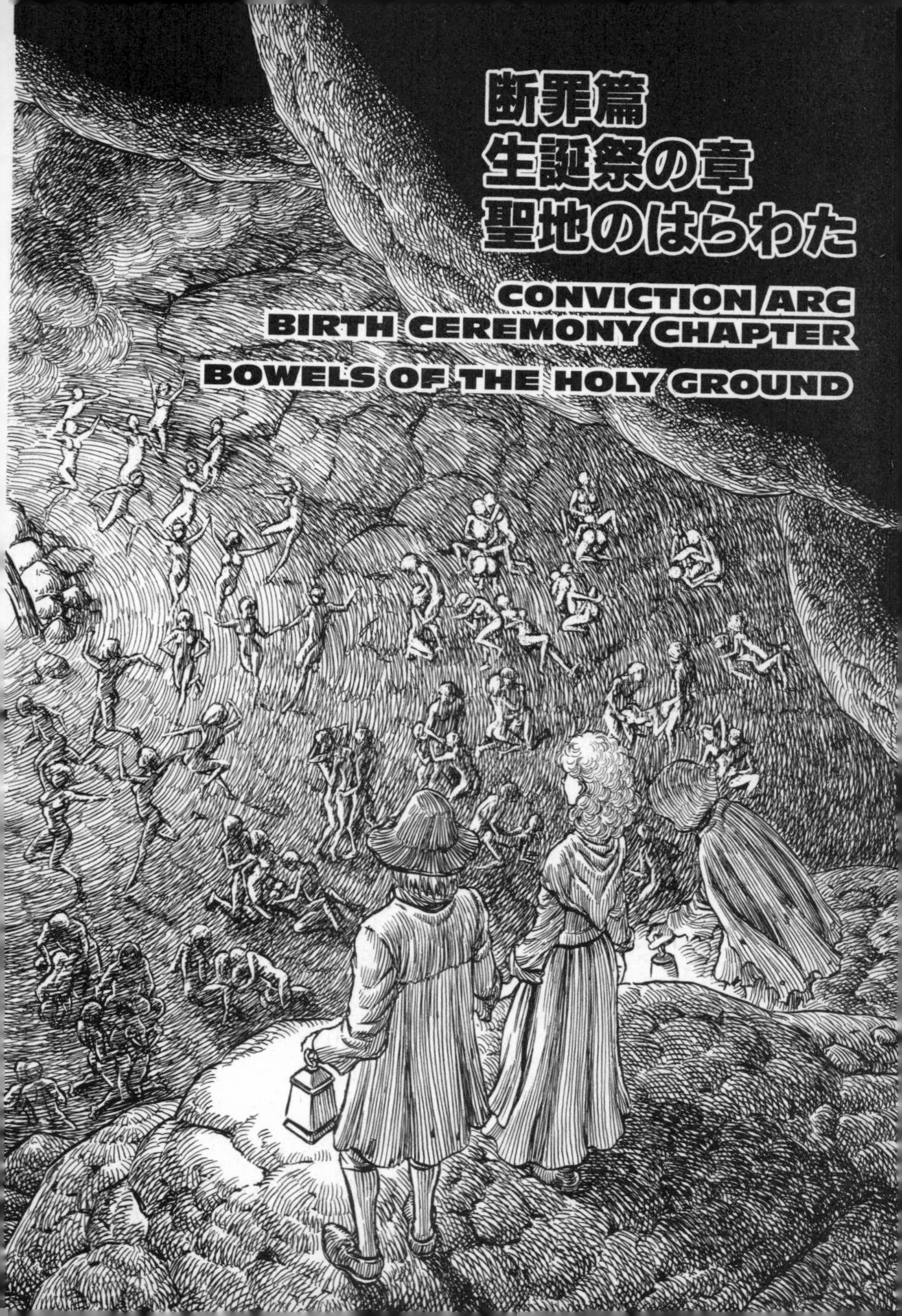
断罪篇
生誕祭の章
聖地のはらわた
CONVICTION ARC
BIRTH CEREMONY CHAPTER
BOWELS OF THE HOLY GROUND

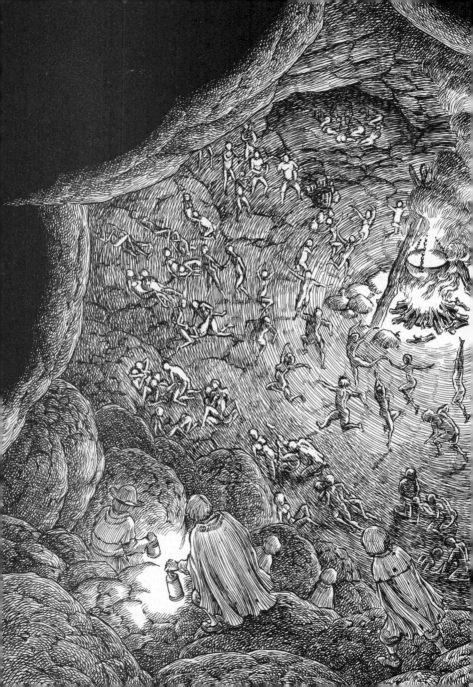

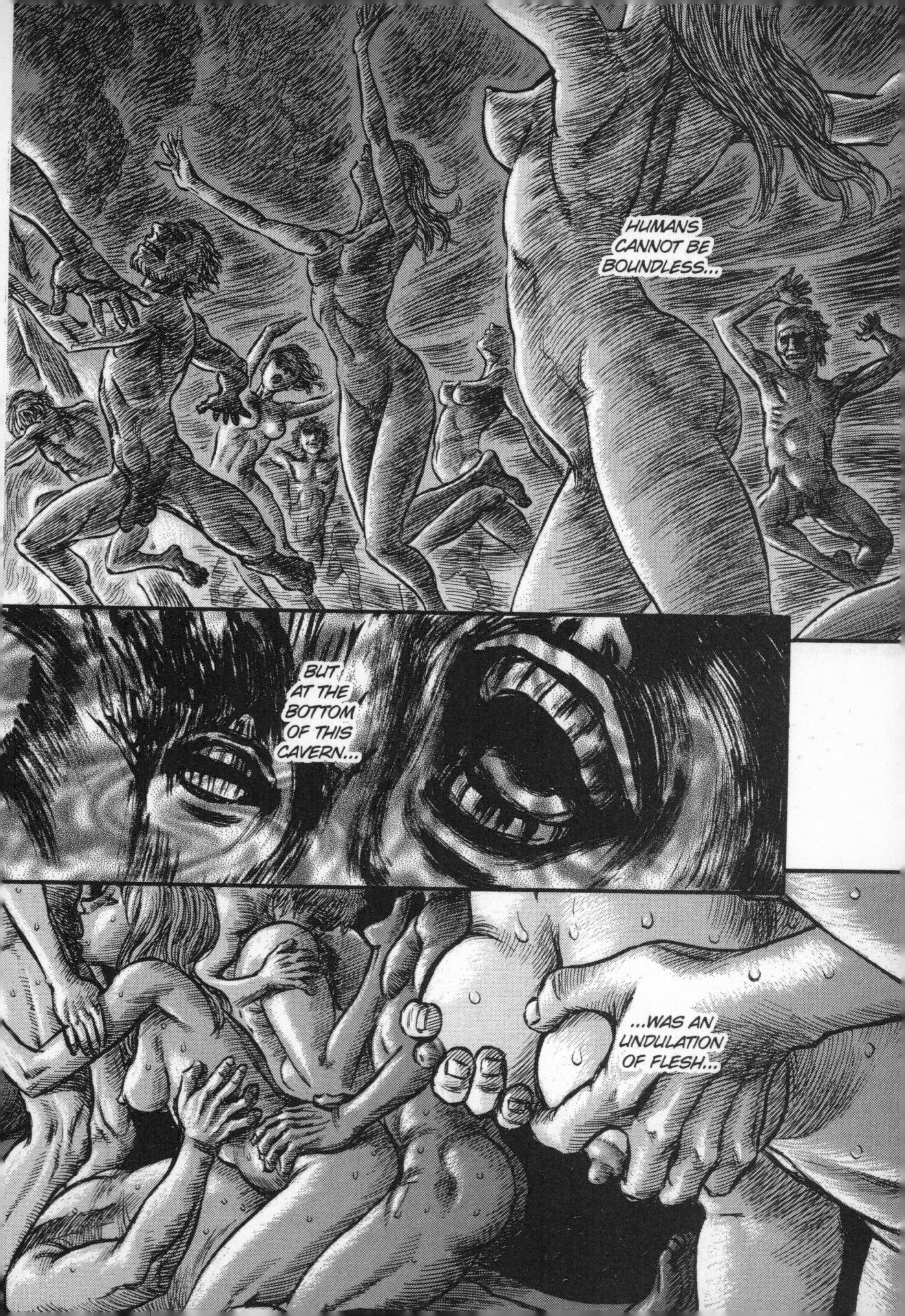
HUMANS CANNOT BE BOUNDLESS...
BUT AT THE BOTTOM OF THIS CAVERN...
...WAS AN UNDULATION OF FLESH...

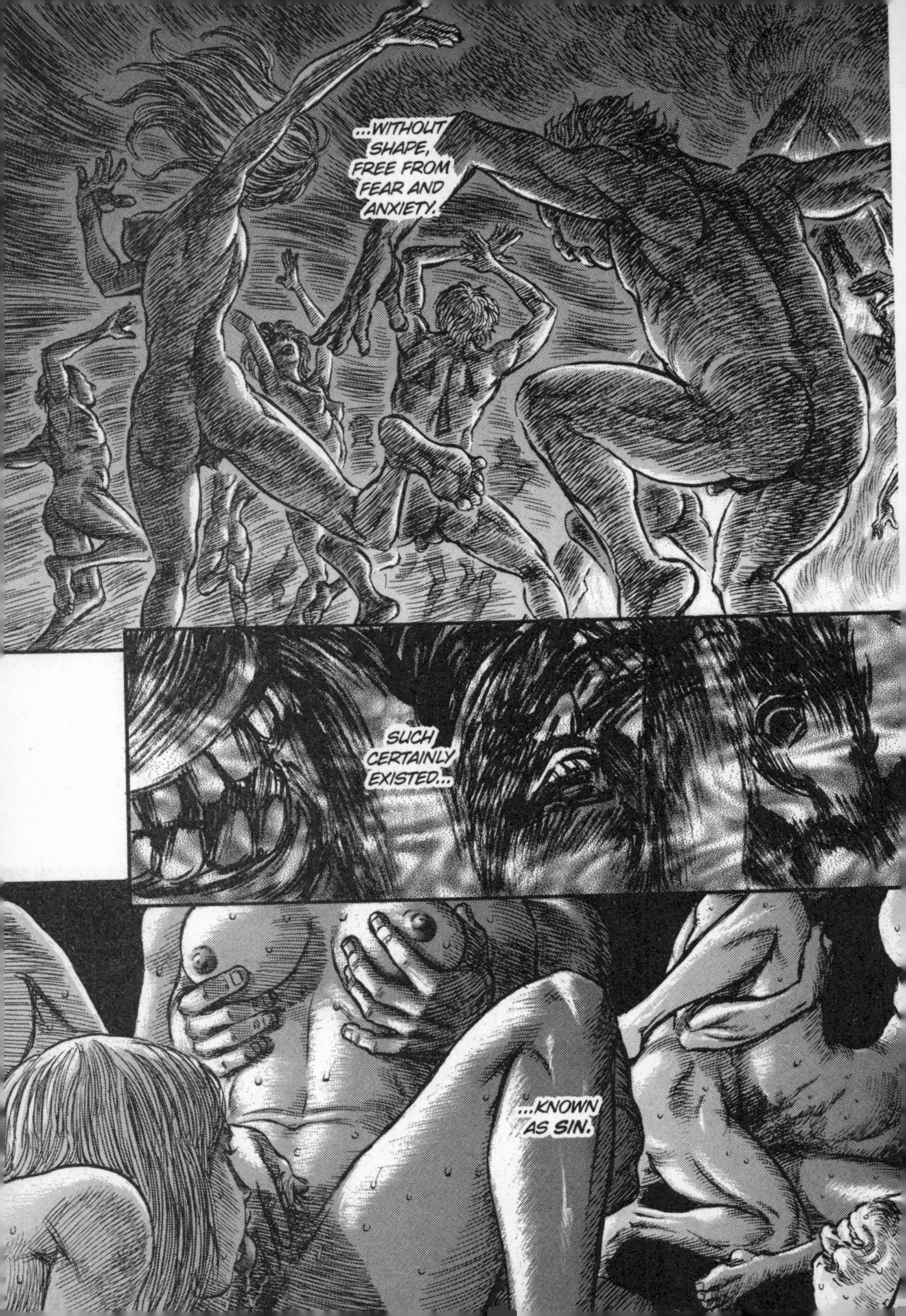
...WITHOUT SHAPE, FREE FROM FEAR AND ANXIETY.
SUCH CERTAINLY EXISTED...
...KNOWN AS SIN.

*FX: GLOOP GLOOP GLOOP GLOOP

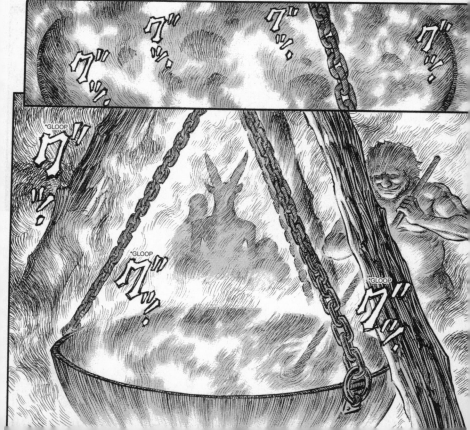

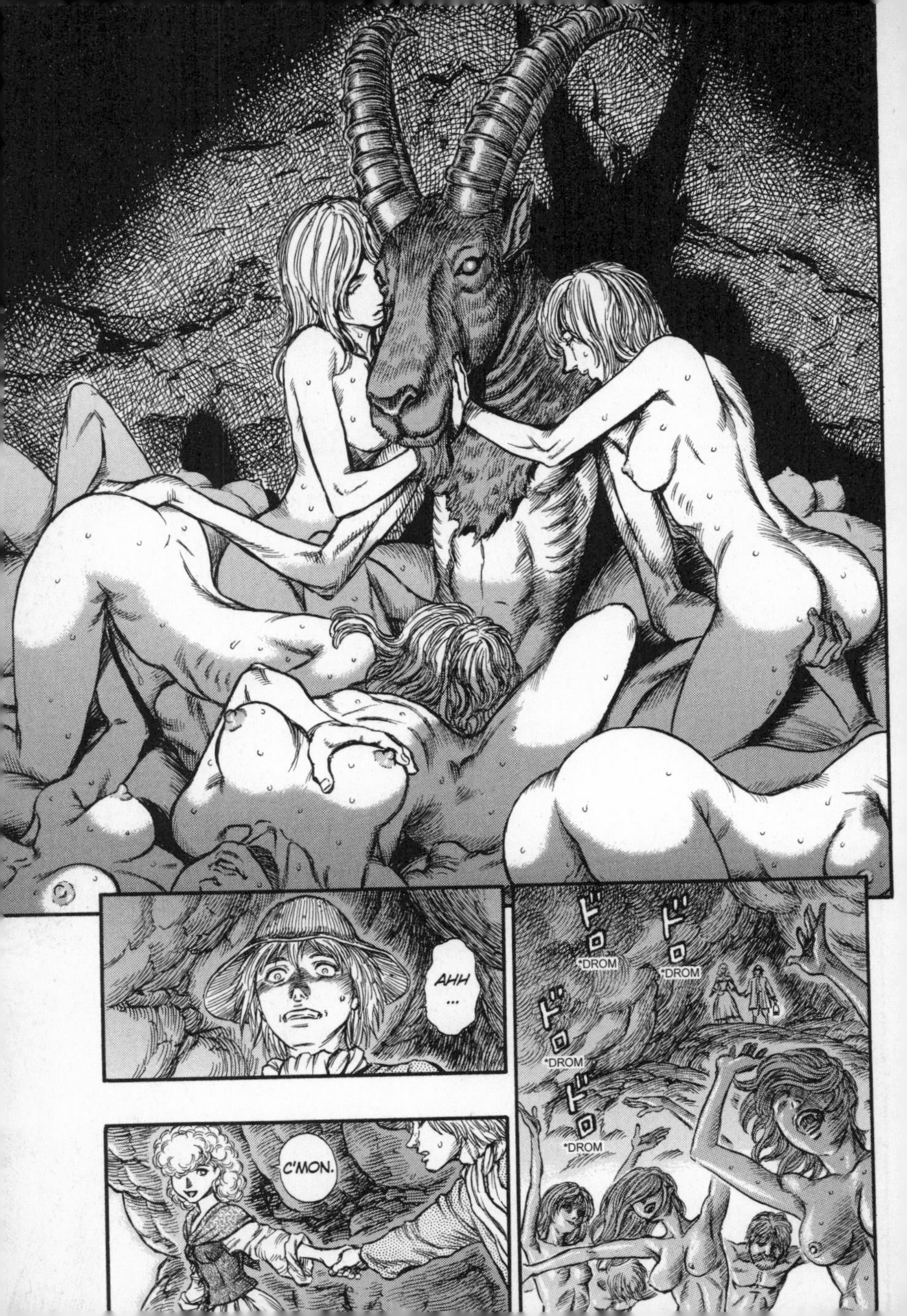
ドロ
*DROM
ドロ
*DROM
ドロ
*DROM
ドロ
*DROM
AHH ...
C'MON.

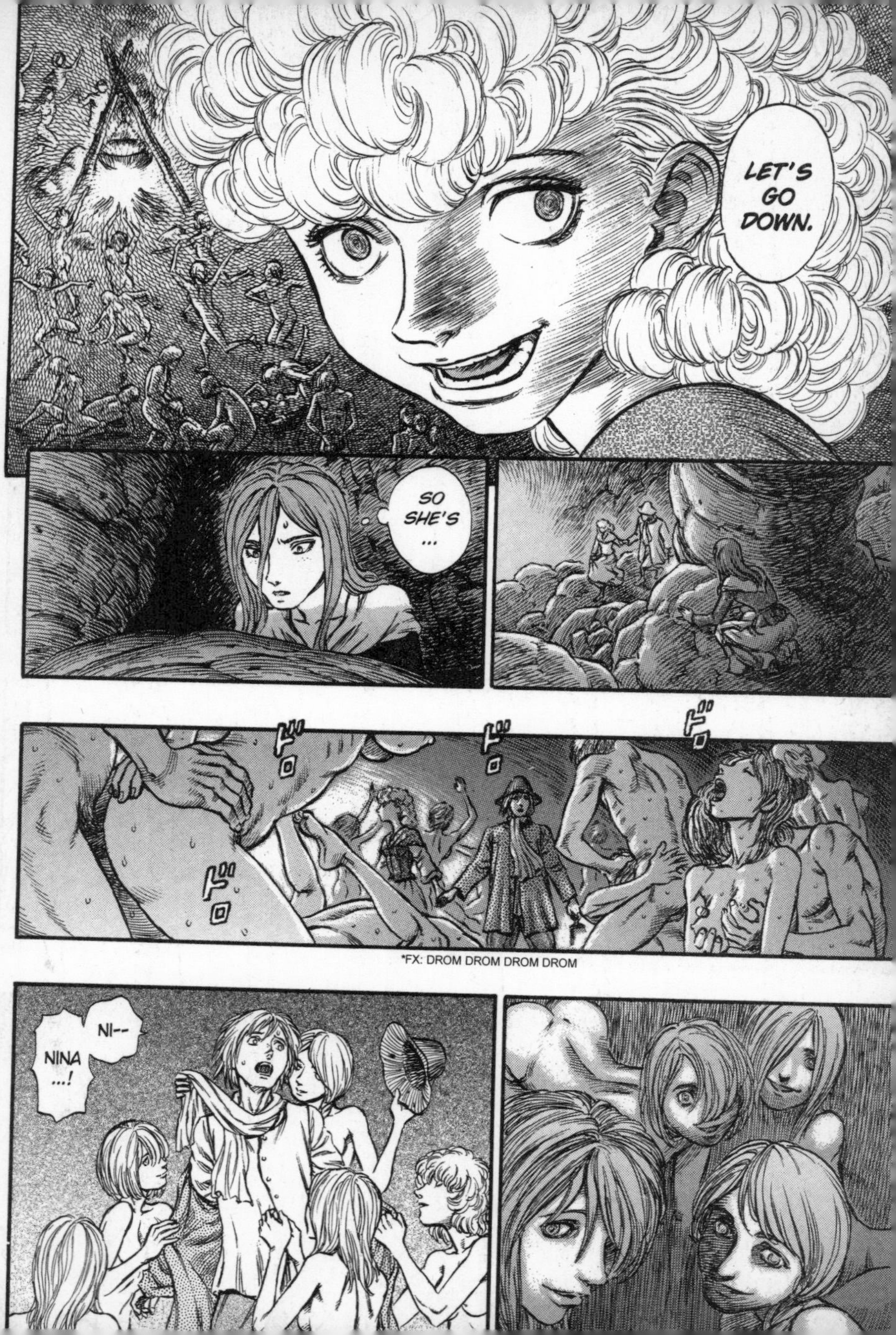
LET'S GO DOWN.
SO SHE'S ...
*FX: DROM DROM DROM DROM
NI-- NINA ...!

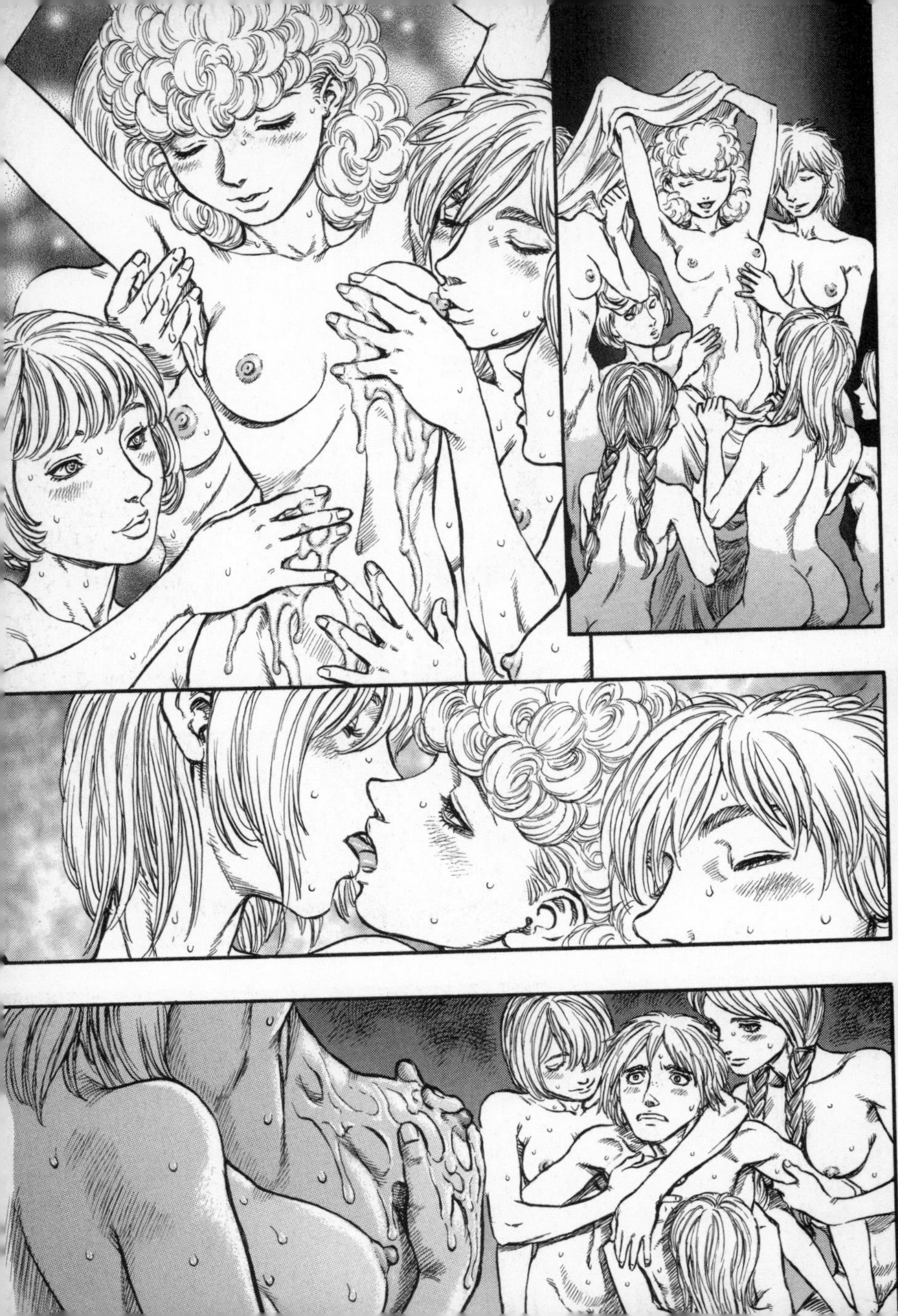

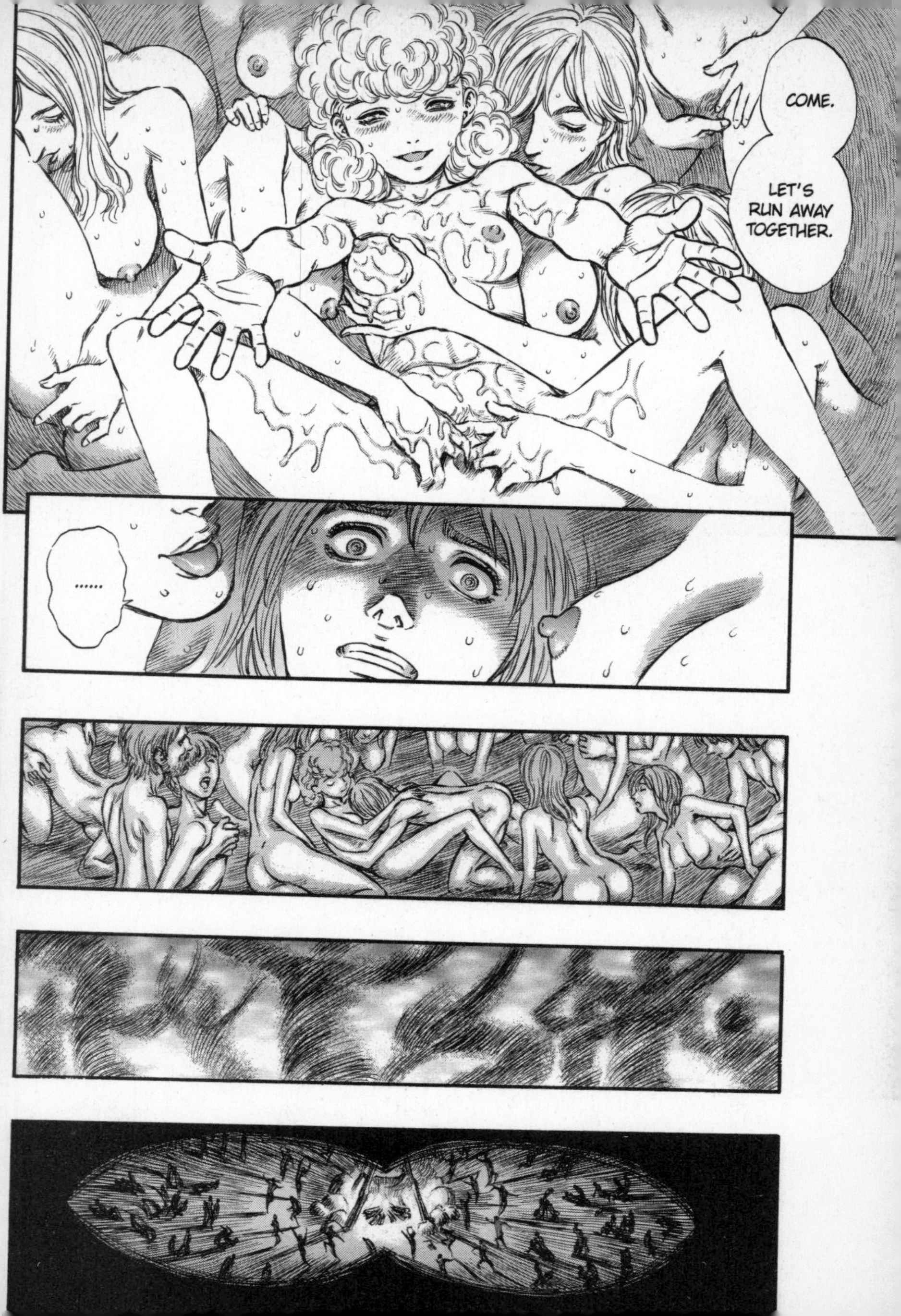
COME.
LET'S RUN AWAY TOGETHER.
......

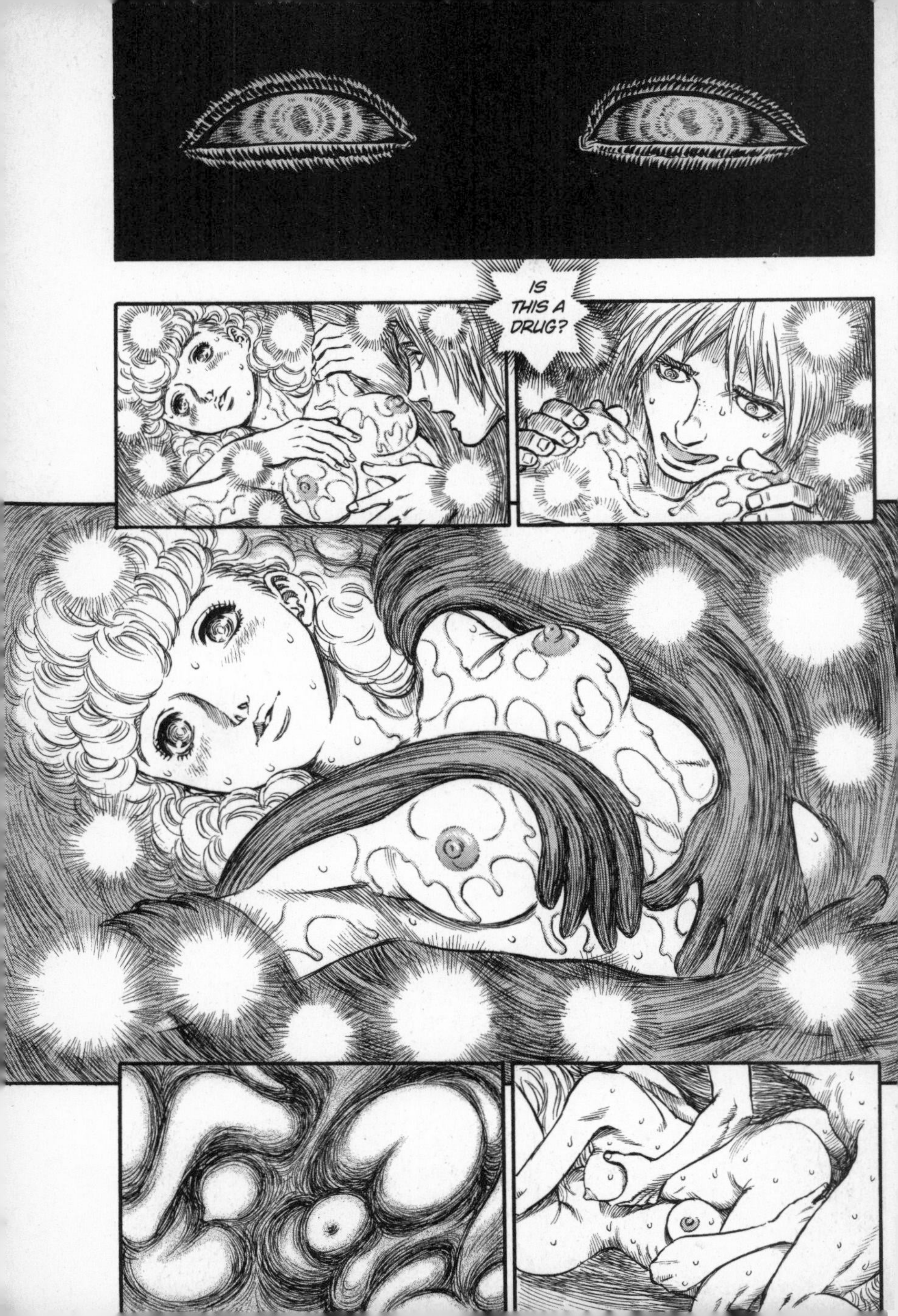
IS THIS A DRUG?

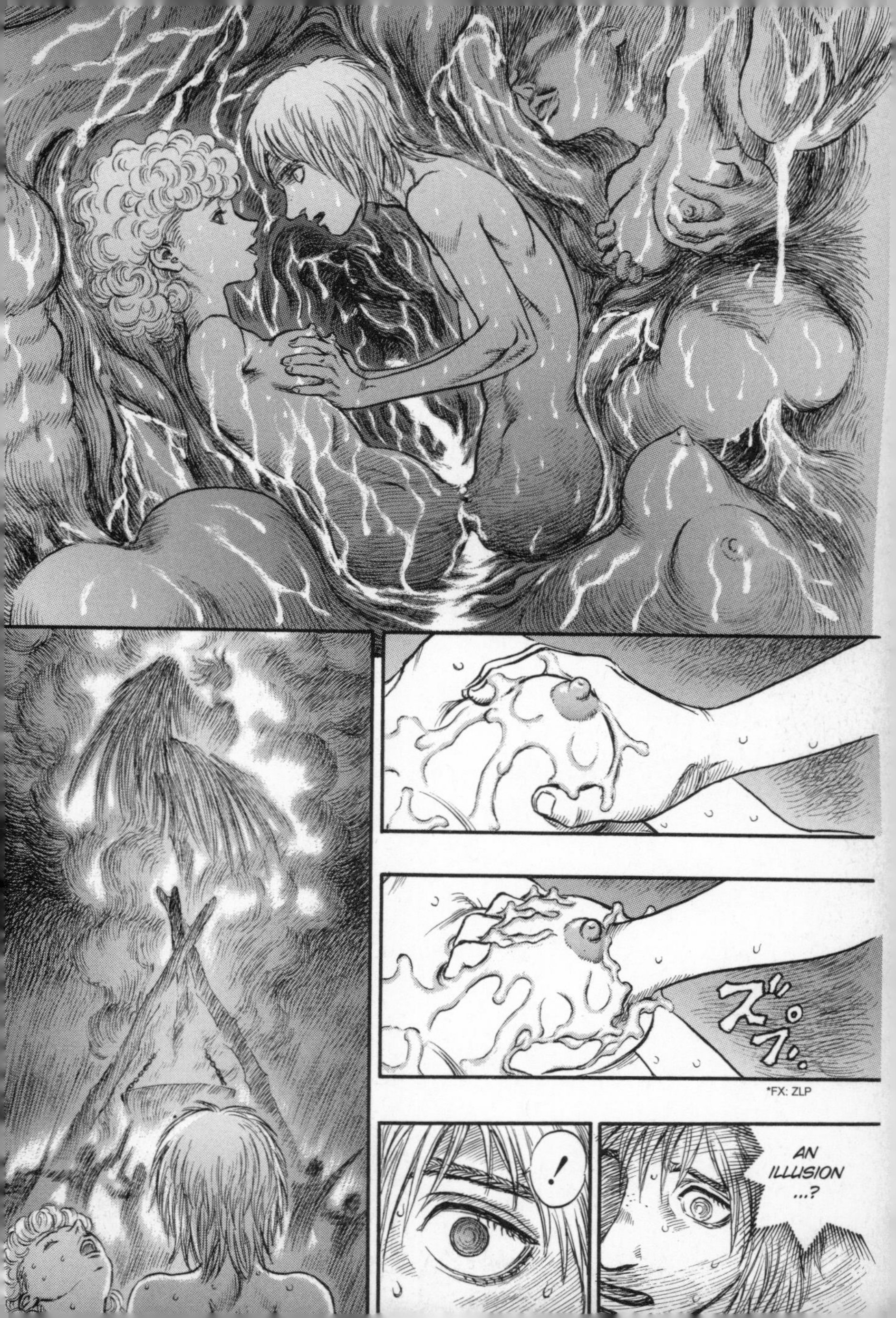
ズプ
*FX: ZLP
AN ILLUSION ...?
!

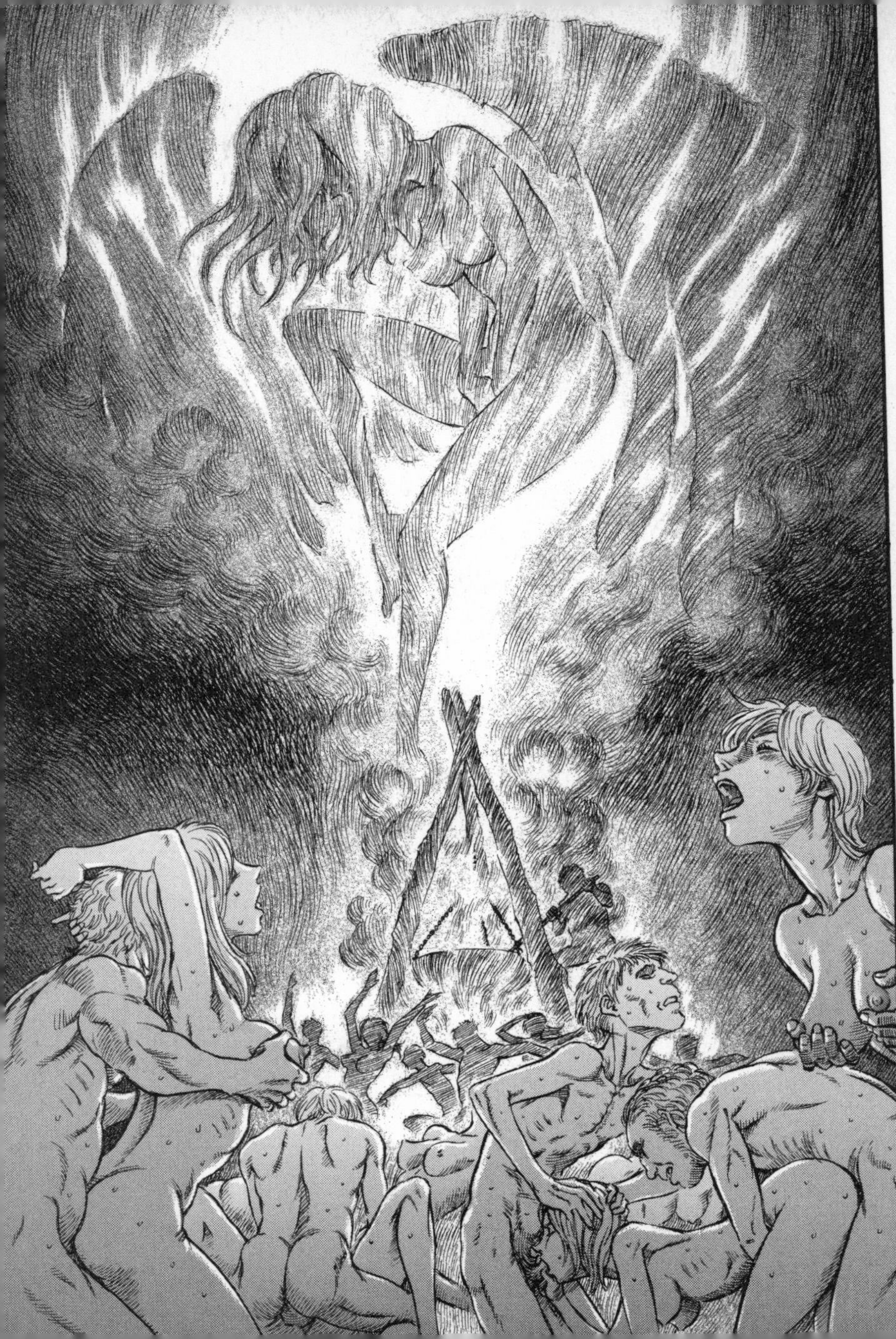

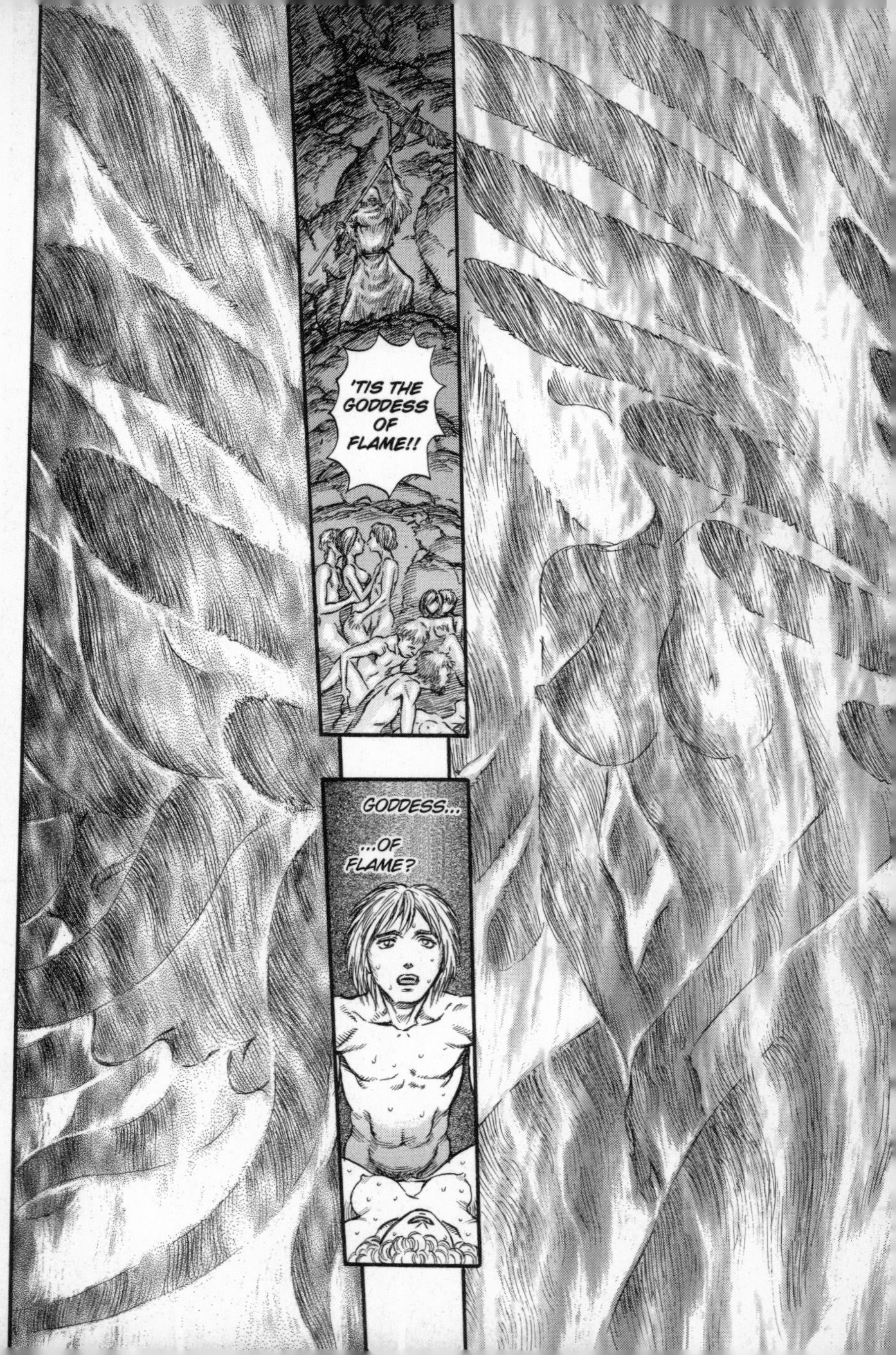
'TIS THE GODDESS OF FLAME!!
GODDESS...
...OF FLAME?

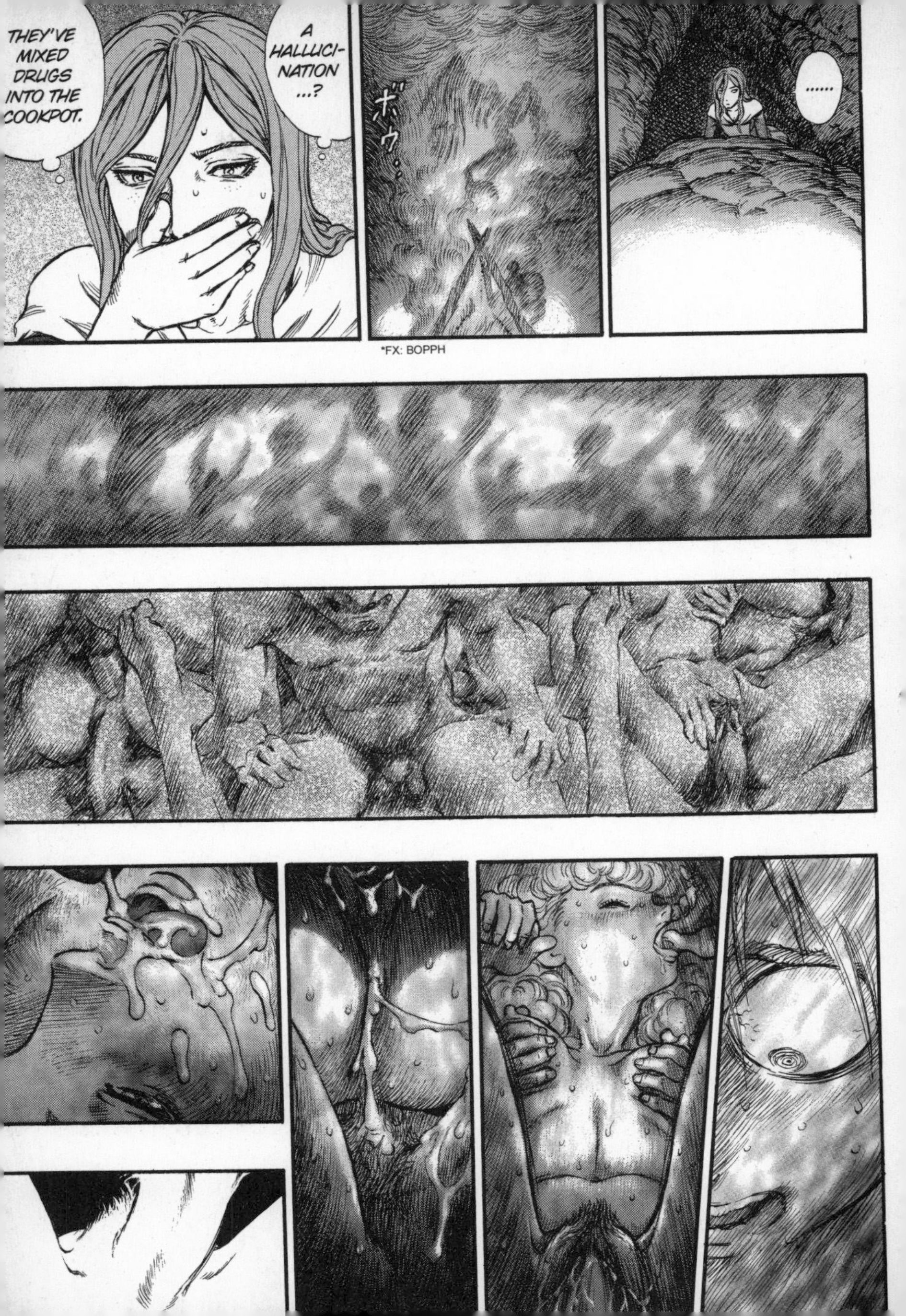
......
ボウ
*FX: BOPPH
A HALLUCI-NATION ...?
THEY'VE MIXED DRUGS INTO THE COOKPOT.

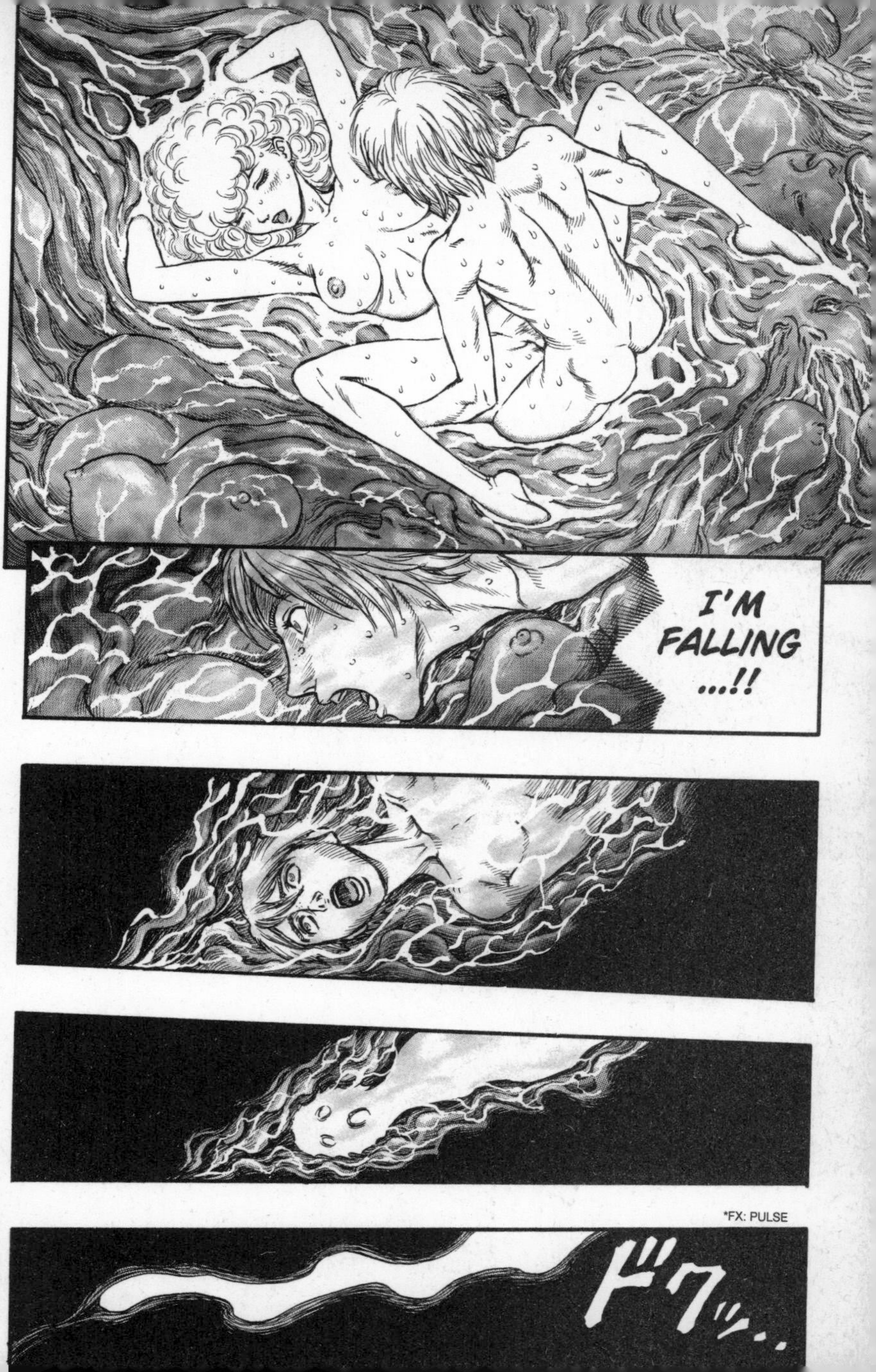
I'M FALLING ...!!
*FX: PULSE
ドクッ..

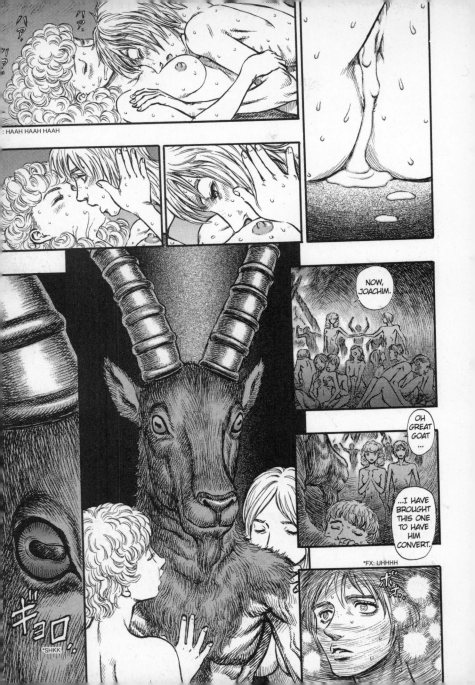

: HAAH HAAH HAAH

NOW, JOACHIM.

OH GREAT GOAT...

...I HAVE BROUGHT THIS ONE TO HAVE HIM CONVERT.

*FX: UHHHH

*SHKK

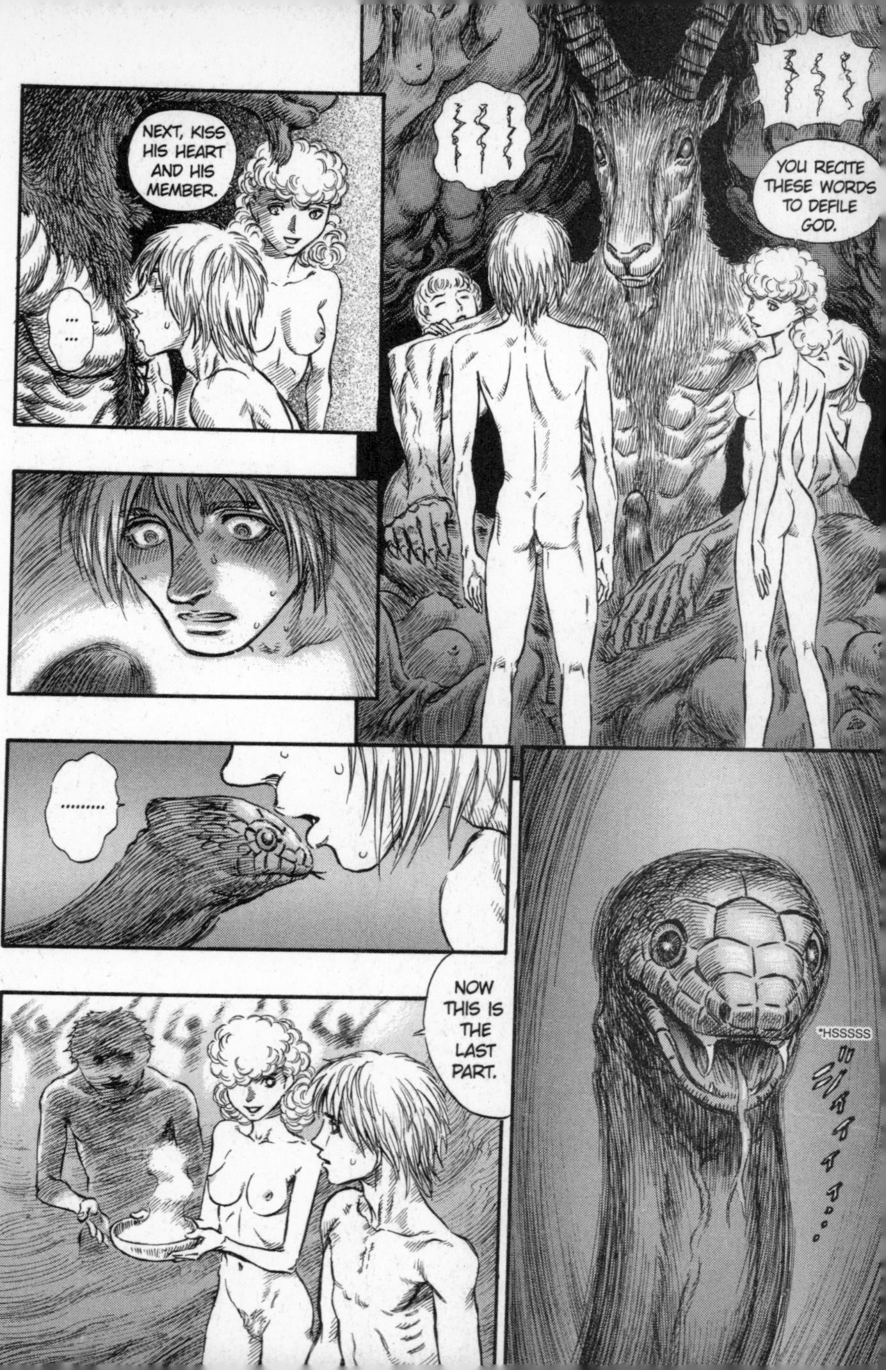
YOU RECITE THESE WORDS TO DEFILE GOD.
NEXT, KISS HIS HEART AND HIS MEMBER.
... ...
*HSSSSS
....
NOW THIS IS THE LAST PART.

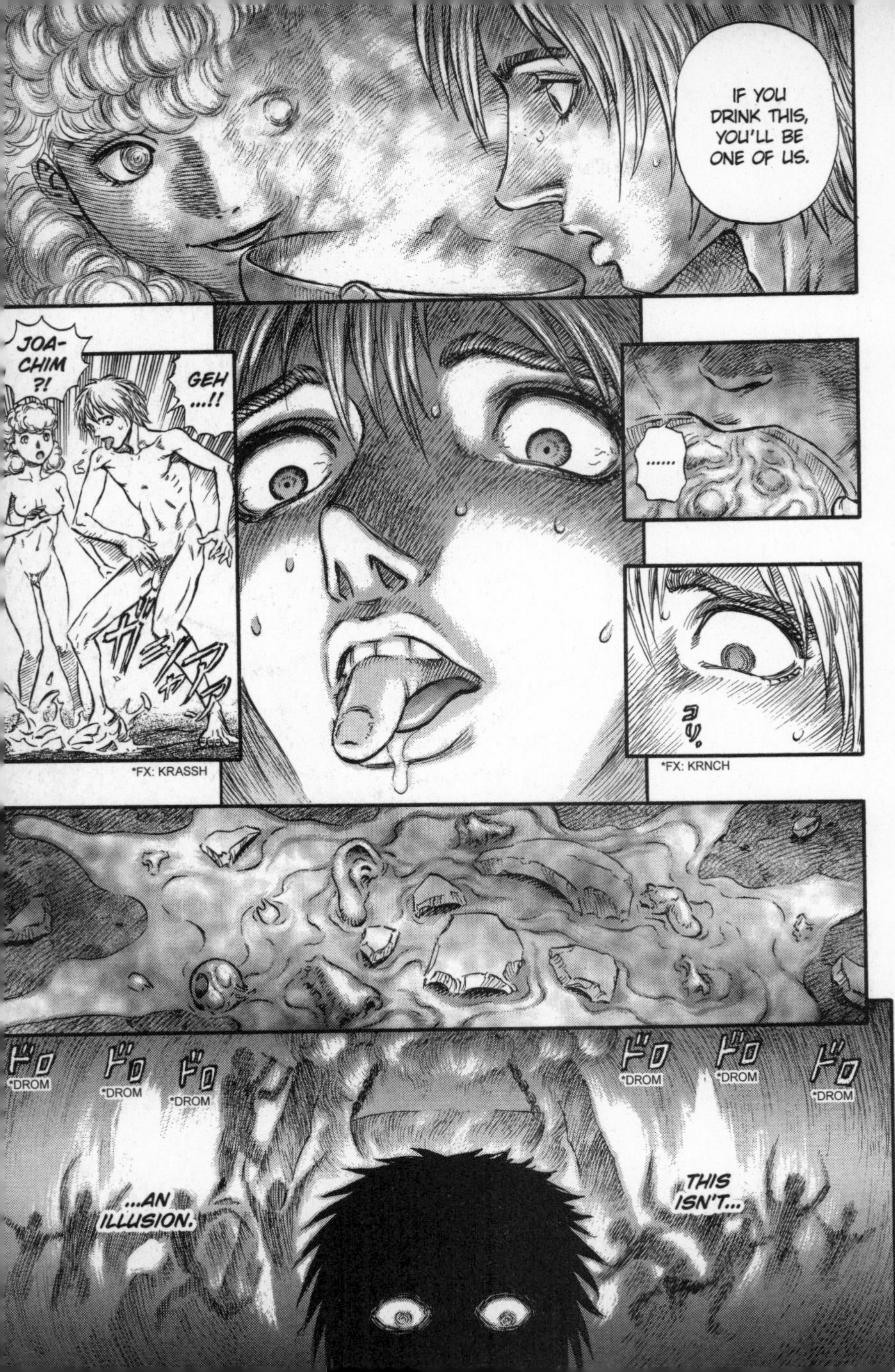
IF YOU DRINK THIS, YOU'LL BE ONE OF US.
......
*FX: KRNCH
GEH ...!!
JOA-CHIM ?!
*FX: KRASSH
*DROM
*DROM
*DROM
*DROM
*DROM
*DROM
THIS ISN'T...
...AN ILLUSION.

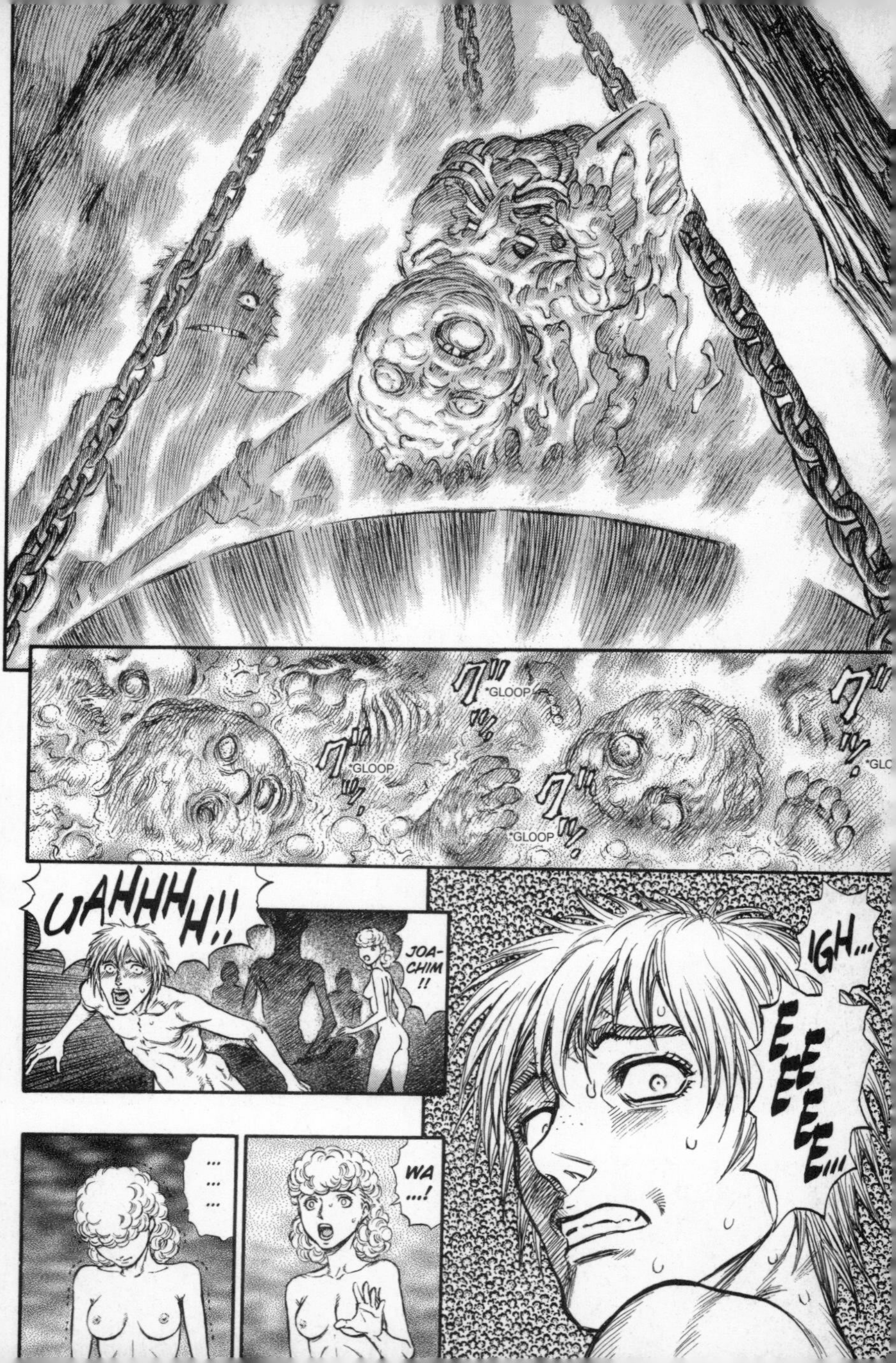
*GLO
*GLOOP
*GLOOP
*GLOOP
IGH...
EEEEEE...!!
UAHHHH!!
JOA-CHIM!!
WA...!
... ...

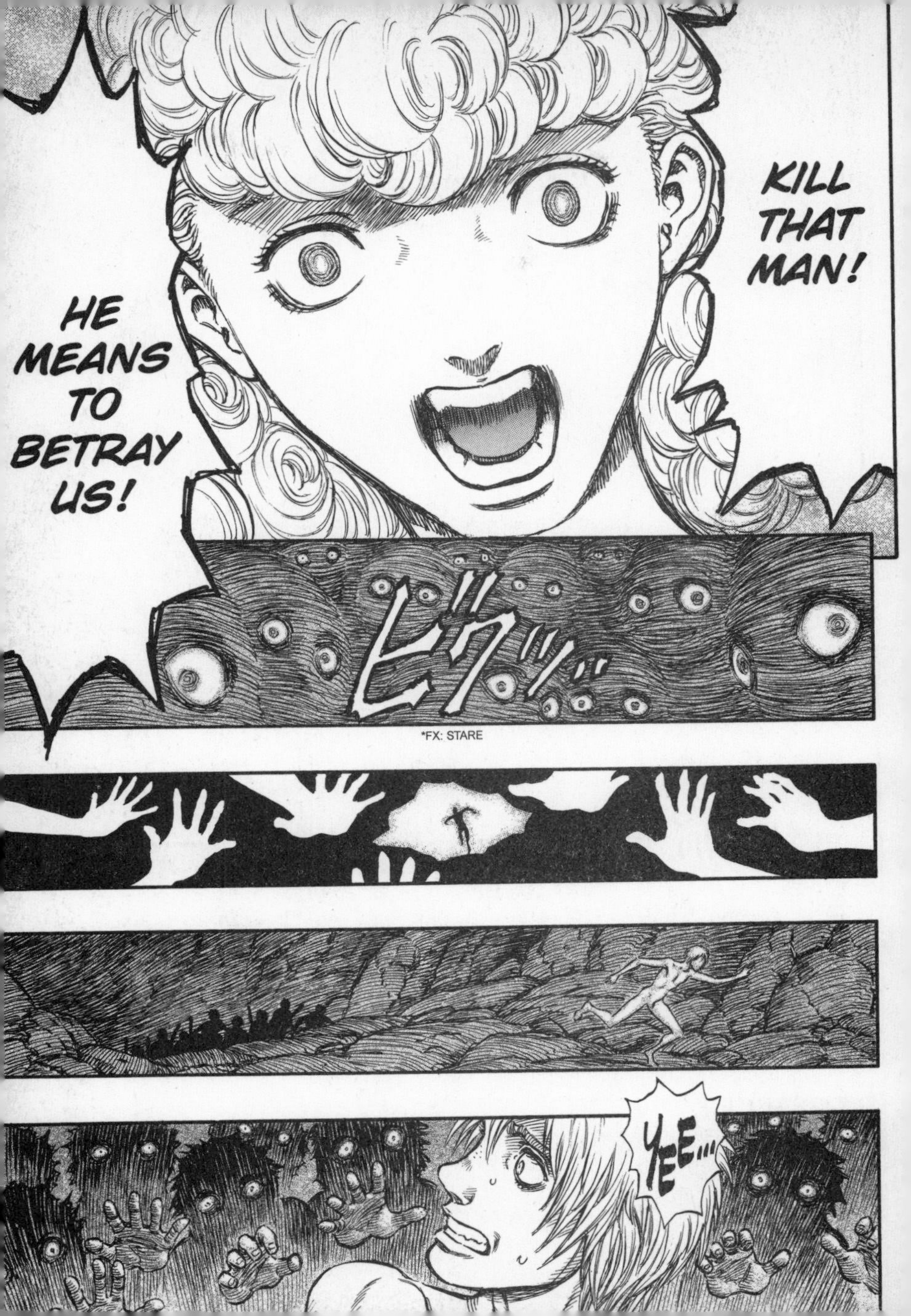
KILL THAT MAN!
HE MEANS TO BETRAY US!
ビクッ
*FX: STARE
YEE...

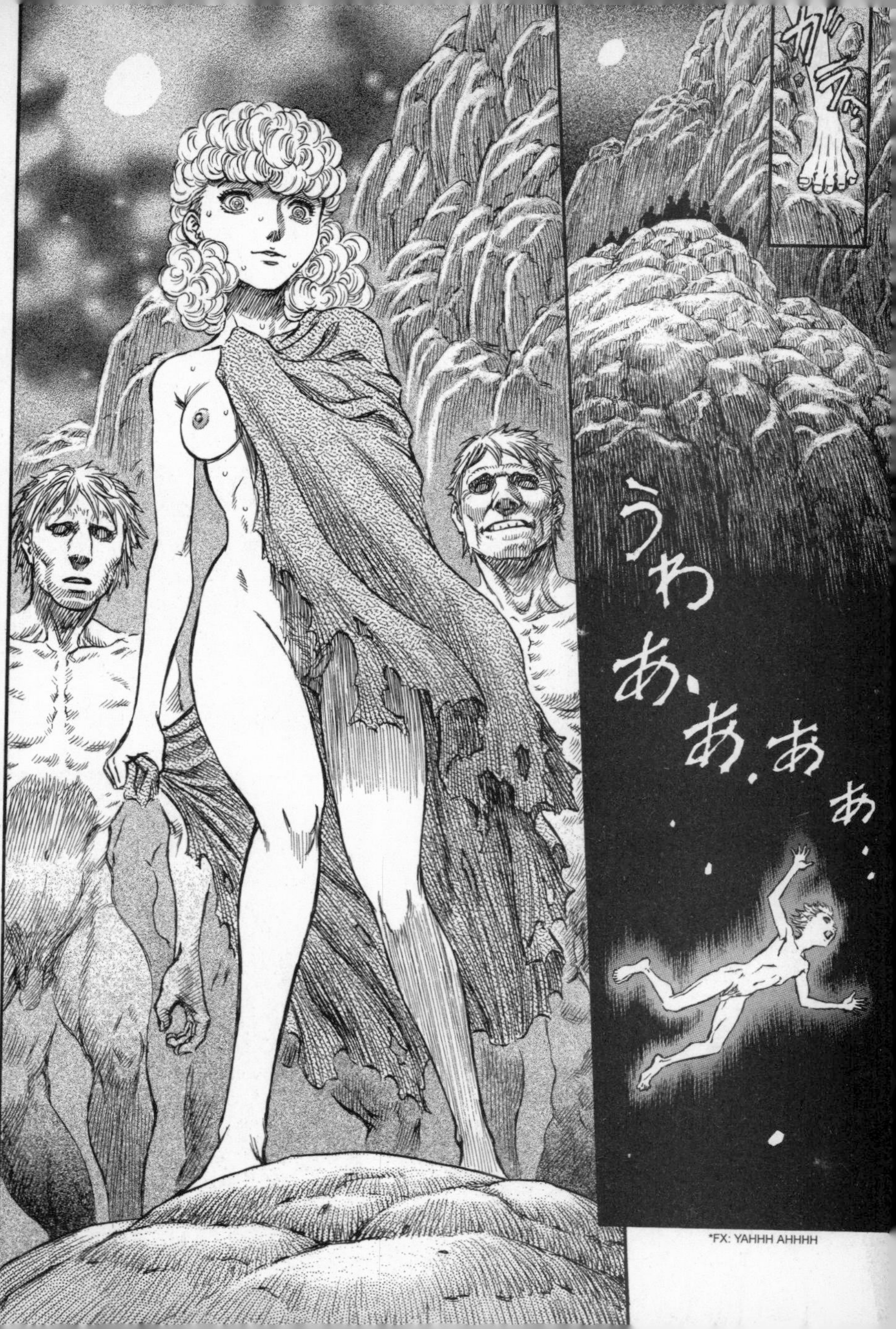
ガラ…
うわあああ…
*FX: YAHHH AHHHH

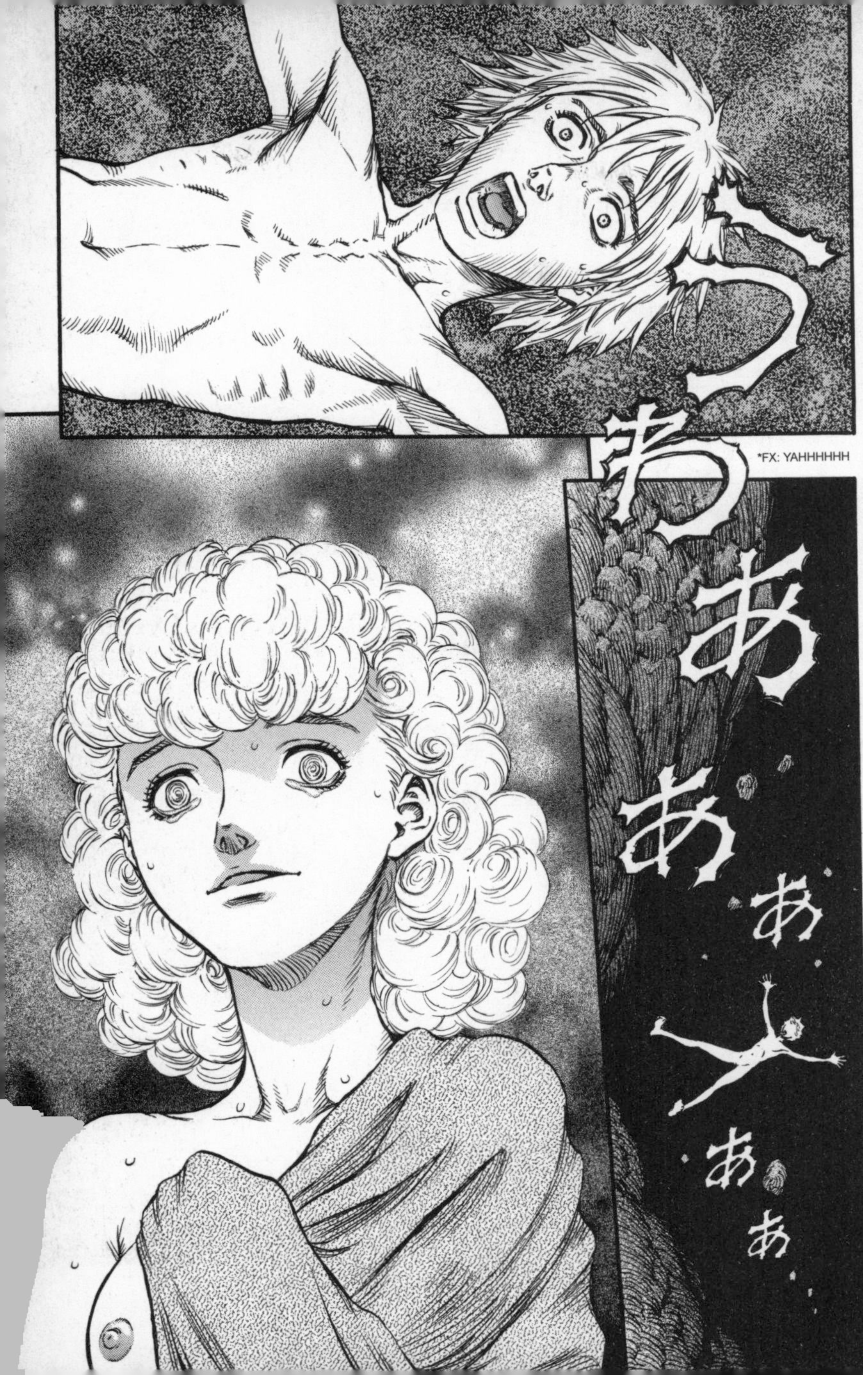
っわあああああ
*FX: YAHHHHHH

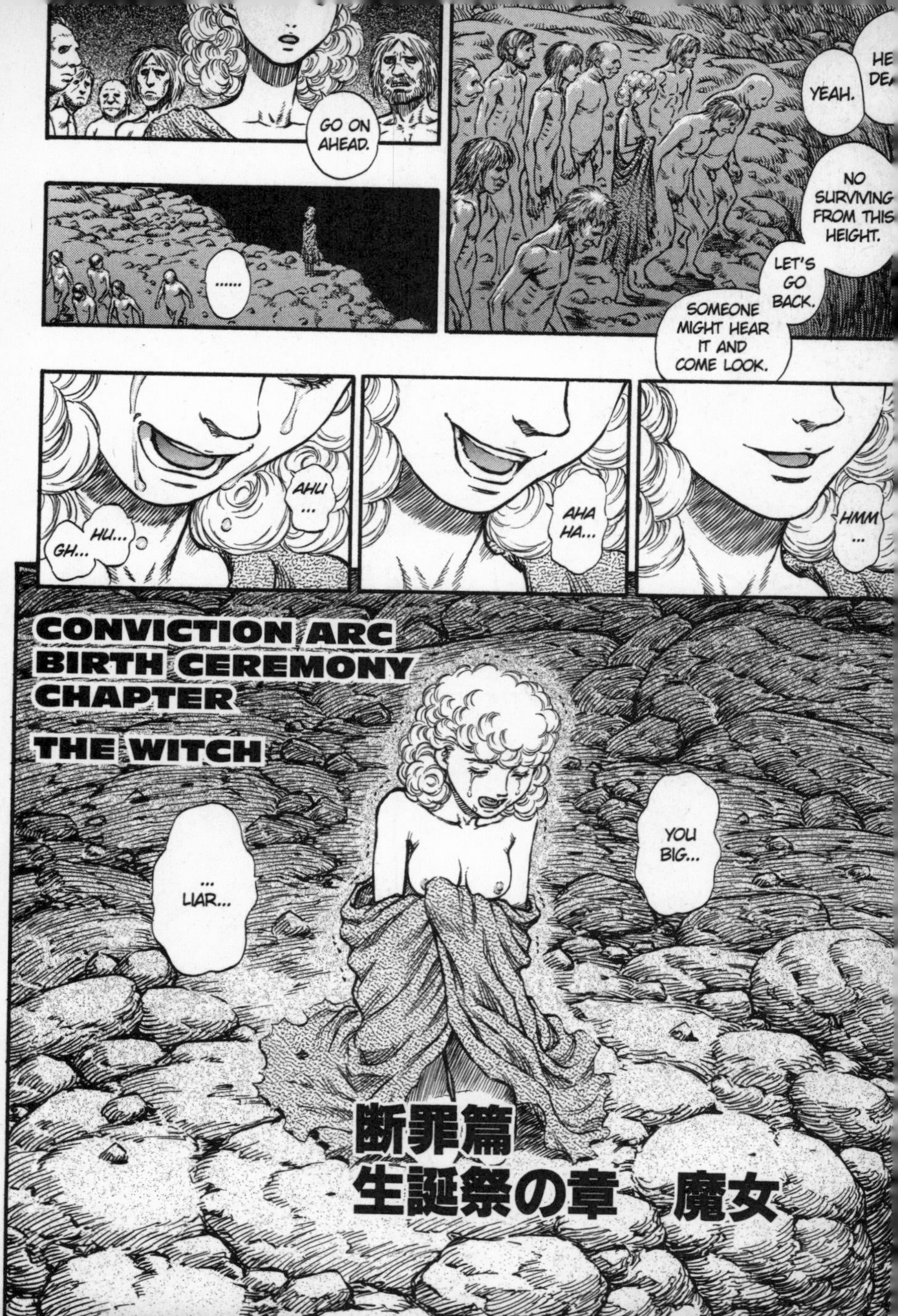
YEAH.
NO SURVIVING FROM THIS HEIGHT.
LET'S GO BACK.
SOMEONE MIGHT HEAR IT AND COME LOOK.
GO ON AHEAD.
......
HMM ...
AHA HA...
AHU ...
HU... GH...
CONVICTION ARC BIRTH CEREMONY CHAPTER
THE WITCH
YOU BIG...
... LIAR...
断罪篇
生誕祭の章　魔女

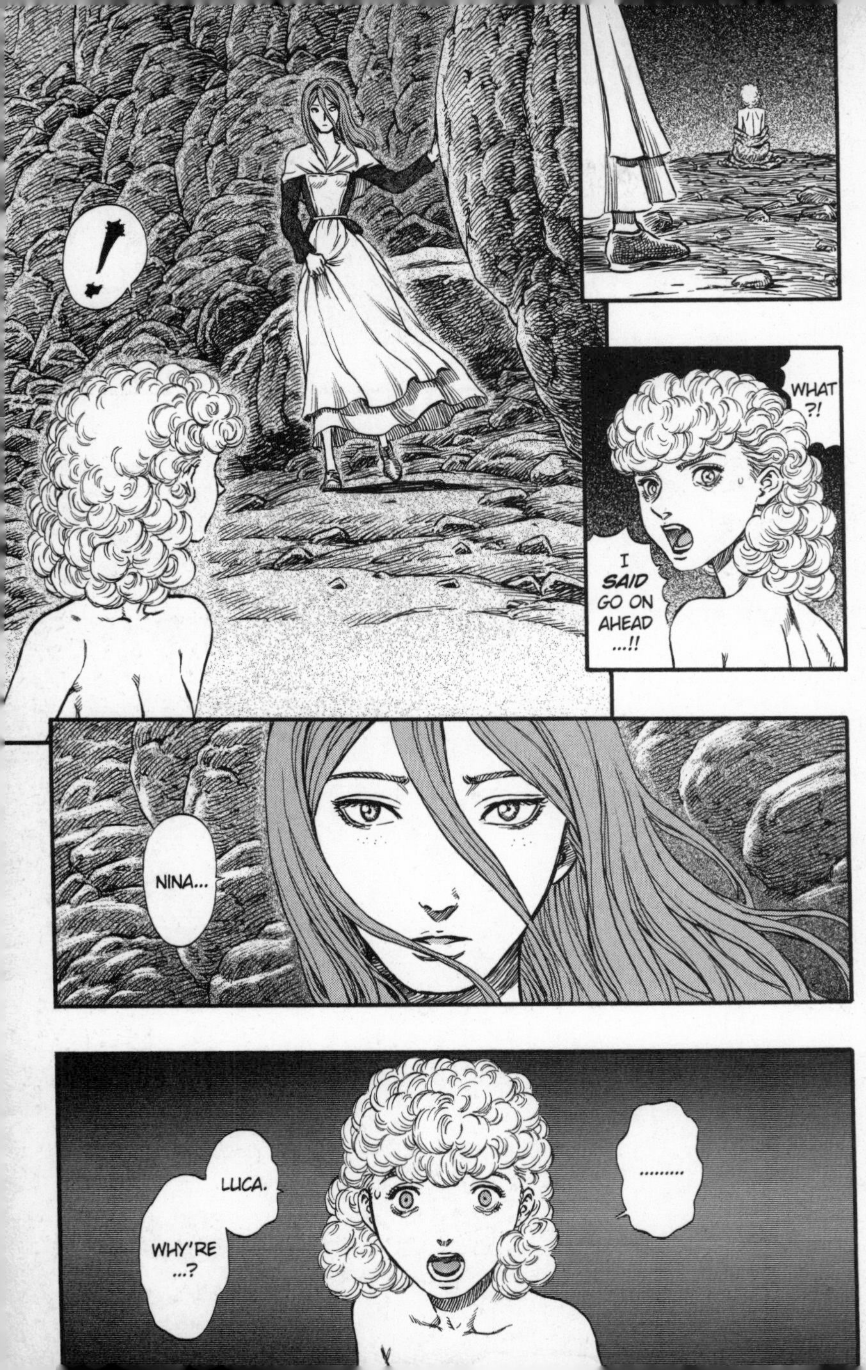
WHAT ?!
I SAID GO ON AHEAD ...!!
!
NINA...
....
LUCA.
WHY'RE ...?

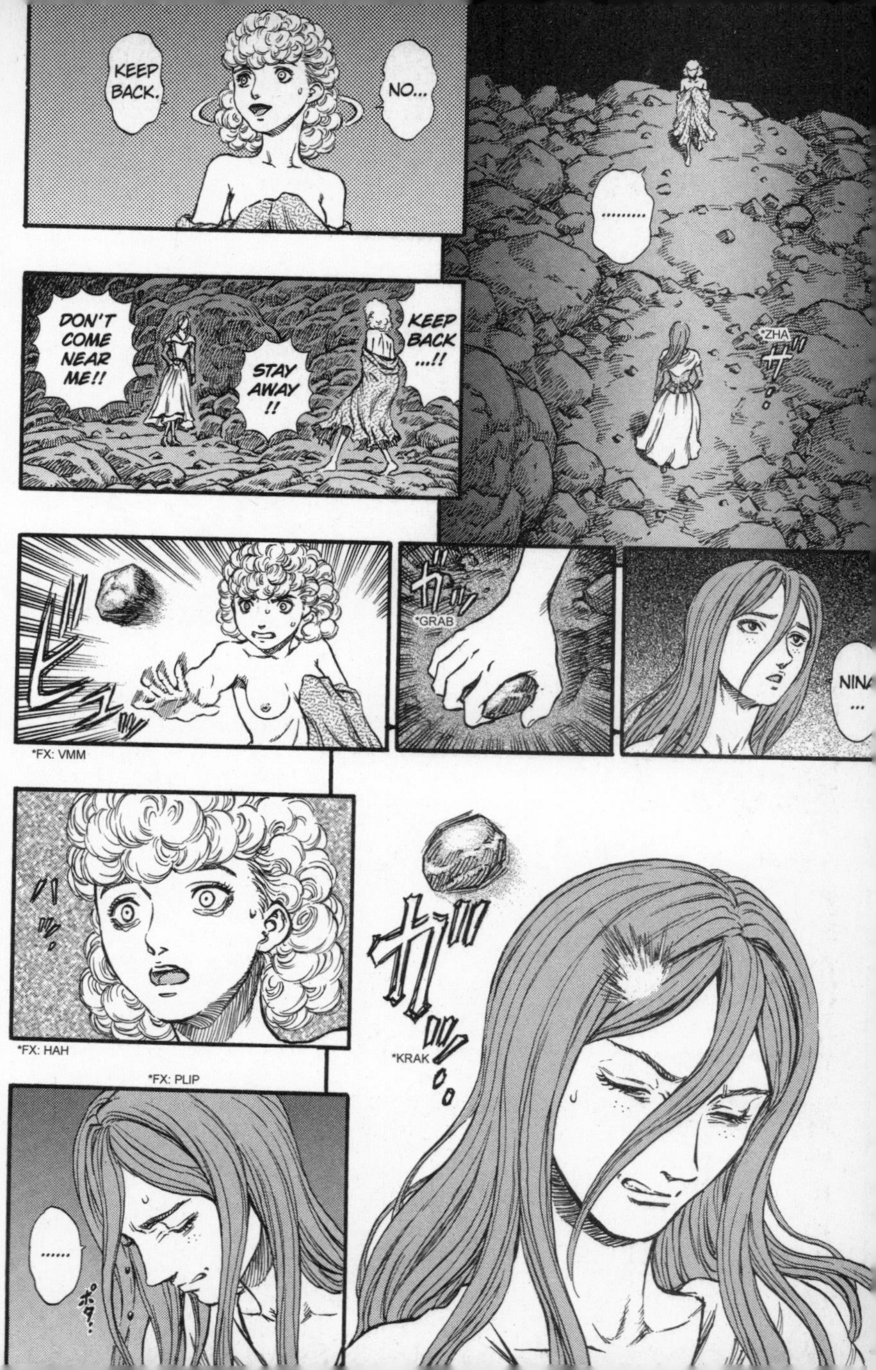
....
*ZHA
NO...
KEEP BACK.
KEEP BACK ...!!
STAY AWAY !!
DON'T COME NEAR ME!!
NINA ...
*GRAB
*FX: VMM
*KRAK
*FX: HAH
*FX: PLIP
......

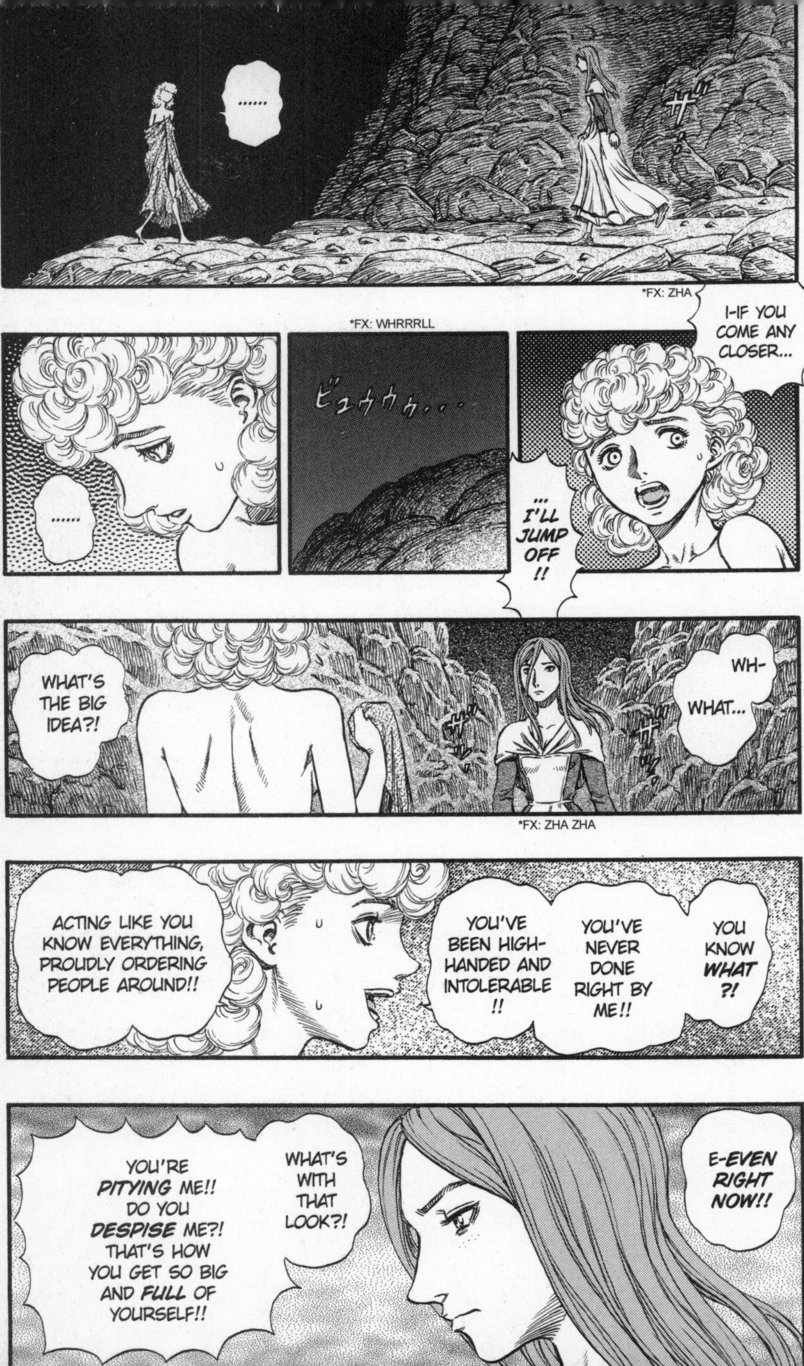
......
*FX: ZHA
I-IF YOU COME ANY CLOSER...
...I'LL JUMP OFF!!
*FX: WHRRRLL
......
WH- WHAT...
WHAT'S THE BIG IDEA?!
*FX: ZHA ZHA
YOU KNOW WHAT?!
YOU'VE NEVER DONE RIGHT BY ME!!
YOU'VE BEEN HIGH-HANDED AND INTOLERABLE!!
ACTING LIKE YOU KNOW EVERYTHING, PROUDLY ORDERING PEOPLE AROUND!!
E-EVEN RIGHT NOW!!
WHAT'S WITH THAT LOOK?!
YOU'RE PITYING ME!! DO YOU DESPISE ME?! THAT'S HOW YOU GET SO BIG AND FULL OF YOURSELF!!

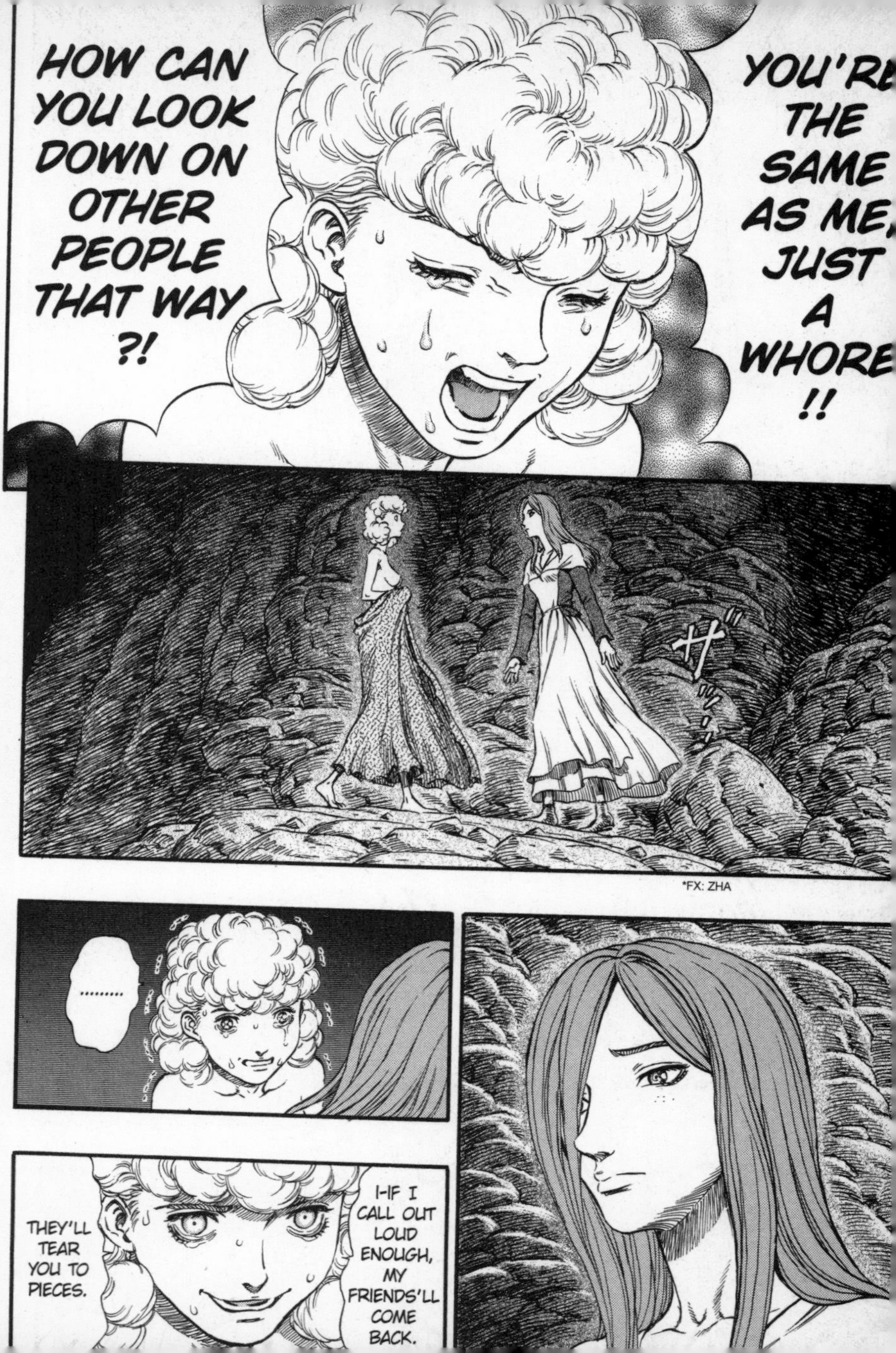
YOU'RE THE SAME AS ME, JUST A WHORE!!
HOW CAN YOU LOOK DOWN ON OTHER PEOPLE THAT WAY?!
*FX: ZHA
....
I-IF I CALL OUT LOUD ENOUGH, MY FRIENDS'LL COME BACK.
THEY'LL TEAR YOU TO PIECES.

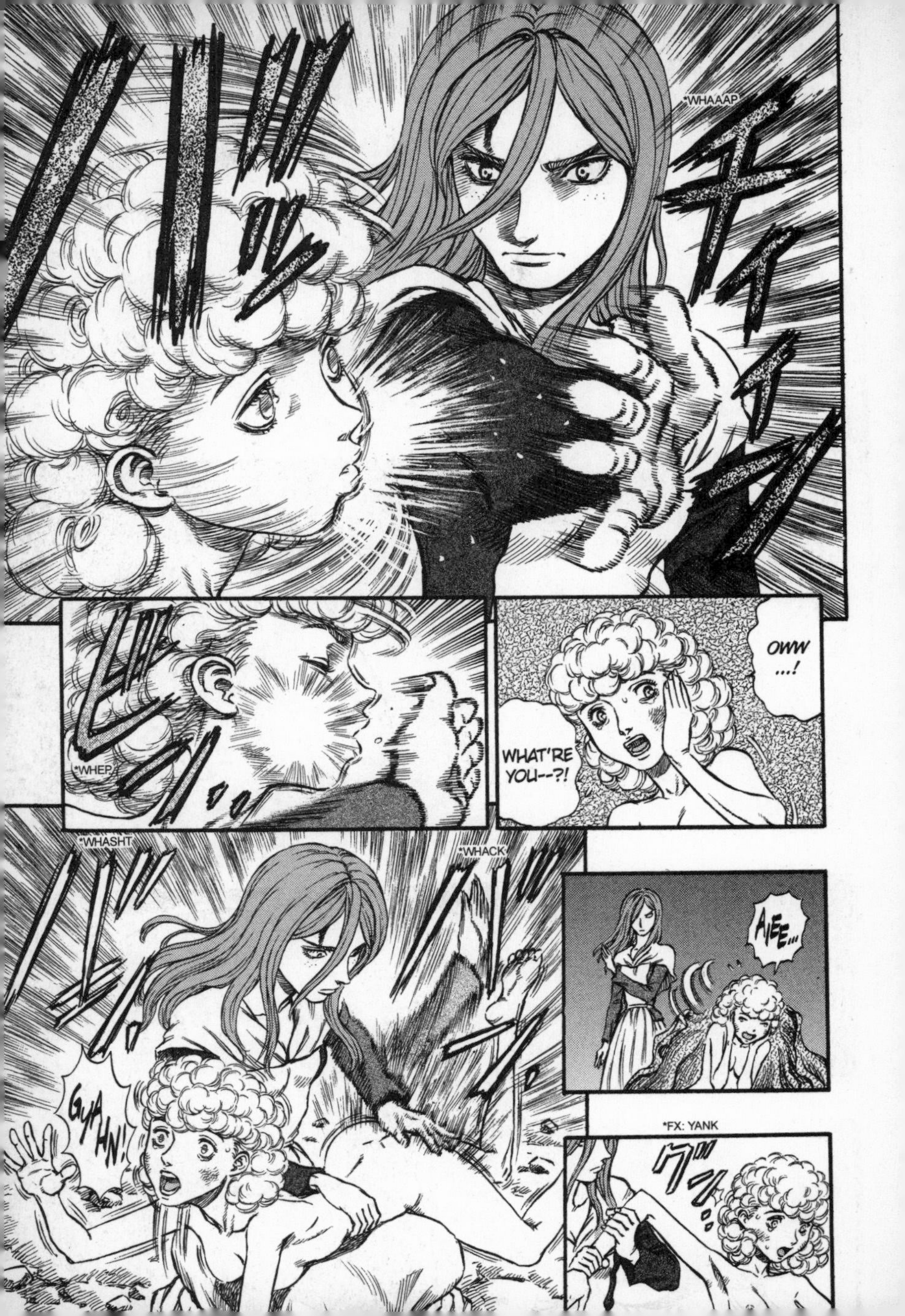
*WHAAAP
OWW ...!
WHAT'RE YOU--?!
*WHEP
AIEE...
*FX: YANK
*WHASHT
*WHACK
GYAHN!

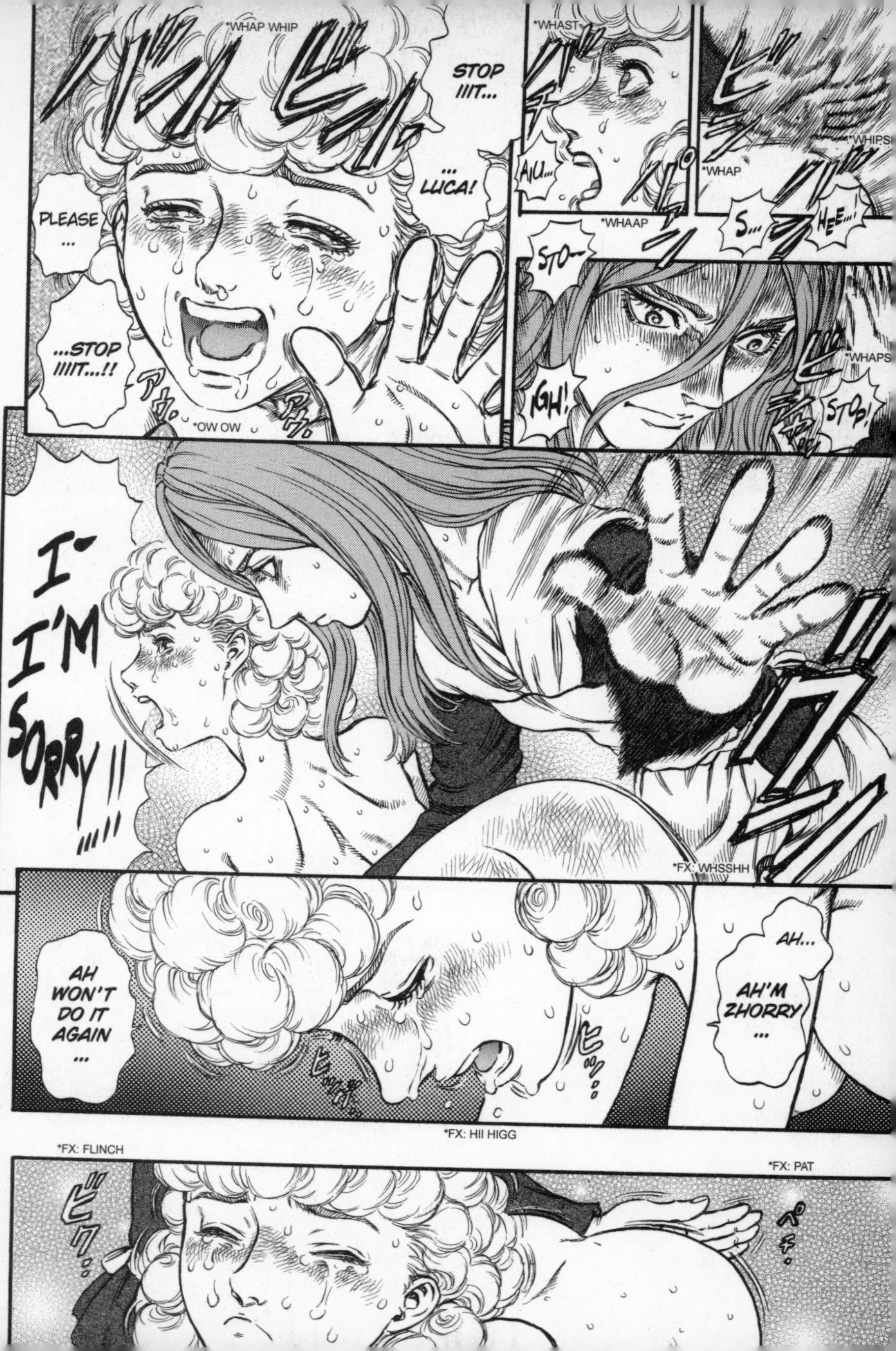
*WHIPS
*WHAP
S...
HEE...!
*WHAST
AU...
*WHAAP
STO--
*WHAPS
GH!
STOP!
*WHAP WHIP
STOP IIIT...
...LUCA!
PLEASE ...
...STOP IIIIT...!!
*OW OW
I- I'M I'M SORRY!!
*FX: WHSSHH
AH... AH'M ZHORRY ...
AH WON'T DO IT AGAIN ...
*FX: HII HIGG
*FX: PAT
*FX: FLINCH

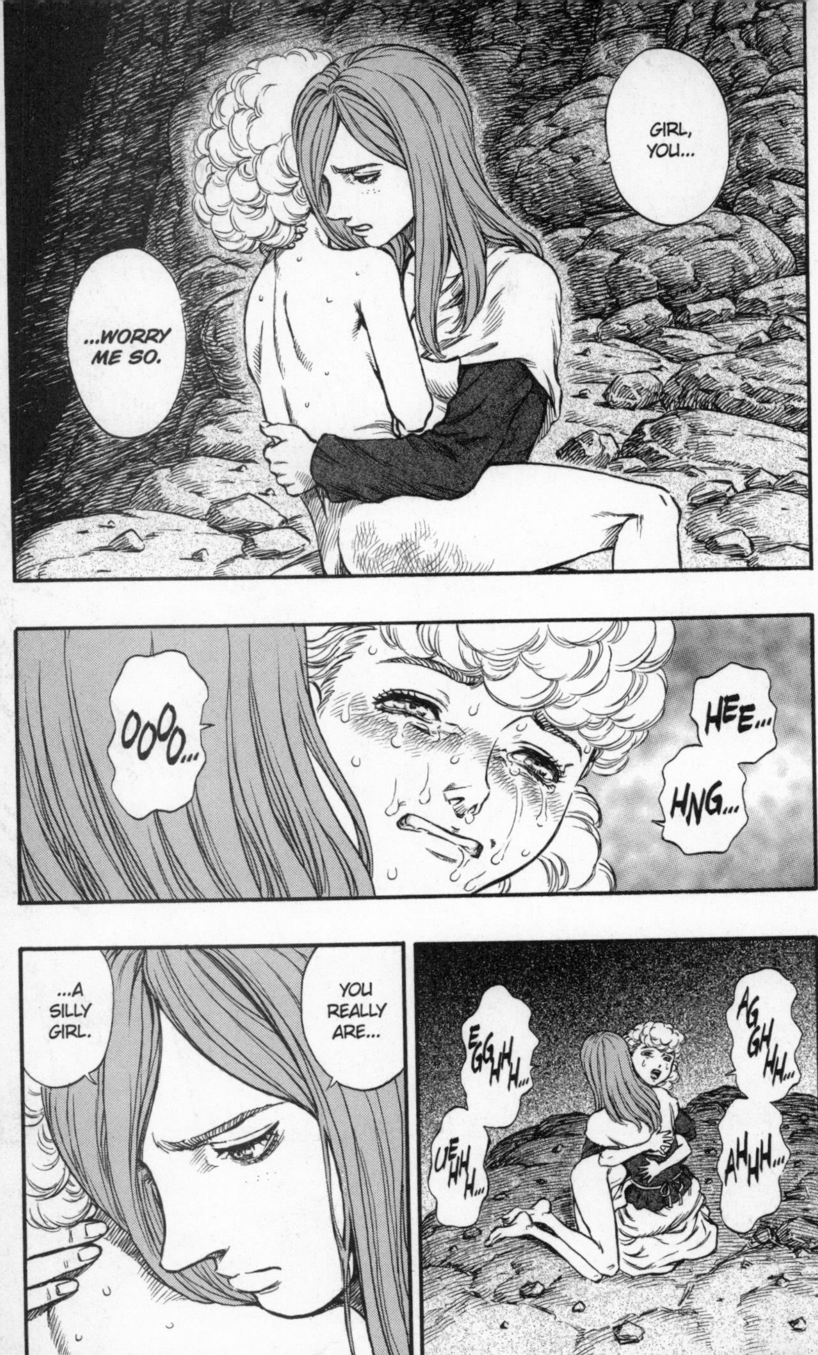
GIRL, YOU...
...WORRY ME SO.
HEE...
HNG...
OOOO...
AGGHHH...
EGGHHH...
AHHH...
UEHHH...
YOU REALLY ARE...
...A SILLY GIRL.

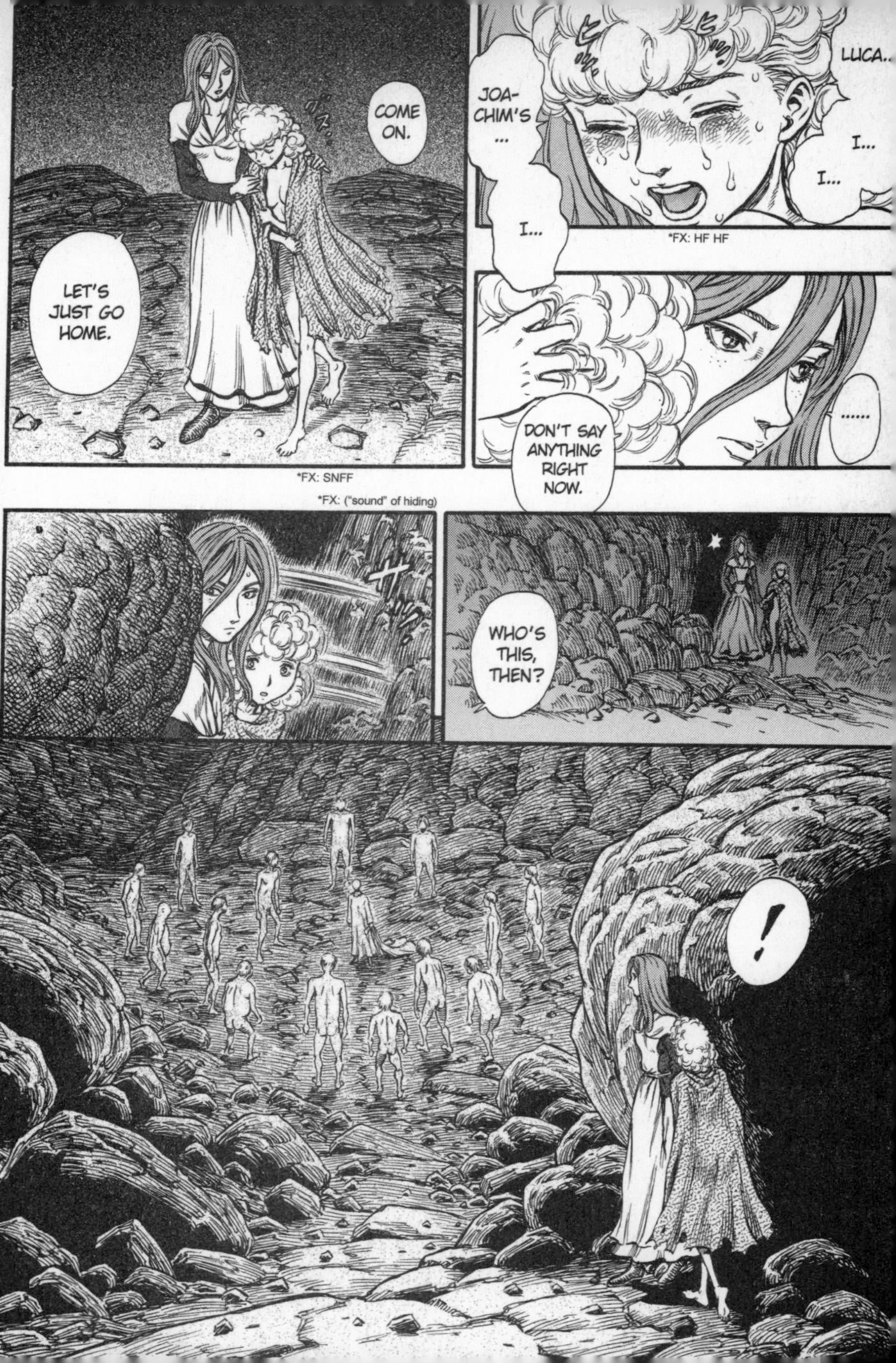
LUCA...
I...
I...
JOA-CHIM'S ...
I...
*FX: HF HF
......
DON'T SAY ANYTHING RIGHT NOW.
COME ON.
LET'S JUST GO HOME.
*FX: SNFF
WHO'S THIS, THEN?
*FX: ("sound" of hiding)
!

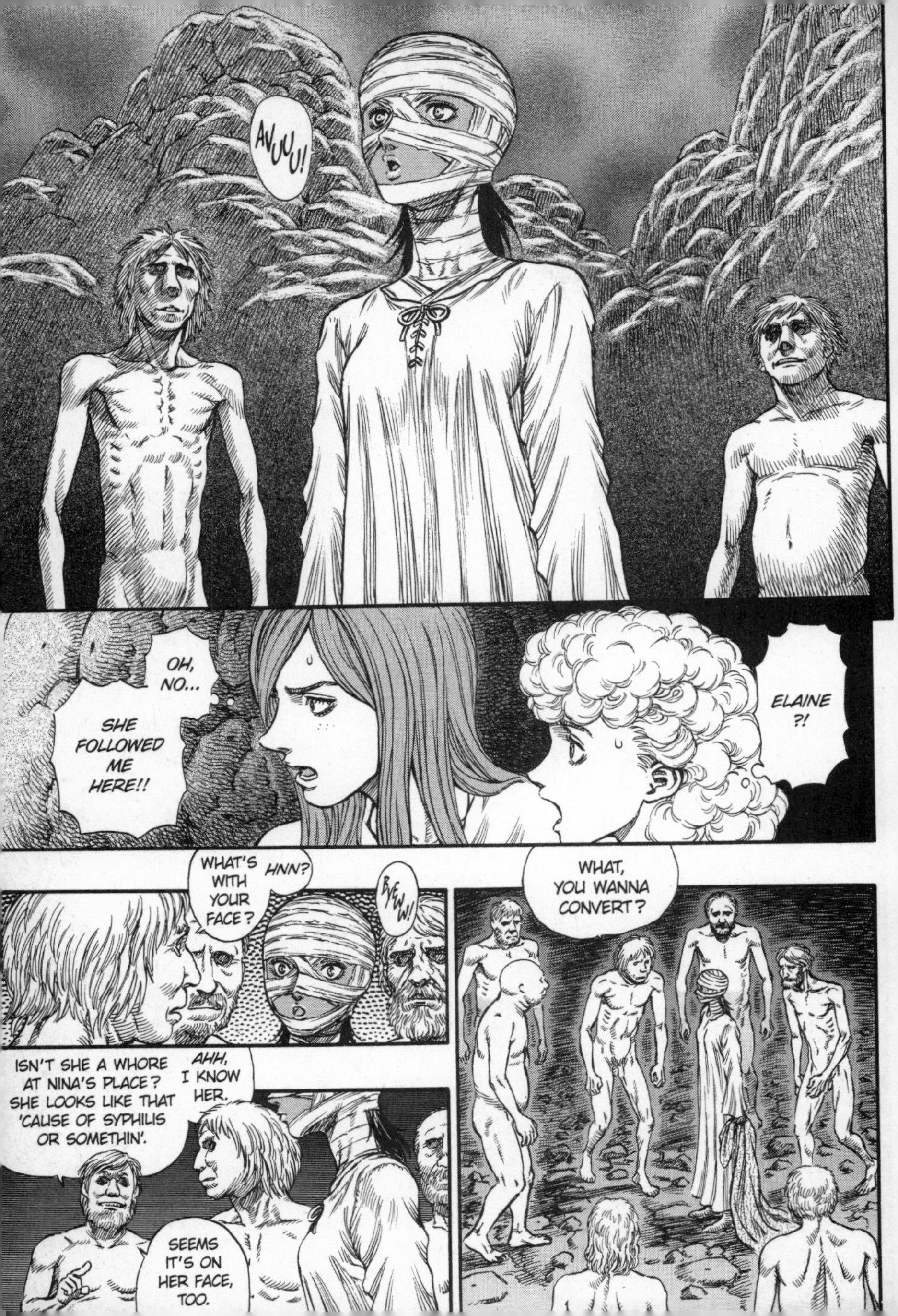
AVUUU!
ELAINE ?!
OH, NO...
SHE FOLLOWED ME HERE!!
WHAT, YOU WANNA CONVERT?
BYEW!
HNN?
WHAT'S WITH YOUR FACE?
AHH, I KNOW HER.
ISN'T SHE A WHORE AT NINA'S PLACE? SHE LOOKS LIKE THAT 'CAUSE OF SYPHILIS OR SOMETHIN'.
SEEMS IT'S ON HER FACE, TOO.

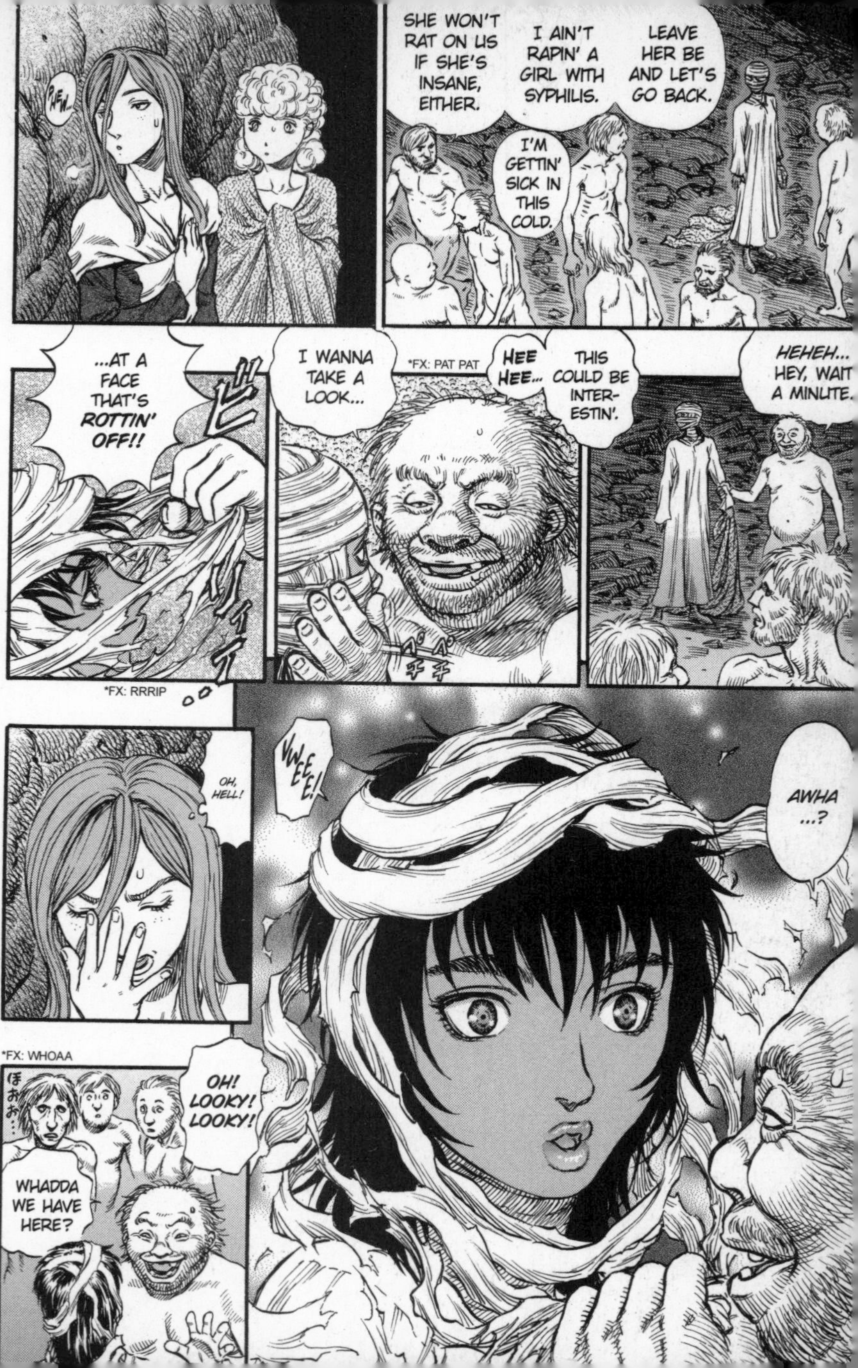
LEAVE HER BE AND LET'S GO BACK.
I AIN'T RAPIN' A GIRL WITH SYPHILIS.
SHE WON'T RAT ON US IF SHE'S INSANE, EITHER.
I'M GETTIN' SICK IN THIS COLD.
PHEW...
HEHEH... HEY, WAIT A MINUTE.
THIS COULD BE INTER-ESTIN'.
HEE HEE...
*FX: PAT PAT
I WANNA TAKE A LOOK...
...AT A FACE THAT'S ROTTIN' OFF!!
*FX: RRRIP
AWHA ...?
VWEEE!
OH, HELL!
*FX: WHOAA
OH! LOOKY! LOOKY!
WHADDA WE HAVE HERE?

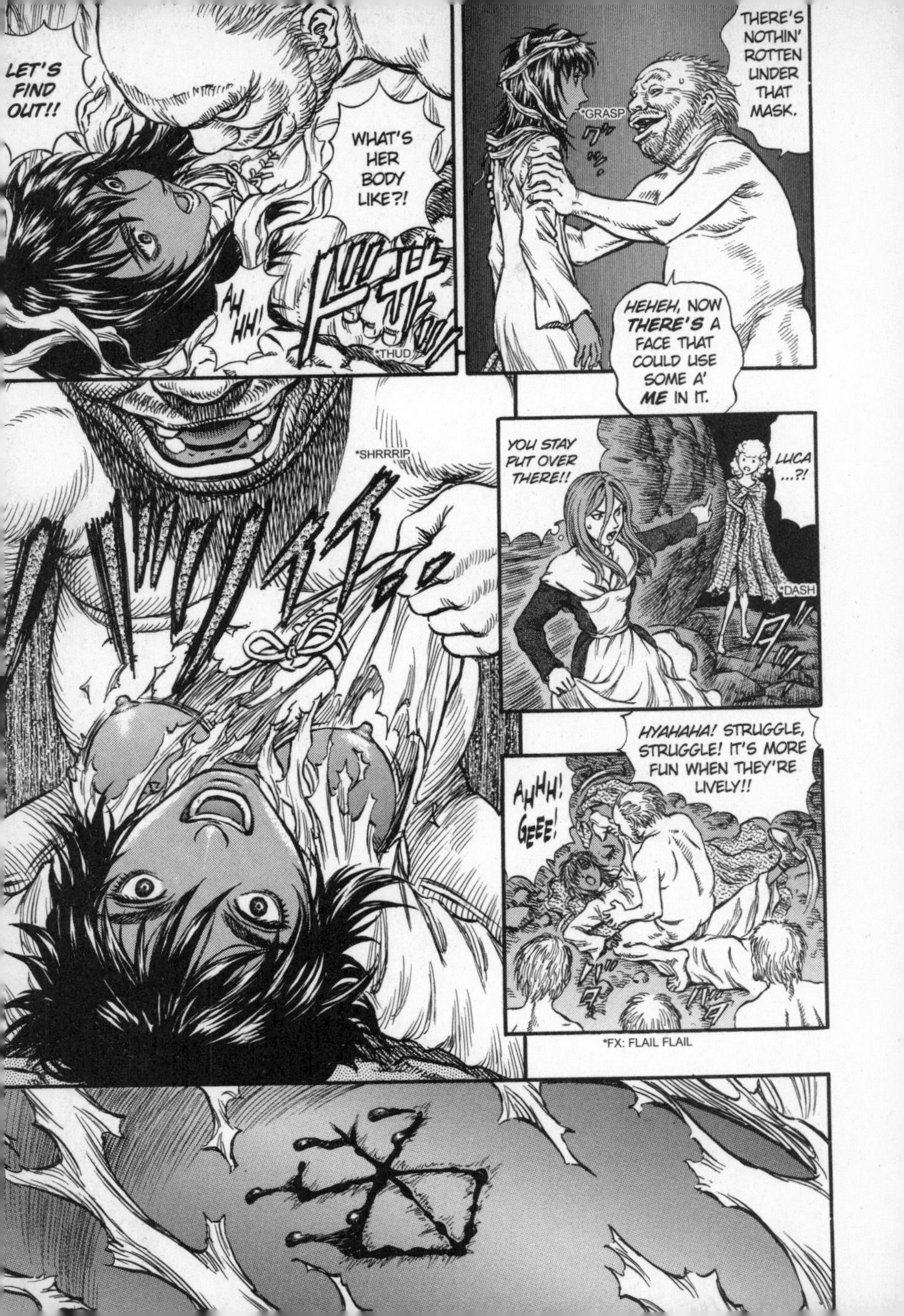
THERE'S NOTHIN' ROTTEN UNDER THAT MASK.
*GRASP
HEHEH, NOW THERE'S A FACE THAT COULD USE SOME A' ME IN IT.
WHAT'S HER BODY LIKE?!
LET'S FIND OUT!!
AHHH!
*THUD
LUCA ...?!
YOU STAY PUT OVER THERE!!
*DASH
HYAHAHA! STRUGGLE, STRUGGLE! IT'S MORE FUN WHEN THEY'RE LIVELY!!
AHHH! GEEE!
*FX: FLAIL FLAIL
*SHRRRIP

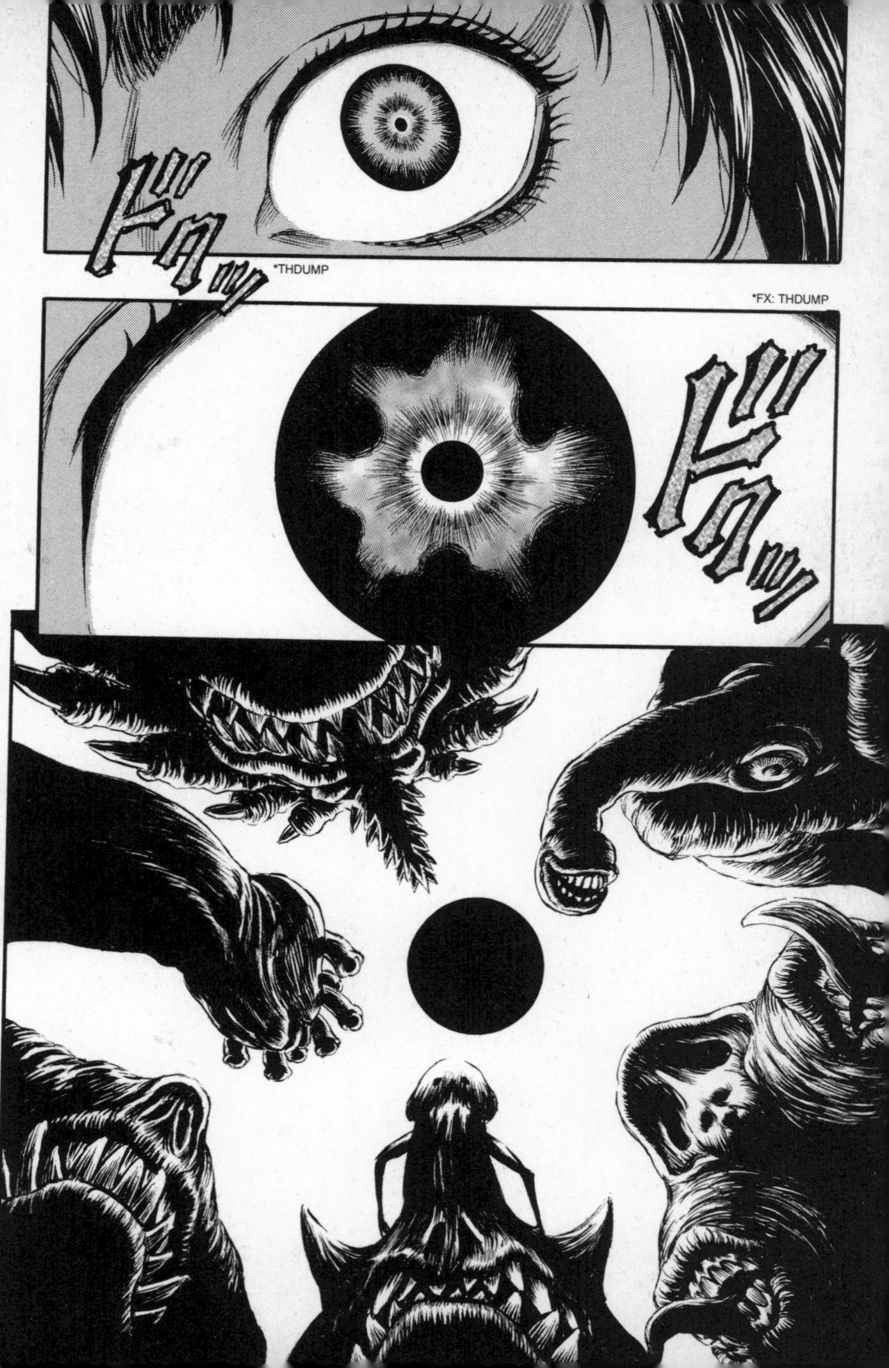
ドクッ
*THDUMP
ドクッ
*FX: THDUMP

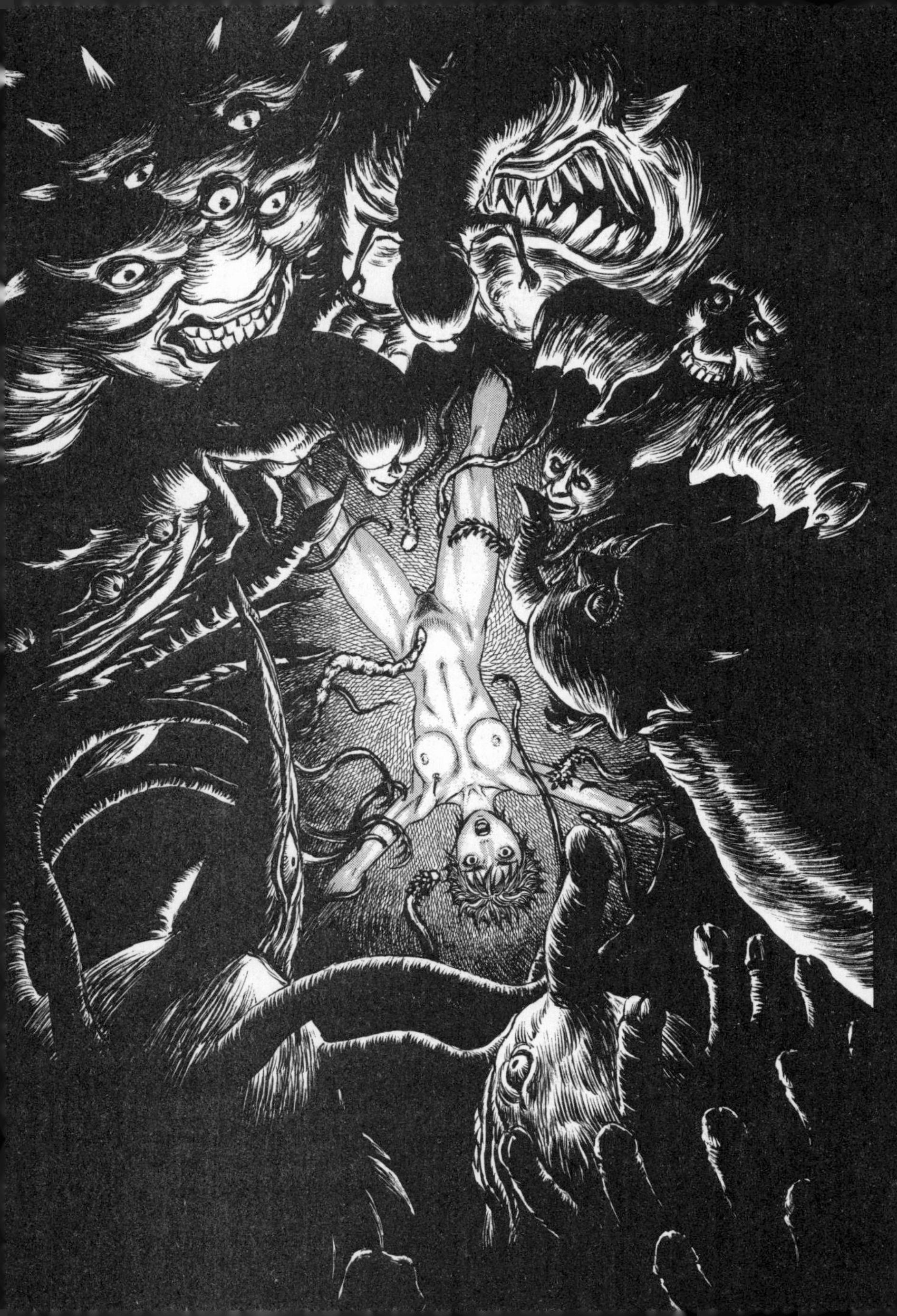

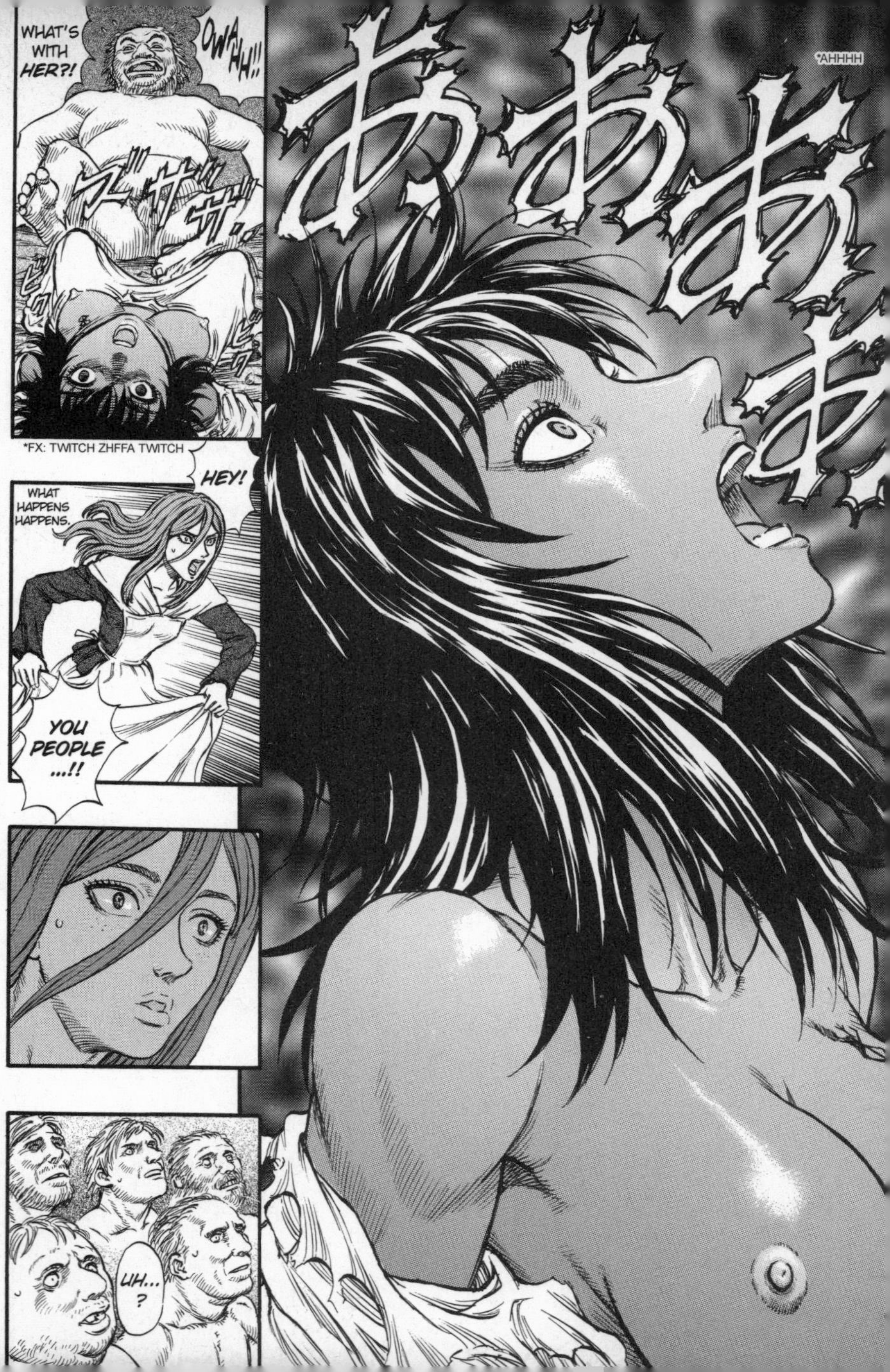

あああああ
*AHHHH
OWAHH!!
WHAT'S WITH HER?!
*FX: TWITCH ZHFFA TWITCH
HEY!
WHAT HAPPENS HAPPENS.
YOU PEOPLE ...!!
UH... ?

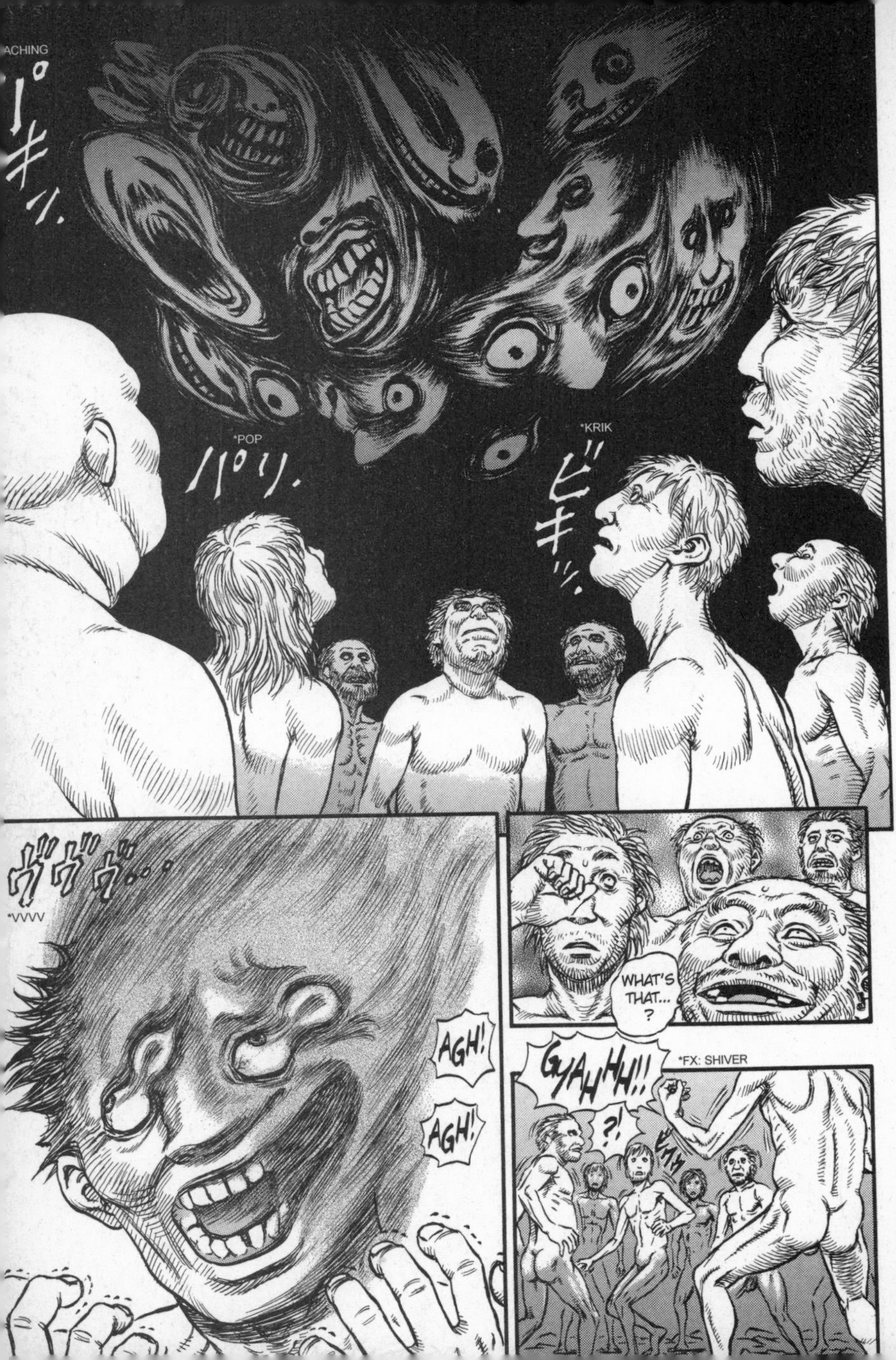
*ACHING
ポキン.
*KRIK
ビキッ.
*POP
パリ.
WHAT'S THAT... ?
*FX: SHIVER
GYAHHH!!
?!
ヴヴヴ...
*VVVV
AGH!
AGH!

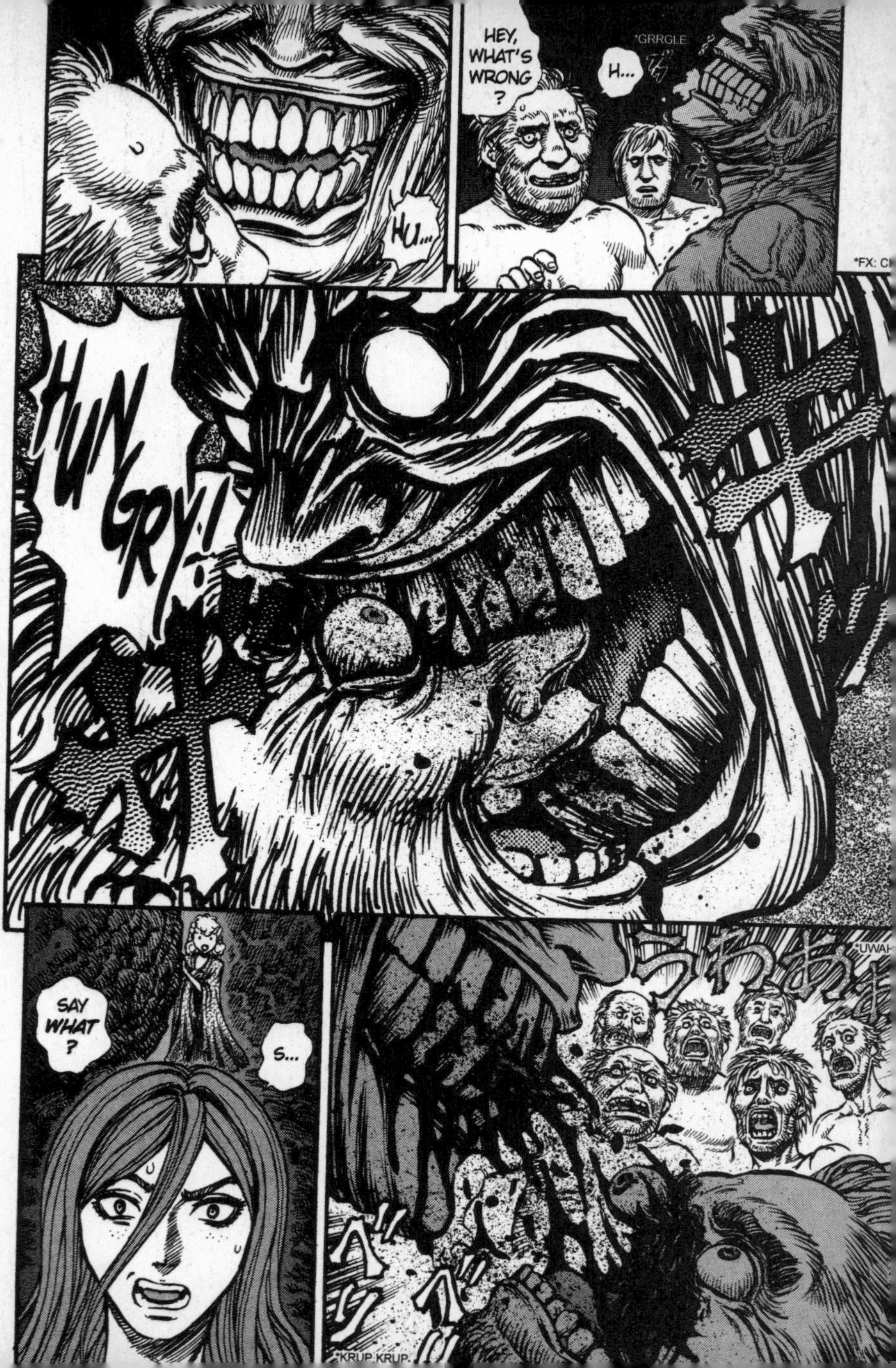
HEY, WHAT'S WRONG ?
H...
*GRRGLE
*FX: C
HU...
HUNGRY!!
*UWAH
S...
SAY WHAT ?
*KRUP KRUP

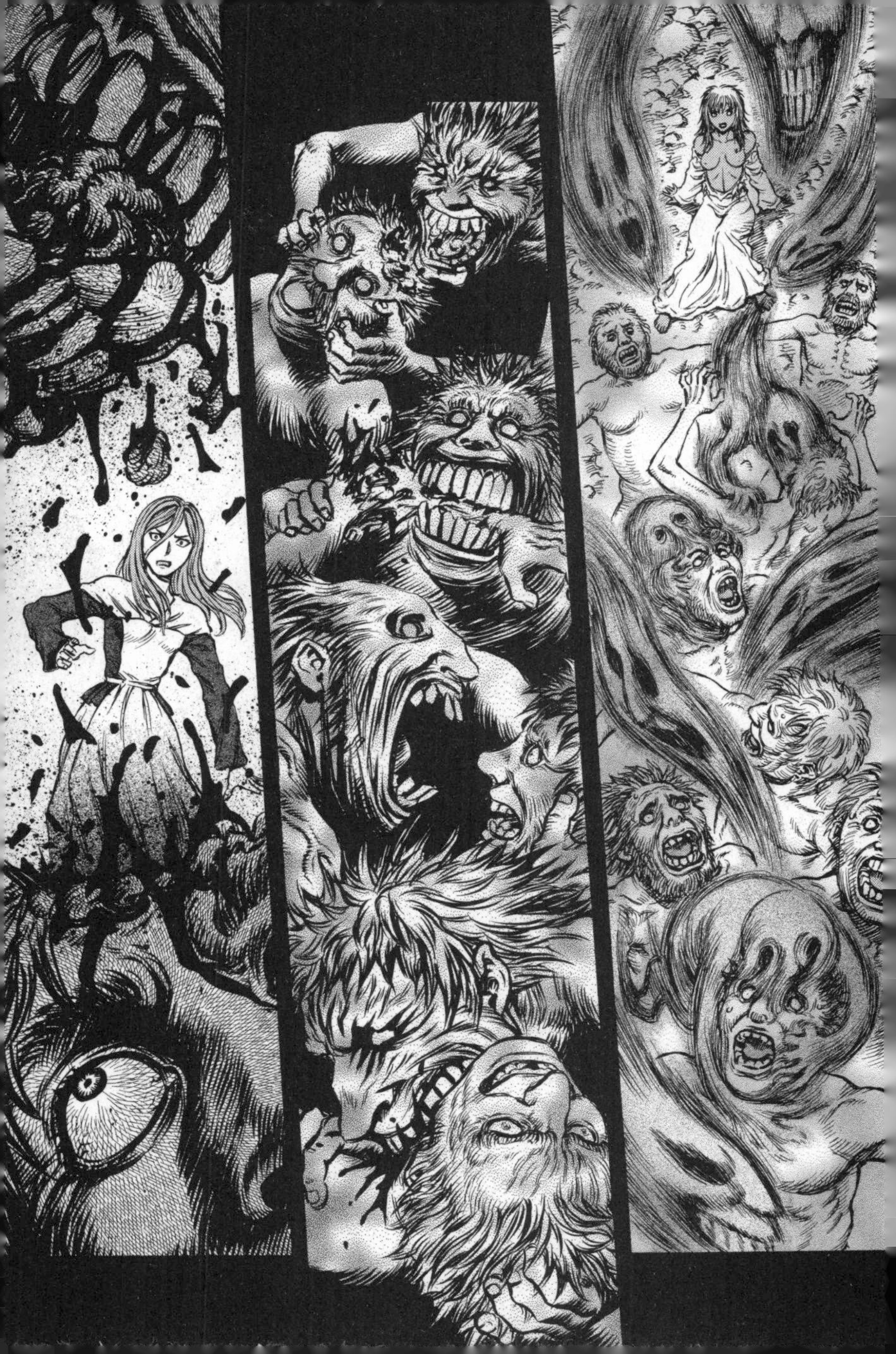

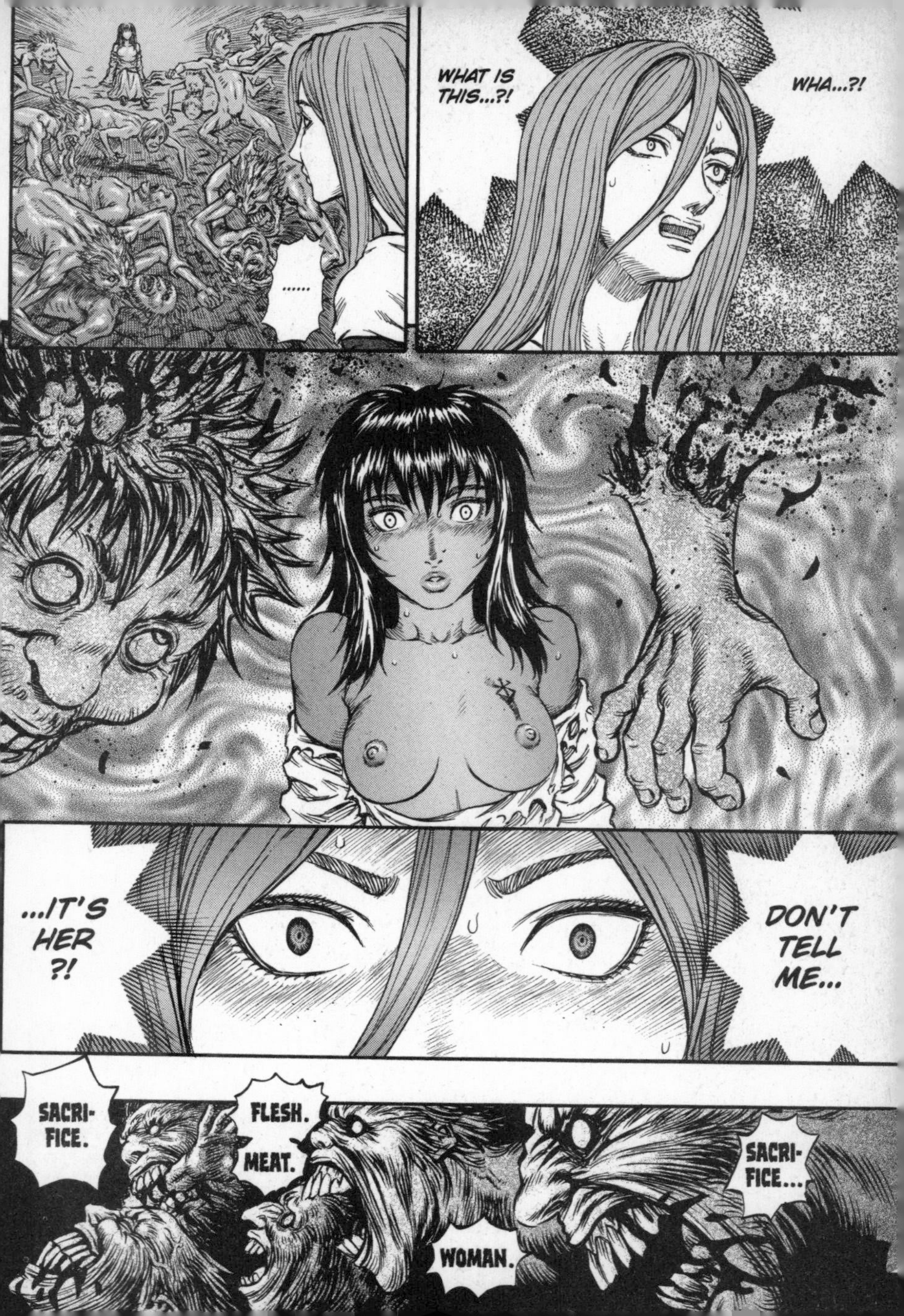
WHA...?!
WHAT IS THIS...?!
......
DON'T TELL ME...
...IT'S HER ?!
SACRI-FICE...
FLESH.
MEAT.
SACRI-FICE.
WOMAN.

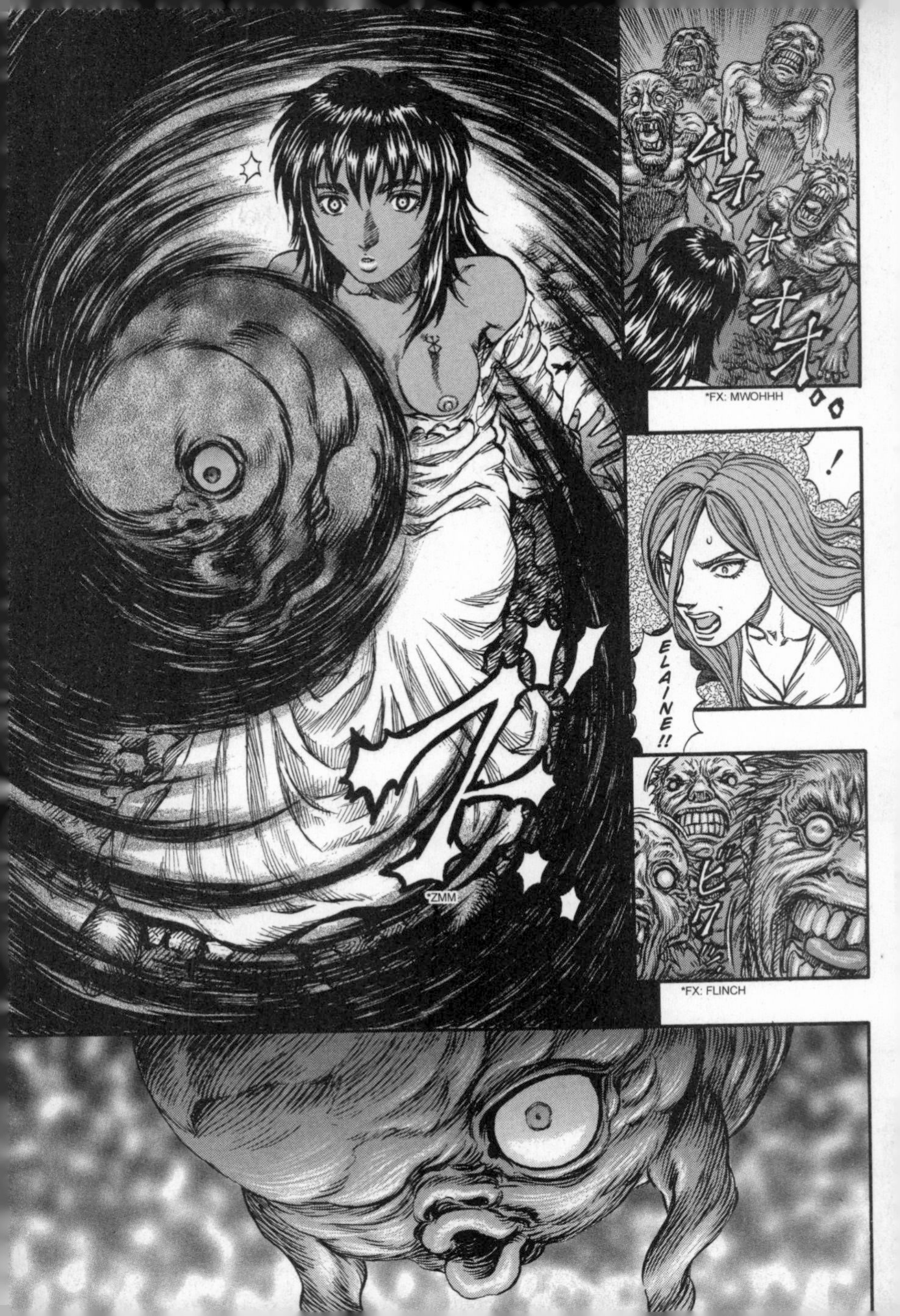
*FX: MWOHHH
!
ELAINE!!
*FX: FLINCH
*ZMM

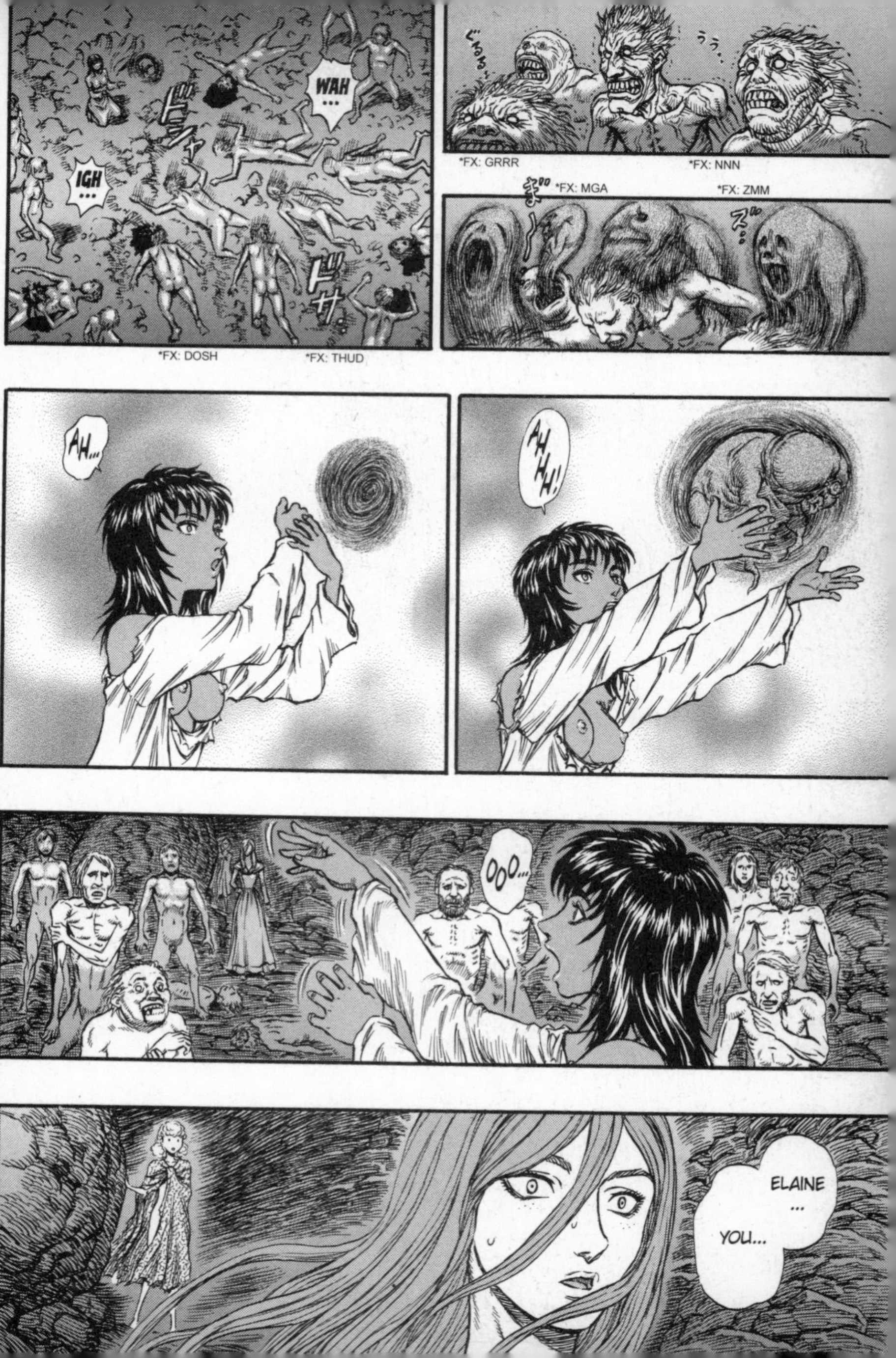
*FX: NNN
*FX: GRRR
*FX: ZMM
*FX: MGA
WAH...
IGH...
*FX: THUD
*FX: DOSH
AHHH!
AH...
OOO...
ELAINE ...
YOU...

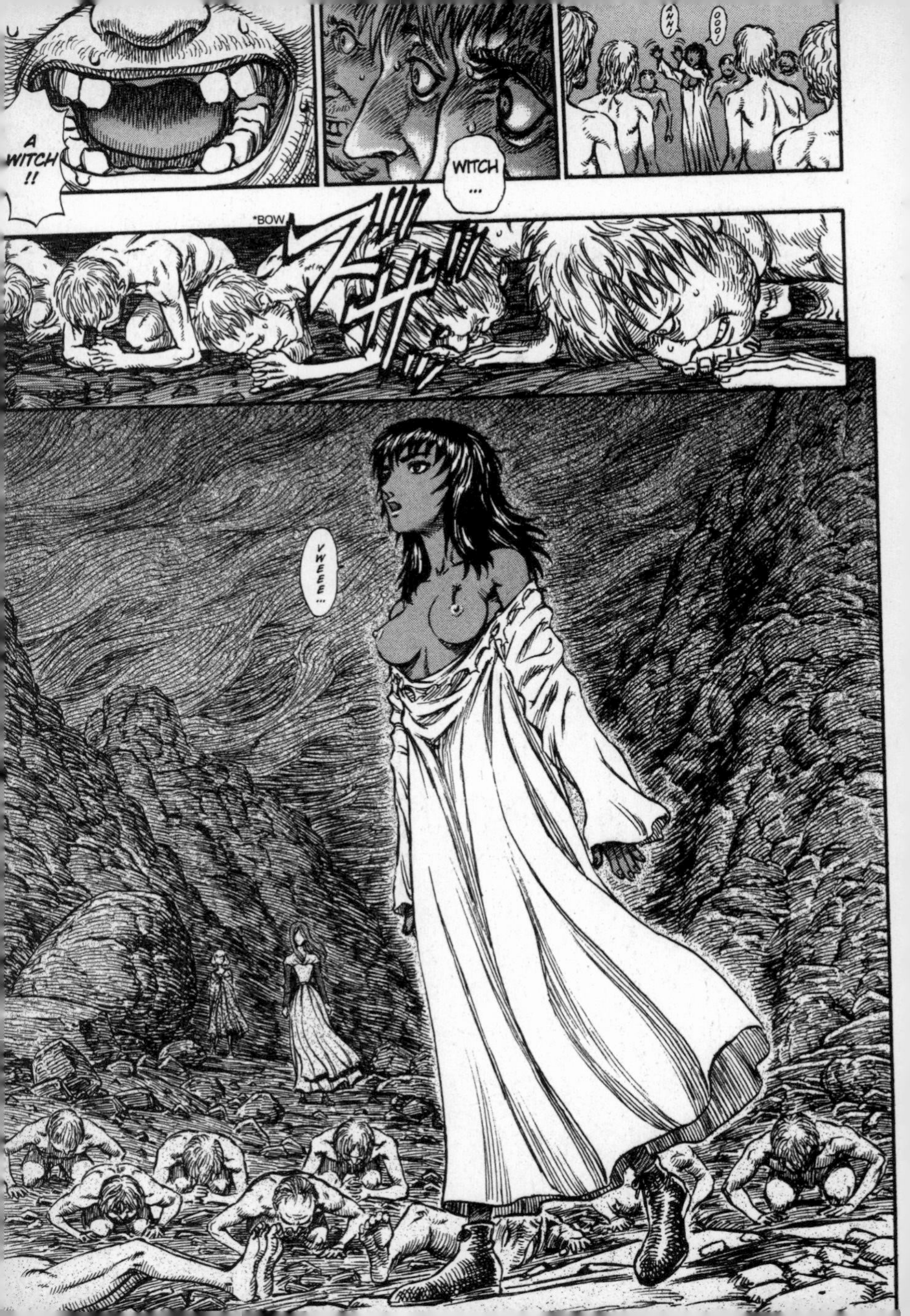
OOO!
AHH!
WITCH ...
A WITCH !!
*BOW
VWEEE ...

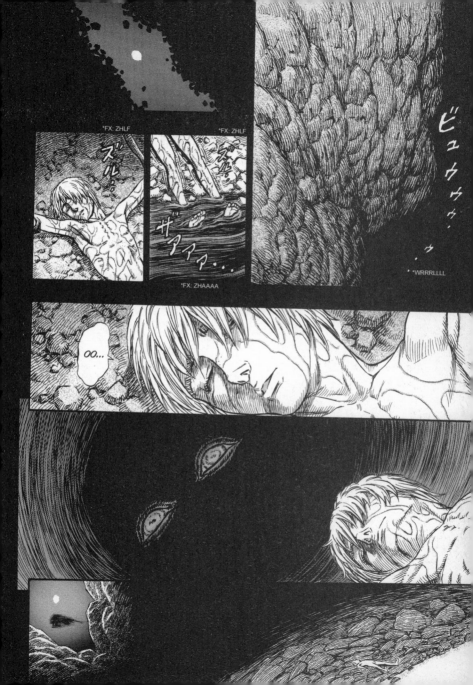

*FX: ZHLF

*FX: ZHLF

ズル

ザァァ・・・・

*FX: ZHAAAA

ビュウウ・・
ゥ

* *WRRRLLLL

OO...

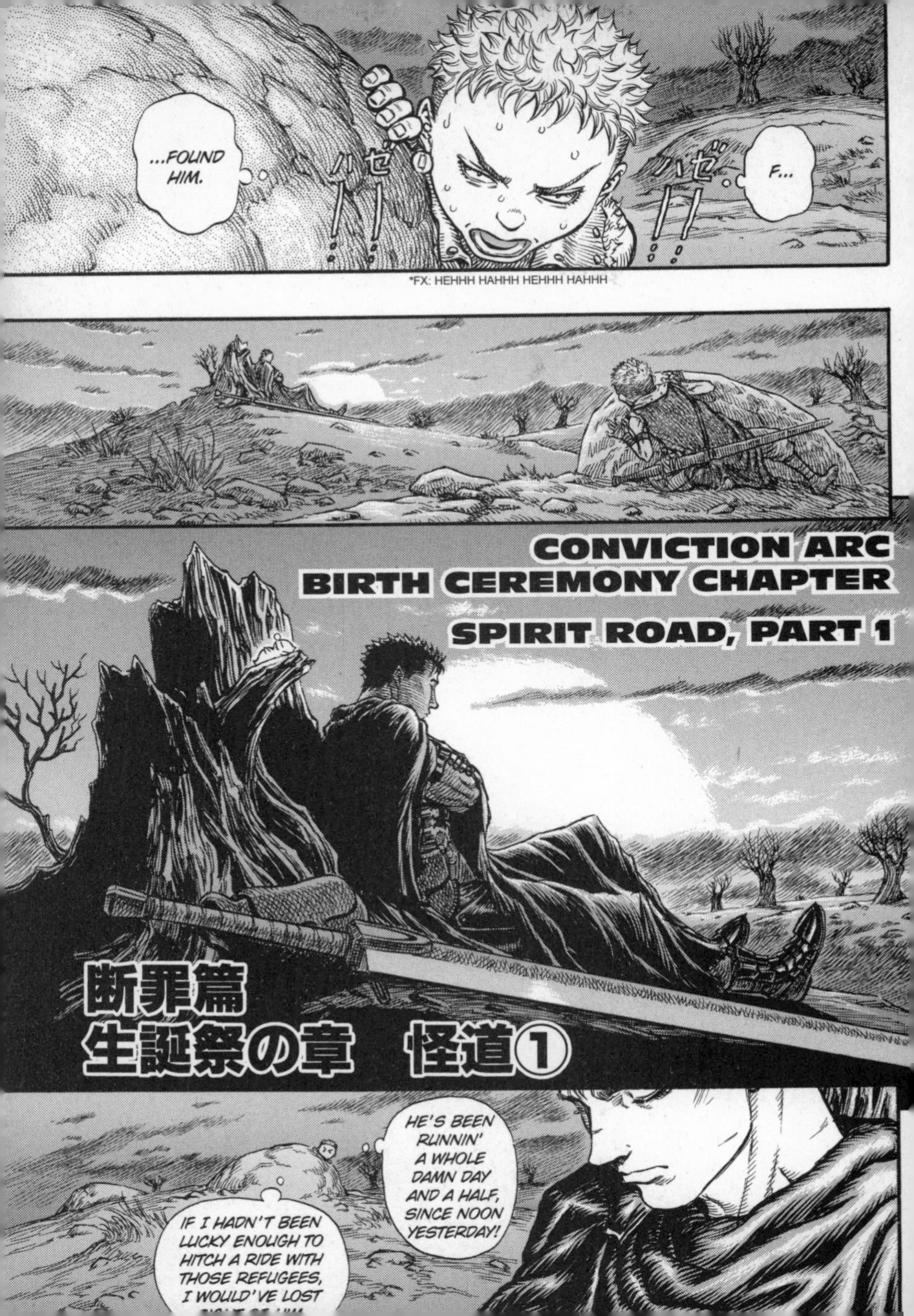
F...
ハゼ!!
ハゼ!!
...FOUND HIM.
*FX: HEHHH HAHHH HEHHH HAHHH
CONVICTION ARC
BIRTH CEREMONY CHAPTER
SPIRIT ROAD, PART 1
断罪篇
生誕祭の章　怪道①
HE'S BEEN RUNNIN' A WHOLE DAMN DAY AND A HALF, SINCE NOON YESTERDAY!
IF I HADN'T BEEN LUCKY ENOUGH TO HITCH A RIDE WITH THOSE REFUGEES, I WOULD'VE LOST

*FX: SHMP

*FX: GRASP

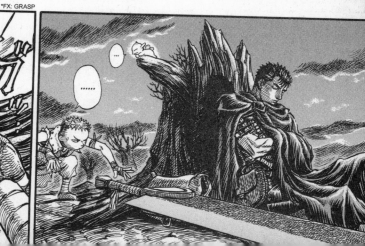

...

......

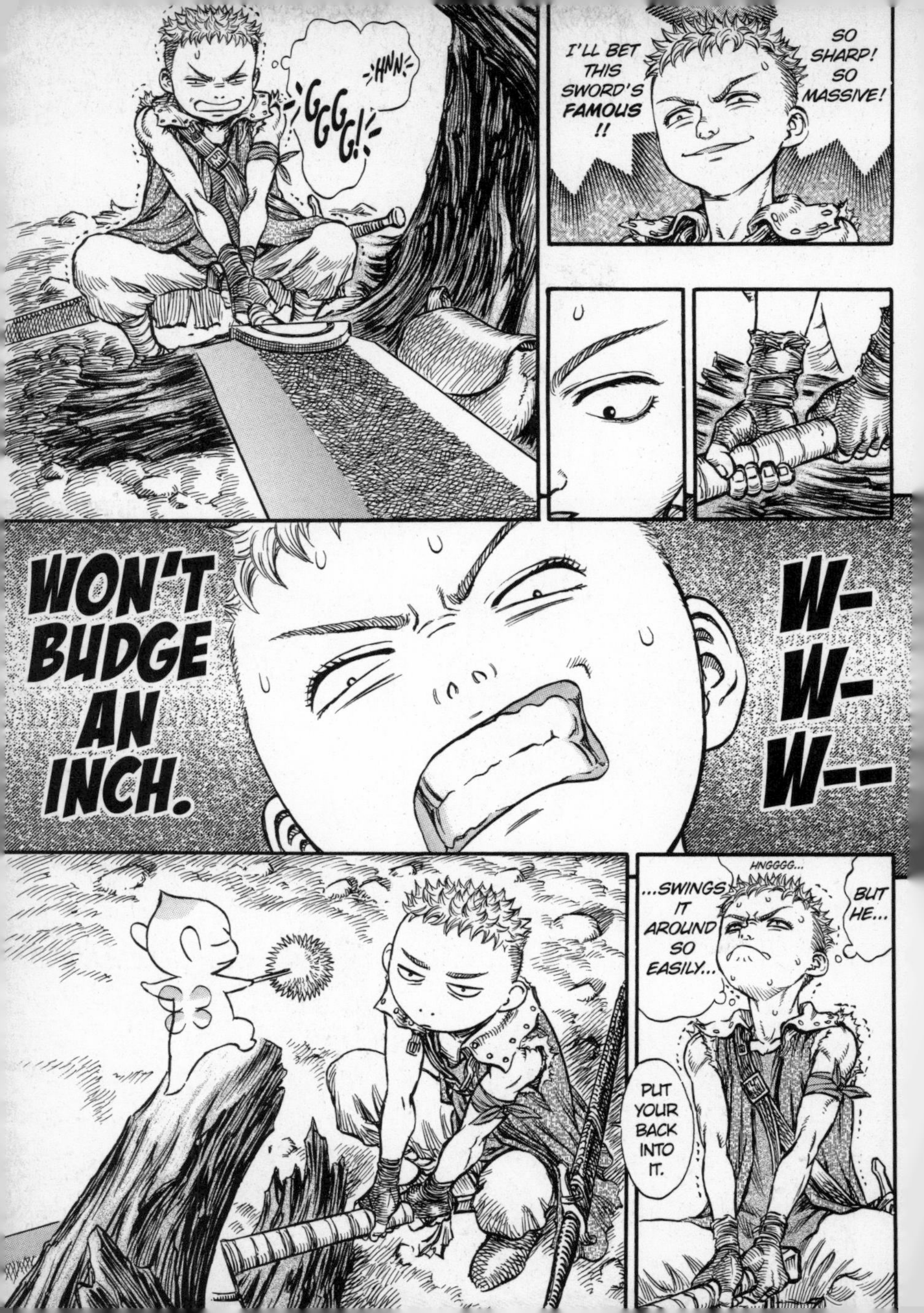
SO SHARP! SO MASSIVE!
I'LL BET THIS SWORD'S FAMOUS !!
HNN
GGGG!
W-W-W--
WON'T BUDGE AN INCH.
BUT HE...
HNGGGG...
...SWINGS IT AROUND SO EASILY...
PUT YOUR BACK INTO IT.

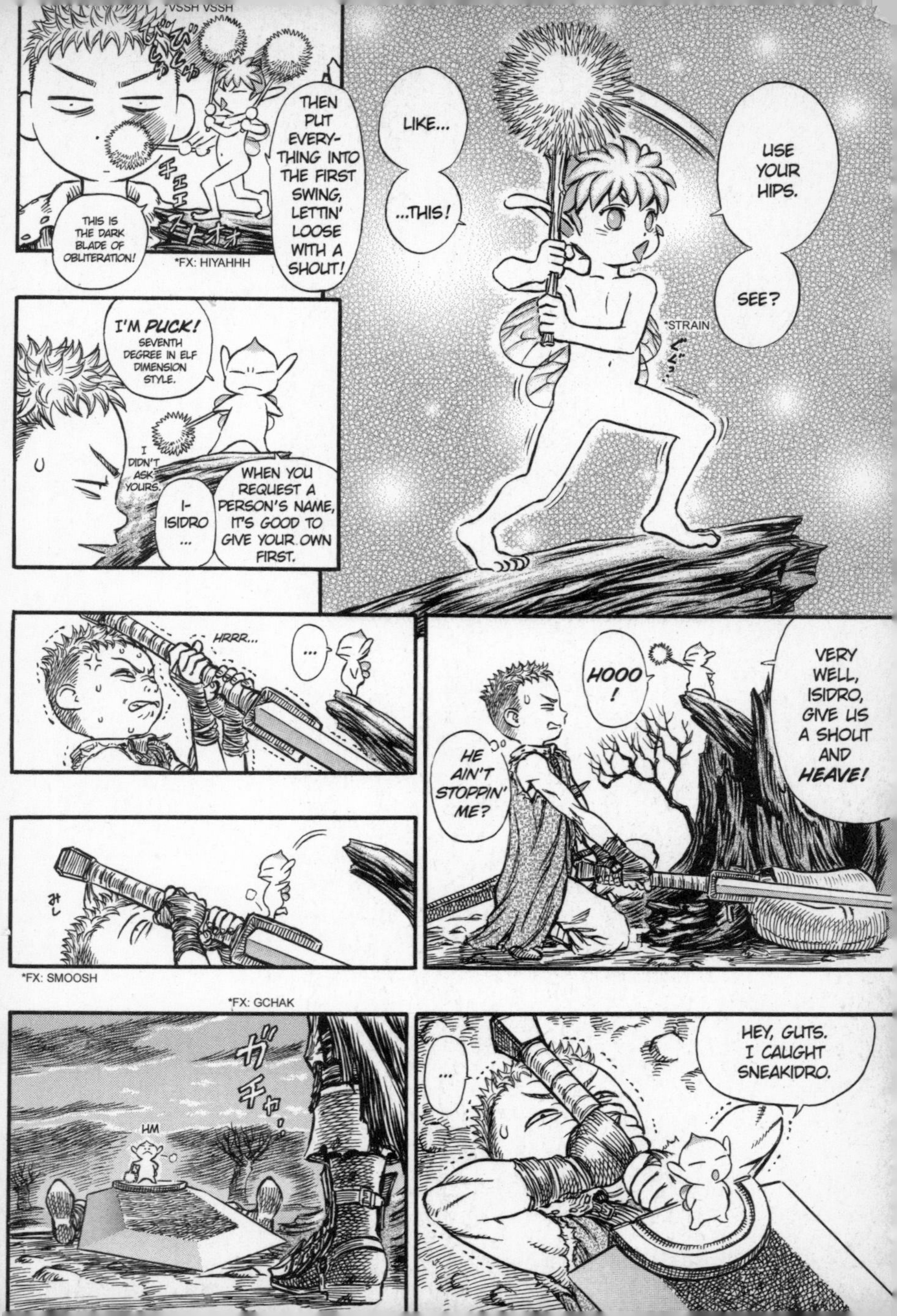
USE YOUR HIPS.
LIKE...
...THIS!
SEE?
*STRAIN
VSSH VSSH
THEN PUT EVERY-THING INTO THE FIRST SWING, LETTIN' LOOSE WITH A SHOUT!
THIS IS THE DARK BLADE OF OBLITERATION!
*FX: HIYAHHH
I'M PUCK! SEVENTH DEGREE IN ELF DIMENSION STYLE.
WHEN YOU REQUEST A PERSON'S NAME, IT'S GOOD TO GIVE YOUR OWN FIRST.
I-ISIDRO...
I DIDN'T ASK YOURS.
VERY WELL, ISIDRO, GIVE US A SHOUT AND HEAVE!
HOOO!
HE AIN'T STOPPIN' ME?
HRRR...
...
*FX: SMOOSH
HEY, GUTS. I CAUGHT SNEAKIDRO.
...
*FX: GCHAK
HM

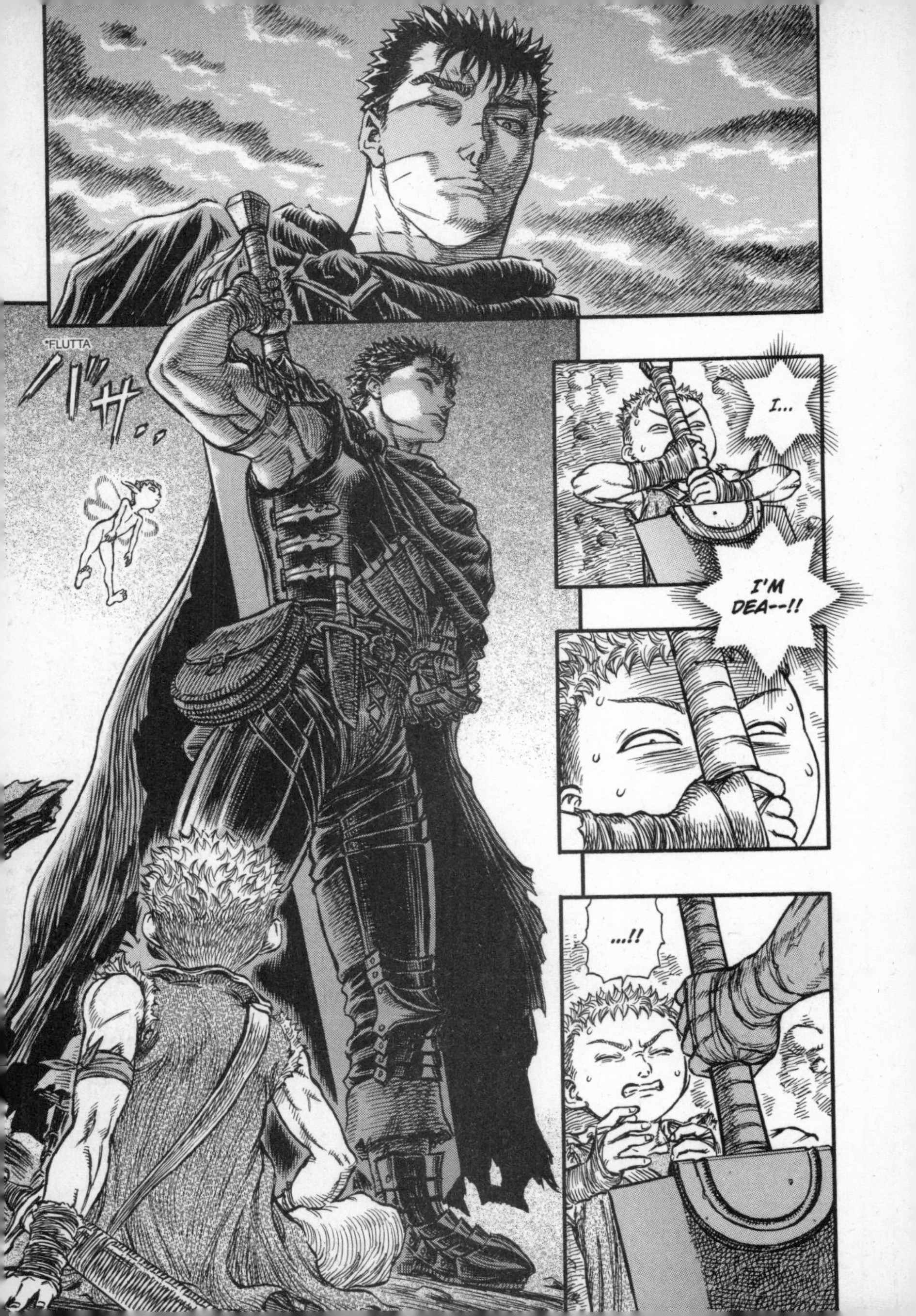
I...
I'M DEA--!!
...!!
ノバサ。。
*FLUTTA

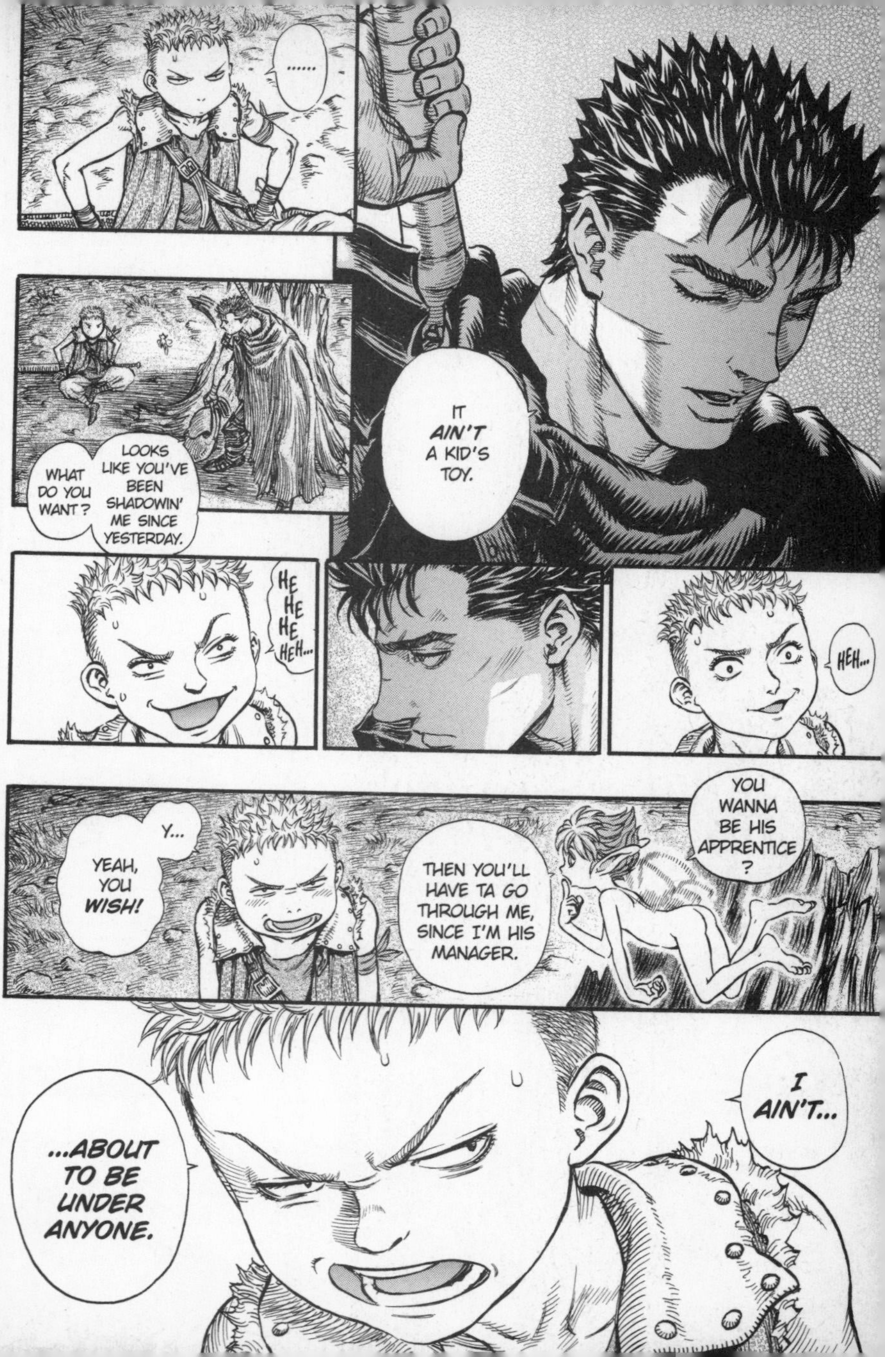
IT AIN'T A KID'S TOY.
......
LOOKS LIKE YOU'VE BEEN SHADOWIN' ME SINCE YESTERDAY.
WHAT DO YOU WANT?
HEH...
HE HE HE HE HEH...
YOU WANNA BE HIS APPRENTICE?
THEN YOU'LL HAVE TA GO THROUGH ME, SINCE I'M HIS MANAGER.
Y...
YEAH, YOU WISH!
I AIN'T...
...ABOUT TO BE UNDER ANYONE.

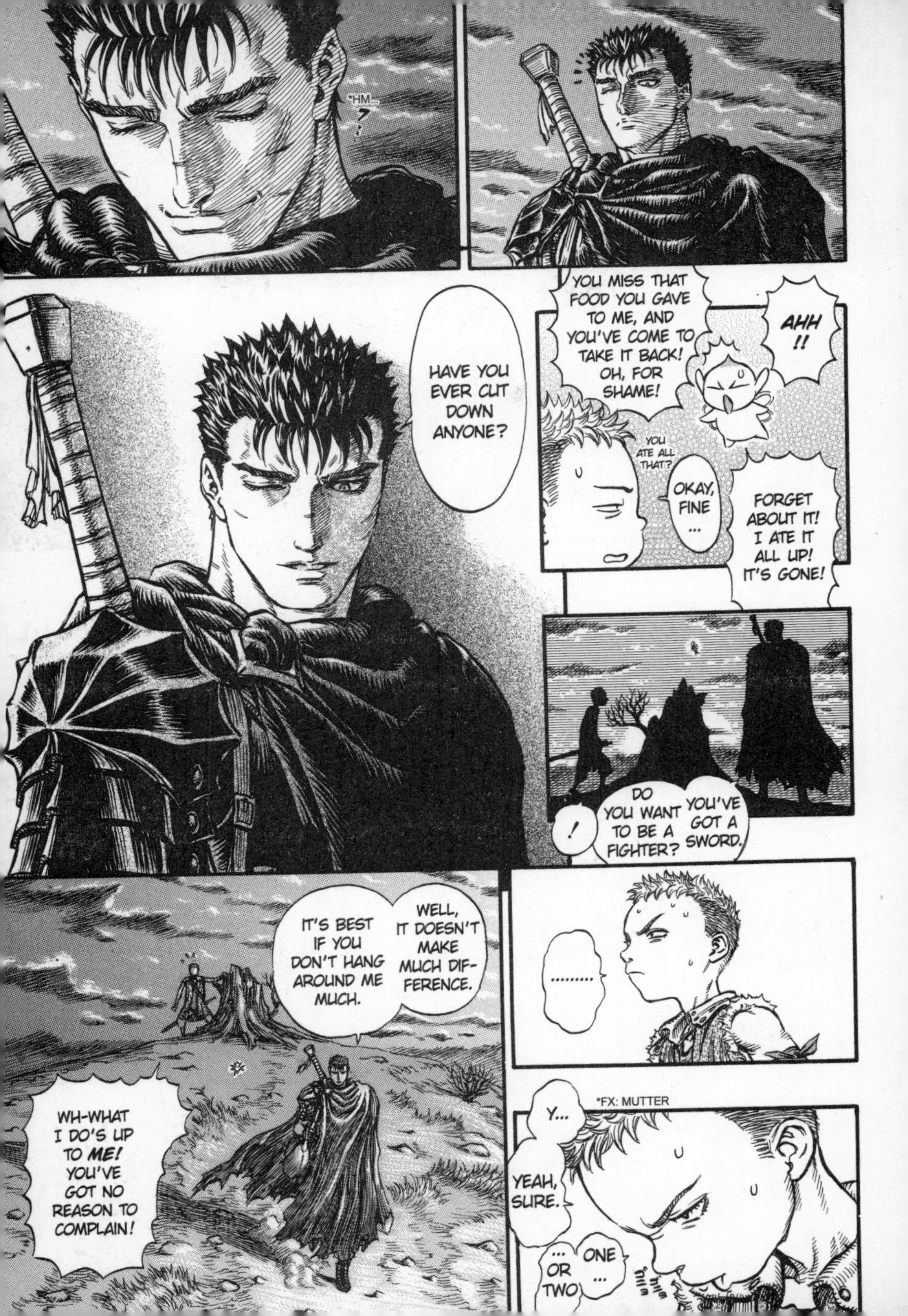
*HM...
?
AHH !!
YOU MISS THAT FOOD YOU GAVE TO ME, AND YOU'VE COME TO TAKE IT BACK! OH, FOR SHAME!
FORGET ABOUT IT! I ATE IT ALL UP! IT'S GONE!
YOU ATE ALL THAT?
OKAY, FINE ...
YOU'VE GOT A SWORD.
DO YOU WANT TO BE A FIGHTER?
!
HAVE YOU EVER CUT DOWN ANYONE?
....
*FX: MUTTER
Y...
YEAH, SURE.
ONE ...
... OR TWO
WELL, IT DOESN'T MAKE MUCH DIF-FERENCE.
IT'S BEST IF YOU DON'T HANG AROUND ME MUCH.
WH-WHAT I DO'S UP TO *ME!* YOU'VE GOT NO REASON TO COMPLAIN!

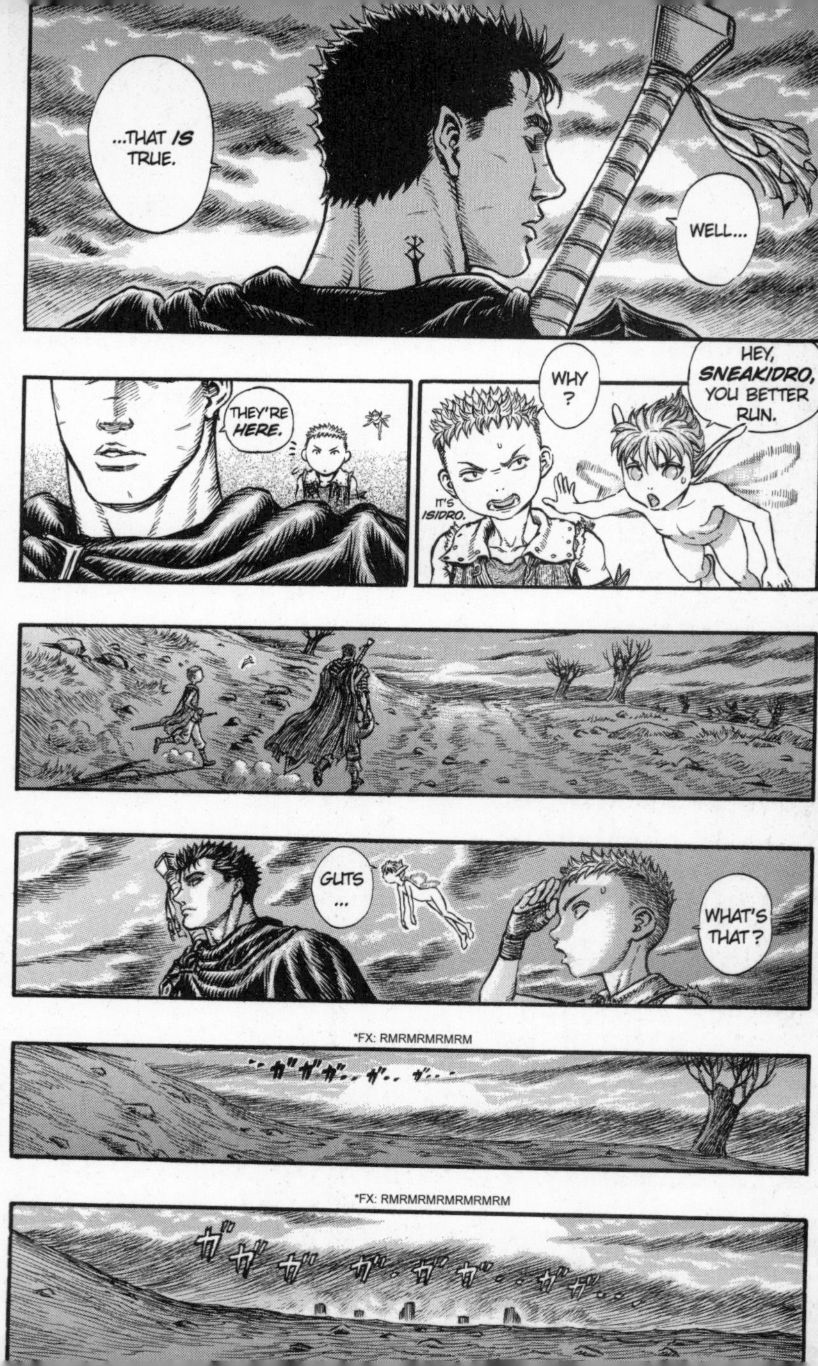
WELL...
...THAT *IS* TRUE.
HEY, *SNEAKIDRO,* YOU BETTER RUN.
WHY?
IT'S *ISIDRO.*
THEY'RE *HERE.*
WHAT'S THAT?
GUTS...
*FX: RMRMRMRMRM
*FX: RMRMRMRMRMRMRM

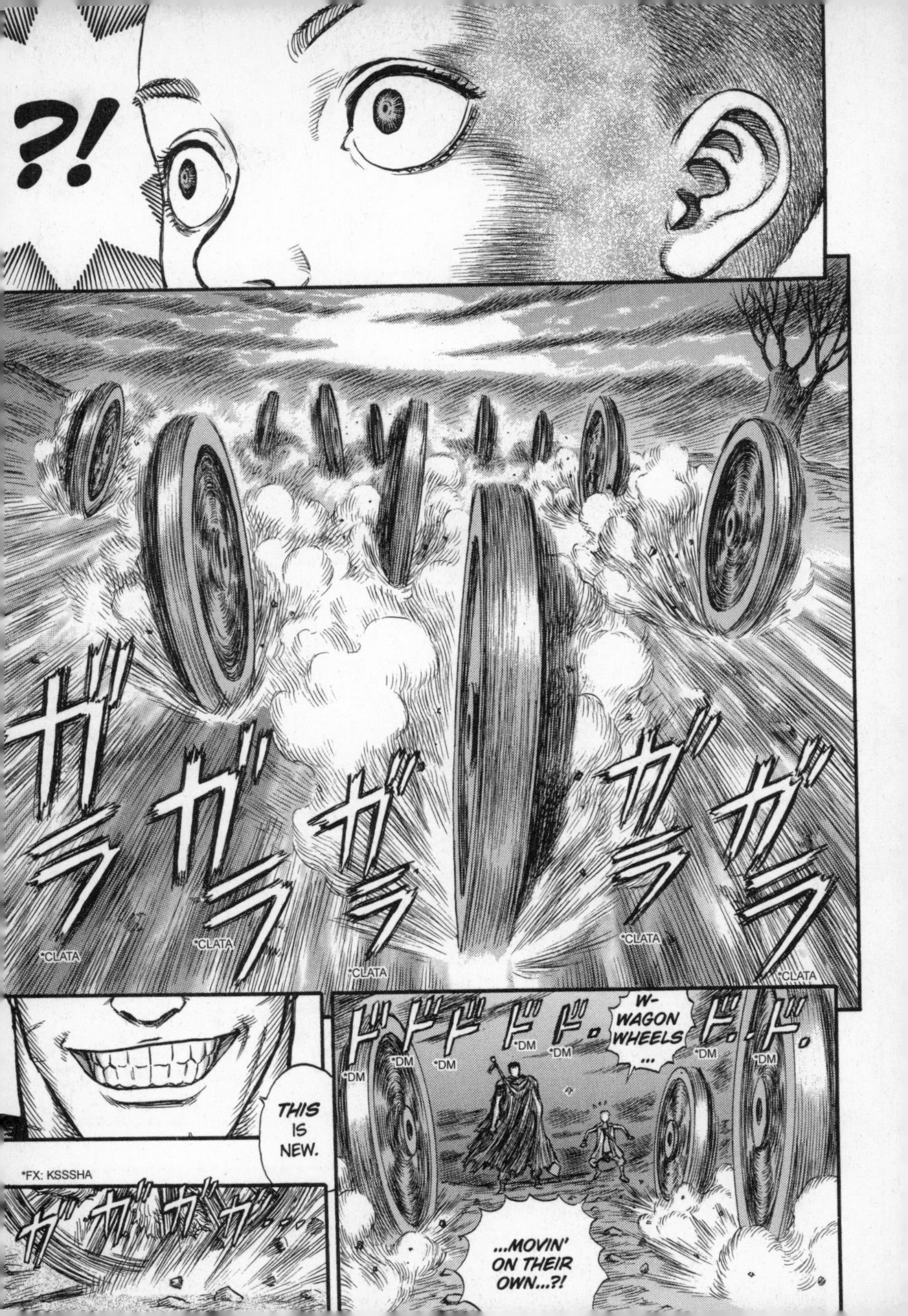
?!
ガラ
*CLATA
ガラ
*CLATA
ガラ
*CLATA
ガラ
*CLATA
ガラ
*CLATA
ドドドドド。
*DM
*DM
*DM
*DM
*DM
W-WAGON WHEELS...
ド。ド。
*DM
*DM
...MOVIN' ON THEIR OWN...?!
THIS IS NEW.
*FX: KSSSHA
ガガガガ...

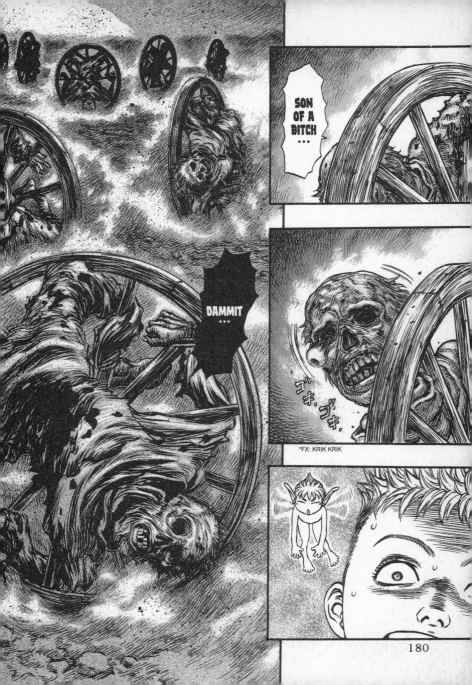

SON OF A BITCH ...

DAMMIT ...

*FX: KRIK KRIK

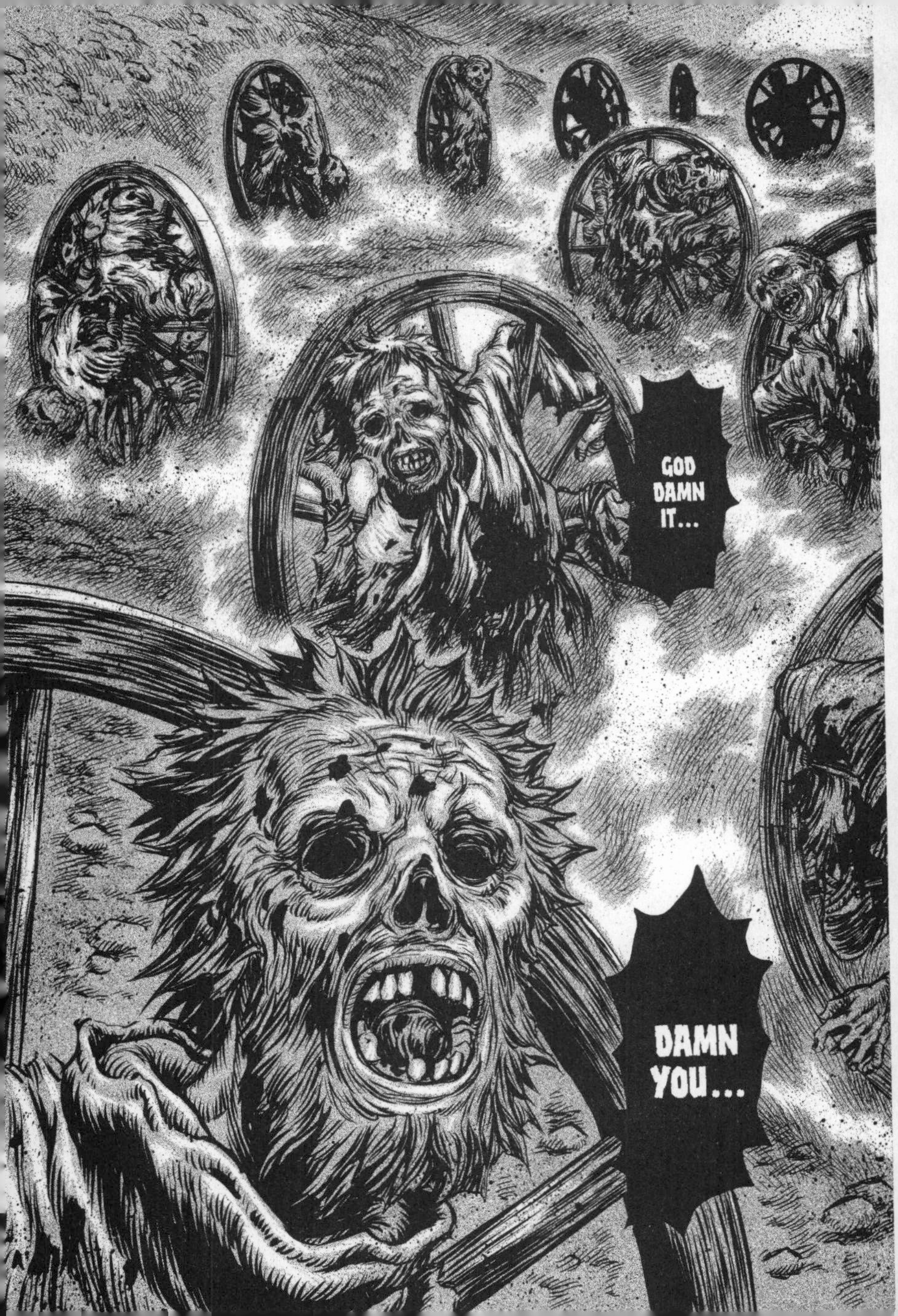
GOD DAMN IT...
DAMN YOU...

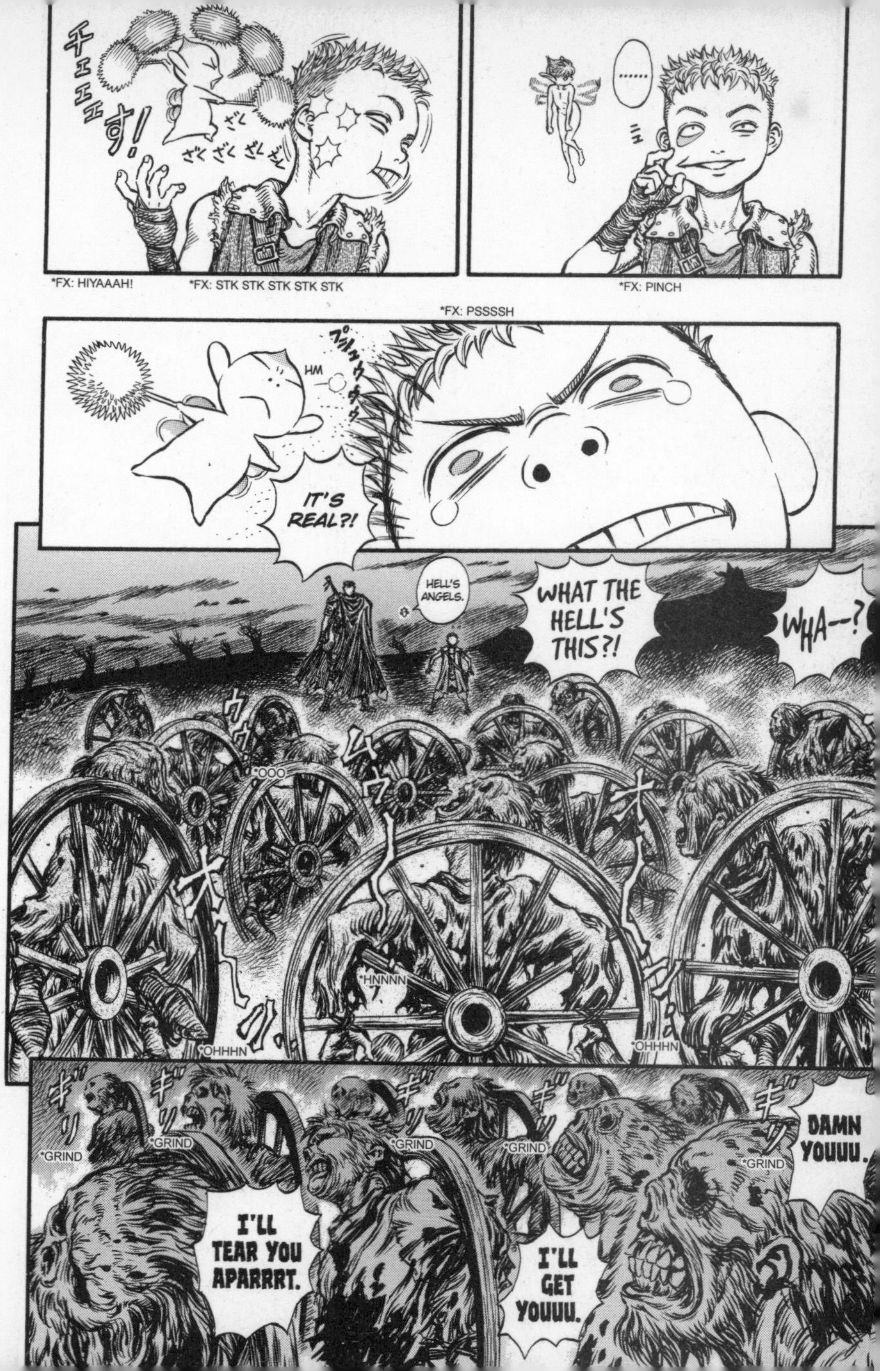

......
*FX: PINCH
*FX: HIYAAAH!
*FX: STK STK STK STK STK
*FX: PSSSSH
HM
IT'S REAL?!
WHA--?
WHAT THE HELL'S THIS?!
HELL'S ANGELS.
*OOO
*HNNNN
*OHHHN
*OHHHN
*GRIND
*GRIND
*GRIND
*GRIND
*GRIND
DAMN YOUUU.
I'LL GET YOUUU.
I'LL TEAR YOU APARRRT.

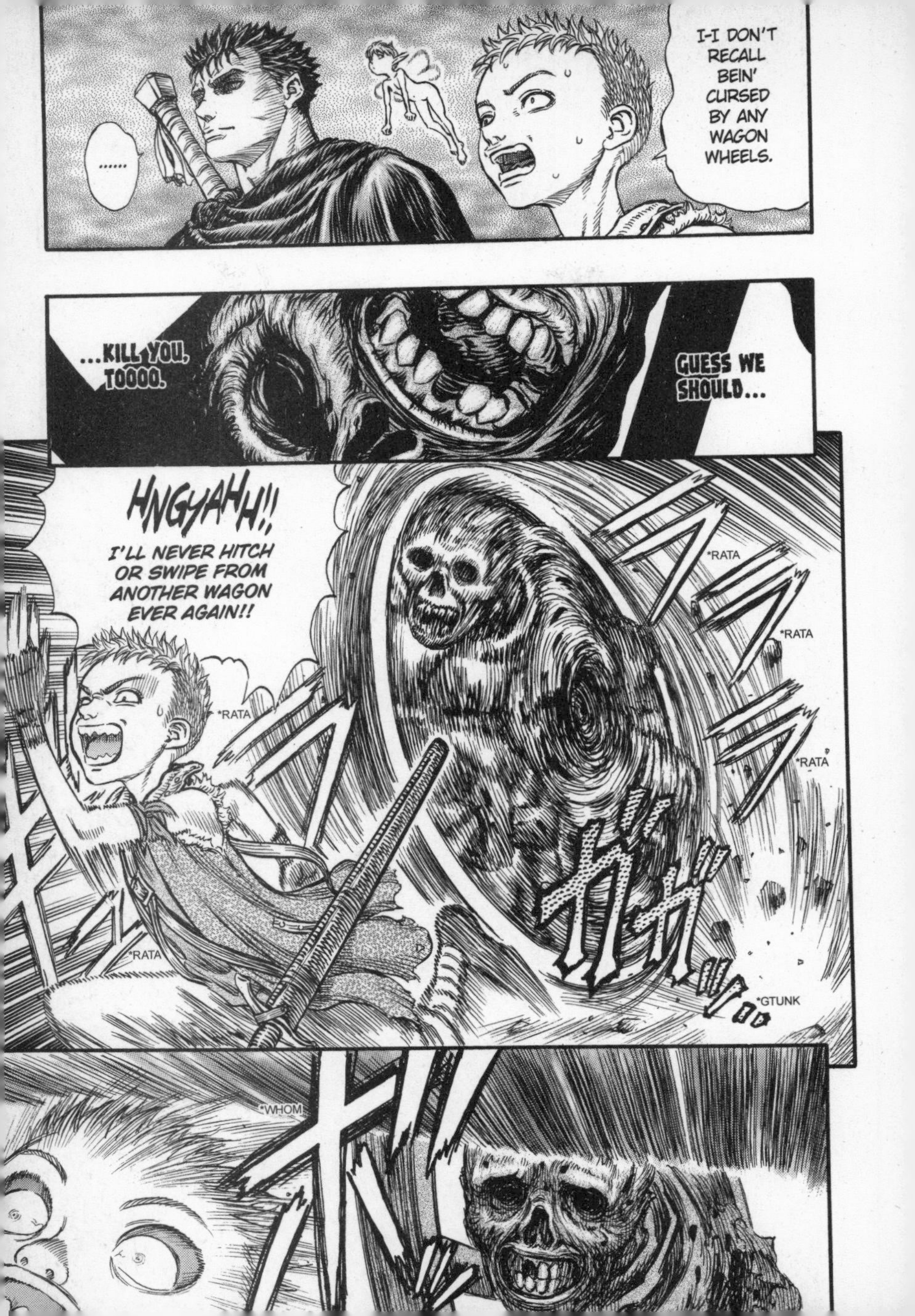
I-I DON'T RECALL BEIN' CURSED BY ANY WAGON WHEELS.
......
GUESS WE SHOULD...
...KILL YOU, TOOOO.
*RATA
*RATA
*RATA
HNGYAHH!!
I'LL NEVER HITCH OR SWIPE FROM ANOTHER WAGON EVER AGAIN!!
*RATA
*RATA
*GTUNK
*WHOM

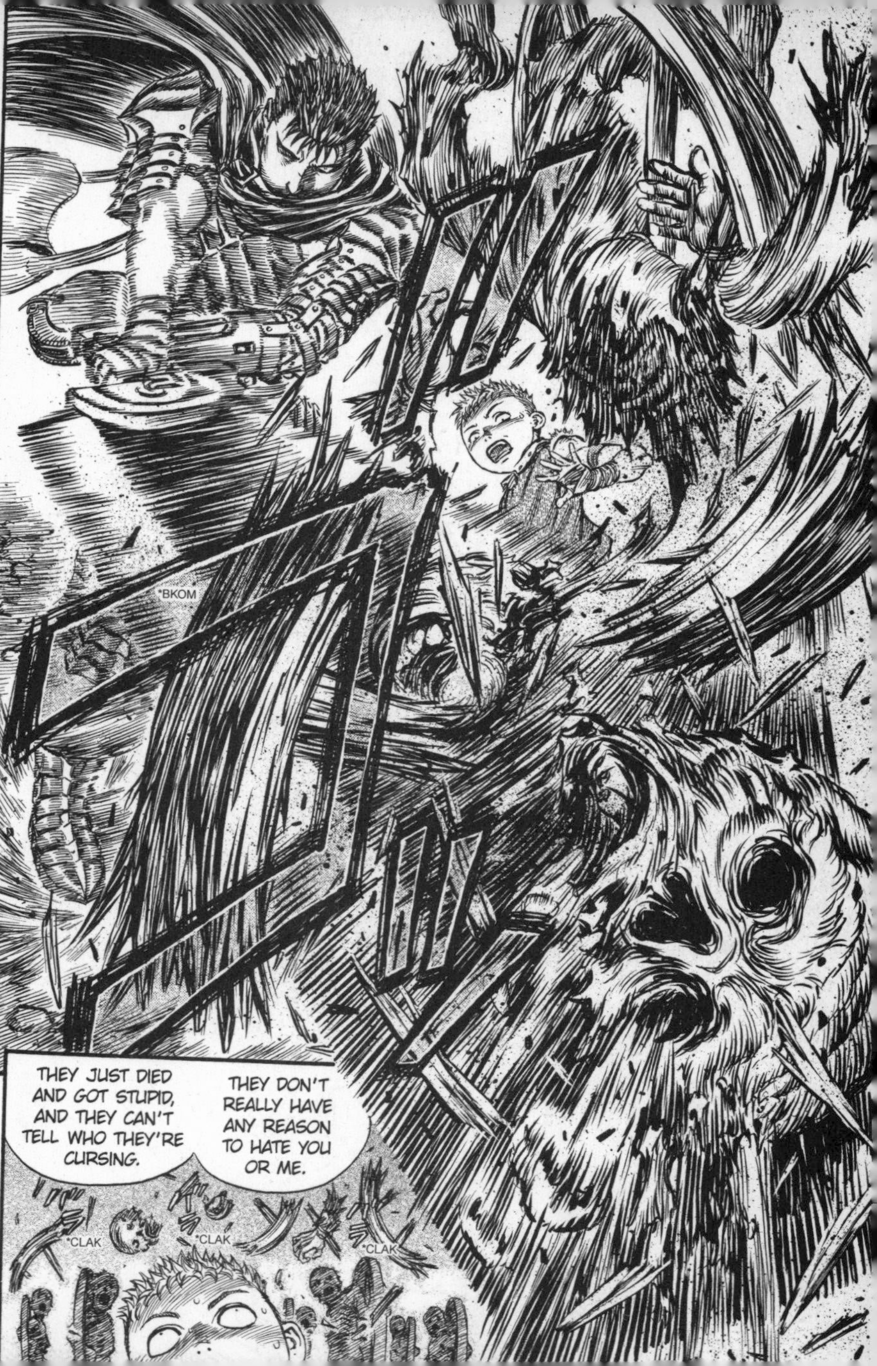
*BKOM
THEY DON'T REALLY HAVE ANY REASON TO HATE YOU OR ME.
THEY JUST DIED AND GOT STUPID, AND THEY CAN'T TELL WHO THEY'RE CURSING.
*CLAK
*CLAK
*CLAK

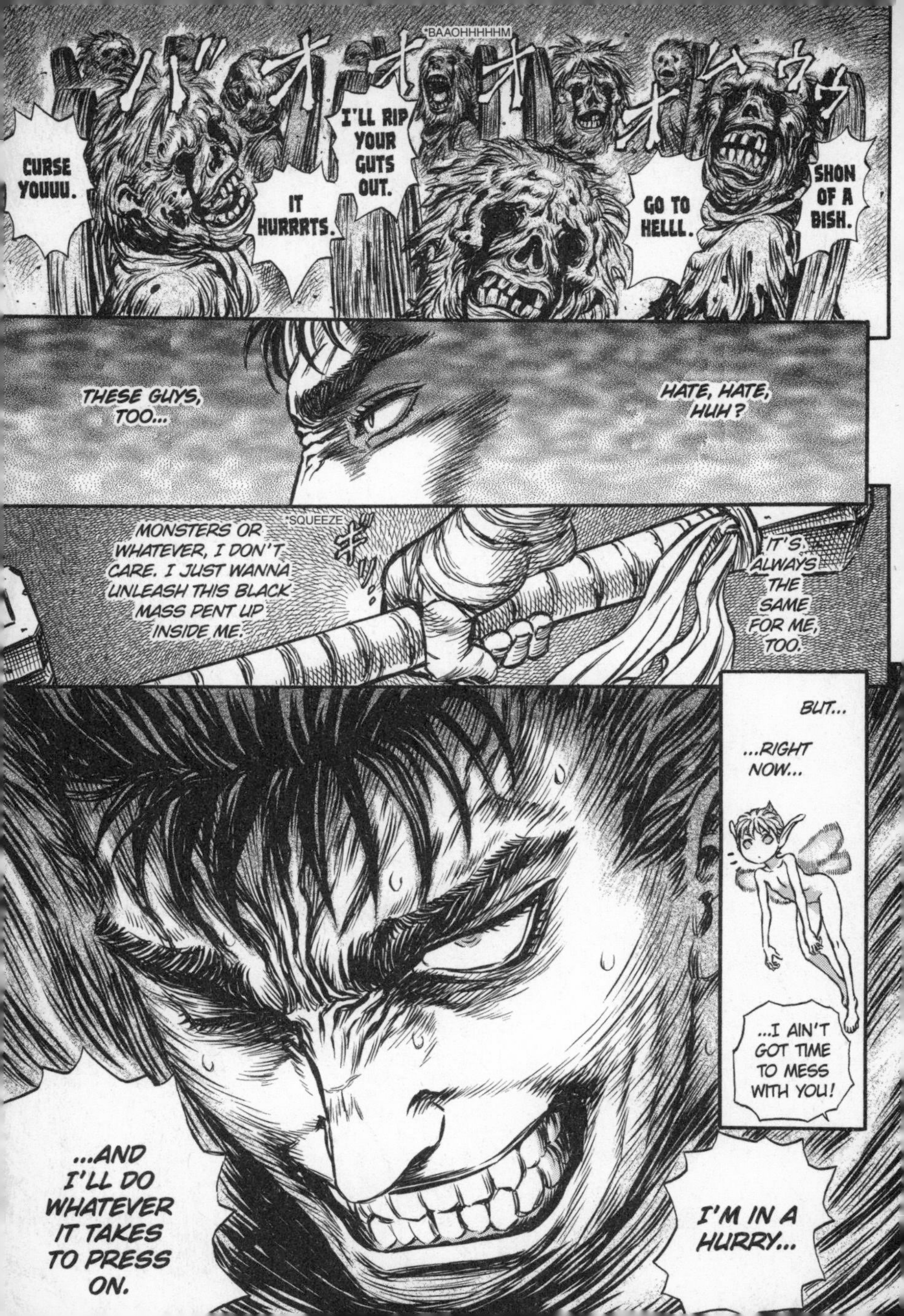
*BAAOHHHHHM
SHON OF A BISH.
GO TO HELLL.
I'LL RIP YOUR GUTS OUT.
IT HURRRTS.
CURSE YOUUU.
HATE, HATE, HUH?
THESE GUYS, TOO...
IT'S ALWAYS THE SAME FOR ME, TOO.
*SQUEEZE
MONSTERS OR WHATEVER, I DON'T CARE. I JUST WANNA UNLEASH THIS BLACK MASS PENT UP INSIDE ME.
BUT...
...RIGHT NOW...
...I AIN'T GOT TIME TO MESS WITH YOU!
I'M IN A HURRY...
...AND I'LL DO WHATEVER IT TAKES TO PRESS ON.

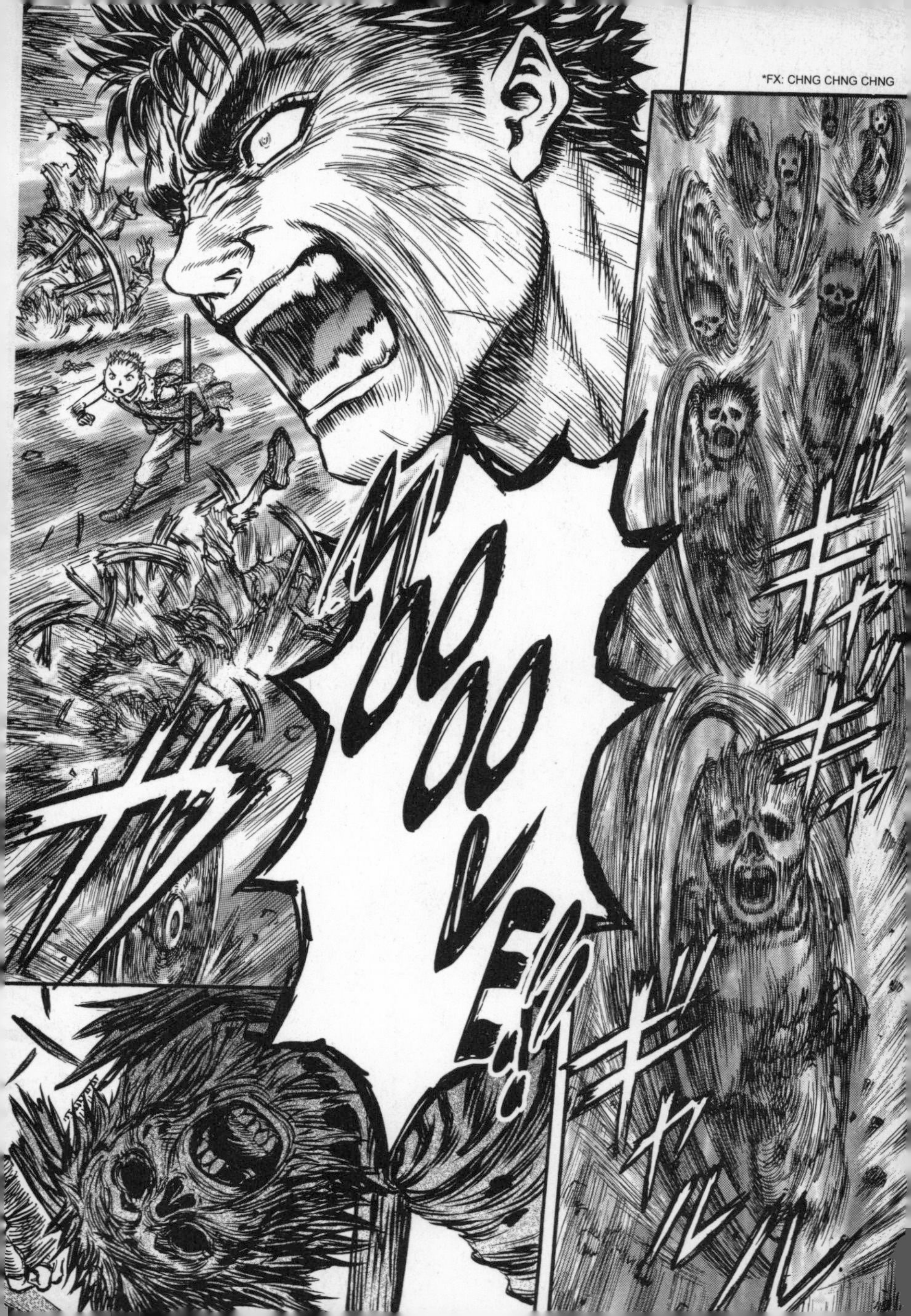
*FX: CHNG CHNG CHNG

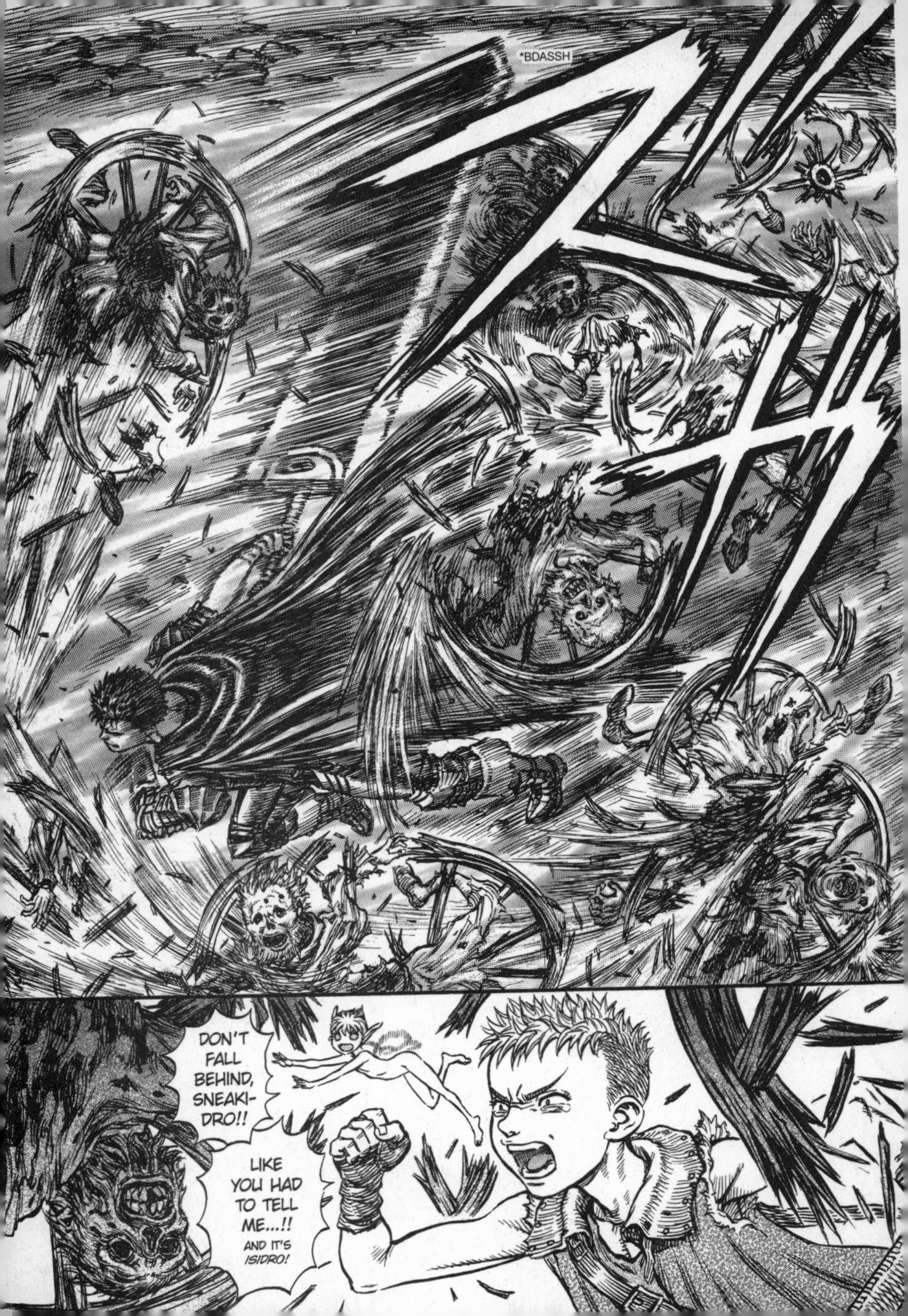
*BDASSH
DON'T FALL BEHIND, SNEAKI-DRO!!
LIKE YOU HAD TO TELL ME...!!
AND IT'S *ISIDRO!*

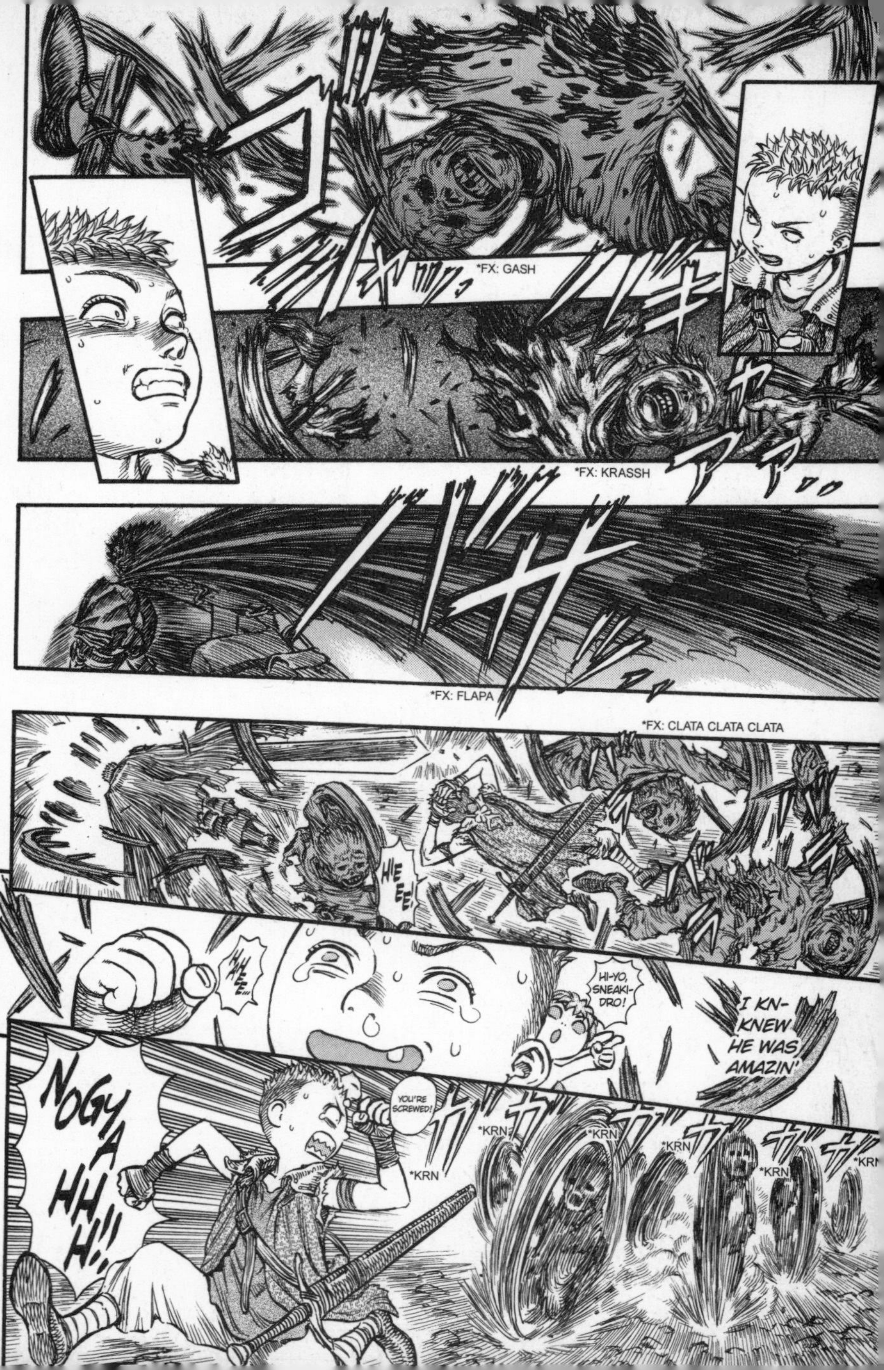
*FX: GASH
*FX: KRASSH
*FX: FLAPA
*FX: CLATA CLATA CLATA
HIEEE!
I KN-KNEW HE WAS AMAZIN'
HI-YO, SNEAKIDRO!
HIHEE...
YOU'RE SCREWED!
NOGYAHHHH!!!
*KRN
*KRN
*KRN
*KRN
*KRN
*KRN

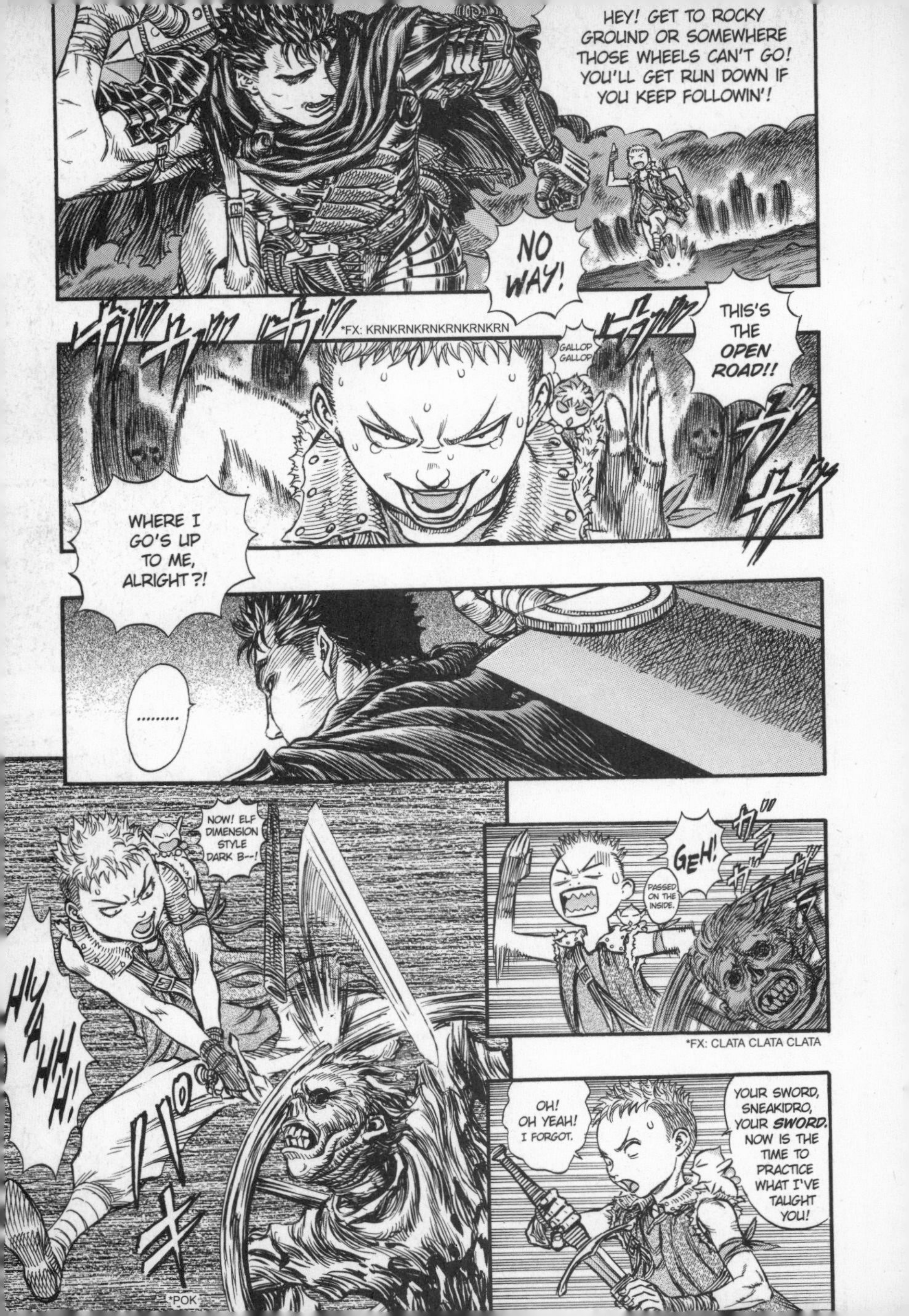
HEY! GET TO ROCKY GROUND OR SOMEWHERE THOSE WHEELS CAN'T GO! YOU'LL GET RUN DOWN IF YOU KEEP FOLLOWIN'!
NO WAY!
*FX: KRNKRNKRNKRNKRNKRN
THIS'S THE OPEN ROAD!!
GALLOP GALLOP
WHERE I GO'S UP TO ME, ALRIGHT?!
....
GEH!
PASSED ON THE INSIDE.
*FX: CLATA CLATA CLATA
YOUR SWORD, SNEAKIDRO, YOUR SWORD. NOW IS THE TIME TO PRACTICE WHAT I'VE TAUGHT YOU!
OH! OH YEAH! I FORGOT.
NOW! ELF DIMENSION STYLE DARK B--!
*POK

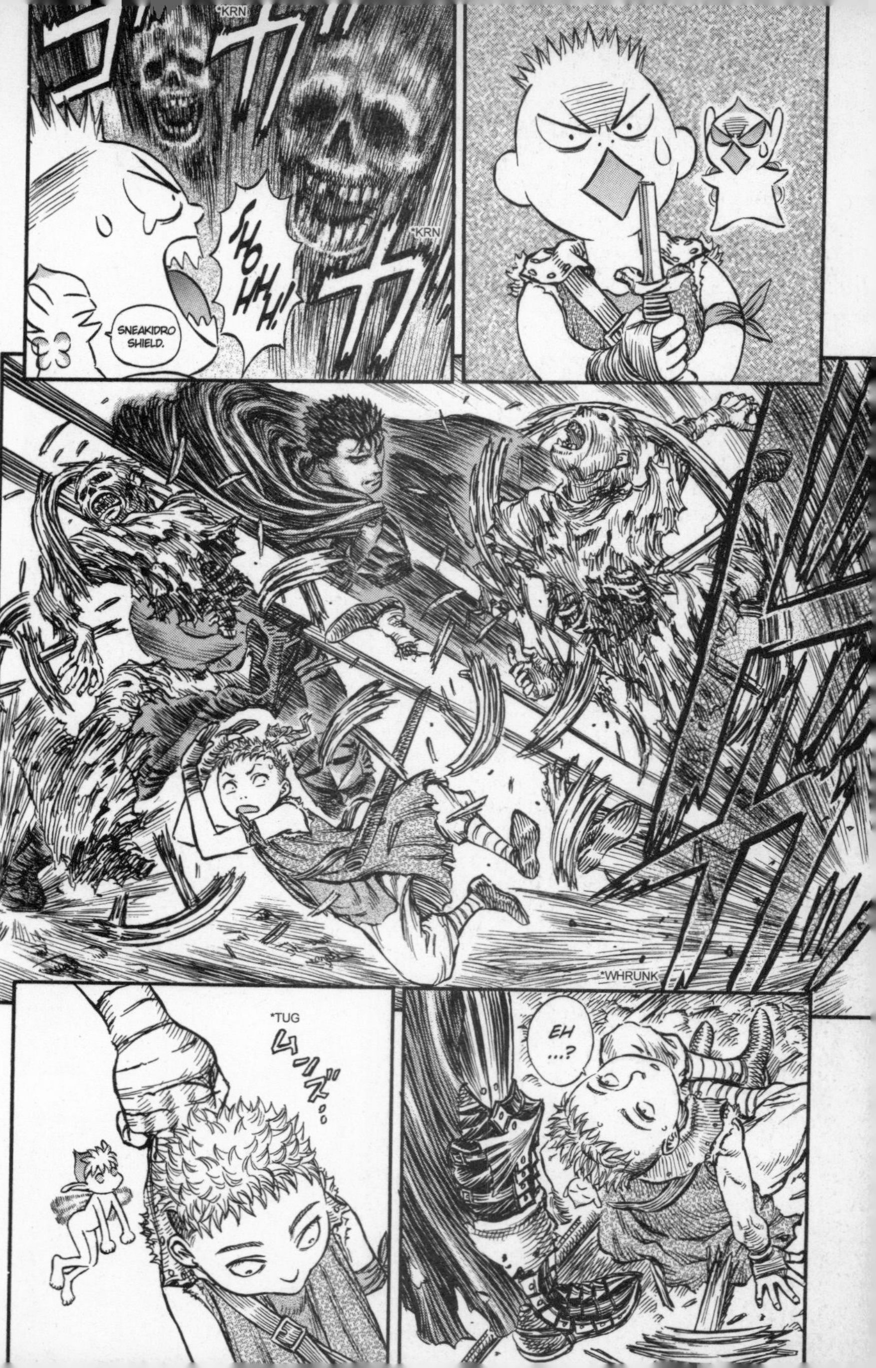
*KRN
SHOHHH!
*KRN
SNEAKIDRO SHIELD.
*WHRUNK
EH ...?
*TUG

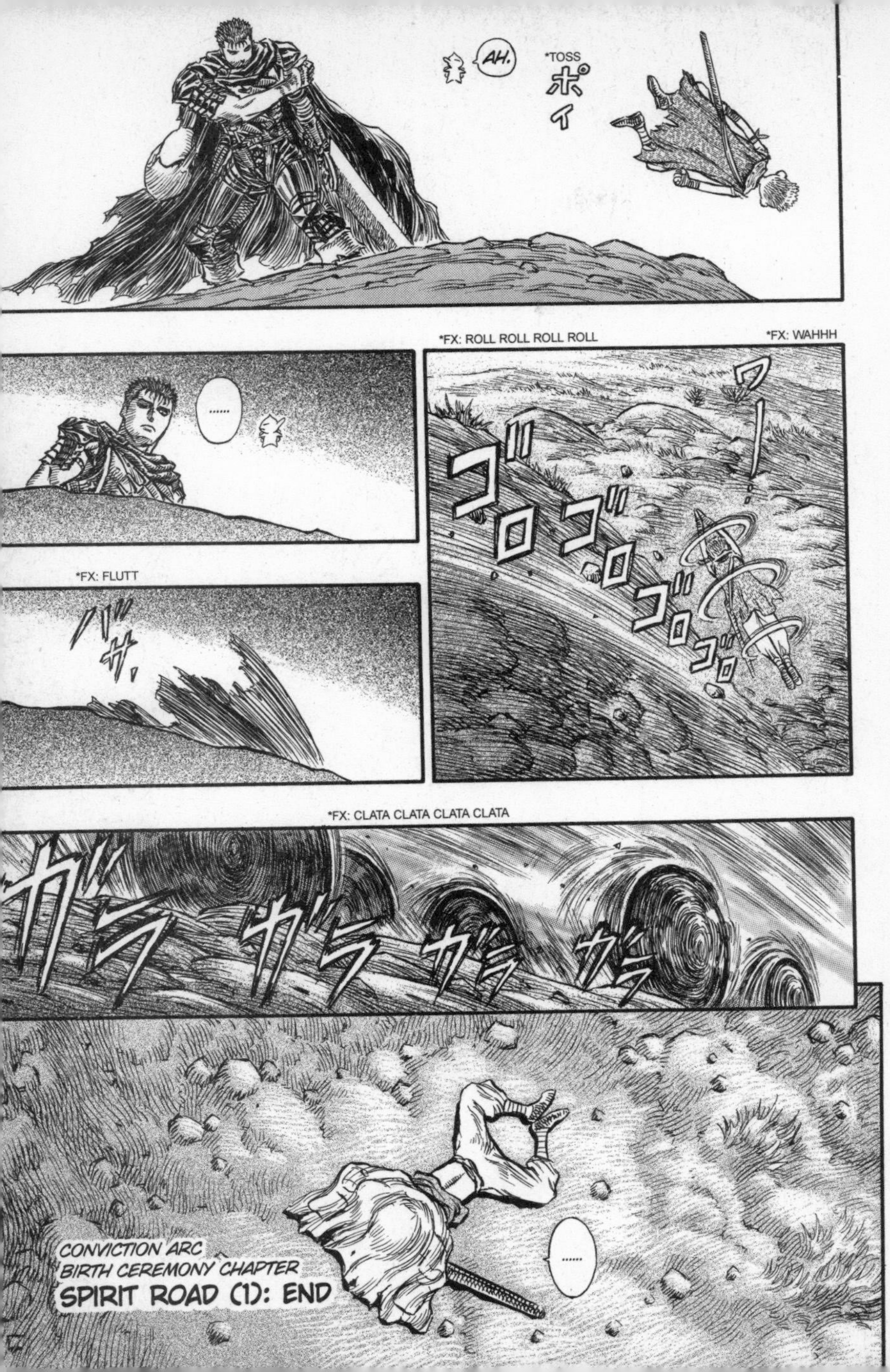
AH.
*TOSS
ポイ
*FX: WAHHH
ワーー
*FX: ROLL ROLL ROLL ROLL
ゴロゴロゴロゴロ
......
*FX: FLUTT
バサ
*FX: CLATA CLATA CLATA CLATA
ガラガラガラガラ
......
CONVICTION ARC
BIRTH CEREMONY CHAPTER
SPIRIT ROAD (1): END

BERSERK

断罪篇 生誕祭の章 怪道②

CONVICTION ARC
BIRTH CEREMONY CHAPTER
SPIRIT ROAD, PART 2

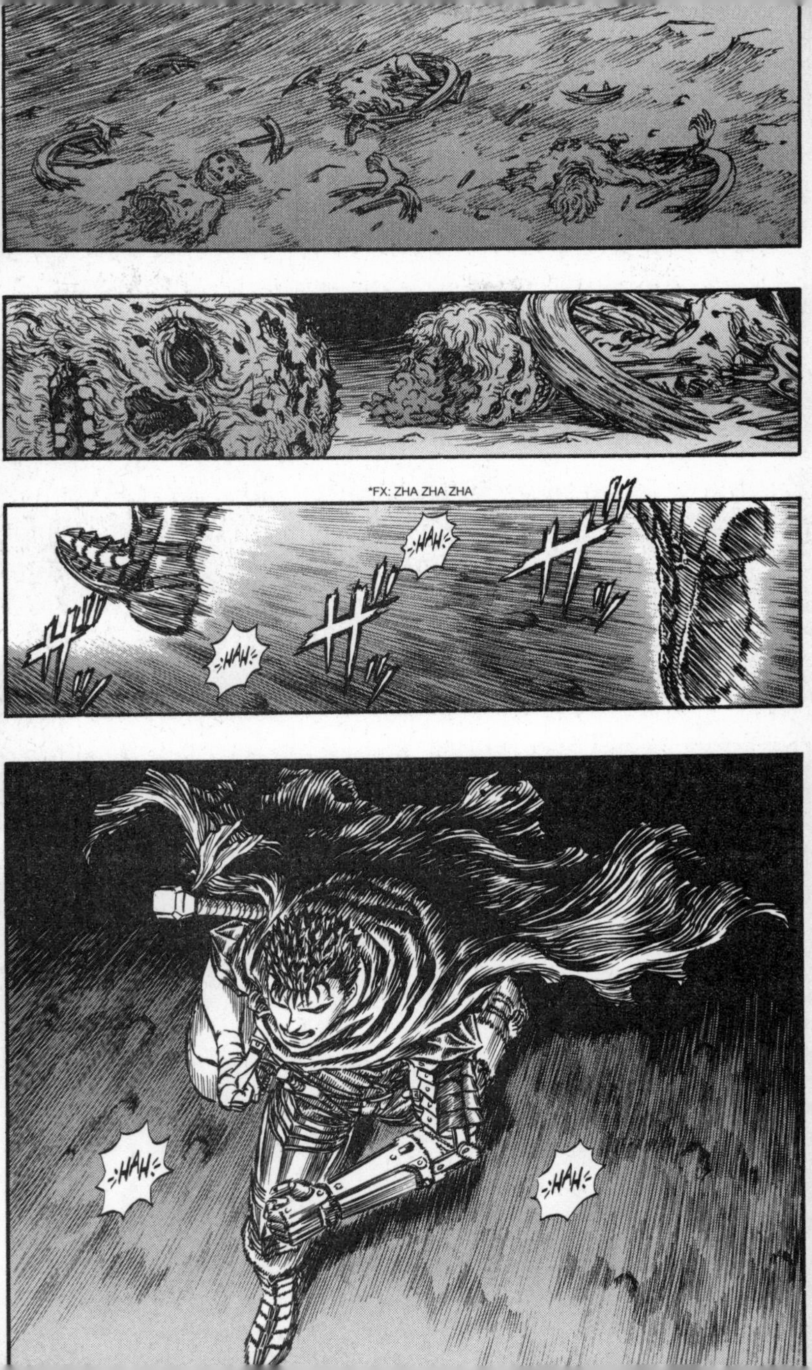
*FX: ZHA ZHA ZHA
HAH
HAH
HAH
HAH

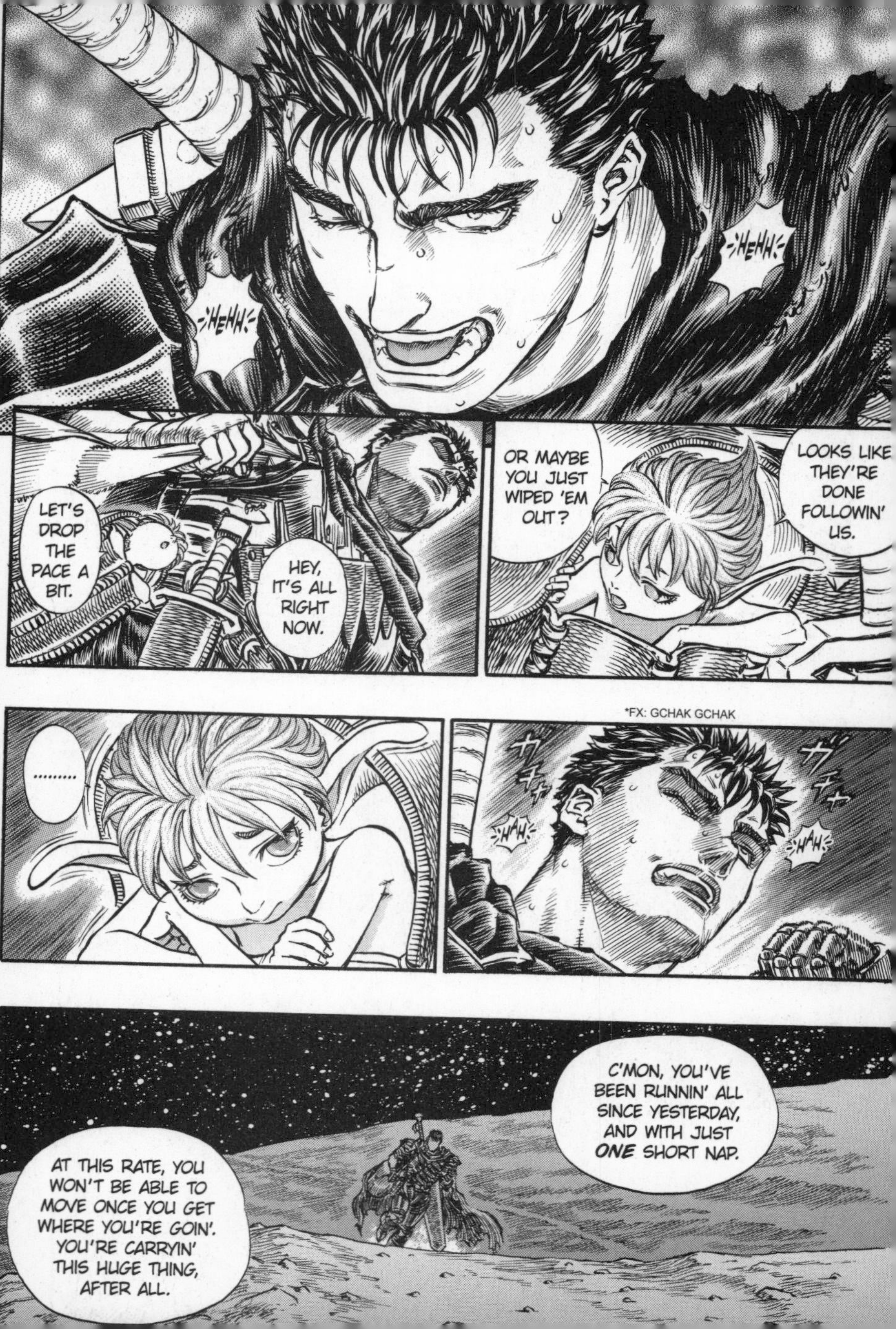
HEHH
HEHH
LOOKS LIKE THEY'RE DONE FOLLOWIN' US.
OR MAYBE YOU JUST WIPED 'EM OUT?
HEY, IT'S ALL RIGHT NOW.
LET'S DROP THE PACE A BIT.
*FX: GCHAK GCHAK
HAH
HAH
....
C'MON, YOU'VE BEEN RUNNIN' ALL SINCE YESTERDAY, AND WITH JUST ONE SHORT NAP.
AT THIS RATE, YOU WON'T BE ABLE TO MOVE ONCE YOU GET WHERE YOU'RE GOIN'. YOU'RE CARRYIN' THIS HUGE THING, AFTER ALL.

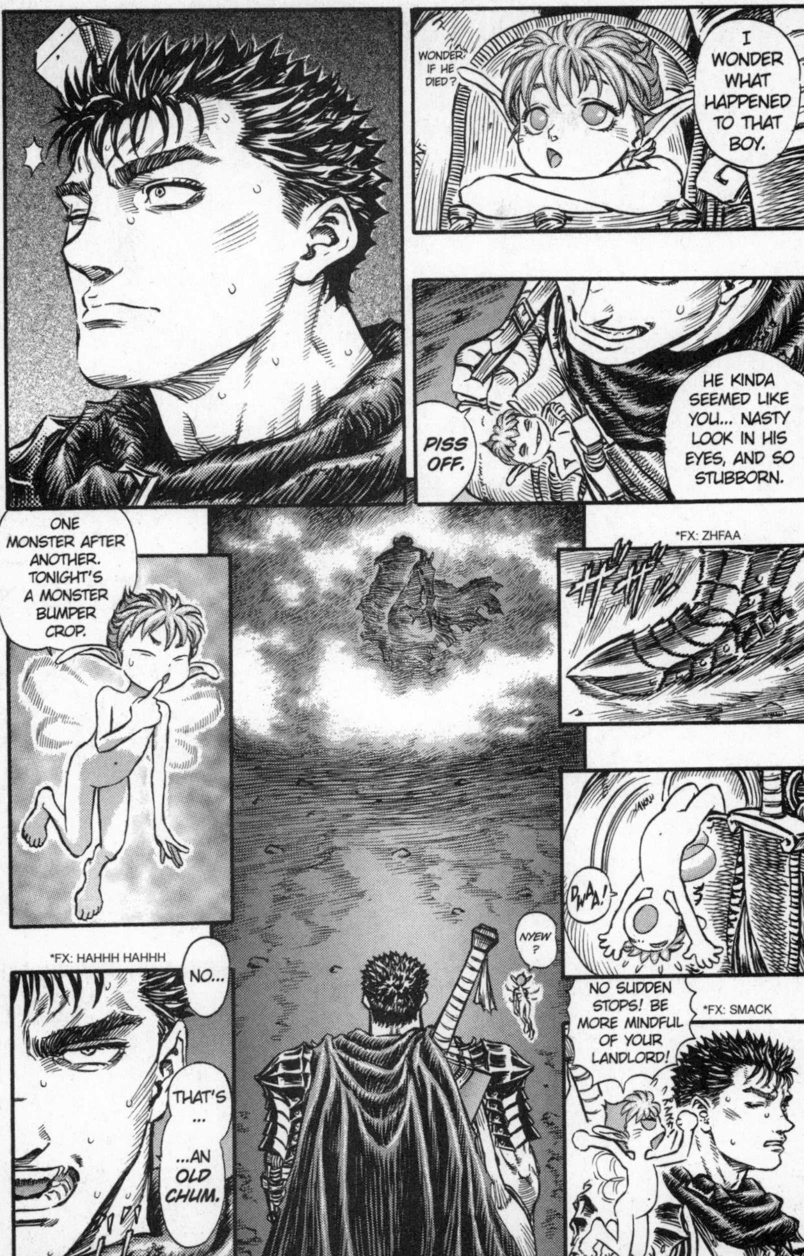
I WONDER WHAT HAPPENED TO THAT BOY.
WONDER? IF HE DIED?
HE KINDA SEEMED LIKE YOU... NASTY LOOK IN HIS EYES, AND SO STUBBORN.
PISS OFF.
*FX: ZHFAA
DWAA!
NO SUDDEN STOPS! BE MORE MINDFUL OF YOUR LANDLORD!
*FX: SMACK
NYEW ?
ONE MONSTER AFTER ANOTHER. TONIGHT'S A MONSTER BUMPER CROP.
*FX: HAHHH HAHHH
NO...
THAT'S ...
...AN OLD CHUM.

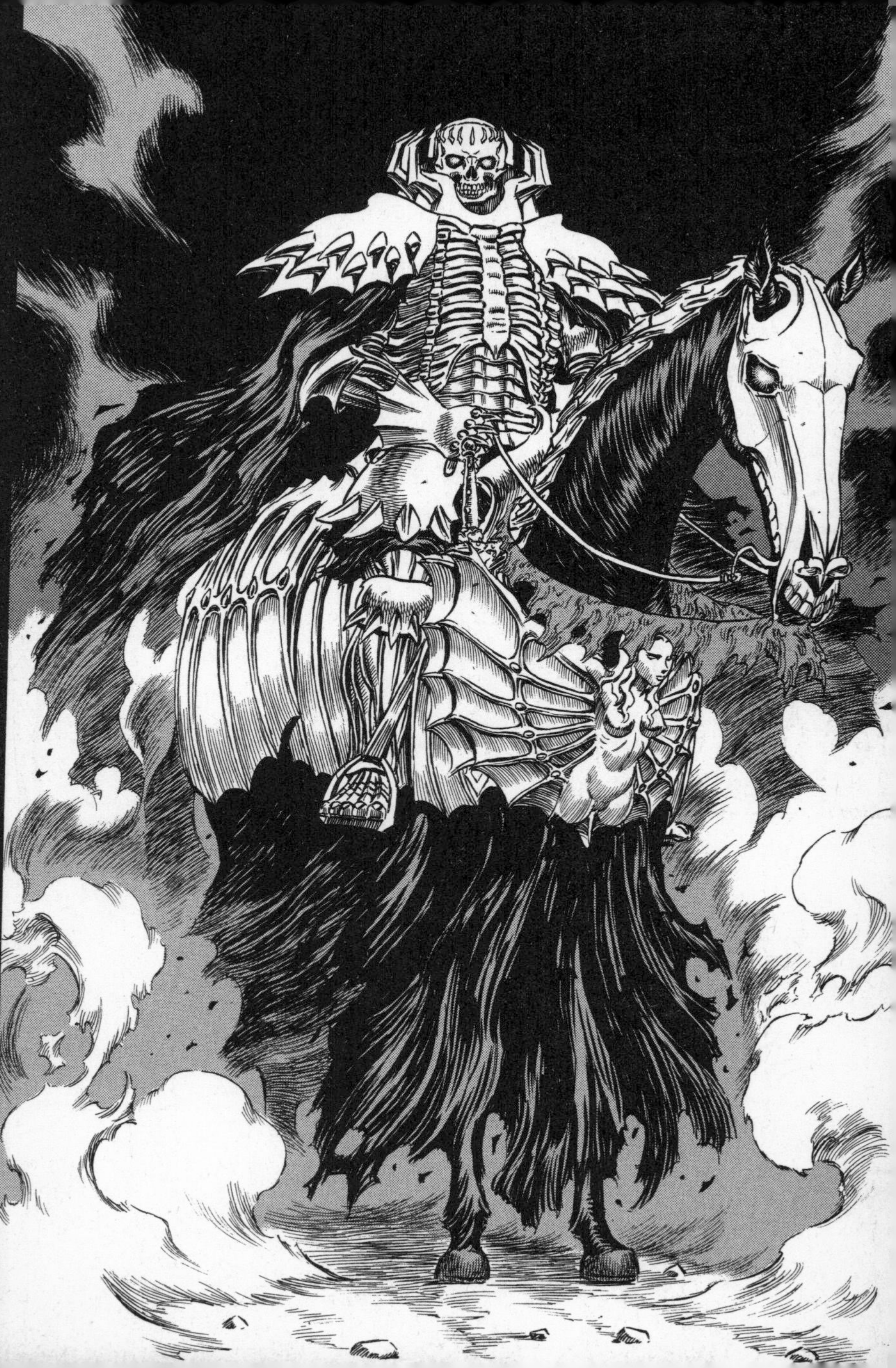

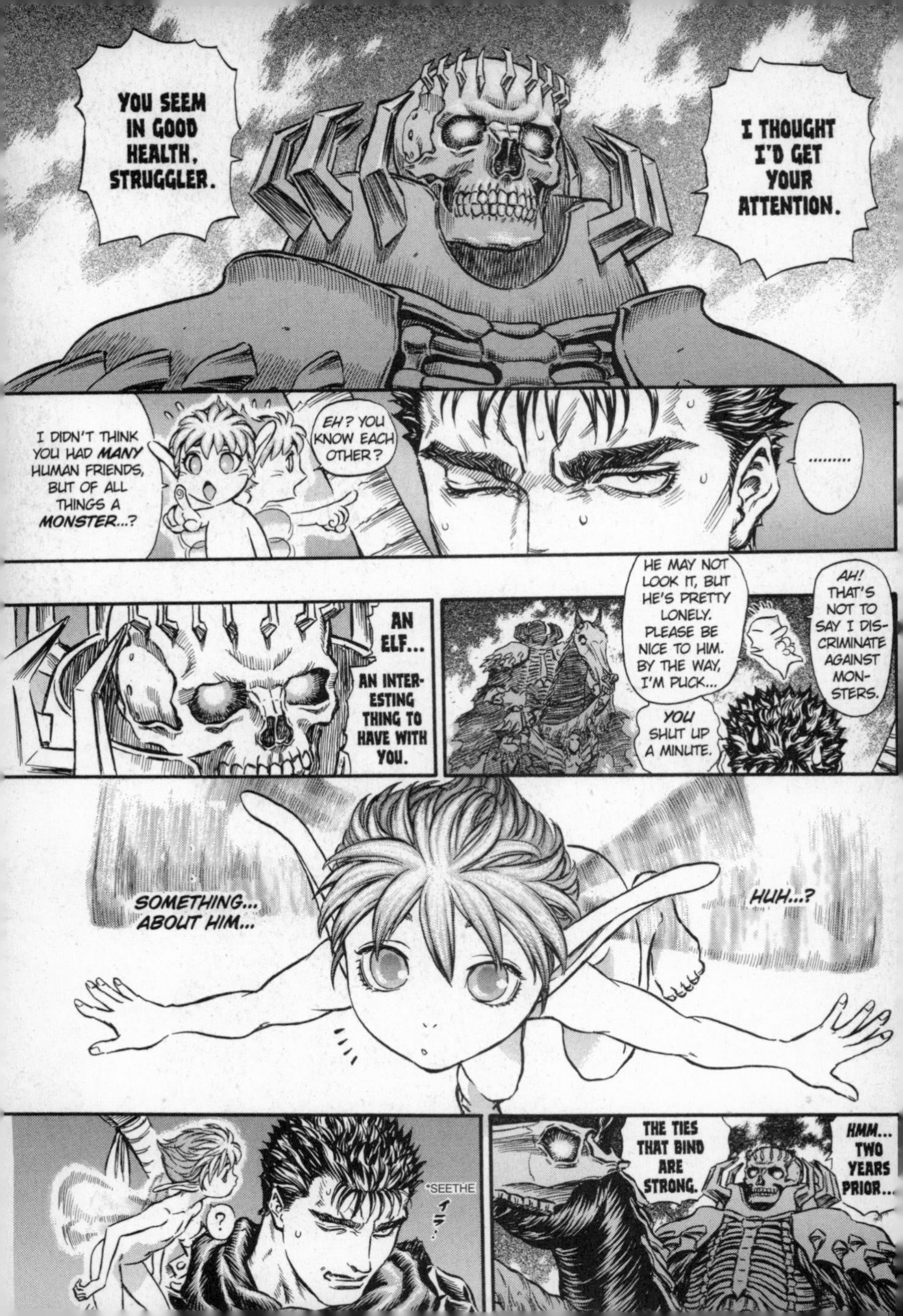

I THOUGHT I'D GET YOUR ATTENTION.
YOU SEEM IN GOOD HEALTH, STRUGGLER.
....
EH? YOU KNOW EACH OTHER?
I DIDN'T THINK YOU HAD MANY HUMAN FRIENDS, BUT OF ALL THINGS A MONSTER...?
AH! THAT'S NOT TO SAY I DIS-CRIMINATE AGAINST MON-STERS.
HE MAY NOT LOOK IT, BUT HE'S PRETTY LONELY. PLEASE BE NICE TO HIM. BY THE WAY, I'M PUCK...
YOU SHUT UP A MINUTE.
AN ELF...
AN INTER-ESTING THING TO HAVE WITH YOU.
HUH...?
SOMETHING... ABOUT HIM...
HMM... TWO YEARS PRIOR...
THE TIES THAT BIND ARE STRONG.
*SEETHE
?

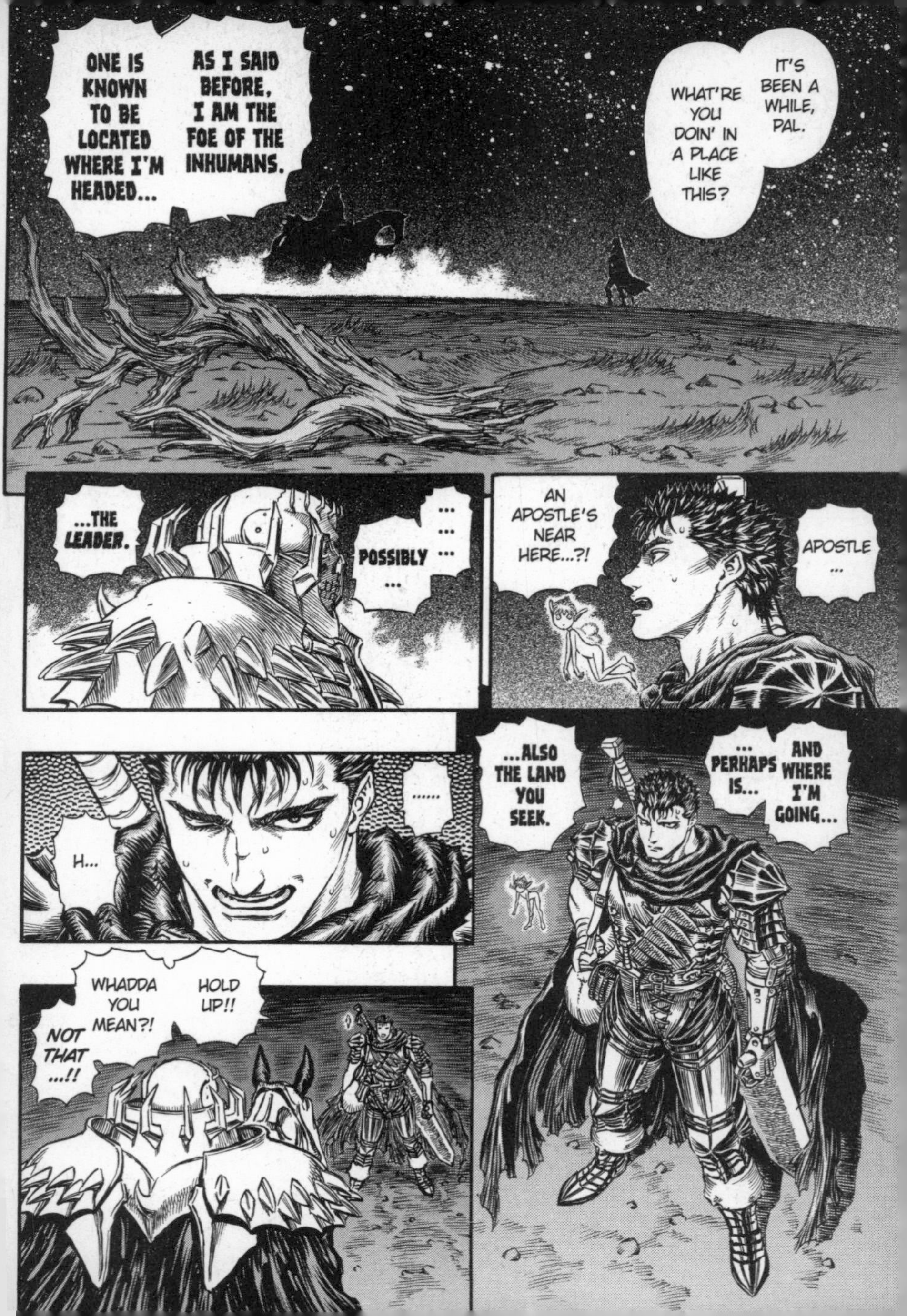
IT'S BEEN A WHILE, PAL.
WHAT'RE YOU DOIN' IN A PLACE LIKE THIS?
AS I SAID BEFORE, I AM THE FOE OF THE INHUMANS.
ONE IS KNOWN TO BE LOCATED WHERE I'M HEADED...
APOSTLE ...
AN APOSTLE'S NEAR HERE...?!
... ...
POSSIBLY ...
...THE *LEADER.*
AND WHERE I'M GOING...
... PERHAPS IS...
...ALSO THE LAND YOU SEEK.
......
H...
HOLD UP!!
WHADDA YOU MEAN?!
NOT THAT ...!!

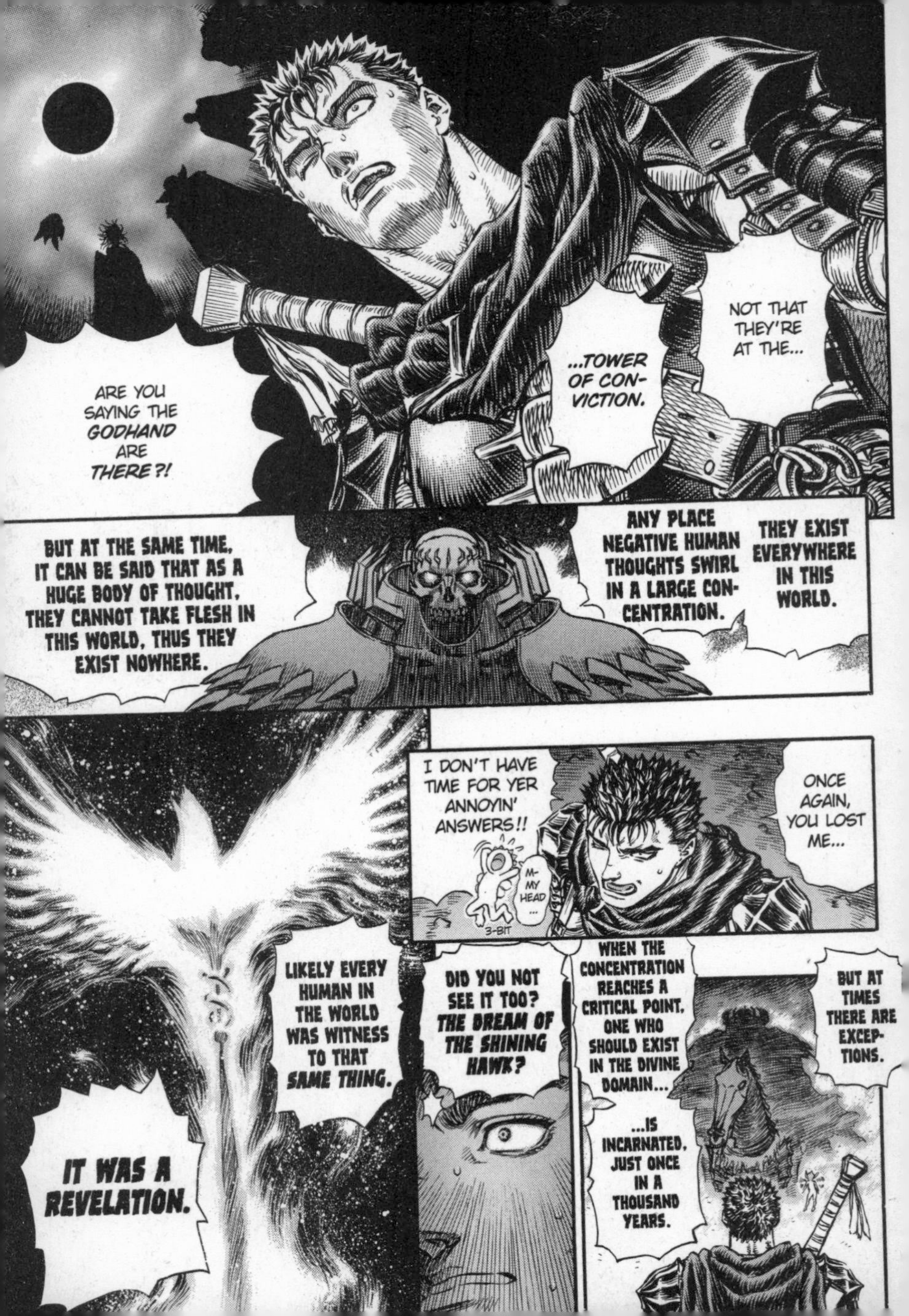
NOT THAT THEY'RE AT THE...
...TOWER OF CON-VICTION.
ARE YOU SAYING THE GODHAND ARE THERE?!
THEY EXIST EVERYWHERE IN THIS WORLD.
ANY PLACE NEGATIVE HUMAN THOUGHTS SWIRL IN A LARGE CON-CENTRATION.
BUT AT THE SAME TIME, IT CAN BE SAID THAT AS A HUGE BODY OF THOUGHT, THEY CANNOT TAKE FLESH IN THIS WORLD, THUS THEY EXIST NOWHERE.
ONCE AGAIN, YOU LOST ME...
I DON'T HAVE TIME FOR YER ANNOYIN' ANSWERS!!
M-MY HEAD ...
3-BIT
BUT AT TIMES THERE ARE EXCEP-TIONS.
WHEN THE CONCENTRATION REACHES A CRITICAL POINT, ONE WHO SHOULD EXIST IN THE DIVINE DOMAIN...
...IS INCARNATED, JUST ONCE IN A THOUSAND YEARS.
DID YOU NOT SEE IT TOO? THE DREAM OF THE SHINING HAWK?
LIKELY EVERY HUMAN IN THE WORLD WAS WITNESS TO THAT SAME THING.
IT WAS A REVELATION.

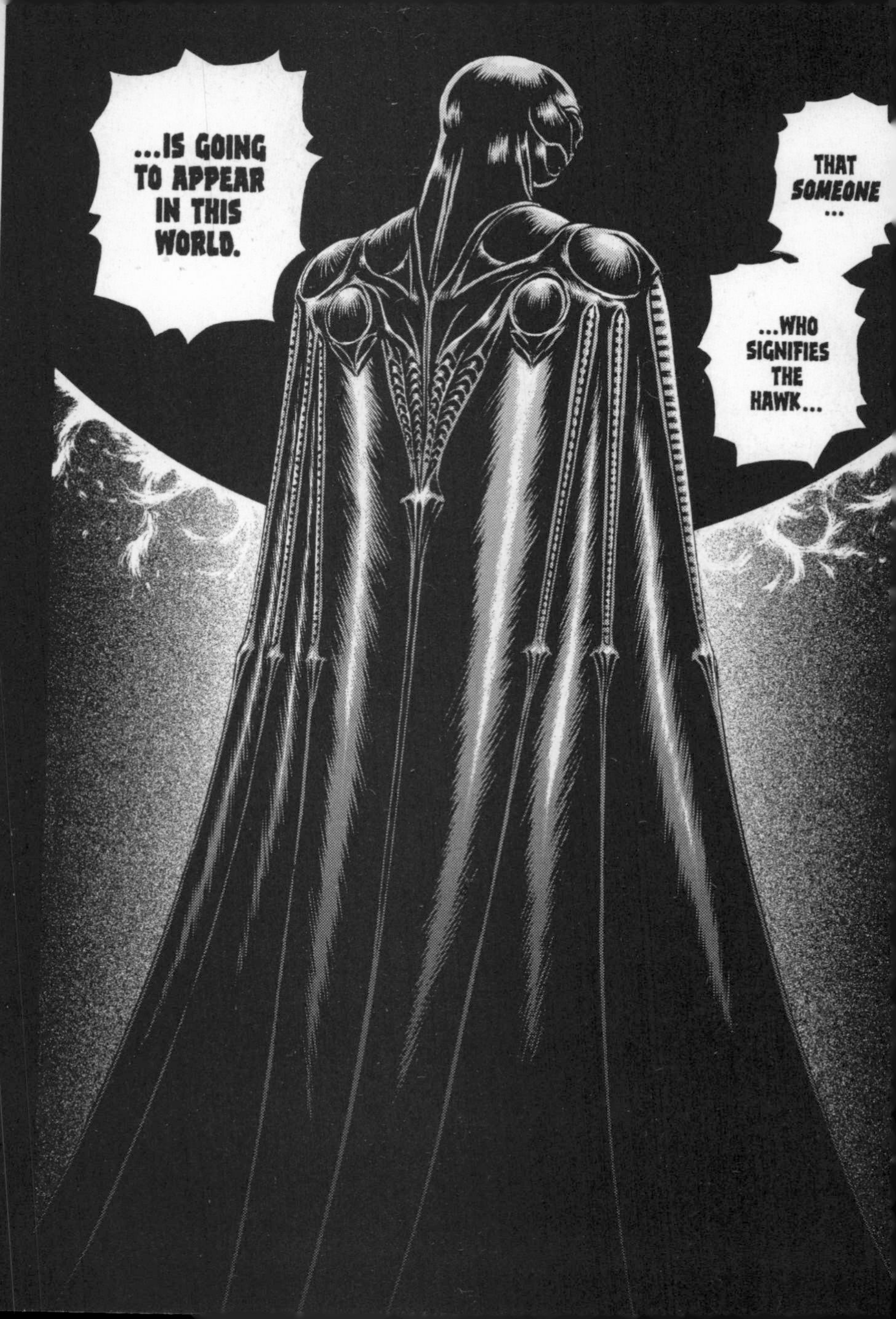
THAT SOMEONE ...
...WHO SIGNIFIES THE HAWK...
...IS GOING TO APPEAR IN THIS WORLD.

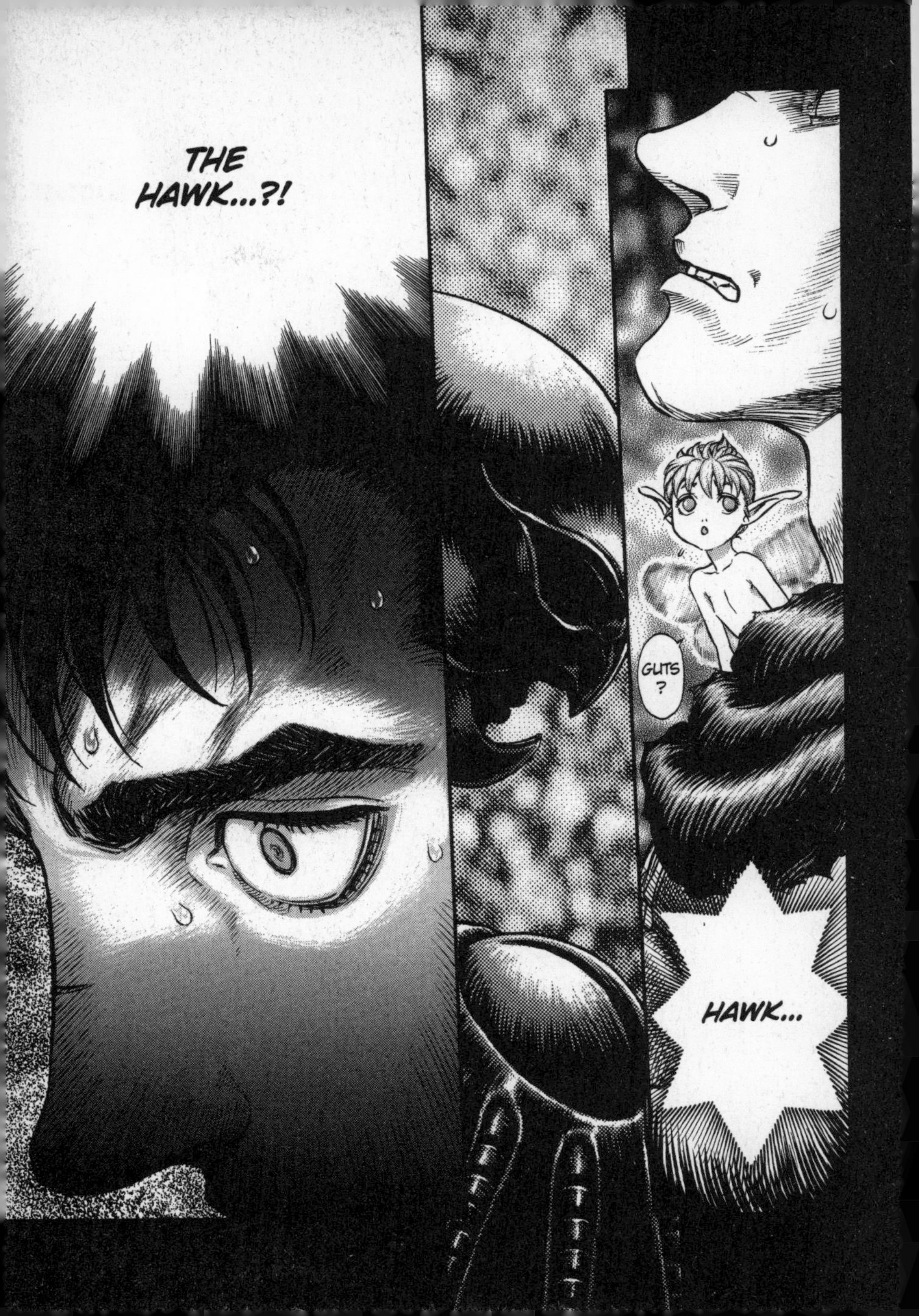
GUTS ?
HAWK...
THE HAWK...?!

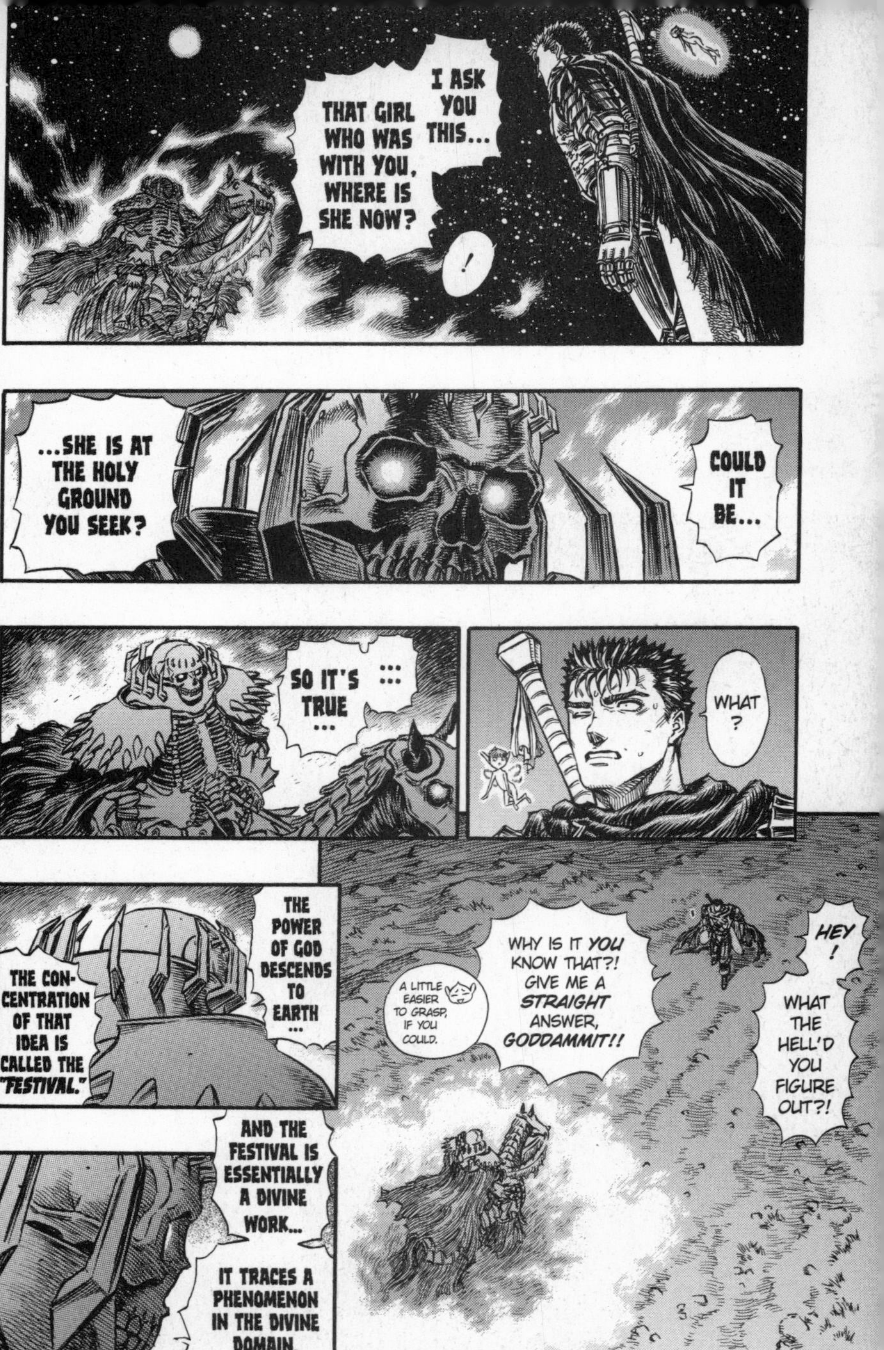
I ASK YOU THIS...
THAT GIRL WHO WAS WITH YOU, WHERE IS SHE NOW?
!
COULD IT BE...
...SHE IS AT THE HOLY GROUND YOU SEEK?
WHAT?
SO IT'S TRUE ... ...
HEY!
WHAT THE HELL'D YOU FIGURE OUT?!
WHY IS IT YOU KNOW THAT?! GIVE ME A STRAIGHT ANSWER, GODDAMMIT!!
A LITTLE EASIER TO GRASP, IF YOU COULD.
THE POWER OF GOD DESCENDS TO EARTH ...
THE CONCENTRATION OF THAT IDEA IS CALLED THE "FESTIVAL."
AND THE FESTIVAL IS ESSENTIALLY A DIVINE WORK...
IT TRACES A PHENOMENON IN THE DIVINE DOMAIN.

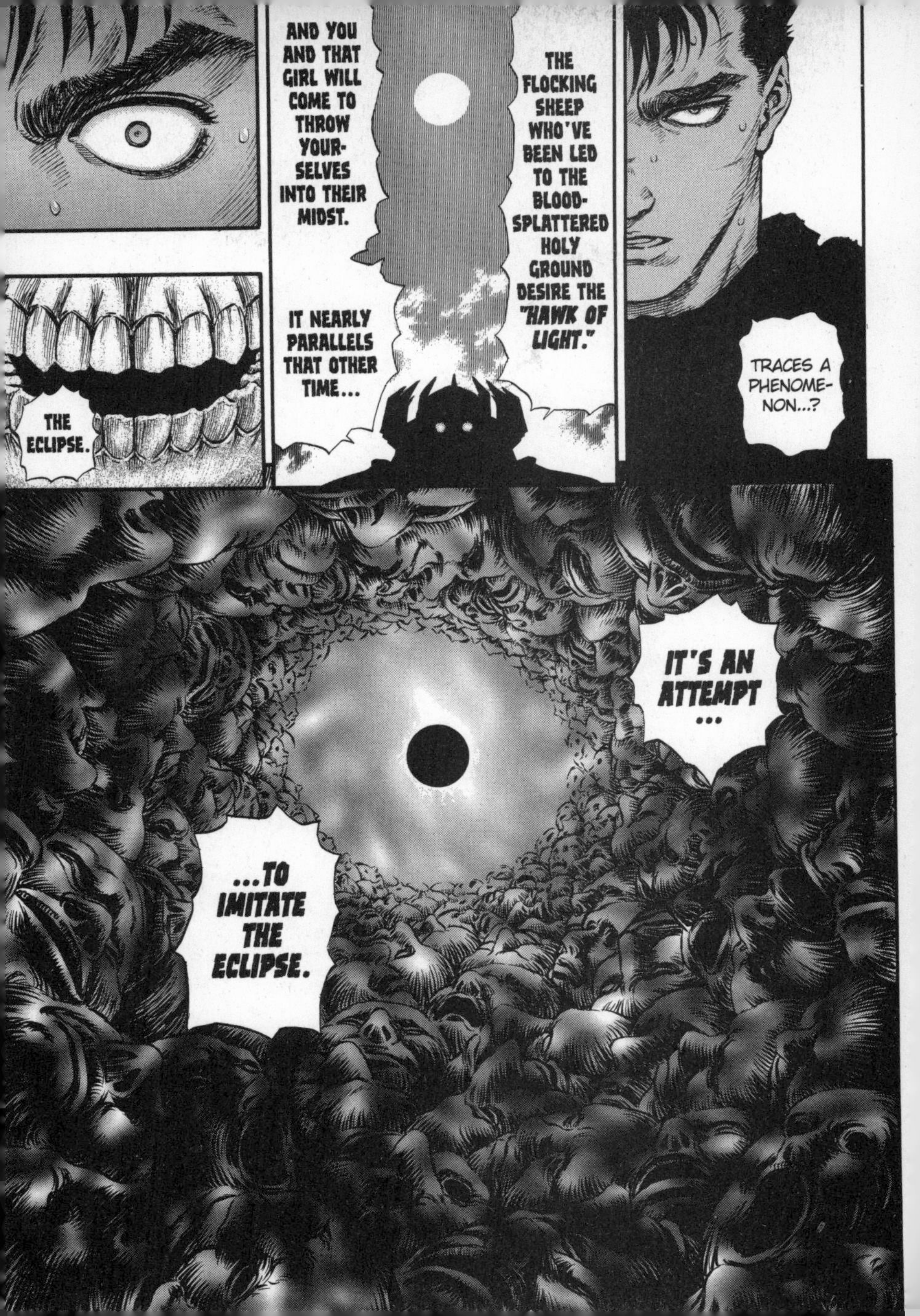
TRACES A PHENOMENON...?
THE FLOCKING SHEEP WHO'VE BEEN LED TO THE BLOOD-SPLATTERED HOLY GROUND DESIRE THE "HAWK OF LIGHT."
AND YOU AND THAT GIRL WILL COME TO THROW YOURSELVES INTO THEIR MIDST.
IT NEARLY PARALLELS THAT OTHER TIME...
THE ECLIPSE.
IT'S AN ATTEMPT...
...TO IMITATE THE ECLIPSE.

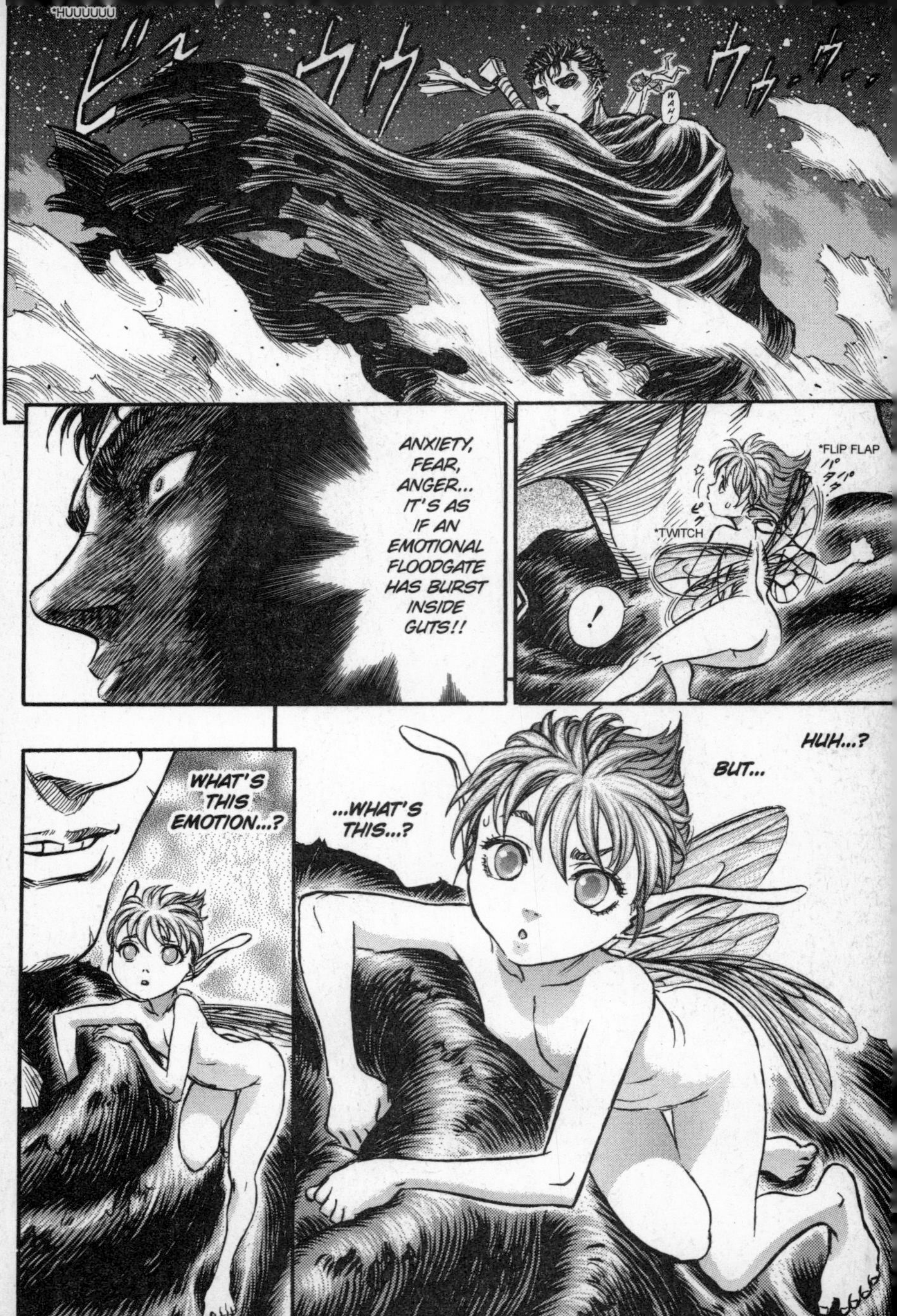
WAH!
*HUUUUUU
*FLIP FLAP
*TWITCH
!
ANXIETY, FEAR, ANGER... IT'S AS IF AN EMOTIONAL FLOODGATE HAS BURST INSIDE GUTS!!
HUH...?
BUT...
...WHAT'S THIS...?
WHAT'S THIS EMOTION...?

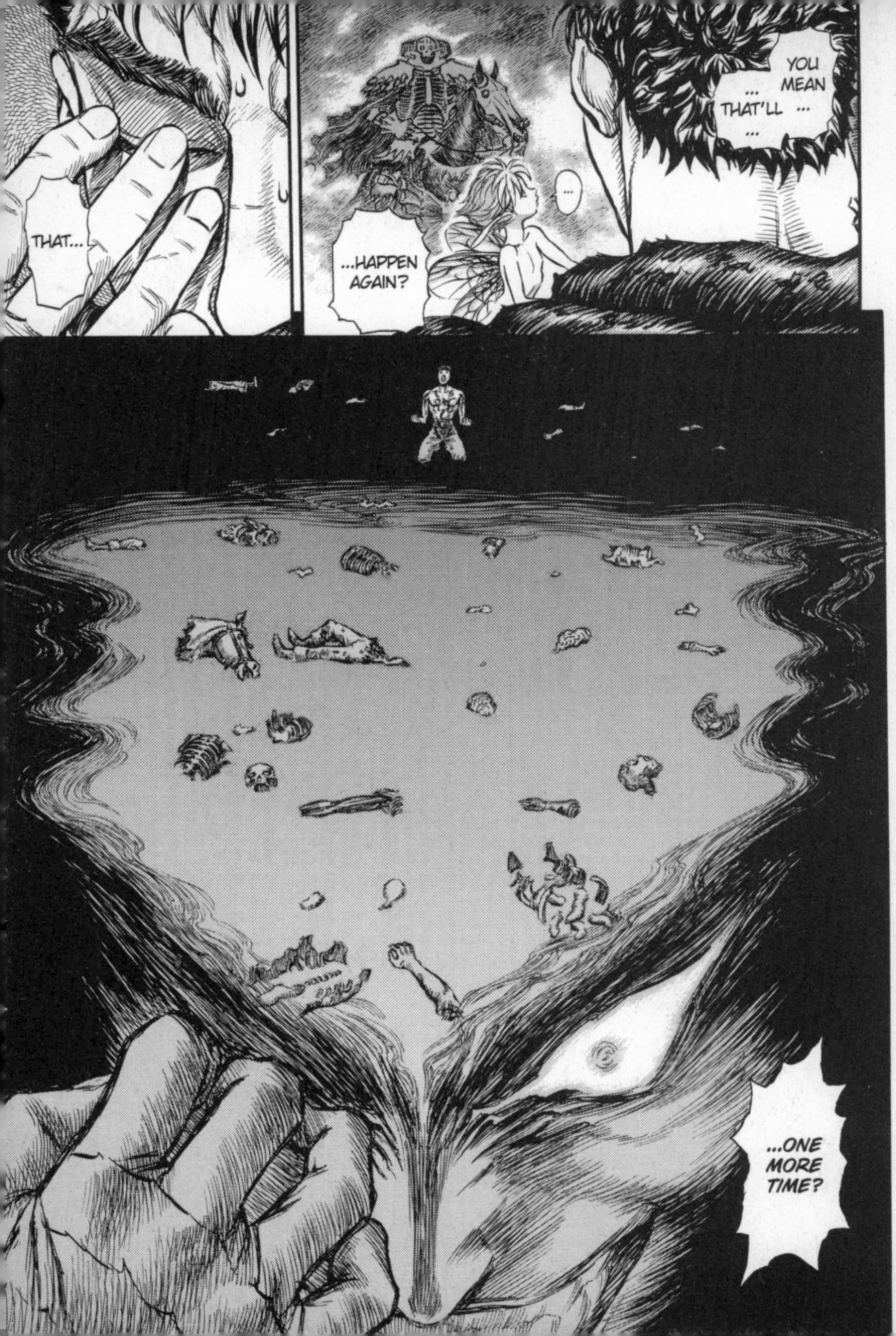
YOU MEAN ... THAT'LL ... ...
...
...HAPPEN AGAIN?
THAT...
...ONE MORE TIME?

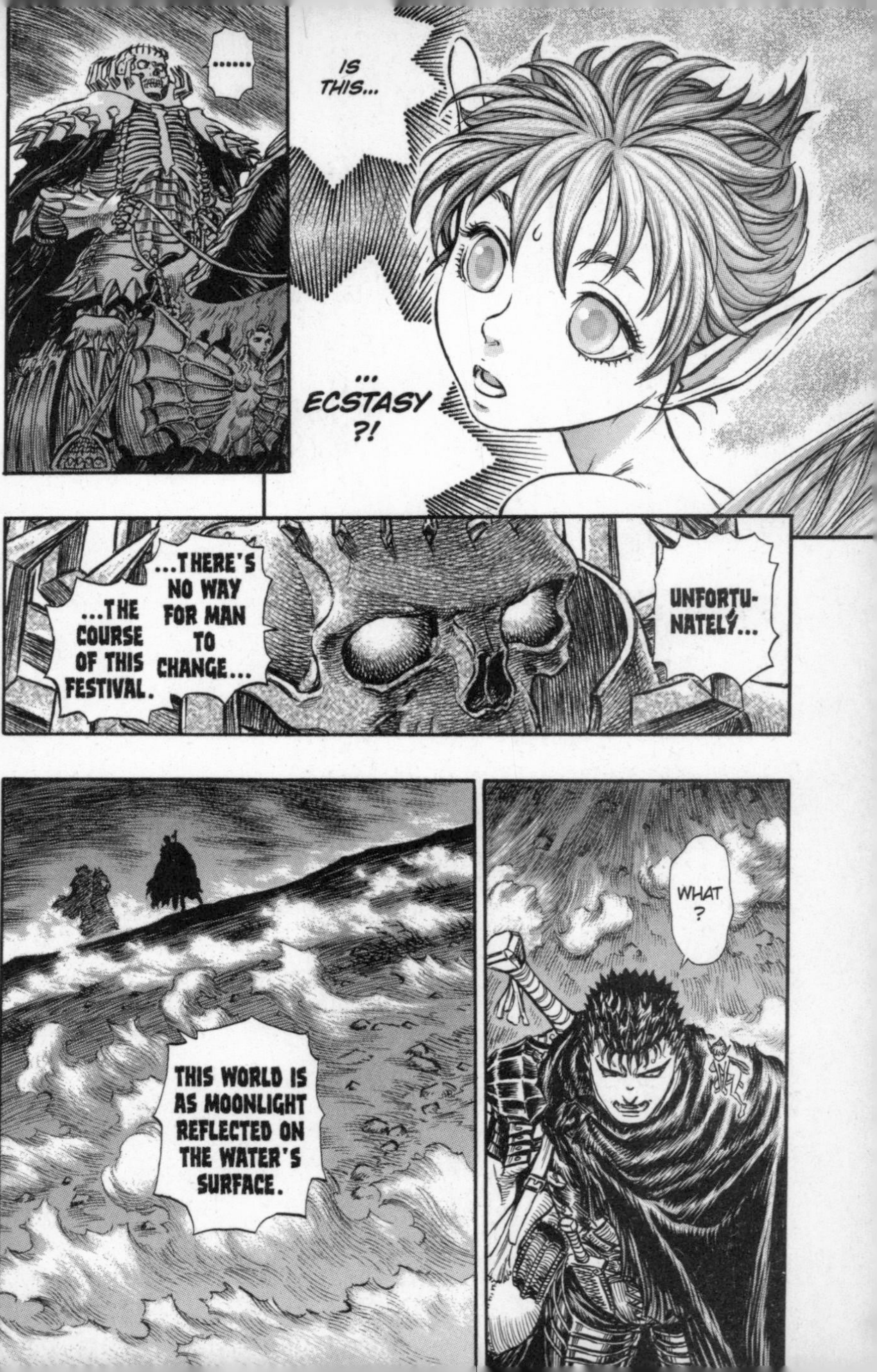
IS THIS...
...ECSTASY ?!
......
UNFORTUNATELY...
...THERE'S NO WAY FOR MAN TO CHANGE...
...THE COURSE OF THIS FESTIVAL.
WHAT ?
THIS WORLD IS AS MOONLIGHT REFLECTED ON THE WATER'S SURFACE.

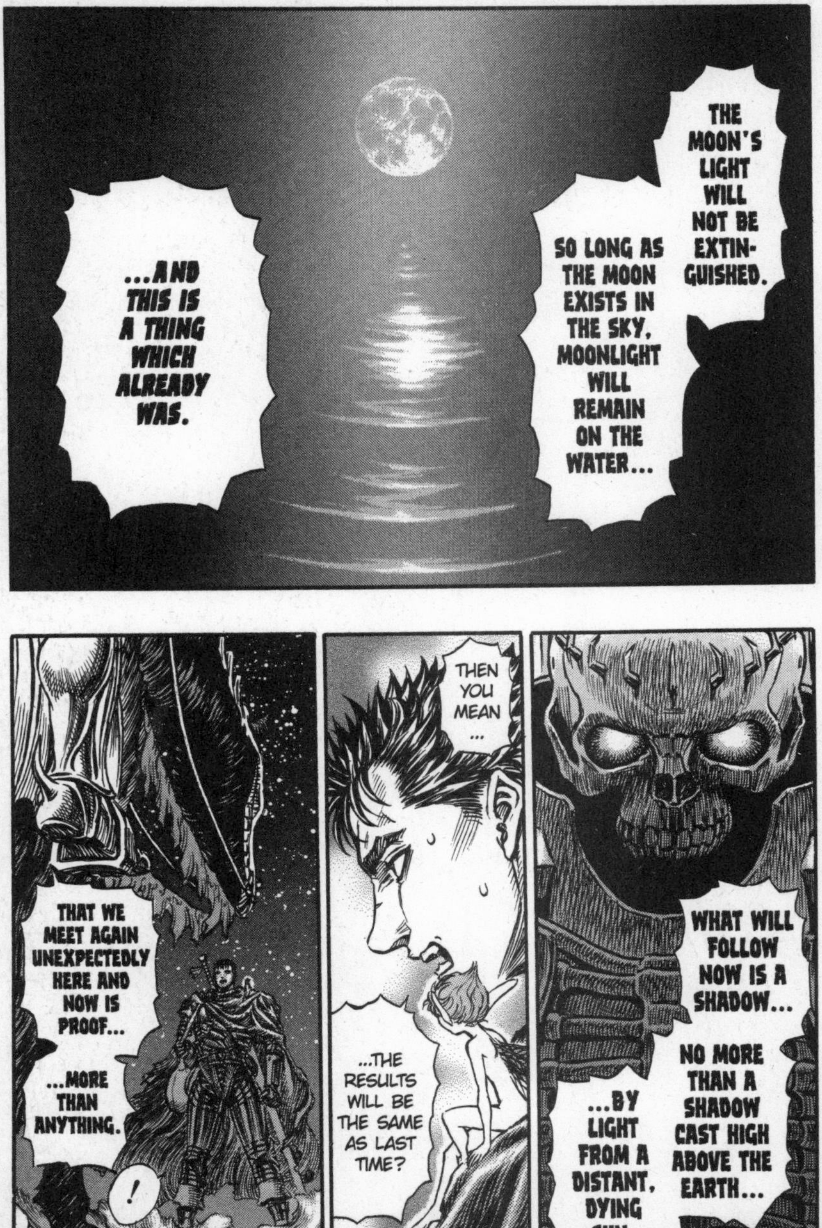
THE MOON'S LIGHT WILL NOT BE EXTINGUISHED.
SO LONG AS THE MOON EXISTS IN THE SKY, MOONLIGHT WILL REMAIN ON THE WATER...
...AND THIS IS A THING WHICH ALREADY WAS.
WHAT WILL FOLLOW NOW IS A SHADOW...
NO MORE THAN A SHADOW CAST HIGH ABOVE THE EARTH...
...BY LIGHT FROM A DISTANT, DYING SUN.
THEN YOU MEAN ...
...THE RESULTS WILL BE THE SAME AS LAST TIME?
THAT WE MEET AGAIN UNEXPECTEDLY HERE AND NOW IS PROOF...
...MORE THAN ANYTHING.
!

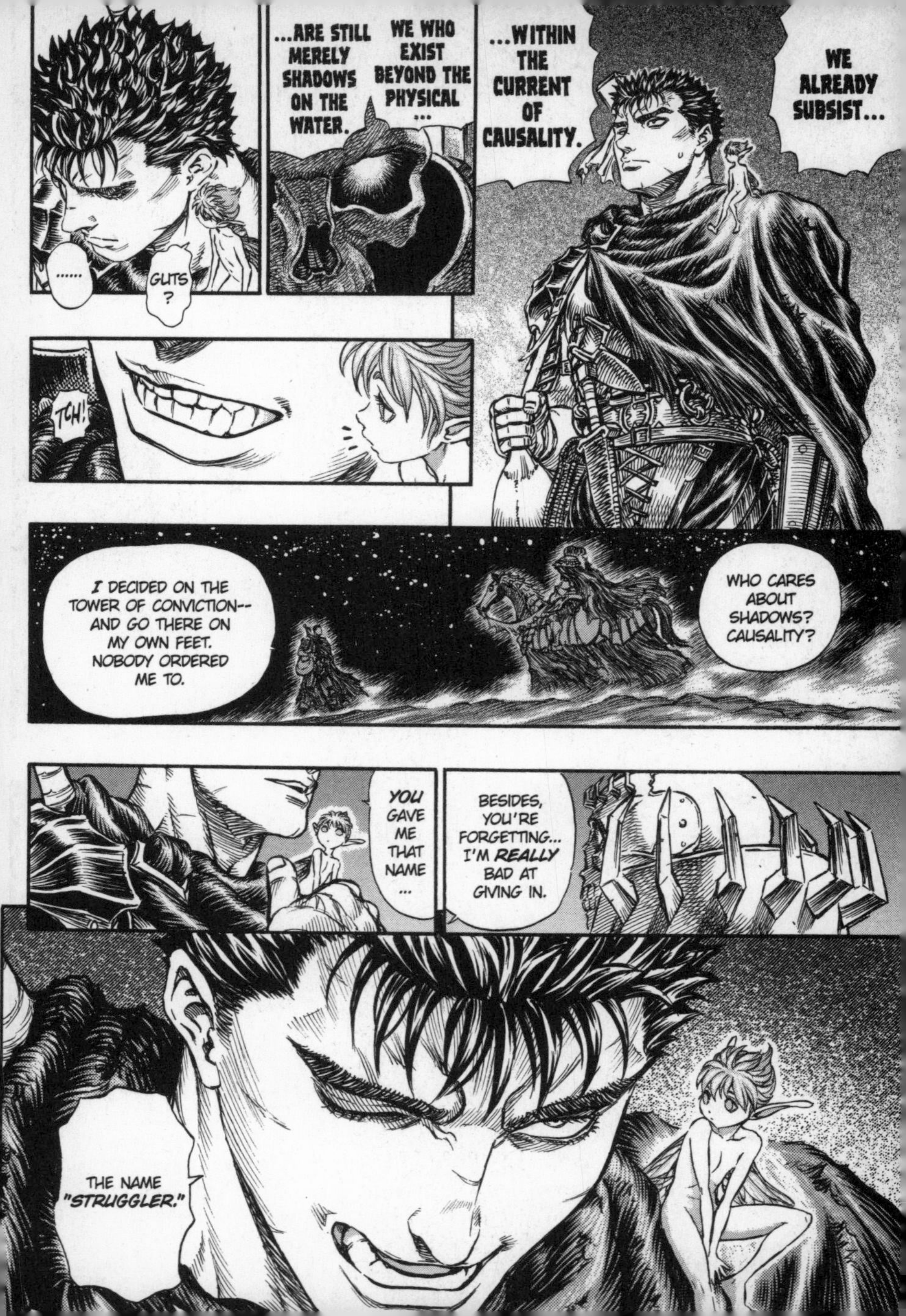
WE ALREADY SUBSIST...
...WITHIN THE CURRENT OF CAUSALITY.
WE WHO EXIST BEYOND THE PHYSICAL...
...ARE STILL MERELY SHADOWS ON THE WATER.
GUTS?
......
TCH!
WHO CARES ABOUT SHADOWS? CAUSALITY?
I DECIDED ON THE TOWER OF CONVICTION--AND GO THERE ON MY OWN FEET. NOBODY ORDERED ME TO.
BESIDES, YOU'RE FORGETTING... I'M ***REALLY*** BAD AT GIVING IN.
YOU GAVE ME THAT NAME...
THE NAME ***"STRUGGLER."***

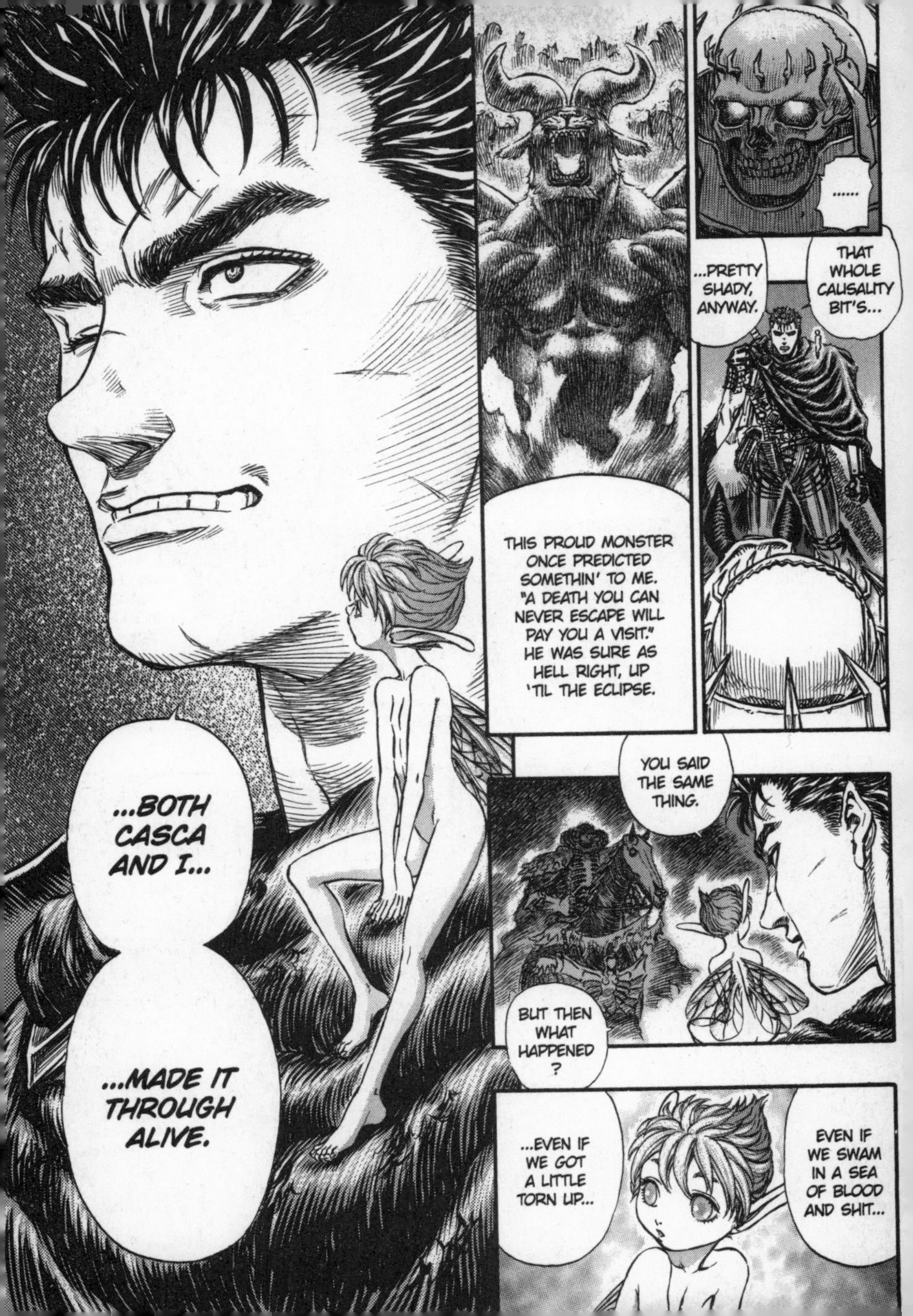
......
THAT WHOLE CAUSALITY BIT'S...
...PRETTY SHADY, ANYWAY.
THIS PROUD MONSTER ONCE PREDICTED SOMETHIN' TO ME. "A DEATH YOU CAN NEVER ESCAPE WILL PAY YOU A VISIT." HE WAS SURE AS HELL RIGHT, UP 'TIL THE ECLIPSE.
YOU SAID THE SAME THING.
BUT THEN WHAT HAPPENED?
EVEN IF WE SWAM IN A SEA OF BLOOD AND SHIT...
...EVEN IF WE GOT A LITTLE TORN UP...
...BOTH CASCA AND I...
...MADE IT THROUGH ALIVE.

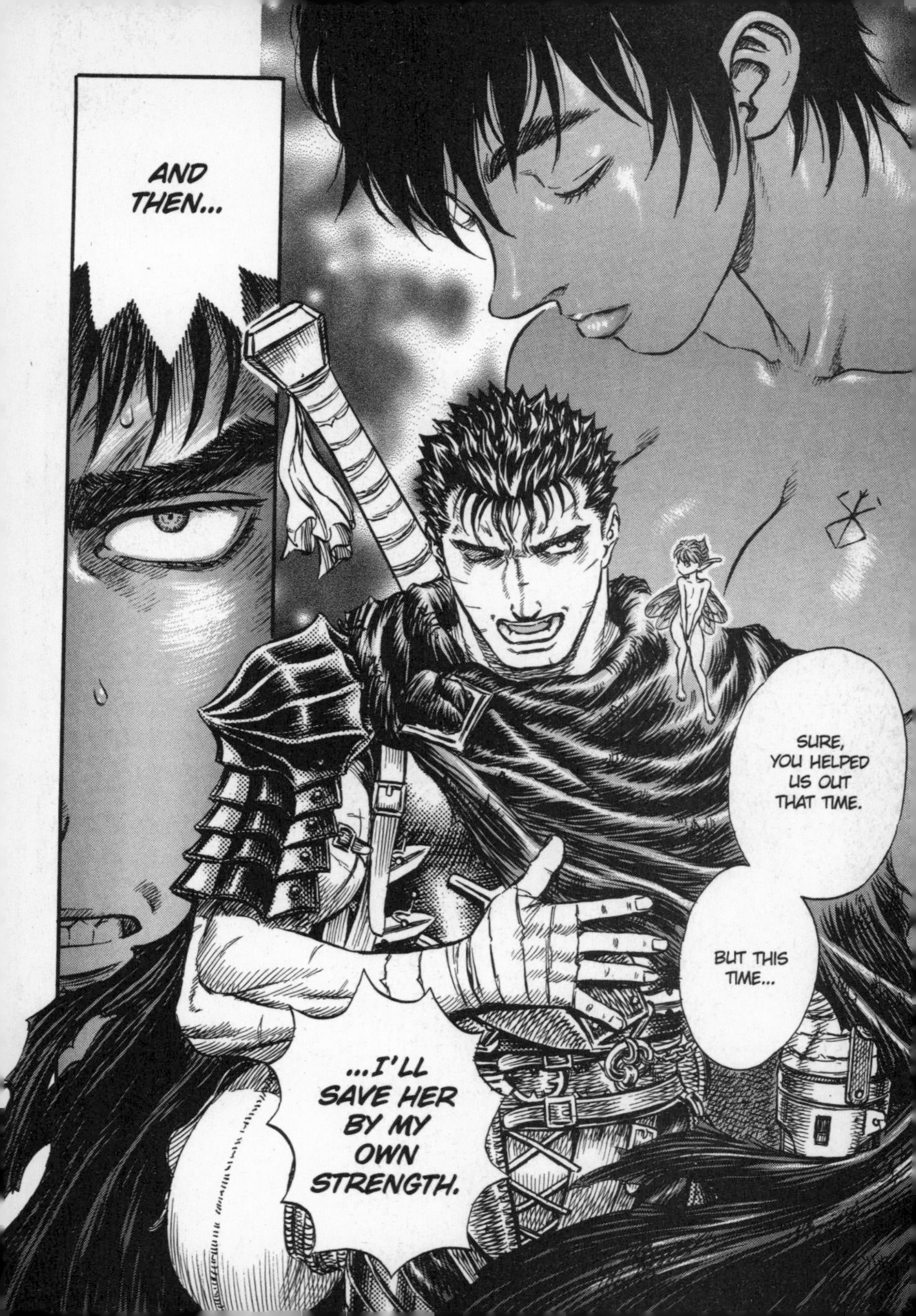
SURE, YOU HELPED US OUT THAT TIME.
BUT THIS TIME...
...I'LL SAVE HER BY MY OWN STRENGTH.
AND THEN...

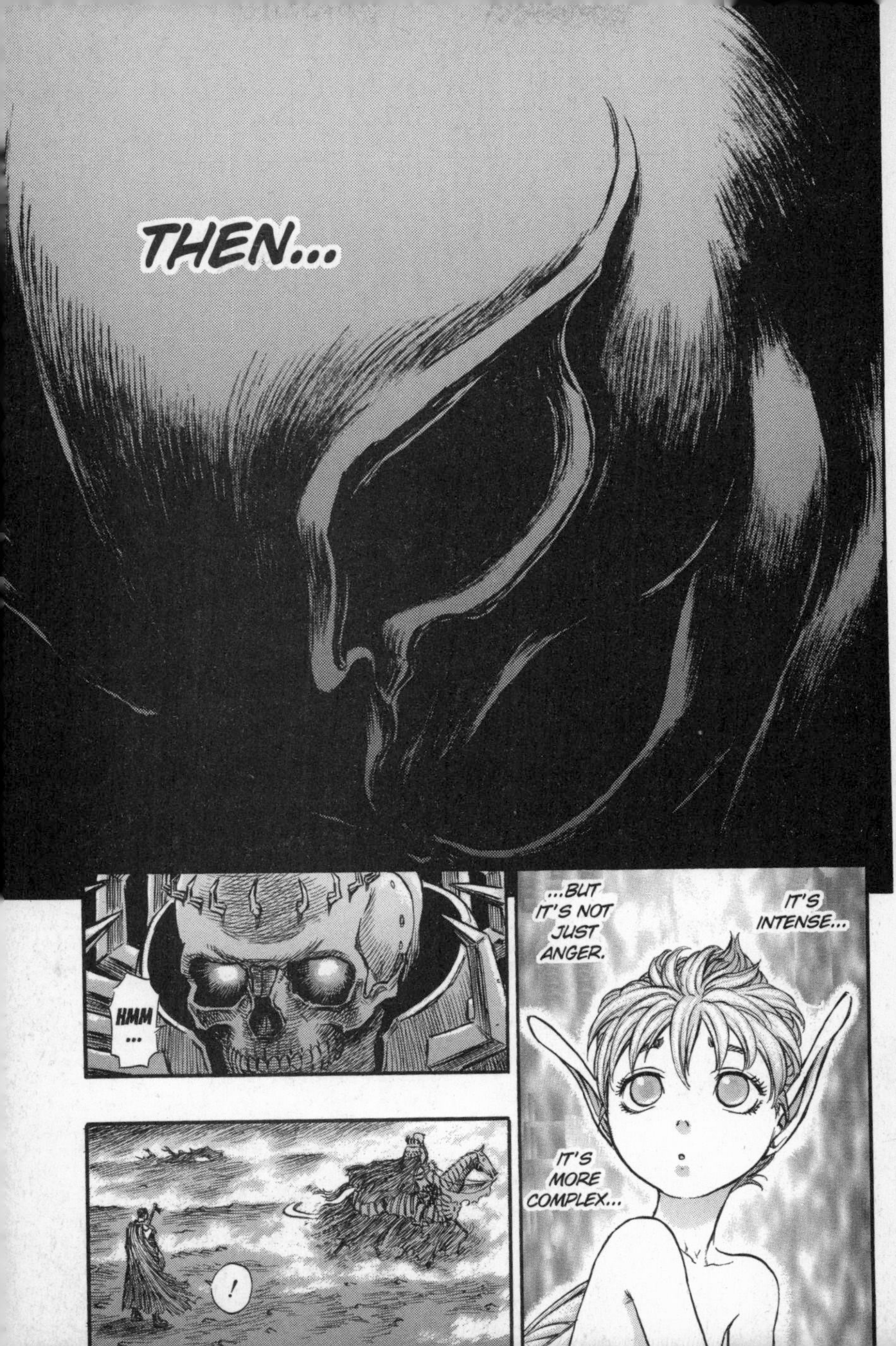
THEN...
IT'S INTENSE...
...BUT IT'S NOT JUST ANGER.
IT'S MORE COMPLEX...
HMM ...
!

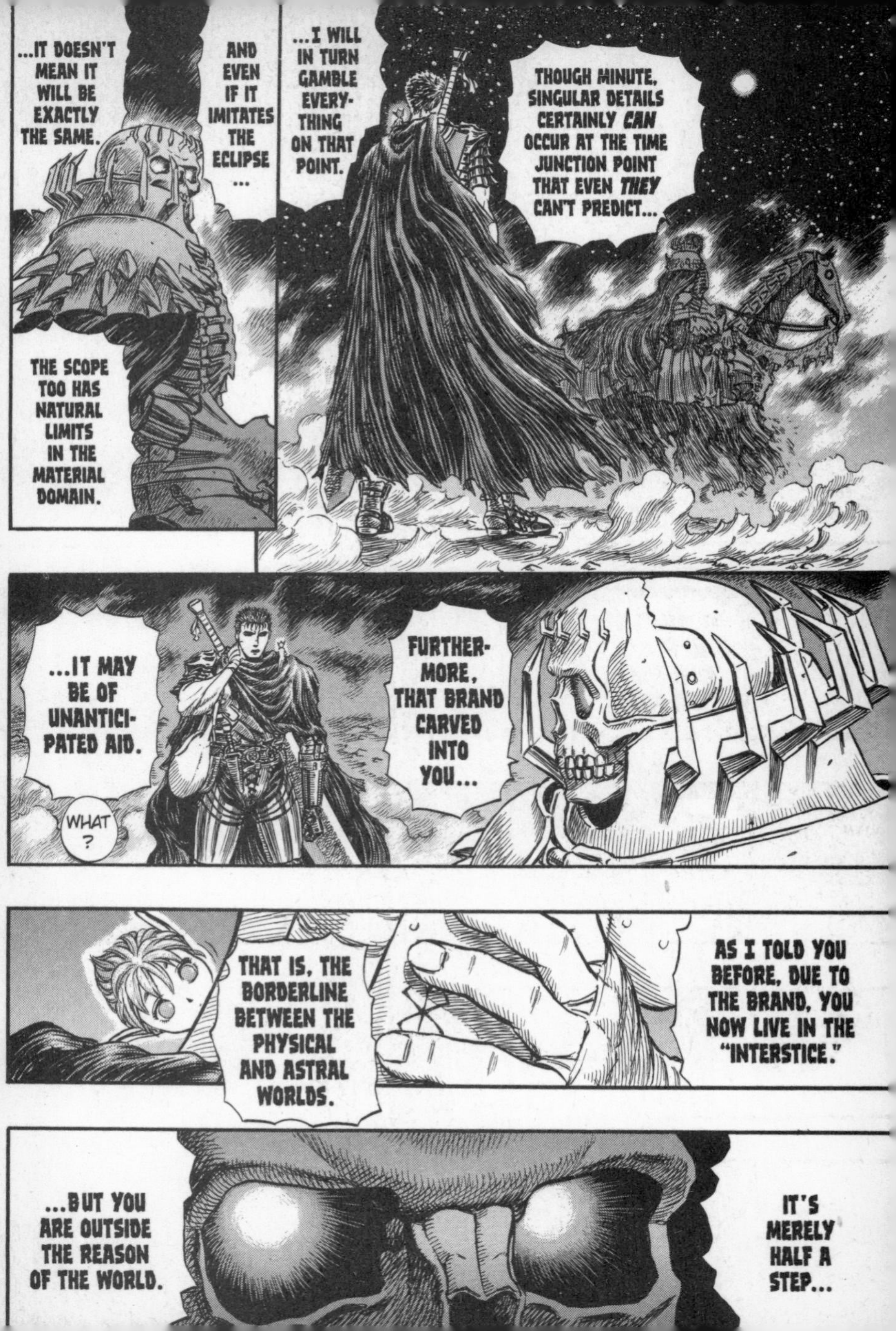
THOUGH MINUTE, SINGULAR DETAILS CERTAINLY *CAN* OCCUR AT THE TIME JUNCTION POINT THAT EVEN *THEY* CAN'T PREDICT...
...I WILL IN TURN GAMBLE EVERY-THING ON THAT POINT.
AND EVEN IF IT IMITATES THE ECLIPSE ...
...IT DOESN'T MEAN IT WILL BE EXACTLY THE SAME.
THE SCOPE TOO HAS NATURAL LIMITS IN THE MATERIAL DOMAIN.
FURTHER-MORE, THAT BRAND CARVED INTO YOU...
...IT MAY BE OF UNANTICI-PATED AID.
WHAT?
AS I TOLD YOU BEFORE, DUE TO THE BRAND, YOU NOW LIVE IN THE "INTERSTICE."
THAT IS, THE BORDERLINE BETWEEN THE PHYSICAL AND ASTRAL WORLDS.
IT'S MERELY HALF A STEP...
...BUT YOU ARE OUTSIDE THE REASON OF THE WORLD.

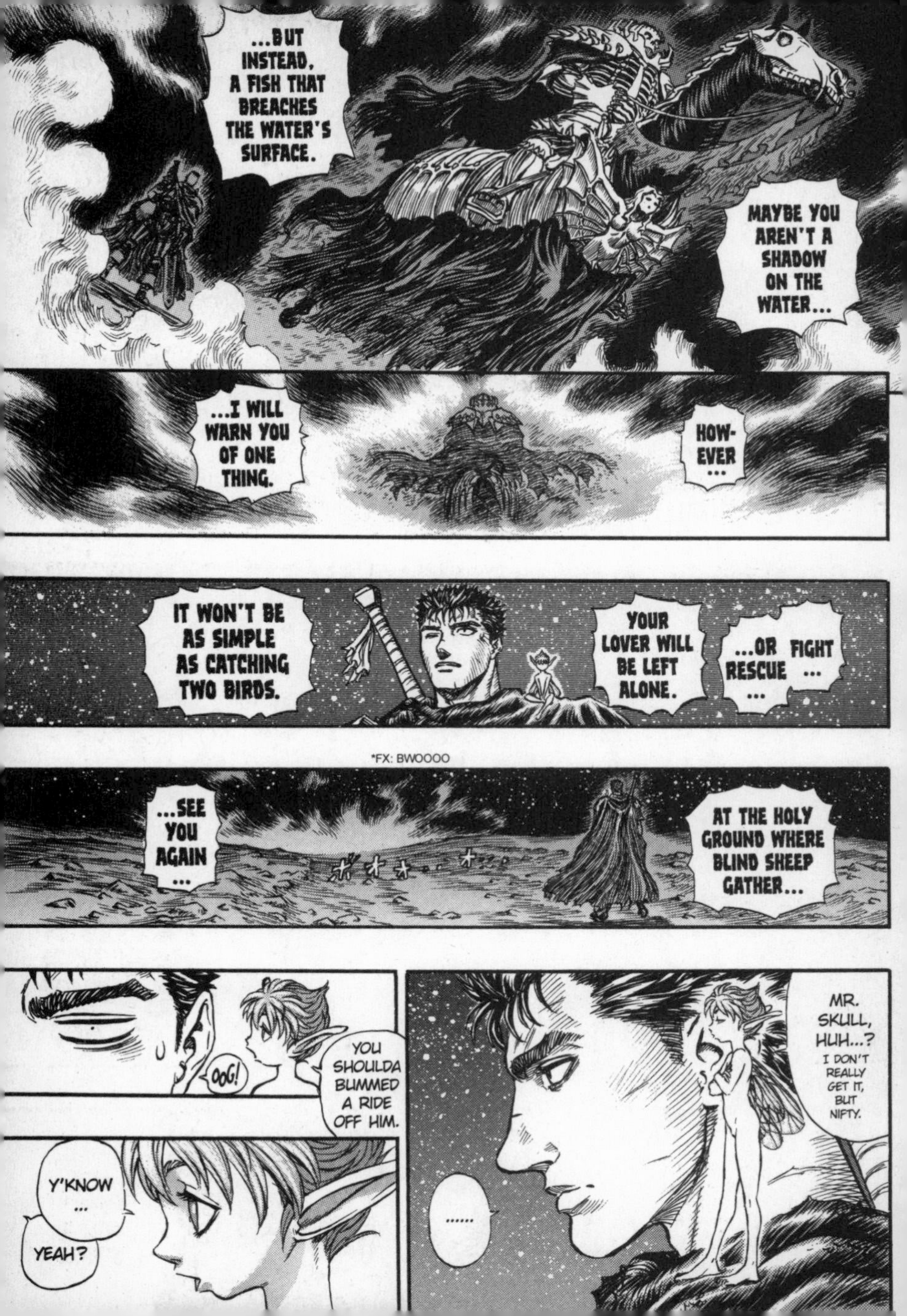
MAYBE YOU AREN'T A SHADOW ON THE WATER...
...BUT INSTEAD, A FISH THAT BREACHES THE WATER'S SURFACE.
HOW-EVER...
...I WILL WARN YOU OF ONE THING.
FIGHT...
...OR RESCUE...
YOUR LOVER WILL BE LEFT ALONE.
IT WON'T BE AS SIMPLE AS CATCHING TWO BIRDS.
*FX: BWOOOO
AT THE HOLY GROUND WHERE BLIND SHEEP GATHER...
...SEE YOU AGAIN...
MR. SKULL, HUH...?
I DON'T REALLY GET IT, BUT NIFTY.
......
OOG!
YOU SHOULDA BUMMED A RIDE OFF HIM.
Y'KNOW...
YEAH?

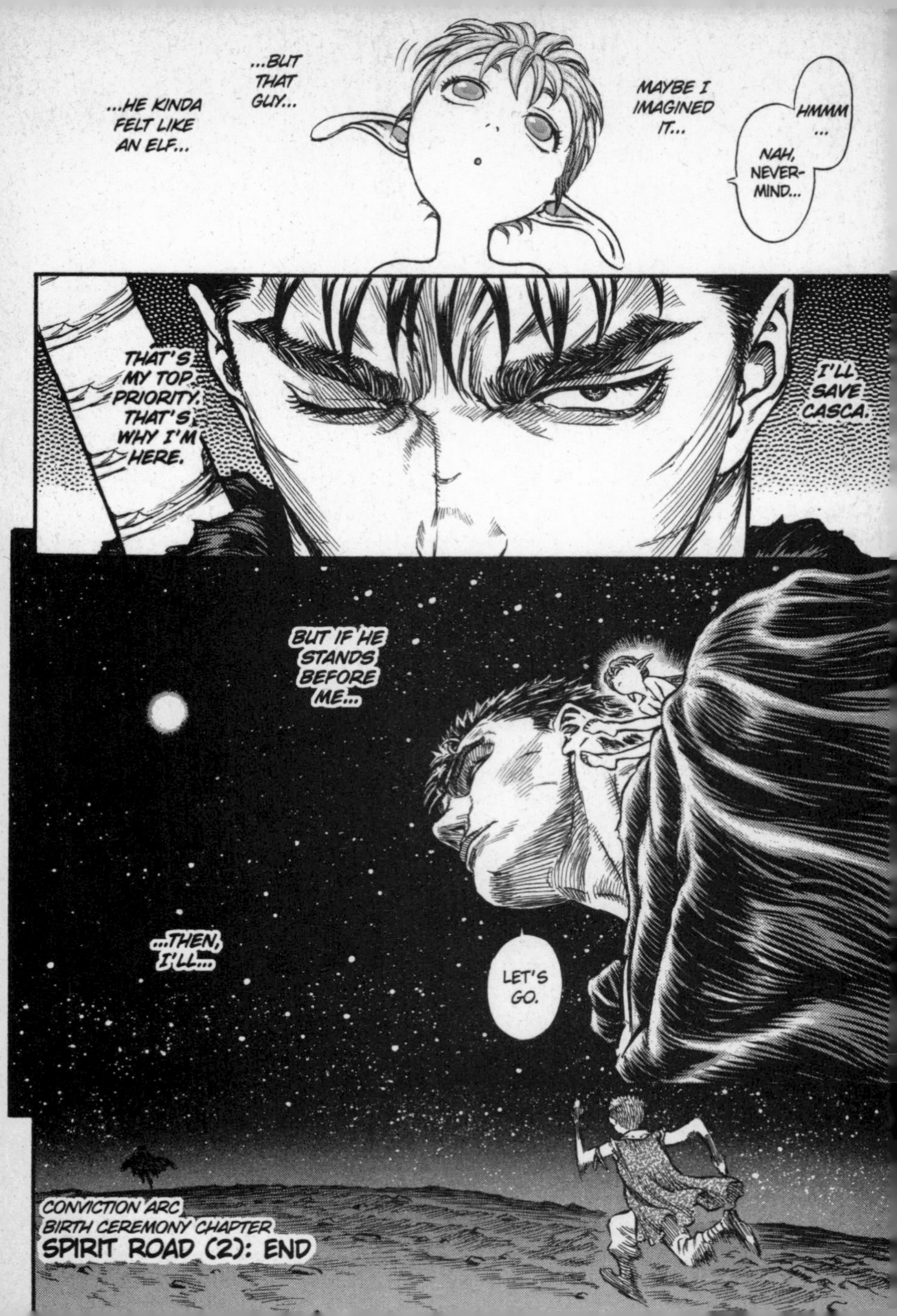
HMMM... NAH, NEVER-MIND...
MAYBE I IMAGINED IT...
...BUT THAT GUY...
...HE KINDA FELT LIKE AN ELF...
I'LL SAVE CASCA.
THAT'S MY TOP PRIORITY. THAT'S WHY I'M HERE.
BUT IF HE STANDS BEFORE ME...
...THEN, I'LL...
LET'S GO.
CONVICTION ARC
BIRTH CEREMONY CHAPTER
SPIRIT ROAD (2): END

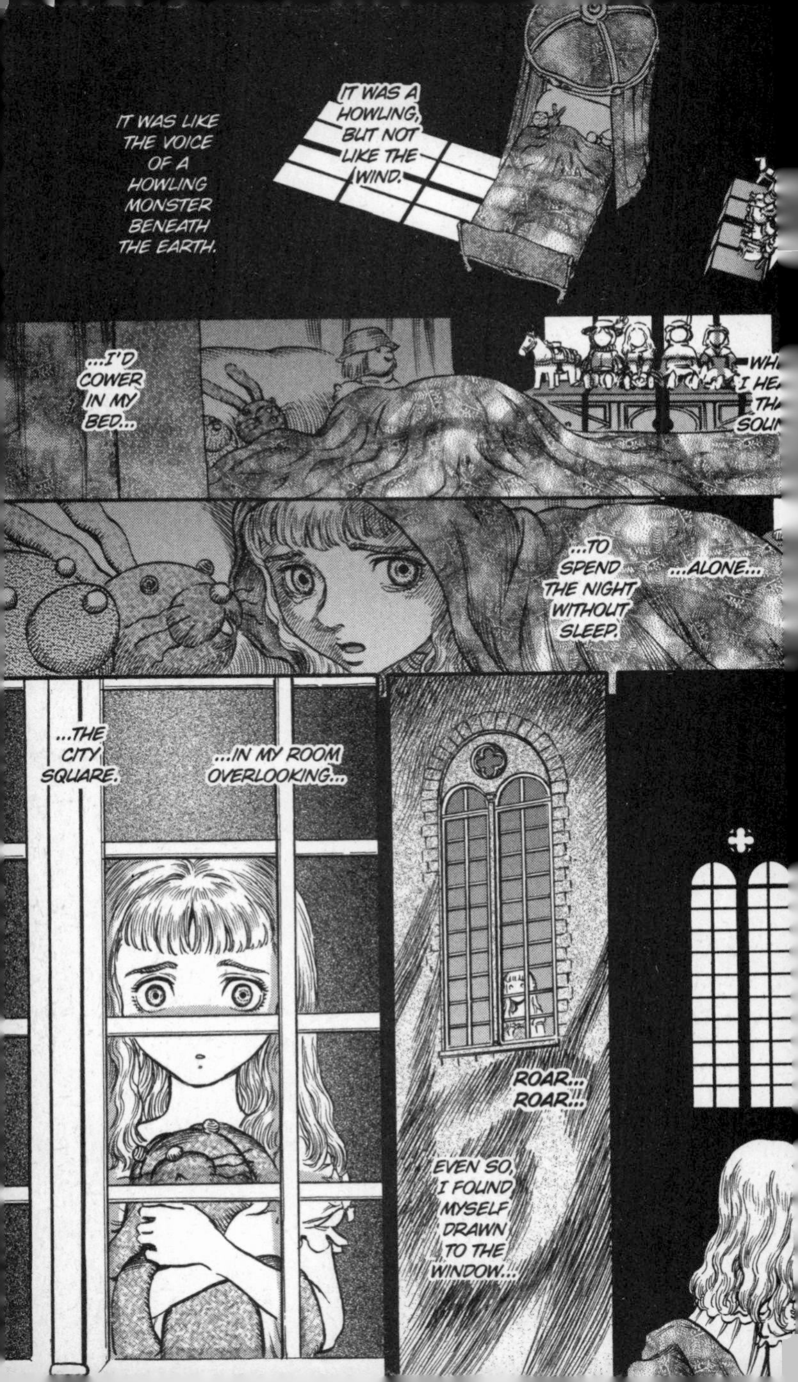
IT WAS A HOWLING, BUT NOT LIKE THE WIND.
IT WAS LIKE THE VOICE OF A HOWLING MONSTER BENEATH THE EARTH.
...I'D COWER IN MY BED...
...ALONE...
...TO SPEND THE NIGHT WITHOUT SLEEP.
ROAR... ROAR...
EVEN SO, I FOUND MYSELF DRAWN TO THE WINDOW...
...IN MY ROOM OVERLOOKING...
...THE CITY SQUARE.

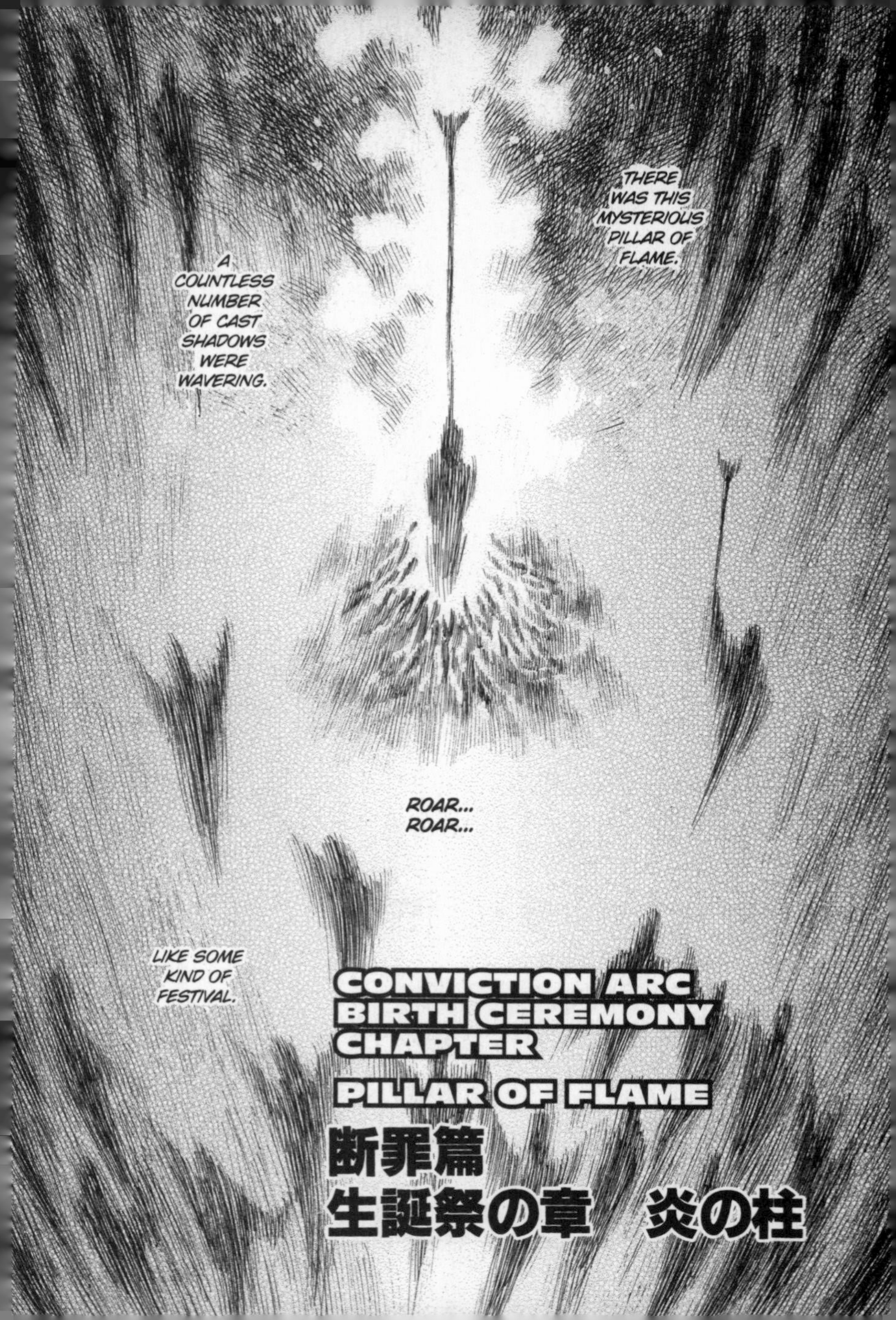
THERE WAS THIS MYSTERIOUS PILLAR OF FLAME.
A COUNTLESS NUMBER OF CAST SHADOWS WERE WAVERING.
ROAR... ROAR...
LIKE SOME KIND OF FESTIVAL.
CONVICTION ARC BIRTH CEREMONY CHAPTER
PILLAR OF FLAME
断罪篇
生誕祭の章　炎の柱

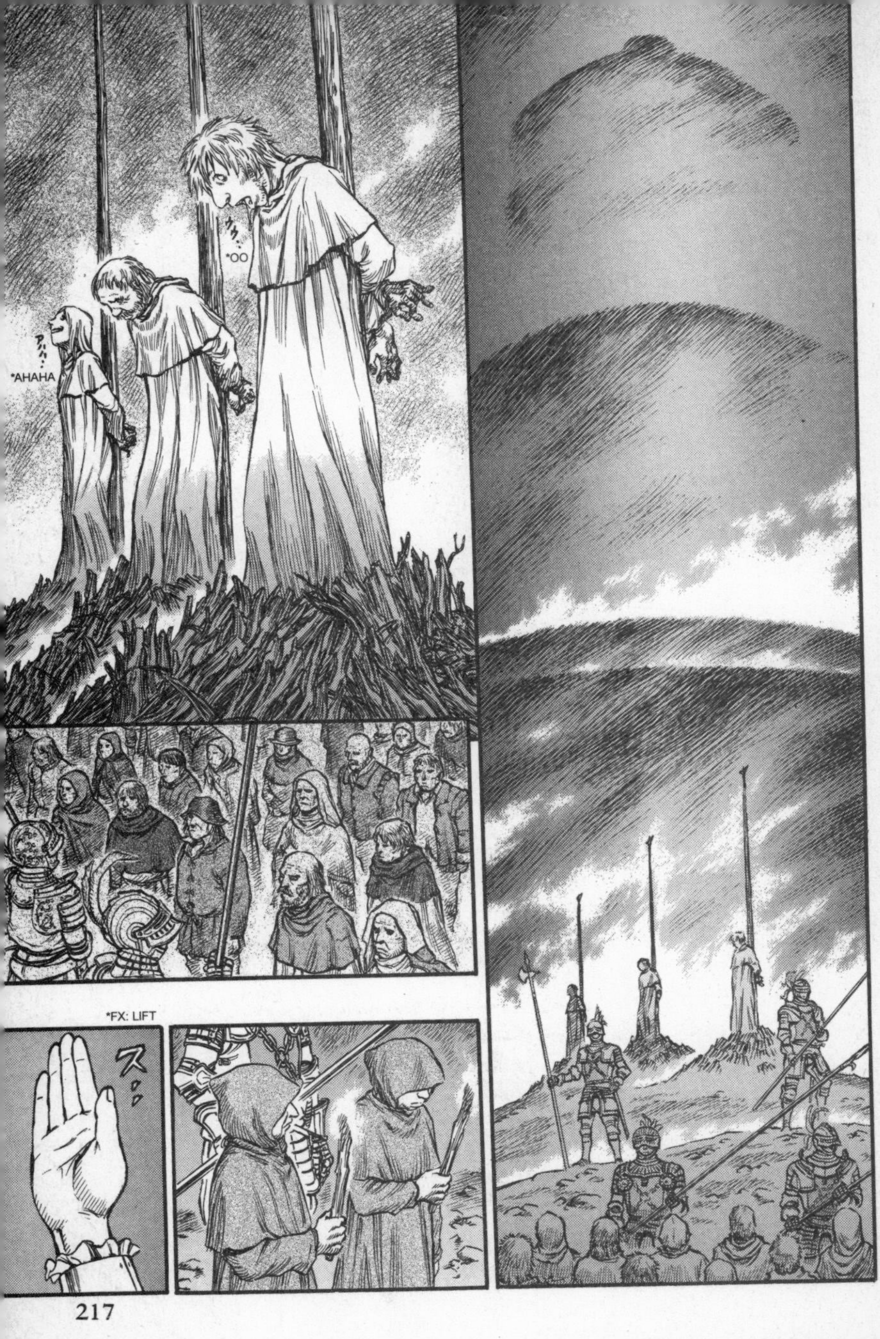
*OO
*AHAHA
*FX: LIFT

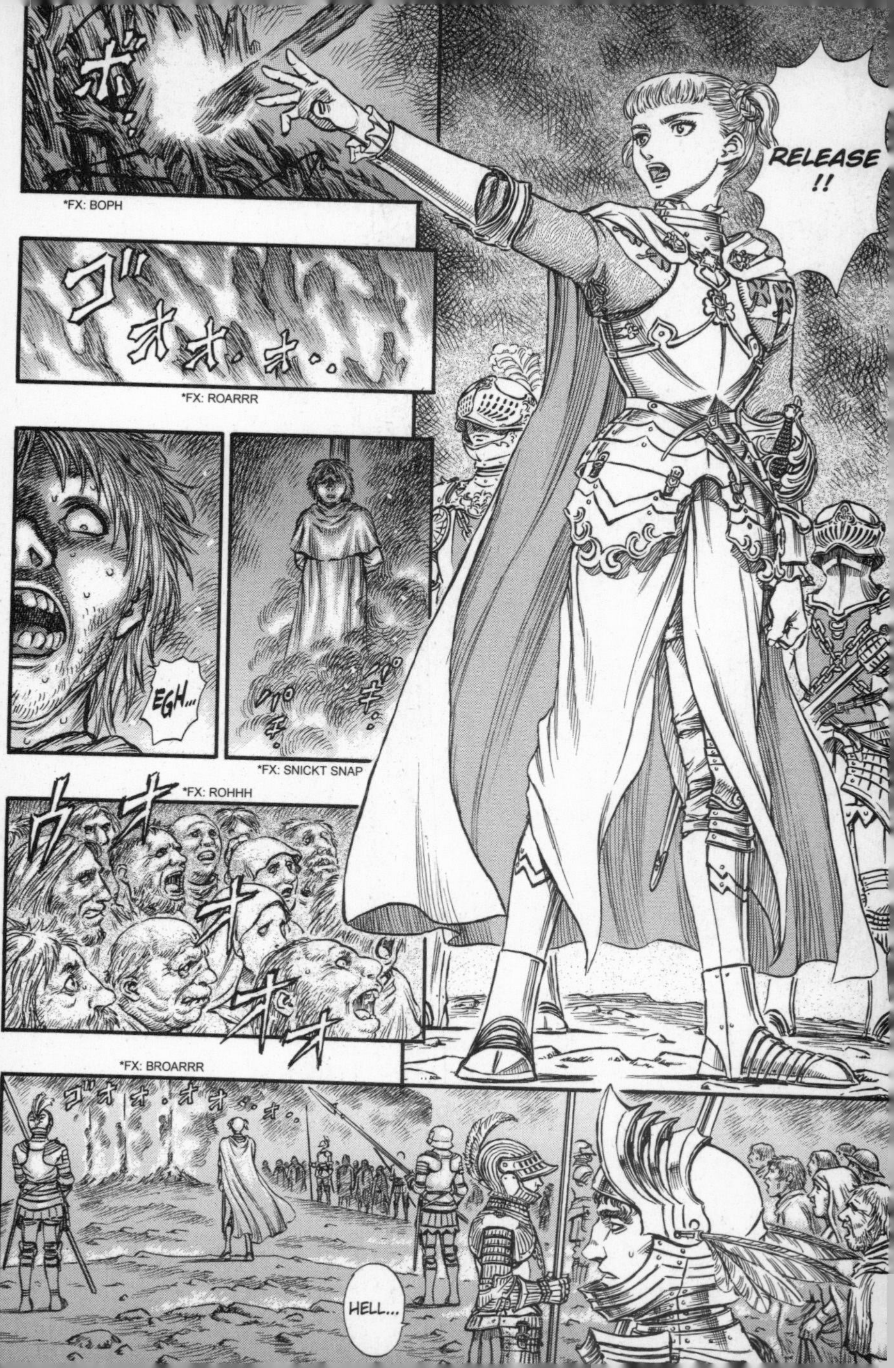
RELEASE !!
*FX: BOPH
*FX: ROARRR
*FX: SNICKT SNAP
EGH...
*FX: ROHHH
*FX: BROARRR
HELL...

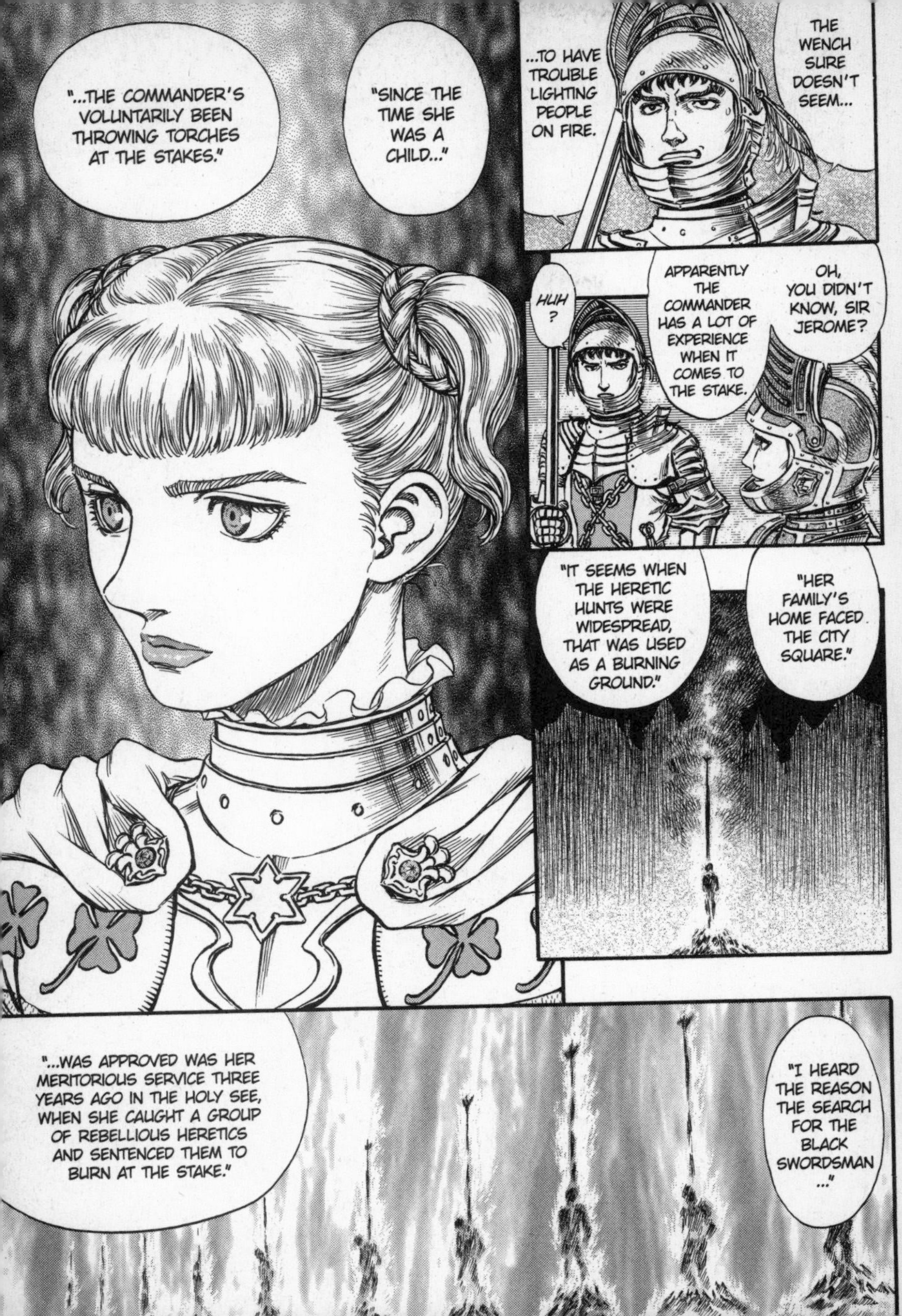
THE WENCH SURE DOESN'T SEEM...
...TO HAVE TROUBLE LIGHTING PEOPLE ON FIRE.
OH, YOU DIDN'T KNOW, SIR JEROME?
APPARENTLY THE COMMANDER HAS A LOT OF EXPERIENCE WHEN IT COMES TO THE STAKE.
HUH?
"HER FAMILY'S HOME FACED THE CITY SQUARE."
"IT SEEMS WHEN THE HERETIC HUNTS WERE WIDESPREAD, THAT WAS USED AS A BURNING GROUND."
"SINCE THE TIME SHE WAS A CHILD..."
"...THE COMMANDER'S VOLUNTARILY BEEN THROWING TORCHES AT THE STAKES."
"I HEARD THE REASON THE SEARCH FOR THE BLACK SWORDSMAN ..."
"...WAS APPROVED WAS HER MERITORIOUS SERVICE THREE YEARS AGO IN THE HOLY SEE, WHEN SHE CAUGHT A GROUP OF REBELLIOUS HERETICS AND SENTENCED THEM TO BURN AT THE STAKE."

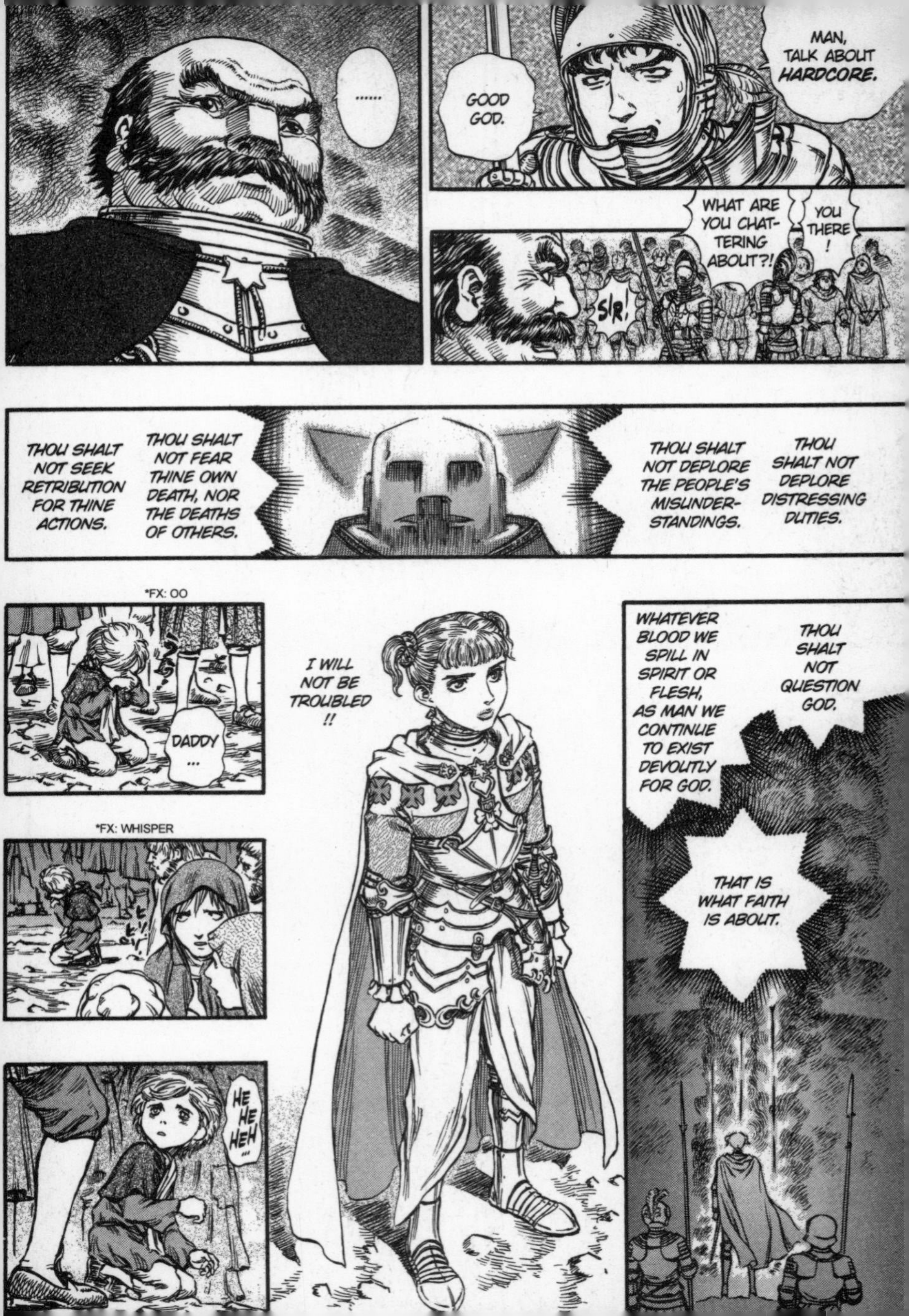
MAN, TALK ABOUT HARDCORE.
GOOD GOD.
YOU THERE!
WHAT ARE YOU CHATTERING ABOUT?!
SIR!
......
THOU SHALT NOT DEPLORE DISTRESSING DUTIES.
THOU SHALT NOT DEPLORE THE PEOPLE'S MISUNDERSTANDINGS.
THOU SHALT NOT FEAR THINE OWN DEATH, NOR THE DEATHS OF OTHERS.
THOU SHALT NOT SEEK RETRIBUTION FOR THINE ACTIONS.
THOU SHALT NOT QUESTION GOD.
WHATEVER BLOOD WE SPILL IN SPIRIT OR FLESH, AS MAN WE CONTINUE TO EXIST DEVOUTLY FOR GOD.
THAT IS WHAT FAITH IS ABOUT.
I WILL NOT BE TROUBLED!!
*FX: OO
DADDY...
*FX: WHISPER
HE HE HEH...

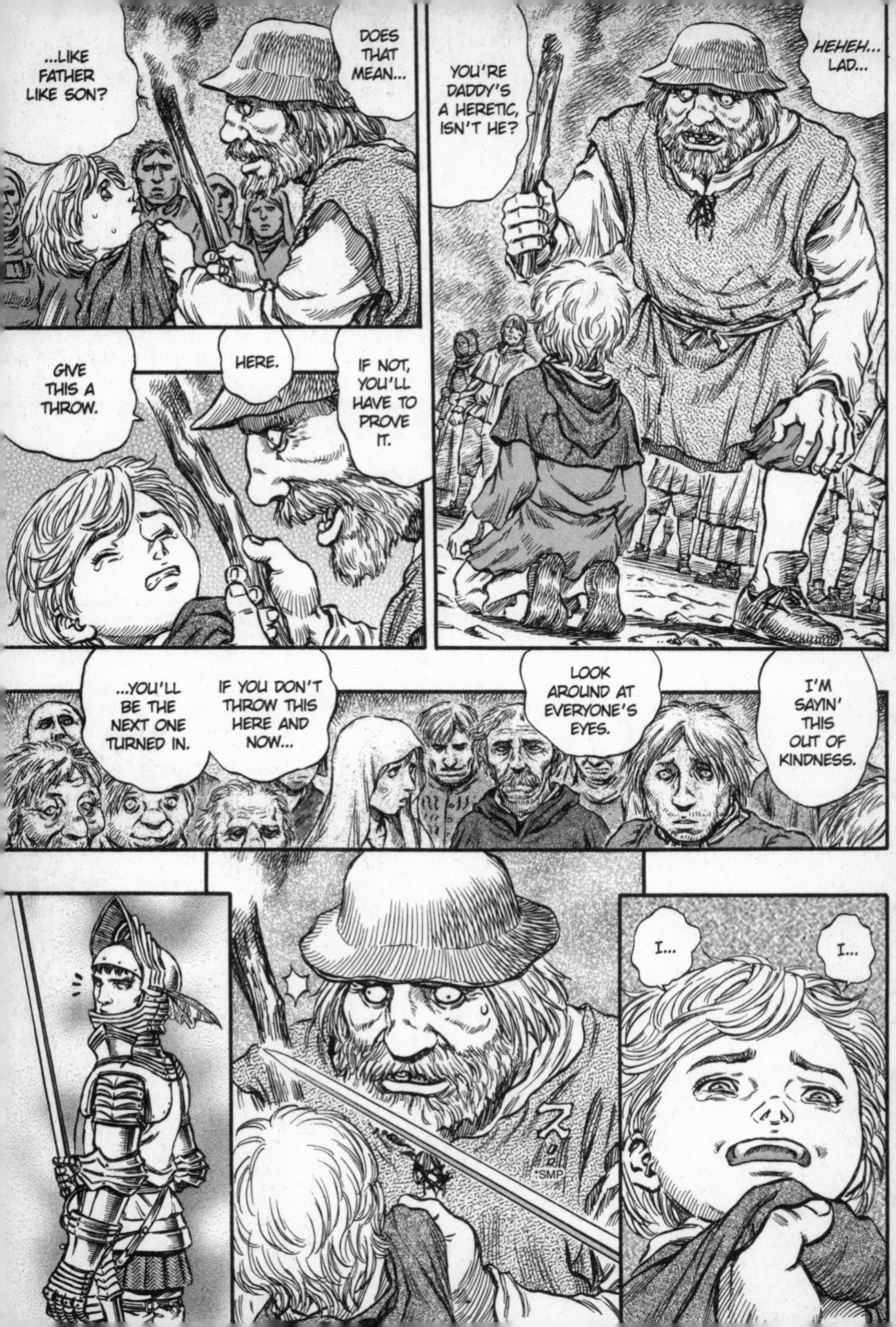

HEHEH... LAD...
YOU'RE DADDY'S A HERETIC, ISN'T HE?
DOES THAT MEAN...
...LIKE FATHER LIKE SON?
IF NOT, YOU'LL HAVE TO PROVE IT.
HERE.
GIVE THIS A THROW.
I'M SAYIN' THIS OUT OF KINDNESS.
LOOK AROUND AT EVERYONE'S EYES.
IF YOU DON'T THROW THIS HERE AND NOW...
...YOU'LL BE THE NEXT ONE TURNED IN.
I...
I...
SMP

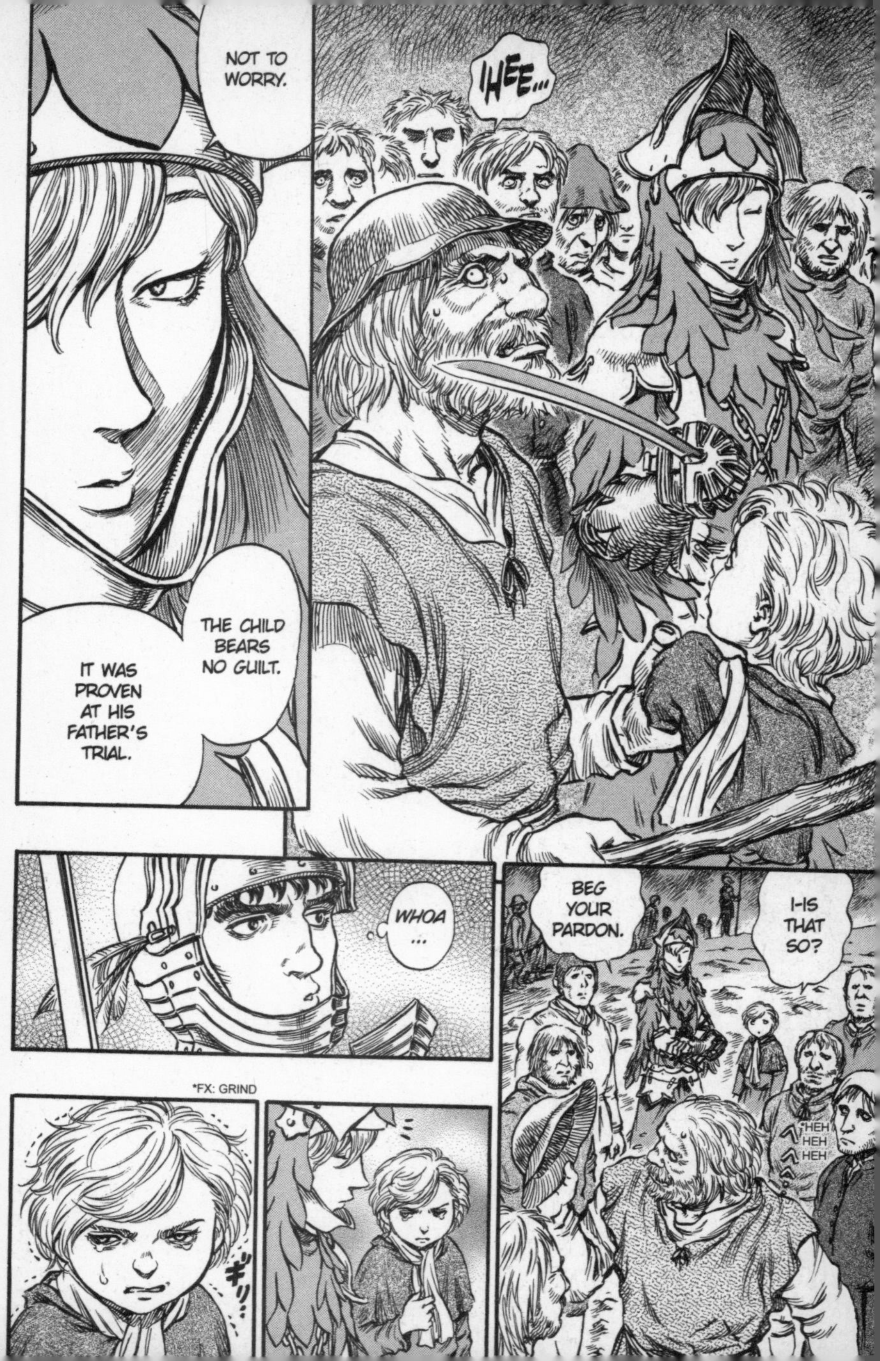
HEE...
NOT TO WORRY.
THE CHILD BEARS NO GUILT.
IT WAS PROVEN AT HIS FATHER'S TRIAL.
I-IS THAT SO?
BEG YOUR PARDON.
*HEH HEH HEH
WHOA ...
*FX: GRIND
ギリ

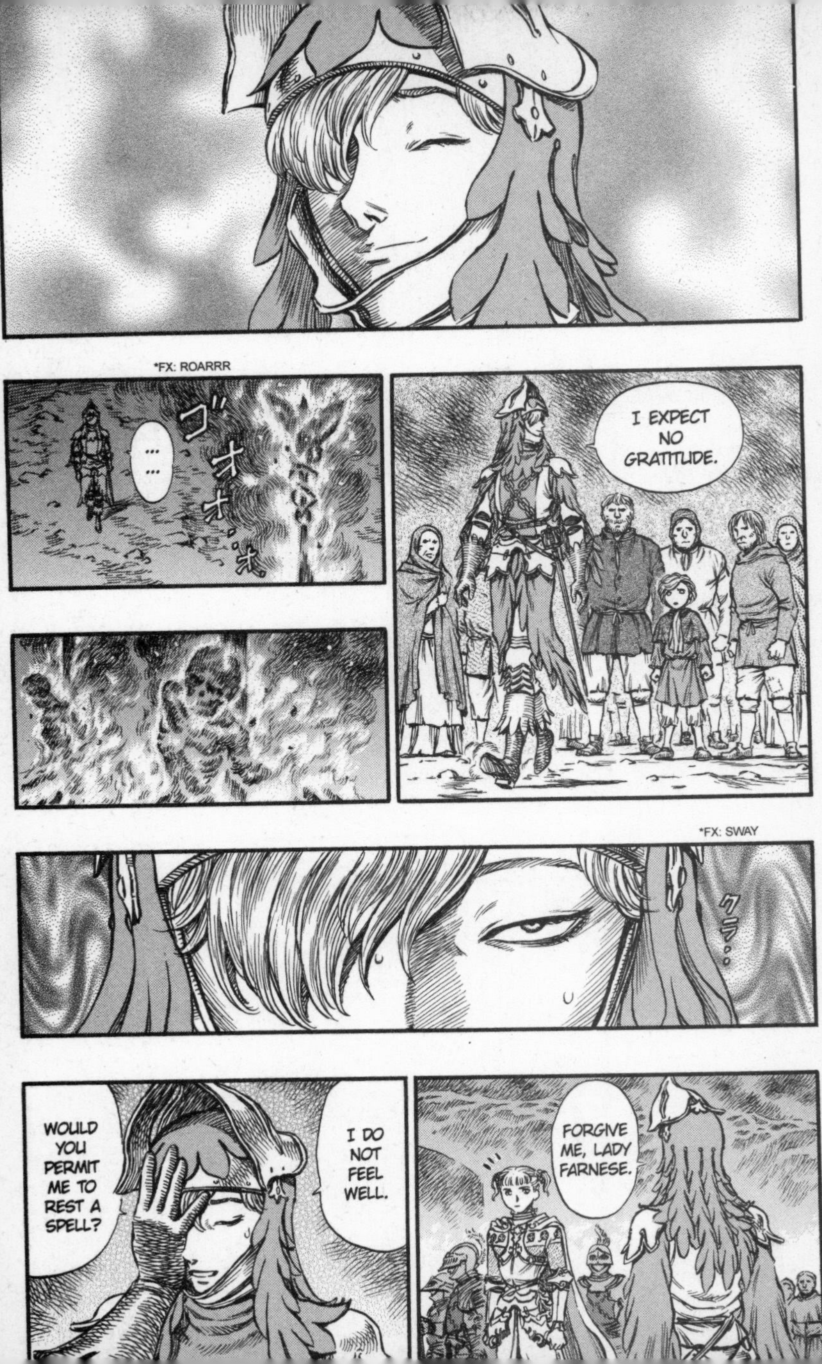
I EXPECT NO GRATITUDE.
*FX: ROARRR
……
……
*FX: SWAY
FORGIVE ME, LADY FARNESE.
I DO NOT FEEL WELL.
WOULD YOU PERMIT ME TO REST A SPELL?

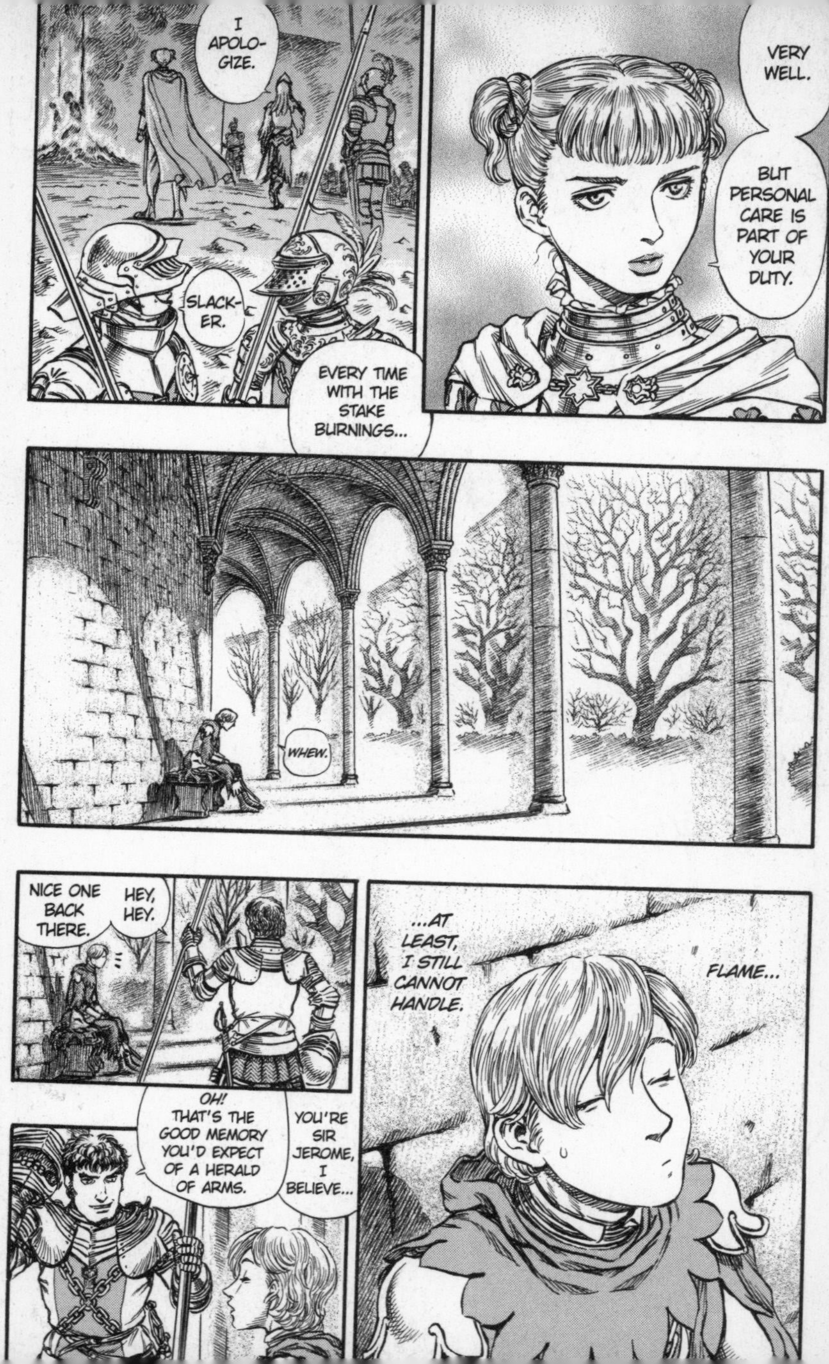
VERY WELL.
BUT PERSONAL CARE IS PART OF YOUR DUTY.
I APOLOGIZE.
SLACKER.
EVERY TIME WITH THE STAKE BURNINGS...
WHEW.
FLAME...
...AT LEAST, I STILL CANNOT HANDLE.
HEY, HEY.
NICE ONE BACK THERE.
YOU'RE SIR JEROME, I BELIEVE...
OH! THAT'S THE GOOD MEMORY YOU'D EXPECT OF A HERALD OF ARMS.

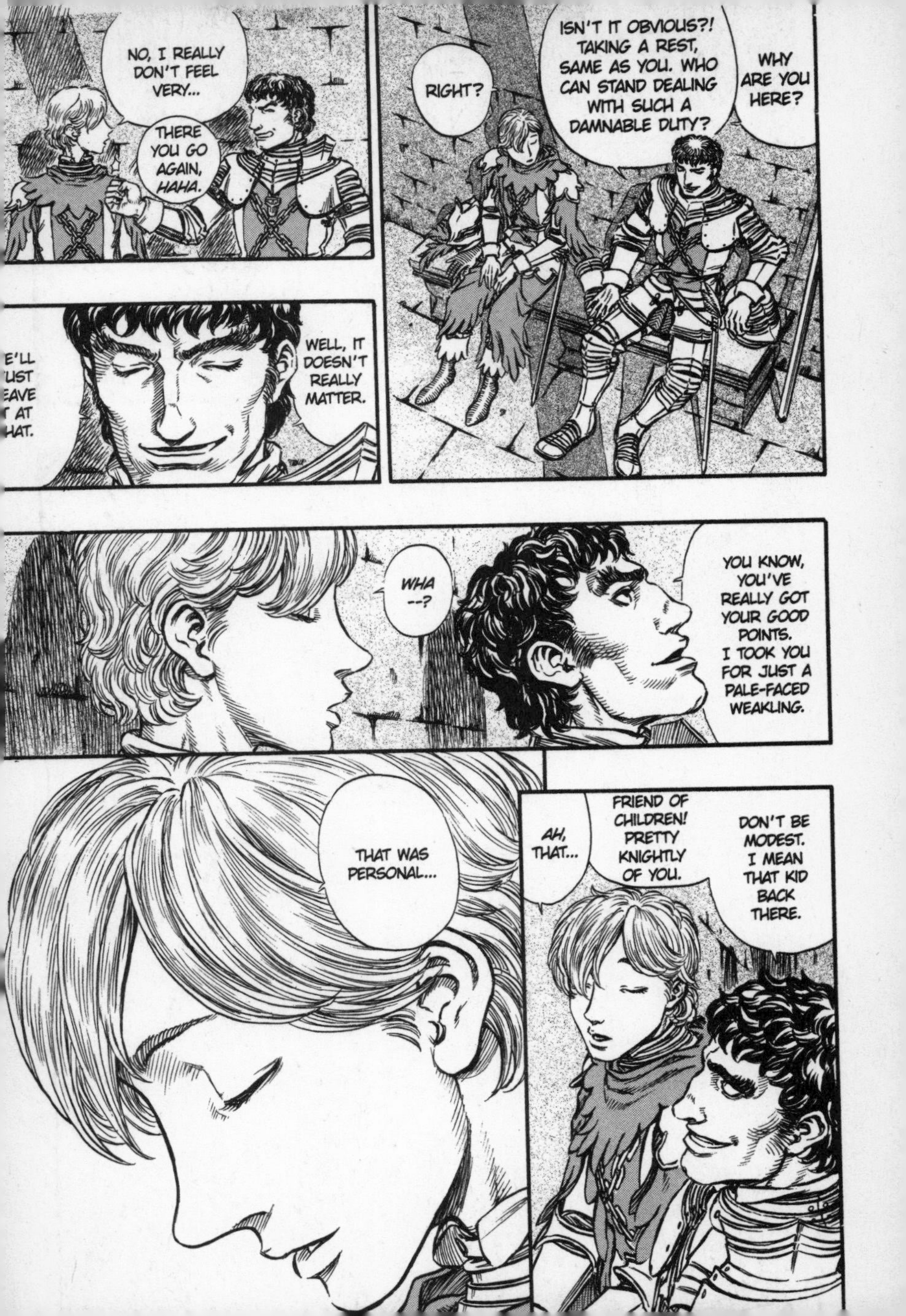
WHY ARE YOU HERE?
ISN'T IT OBVIOUS?! TAKING A REST, SAME AS YOU. WHO CAN STAND DEALING WITH SUCH A DAMNABLE DUTY?
RIGHT?
NO, I REALLY DON'T FEEL VERY...
THERE YOU GO AGAIN, HAHA.
WELL, IT DOESN'T REALLY MATTER.
E'LL UST EAVE T AT HAT.
YOU KNOW, YOU'VE REALLY GOT YOUR GOOD POINTS. I TOOK YOU FOR JUST A PALE-FACED WEAKLING.
WHA--?
DON'T BE MODEST. I MEAN THAT KID BACK THERE.
FRIEND OF CHILDREN! PRETTY KNIGHTLY OF YOU.
AH, THAT...
THAT WAS PERSONAL...

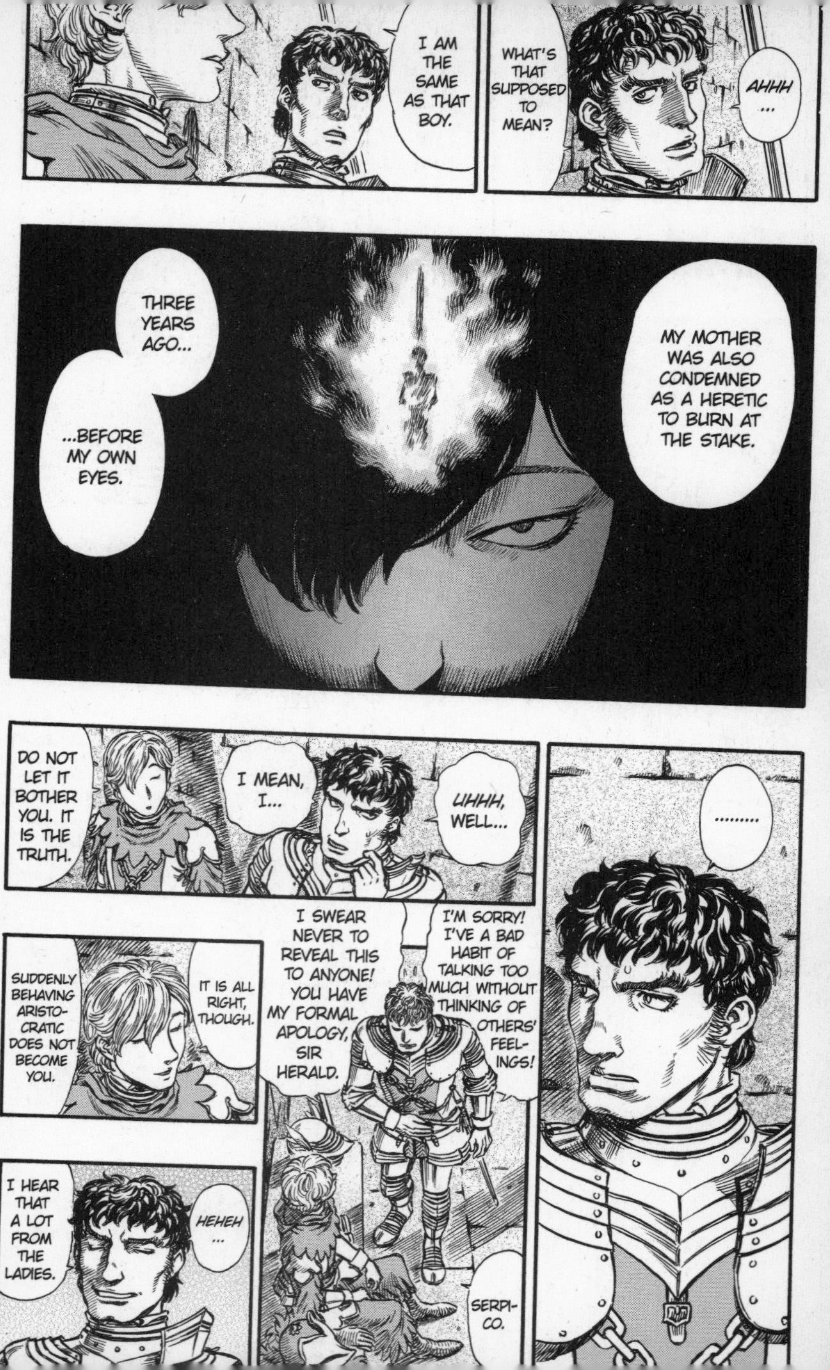
AHHH ...
WHAT'S THAT SUPPOSED TO MEAN?
I AM THE SAME AS THAT BOY.
MY MOTHER WAS ALSO CONDEMNED AS A HERETIC TO BURN AT THE STAKE.
THREE YEARS AGO...
...BEFORE MY OWN EYES.
....
SERPI-CO.
UHHH, WELL...
I MEAN, I...
DO NOT LET IT BOTHER YOU. IT IS THE TRUTH.
I'M SORRY! I'VE A BAD HABIT OF TALKING TOO MUCH WITHOUT THINKING OF OTHERS' FEEL-INGS!
I SWEAR NEVER TO REVEAL THIS TO ANYONE! YOU HAVE MY FORMAL APOLOGY, SIR HERALD.
IT IS ALL RIGHT, THOUGH.
SUDDENLY BEHAVING ARISTO-CRATIC DOES NOT BECOME YOU.
HEHEH ...
I HEAR THAT A LOT FROM THE LADIES.

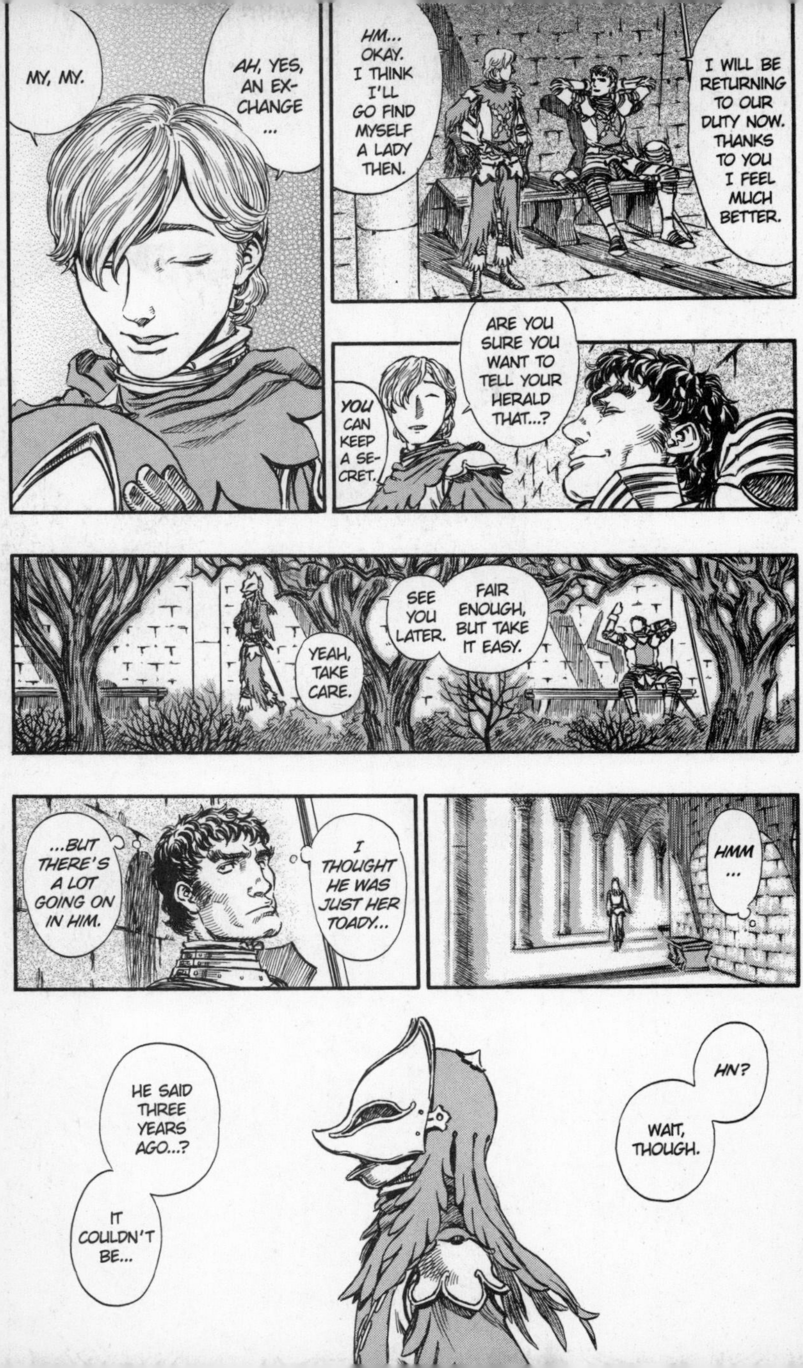
I WILL BE RETURNING TO OUR DUTY NOW. THANKS TO YOU I FEEL MUCH BETTER.
HM... OKAY. I THINK I'LL GO FIND MYSELF A LADY THEN.
ARE YOU SURE YOU WANT TO TELL YOUR HERALD THAT...?
YOU CAN KEEP A SE-CRET.
AH, YES, AN EX-CHANGE ...
MY, MY.
FAIR ENOUGH, BUT TAKE IT EASY.
SEE YOU LATER.
YEAH, TAKE CARE.
HMM ...
I THOUGHT HE WAS JUST HER TOADY...
...BUT THERE'S A LOT GOING ON IN HIM.
HN?
WAIT, THOUGH.
HE SAID THREE YEARS AGO...?
IT COULDN'T BE...

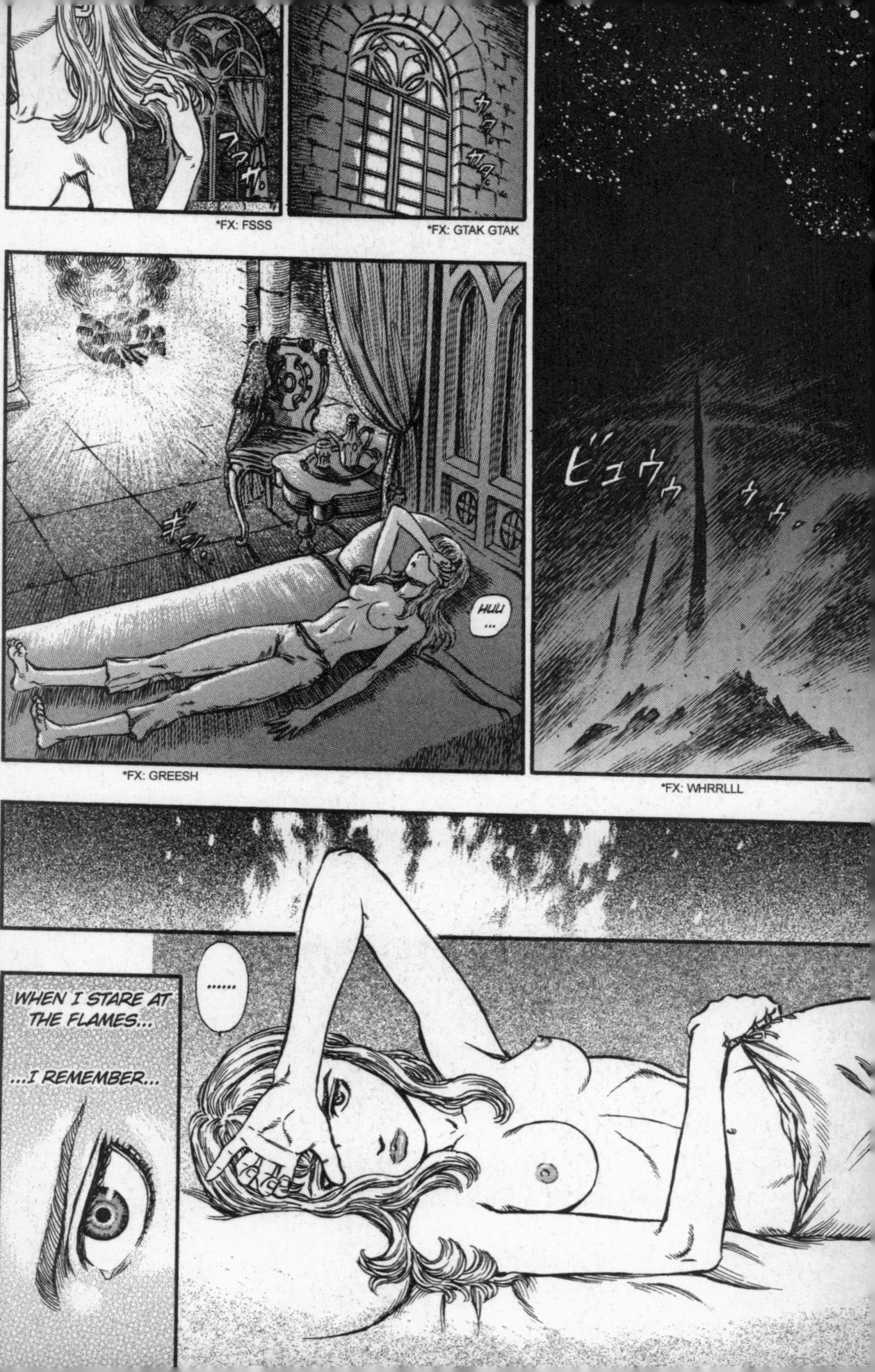
*FX: WHRRLLL
*FX: GTAK GTAK
*FX: FSSS
HUU ...
*FX: GREESH
......
WHEN I STARE AT THE FLAMES...
...I REMEMBER...

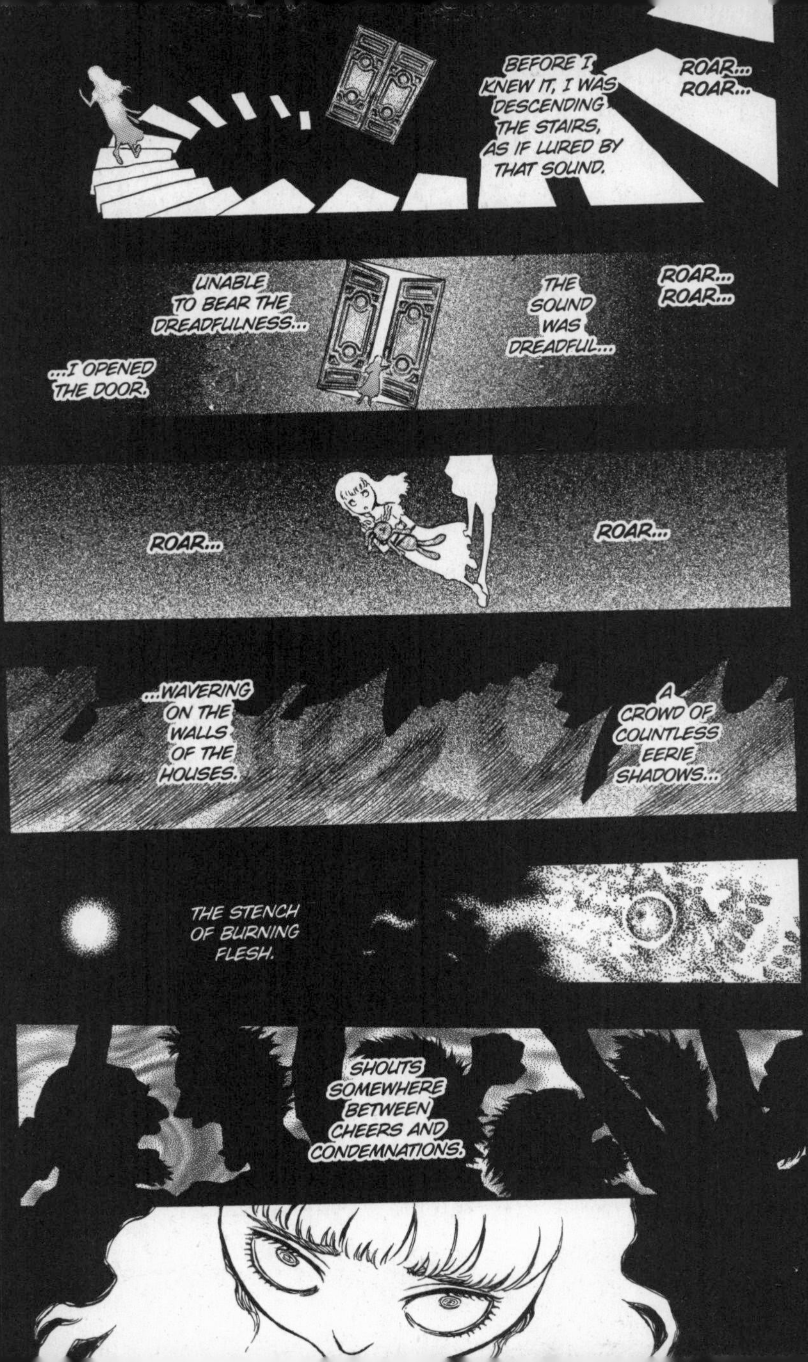
ROAR... ROAR...
BEFORE I KNEW IT, I WAS DESCENDING THE STAIRS, AS IF LURED BY THAT SOUND.
ROAR... ROAR...
THE SOUND WAS DREADFUL...
UNABLE TO BEAR THE DREADFULNESS...
...I OPENED THE DOOR.
ROAR...
ROAR...
A CROWD OF COUNTLESS EERIE SHADOWS...
...WAVERING ON THE WALLS OF THE HOUSES.
THE STENCH OF BURNING FLESH.
SHOUTS SOMEWHERE BETWEEN CHEERS AND CONDEMNATIONS.

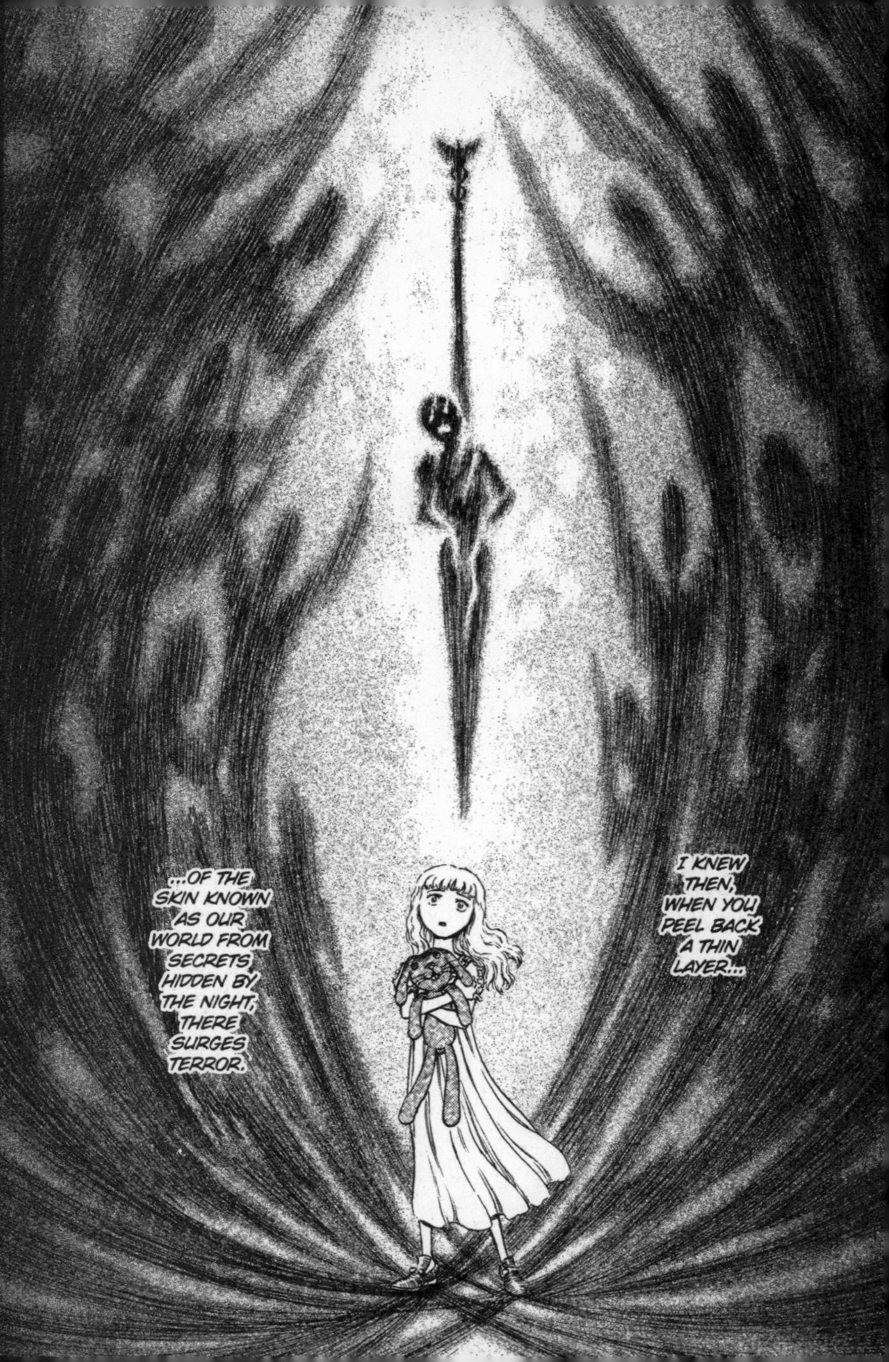
I KNEW THEN, WHEN YOU PEEL BACK A THIN LAYER...
...OF THE SKIN KNOWN AS OUR WORLD FROM SECRETS HIDDEN BY THE NIGHT, THERE SURGES TERROR.

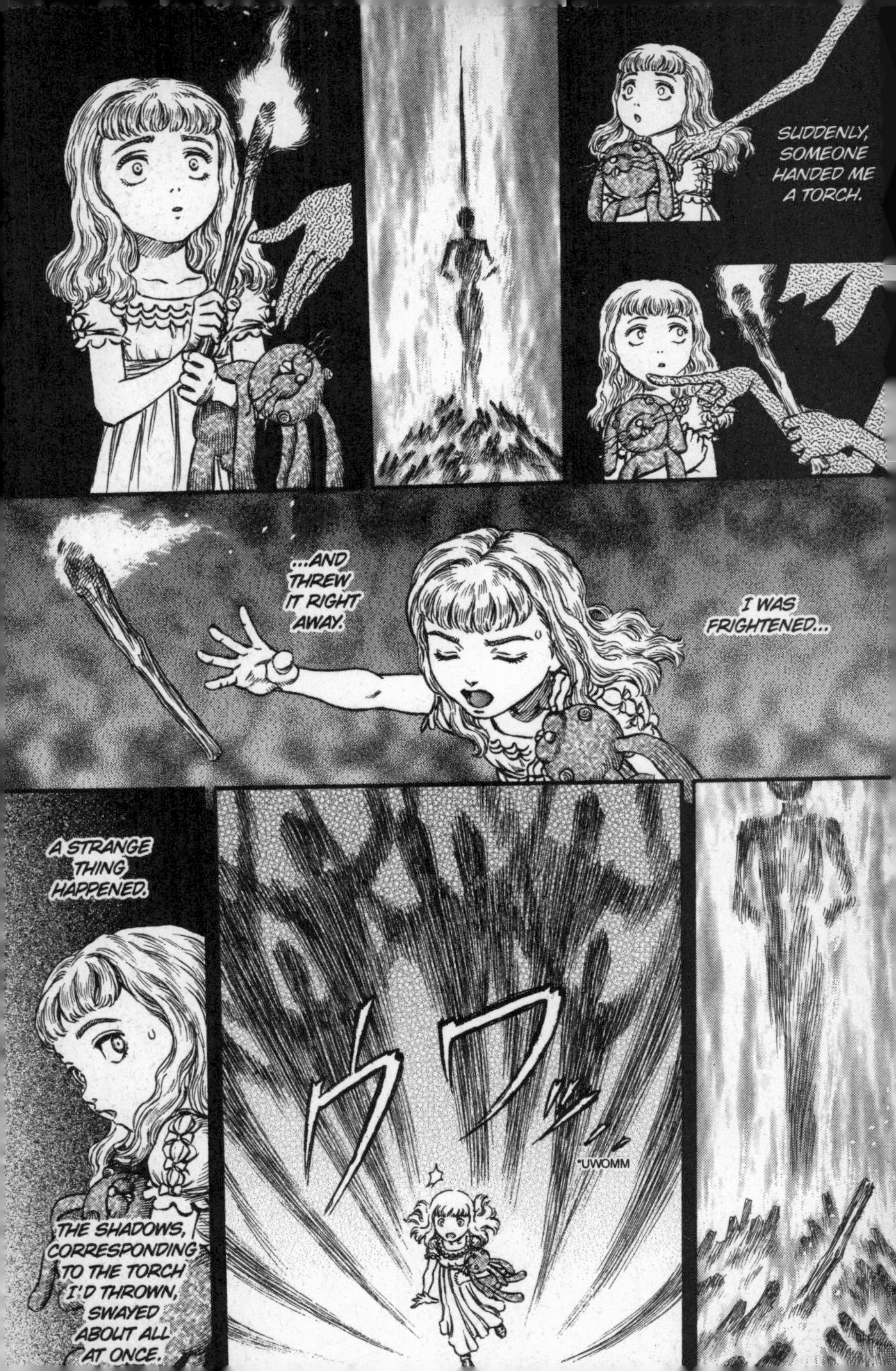
SUDDENLY, SOMEONE HANDED ME A TORCH.
I WAS FRIGHTENED...
...AND THREW IT RIGHT AWAY.
*UWOMM
A STRANGE THING HAPPENED.
THE SHADOWS, CORRESPONDING TO THE TORCH I'D THROWN, SWAYED ABOUT ALL AT ONCE.

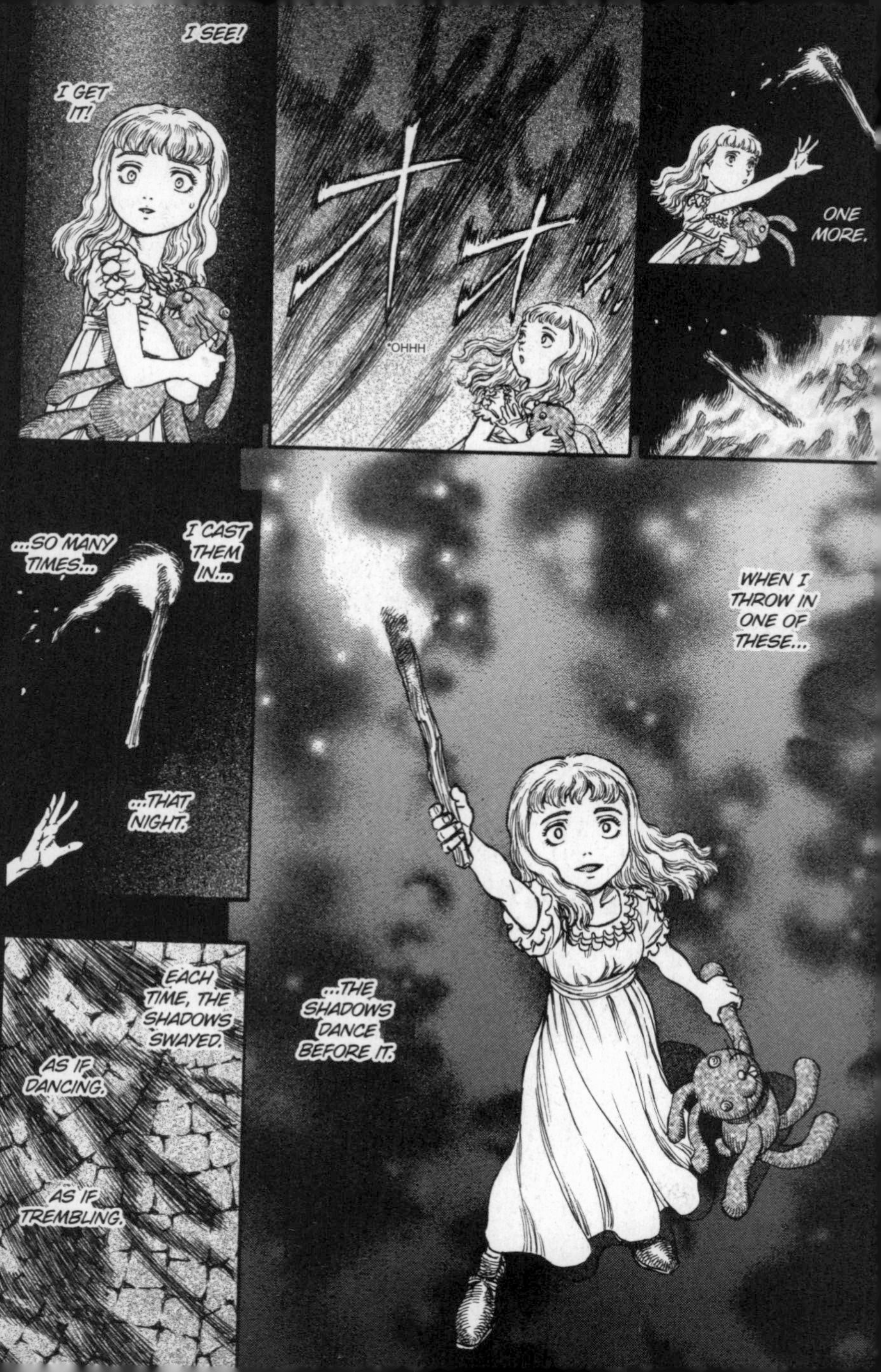

ONE MORE.
*OHHH
I SEE!
I GET IT!
WHEN I THROW IN ONE OF THESE...
...THE SHADOWS DANCE BEFORE IT.
I CAST THEM IN...
...SO MANY TIMES...
...THAT NIGHT.
EACH TIME, THE SHADOWS SWAYED.
AS IF DANCING.
AS IF TREMBLING.

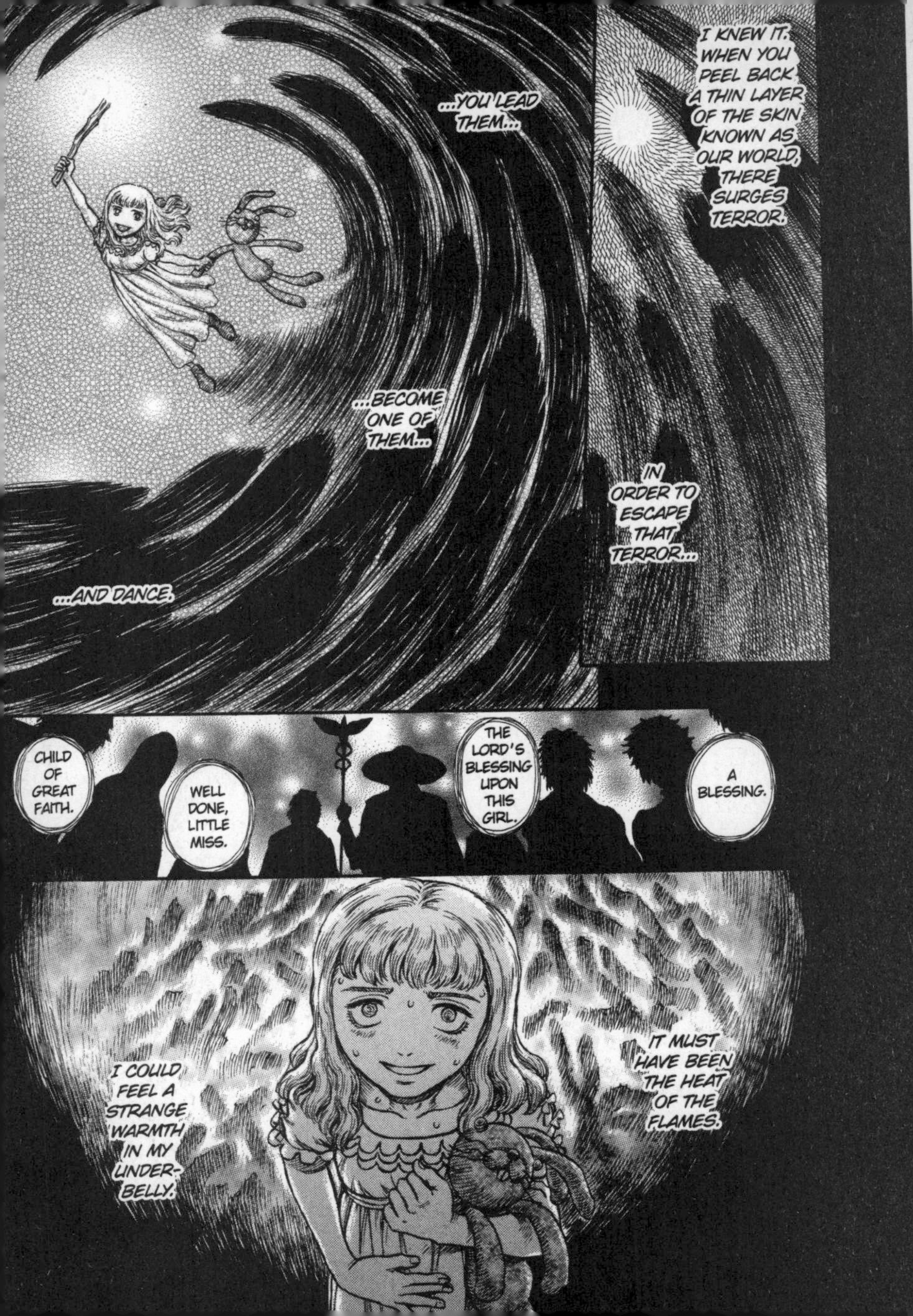
I KNEW IT. WHEN YOU PEEL BACK A THIN LAYER OF THE SKIN KNOWN AS OUR WORLD, THERE SURGES TERROR.
IN ORDER TO ESCAPE THAT TERROR...
...YOU LEAD THEM...
...BECOME ONE OF THEM...
...AND DANCE.
A BLESSING.
THE LORD'S BLESSING UPON THIS GIRL.
WELL DONE, LITTLE MISS.
CHILD OF GREAT FAITH.
IT MUST HAVE BEEN THE HEAT OF THE FLAMES.
I COULD FEEL A STRANGE WARMTH IN MY UNDER-BELLY.

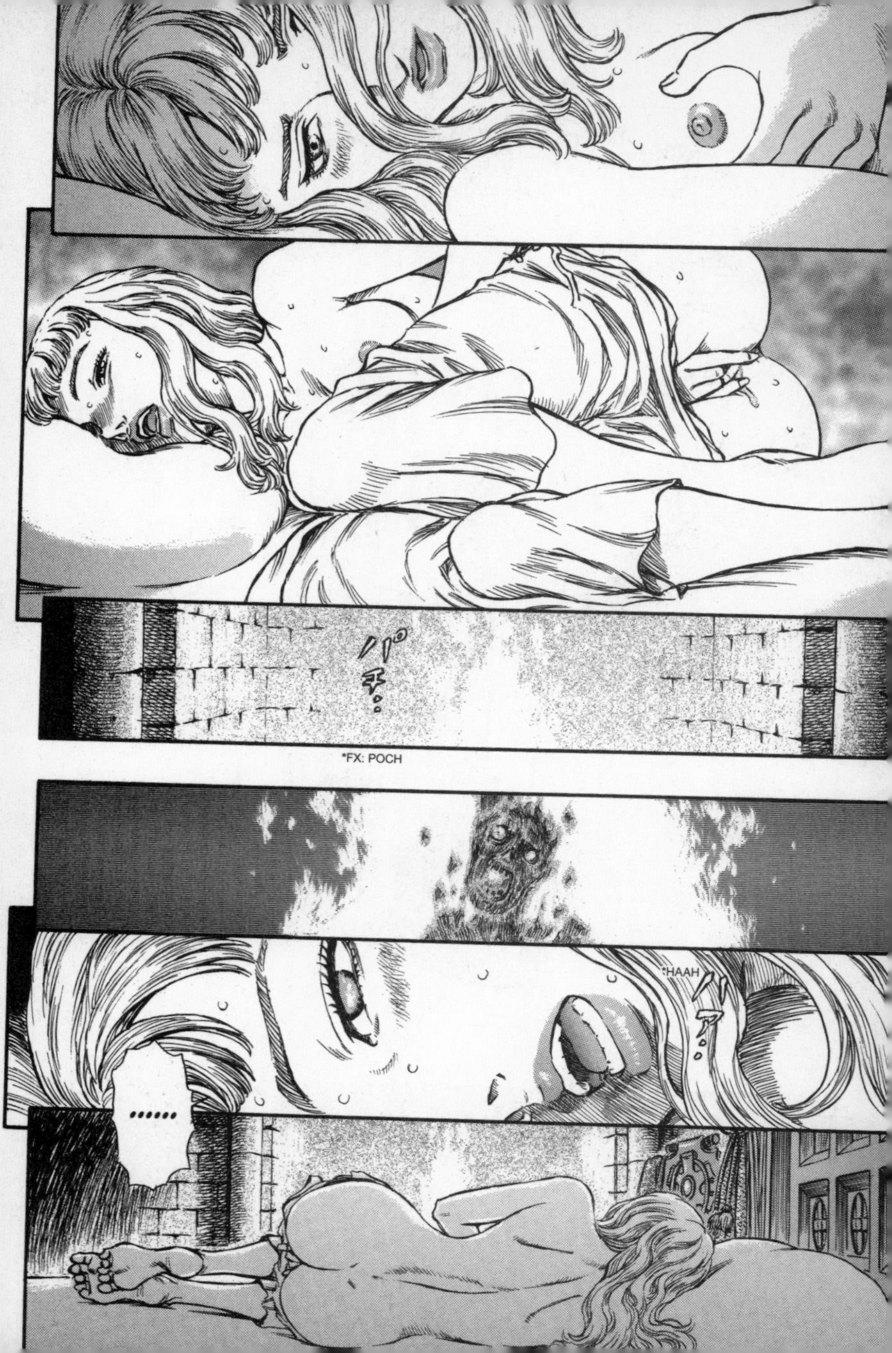

......
*HAAH
*FX: POCH

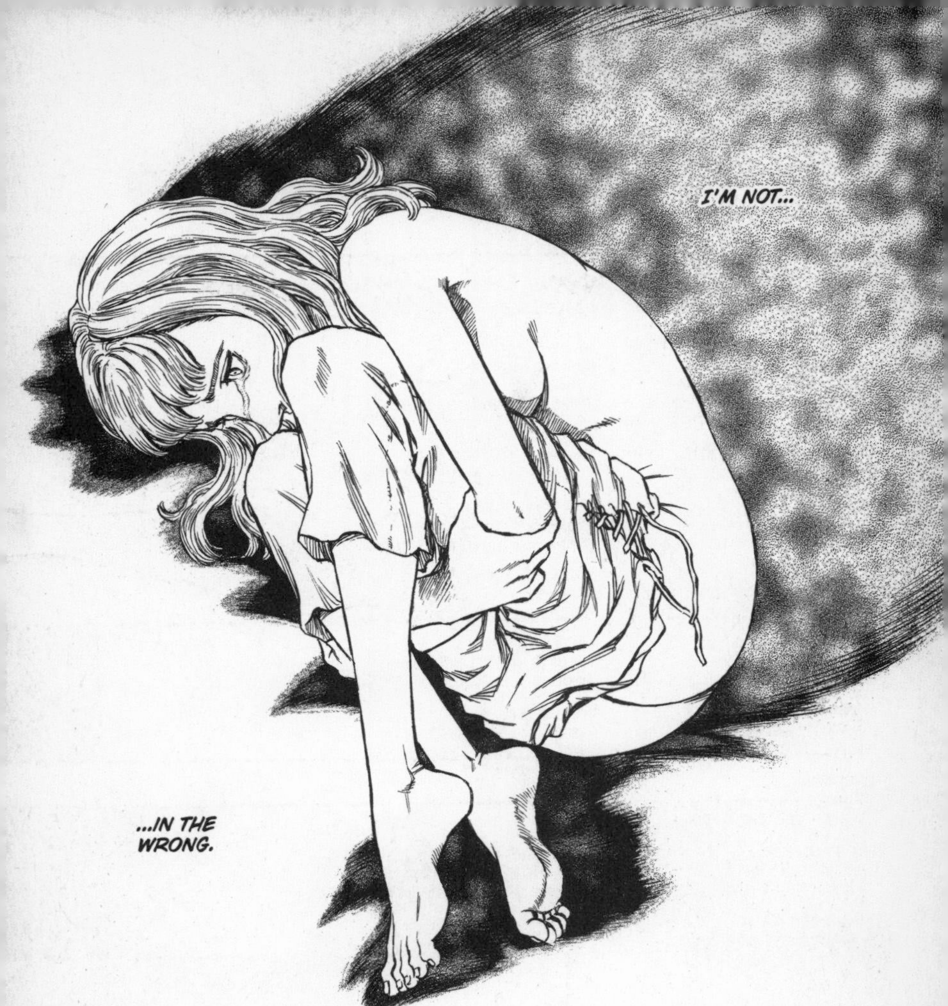
I'M NOT...
...IN THE WRONG.

*FX: WHRRRLLLL

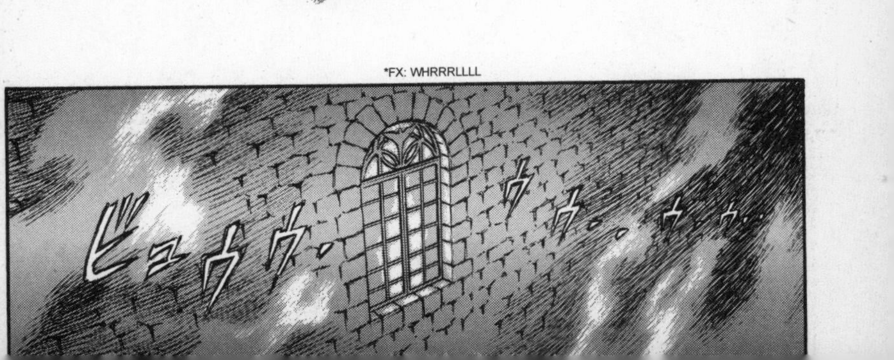
ビュゥウ。ウ。ウ。ウ。

Created by Kentaro Miura, *Berserk* is manga mayhem to the extreme—violent, horrifying, and mercilessly funny—and the wellspring for the internationally popular anime series. Not for the squeamish or the easily offended, *Berserk* asks for no quarter—and offers none!

VOLUME 1:
ISBN-10: 1-59307-020-9
ISBN-13: 978-1-59307-020-5

VOLUME 2:
ISBN-10: 1-59307-021-7
ISBN-13: 978-1-59307-021-2

VOLUME 3:
ISBN-10: 1-59307-022-5
ISBN-13: 978-1-59307-022-9

VOLUME 4:
ISBN-10: 1-59307-203-1
ISBN-13: 978-1-59307-203-2

VOLUME 5:
ISBN-10: 1-59307-251-1
ISBN-13: 978-1-59307-251-3

VOLUME 6:
ISBN-10: 1-59307-252-X
ISBN-13: 978-1-59307-252-0

VOLUME 7:
ISBN-10: 1-59307-328-3
ISBN-13: 978-1-59307-328-2

VOLUME 8:
ISBN-10: 1-59307-329-1
ISBN-13: 978-1-59307-329-9

VOLUME 9:
ISBN-10: 1-59307-330-5
ISBN-13: 978-1-59307-330-5

VOLUME 10:
ISBN-10: 1-59307-331-3
ISBN-13: 978-1-59307-331-2

VOLUME 11:
ISBN-10: 1-59307-470-0
ISBN-13: 978-1-59307-470-8

VOLUME 12:
ISBN-10: 1-59307-484-0
ISBN-13: 978-1-59307-484-5

VOLUME 13:
ISBN-10: 1-59307-500-6
ISBN-13: 978-1-59307-500-2

VOLUME 14:
ISBN-10: 1-59307-501-4
ISBN-13: 978-1-59307-501-9

VOLUME 15:
ISBN-10: 1-59307-577-4
ISBN-13: 978-1-59307-577-4

VOLUME 16:
ISBN-10: 1-59307-706-8
ISBN-13: 978-1-59307-706-8

VOLUME 17:
ISBN-10: 1-59307-742-4
ISBN-13: 978-1-59307-742-6

Presented uncensored in the original Japanese format!
$13.95 Each!

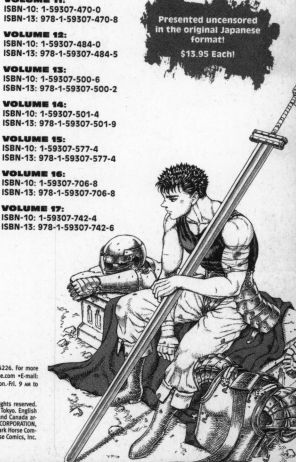

dmpbooks.com

darkhorse.com

AVAILABLE AT YOUR LOCAL COMICS SHOP OR BOOKSTORE
To find a comics shop near your area, call 1-888-266-4226. For more information or to order direct: •On the web: darkhorse.com •E-mail: mailorder@darkhorse.com •Phone: 1-800-862-0052 Mon.-Fri. 9 AM to 5 PM Pacific Time.

BERSERK by Kentaro Miura ©1989 Kentaro Miura. All rights reserved. First published in Japan in 1990 by HAKUSENSHA, INC., Tokyo. English text translation rights in the United States of America and Canada arranged with HAKUSENSHA, INC., Tokyo through TOHAN CORPORATION, Tokyo. English text translation © Digital Manga, Inc. & Dark Horse Comics, Inc. Dark Horse Manga™ is a trademark of Dark Horse Comics, Inc. All rights reserved. (BL7623)